Macao – The Formation of a Global City

Macao, the former Portuguese colony in southeast China, has a long and very interesting history of cultural interaction between China and the West. Held by the Portuguese from the 1550s until its return to China in 1999, Macao was, up to the emergence of Hong Kong in the later nineteenth century, the principal point of entry into China for all Westerners – Dutch, British and others, as well as Portuguese. The relatively relaxed nature of Portuguese colonial rule, intermarriage, the mixing of Chinese and Western cultures, and the fact that Macao served as a safe haven for many Chinese reformers at odds with the Chinese authorities, including Sun Yat-sen, all combined to make Macao a very different and special global place. This book explores how Macao was formed and evolved into a cosmopolitan city over the centuries. It puts forward substantial new research findings and new thinking, and covers a wide range of issues. It is a companion volume to *Macao – Cultural Interaction and Literary Representations*.

C.X. George Wei is Professor and Head of the Department of History at the University of Macau, China.

Routledge Studies in the Modern History of Asia

Macao – The Formation of a Global City

Edited by
C.X. George Wei

Routledge
Taylor & Francis Group

LONDON AND NEW YORK

First published 2014
by Routledge

2 Park Square, Milton Park, Abingdon, Oxon OX14 4RN

711 Third Avenue, New York, NY 10017, USA

Routledge is an imprint of the Taylor & Francis Group, an informa business

First issued in paperback 2016

British Library Cataloguing in Publication Data
A catalogue record for this book is available from the British Library

Library of Congress Cataloging in Publication Data
A catalog request for this book has been made

ISBN 978-1-138-65718-2 (pbk)
ISBN 978-0-415-62584-5 (hbk)
ISBN 978-0-203-79724-2 (ebk)

Typeset in Times New Roman
by Out of House Publishing

Contents

Illustrations

Contributors

Bill K.P. Chou is associate professor in the Department of Government and Public Administration, University of Macau. He obtained his PhD from the University of Hong Kong, and has held visiting positions in UCLA, National University of Singapore, Asian Development Bank Institute and City University of Hong Kong. His research interests include the governance of China, Hong Kong, Macao and Singapore, as well as China's frontiers and foreign policies.

He Sibing received his PhD in US diplomatic history from Miami University, Ohio. He is presently serving as guest professor of overseas Chinese studies at Huaqiao University, China. His research interests are in the areas of Sino–US relations and the Philippine–Chinese and Sino–Philippine relations. He recently completed a monograph entitled *Macao in the Making of Early Sino-American Relations, 1784–1844,* funded by the Instituto Cultural do Governo da RAE de Macau's Academic Research Grant.

Iona Man-Cheong holds a Yale PhD and is associate professor of history at Stony Brook University (SUNY), with teaching fields in Qing and modern Chinese history. Her research interests are presently focused on eighteenth- and nineteenth-century Chinese maritime and transnational history and the Chinese diaspora. She has written papers on Chinese maritime labour and cross-cultural encounters in the 'British metropole, John Anthony: a Chinese sailor in London (1798–1805)' (forthcoming in *Social History*) and 'Macao as eighteenth-century cosmopolis'. Her publications include *The Class of 1761: Examinations, the State and Elites in 18th-Century Qing China* (Stanford University Press, 2002).

Carmen Amado Mendes is professor in the International Relations Department at the School of Economics, University of Coimbra, and leading researcher on the project 'An Analysis of the "One Country, Two Systems" Formula: The Role of Macau in China's Relations with the European Union and the Portuguese Speaking Countries', Centre of Social Studies (CES), University of Coimbra. She is also a board member of the European Association for Chinese Studies. She received her PhD from the School of Oriental and African Studies, University of London, and her Master's degree from the *Institut des Hautes Études Européennes*, University of Strasbourg. Her fields of research focus on China's foreign policy, EU–China relations and Macao. She was president of the International Relations Section and board member of the Portuguese Political Science Association; visiting professor of the University of Macau; post-doctorate scholar of the Institute of Political Studies, Portuguese Catholic University of Lisbon; auditor of the Institute of National Defence and founder of the consulting company ChinaLink and of the Observatory of China in Portugal.

Isabel Morais is associate professor and coordinator of CHERISH (Center of Heritage and History Studies) at the University of Saint Joseph, Macao. She has a doctorate degree in comparative literature from the University of Hong Kong and her research interests include transcultural studies, diasporic memory, gender/ethnicity, and human rights. Her research appears in *Mare Liberum: Revista de História dos Mares* (Lisbon, Portugal), *Journal of Social Sciences* (Guangdong), *Chinese Heritage Centre Bulletin* (Singapore), *Chinese Cross Currents* (Macao Ricci Institute), *Review of Culture* (Macao) and *Transtext(e)s Transcultures: Journal of Global Cultural Studies* (University of Jean Moulin Lyon 3). More recent work is included in the anthologies *Gendering the Fairs: Histories of Women and Gender at World Fairs* (University of Illinois Press, 2010), *Feminist Writing from Ancient Times to Modern World* (Greenwood/ABC-Clio, 2011), *The Making of the Luso-Asian World, Intricacies of Engagement, Vol. 1* (ISEAS Publications, 2011), *The City and the Ocean: Urbanity (Im)migration, Memory, and Imagination* (Cambridge Scholars Publishing, 2012), and *Americans and Macao: Trade, Religion, and Diplomacy on the South China Coast* (Hong Kong University Press, 2012)

Paula Morais is presently research officer at the London School of Economics (LSE) for the EU-FP7 URBACHINA research project looking at sustainable urbanization in China, and teaching assistant in urban design and international planning at the Bartlett School of Planning, UCL. She is concluding a PhD in planning studies, focusing on contemporary urban public space at the Bartlett School of Planning (UCL), where she also co-founded and formerly co-coordinated the China Planning Research Group (CPRG) until October 2011. Her recent research projects include collaboration with CIAUD-FAUTL in Lisbon and the Metropolis' Observatory in Brazil looking at 'Lusophone Metropolises: Genesis and Patterns of Urban Sprawl, a Comparative Perspective'. She also holds a Postgraduate Certificate in Learning and Teaching in Higher Education at CALT (UCL) and is a fellow of the Higher Education Academy. Trained as an architect by FAUP at the University of Porto she has worked in several architecture projects, such as Santiago Calatrava and Frederico Valsassina Arquitectos, and started her own practice in Lisbon with Bernardo Falcão de Azevedo in 2000. Paula also holds a BSc in musical education (4th year degree) awarded in 1987 by the Porto's Music School. She has been board member of Architects Sans Frontiers Portugal since 2003 and was member of 'Orfeão Universitário do Porto' (Music Society) during her architectural studies.

André Murteira is research assistant at the Centre for Overseas Portuguese History at the New University of Lisbon. He has an MA in history of the Portuguese Overseas Expansion from the New University of Lisbon, Portugal, on the subject of Dutch privateering against the Portuguese navigation to Asia between 1595 and 1625. He is currently working on a PhD at the New University of Lisbon on the subject of Dutch privateering against Portuguese navigation in Asia in the first half of the seventeenth century. He is the recipient of grants from the Oriente Foundation (Portugal) and the Foundation for Science and Technology (Portugal). He has published in journals such as *Anaisde História de Além-Mar*, *Oriente*, *Revista de Cultural/Review of Culture*. He is interested in the maritime history of the Portuguese in Asia in the seventeenth century and in the history of Dutch–Portuguese conflicts in Asia in the same period.

Roderich Ptak earned an MA degree in economics from the University of Guelph, Canada; and DPhil and Habil degrees in Chinese studies from Heidelberg, Germany. He has been professor of Chinese studies, first at Heidelberg, then at Mainz-Germersheim, and since 1994 at Munich (chair). In between, he has been a Heisenberg scholar and a guest teacher in Paris, Lisbon and Macao. He has written several books and articles on maritime Chinese history, Macao, traditional Chinese literature and animals in Chinese texts. He is also the co-editor of several book series.

Leonor Diaz de Seabra is assistant professor of the Department of Portuguese at the University of Macau. She earned her PhD in history from the University of Porto (Portugal, 2006) with a dissertation on the Holy House of Mercy of Macao (A Misericórdia de Macau: Irmandade, Poder e CaridadenaIdade do Comércio) and an MA degree in history from the University of Macau (1989–1995) with a thesis on the relations between Macao and Siam (Thailand). These two topics are the main interest of her research areas. She has published several books as well as articles in academic journals.

Rogério Miguel Puga holds a PhD on Anglo-Portuguese Studies (FCSH, New University of Lisbon) and was a lecturer at the Institute of Education and Sciences (ISEC, Lisbon, 2000–2005), assistant professor at the University of Macau (2007–2009) and is now senior researcher at the Centre for English, Translation and Anglo-Portuguese Studies (CETAPS, New University of Lisbon), where he also teaches. He is also a research collaborator at the Centre for Overseas History (CHAM, New University) and the Centre for Comparative Studies (University of Lisbon) as well as editor of the *European Journal of Macao Studies* (Portugal) and subject editor for the *Journal of Romance Studies* (UK). He has published several works on Anglo-Portuguese literary and historical relations, the Portuguese and British empires and Lusophone and Anglophone literatures, namely: *The Portuguese Historical Novel* (Lisbon, 2006), *A World of Euphemism: Representations of Macao in the Work of Austin Coates, City of Broken Promises as Historical Novel and Female Bildungsroman* (Lisbon, 2009), and 'The English Presence and Anglo-Portuguese Relations in Macao (1635–1794)' (Lisbon, 2009).

C.X. George Wei is professor and head of the Department of History at the University of Macau, and guest professor of the Institute of History Research at the Shanghai Academy of Social Science. He earned his PhD in history from Washington University, St. Louis, Missouri and taught at Susquehanna University, Pennsylvania; Walla Walla College, Washington and the University of Toledo, Ohio. He is author of *Sino-American Economic Relations, 1944–1949* (1997), editor of *China–Taiwan Relations in a Global Context: Taiwan's Foreign Policy and Relations* (2011), co-editor of *Challenges to Chinese Foreign Policy* (2009), *Exploring Nationalisms of China: Themes and Conflicts* (2002) and *Chinese Nationalism in Perspective: Historical and Recent Cases* (2001), *Asian Diplomatic History* (in Chinese – Vol. I, *The Development of Asian Diplomacy*, 2009; Vol. II, *Asian Diplomacy and Taiwan*, 2011; Vol. III, *Asian Diplomacy and the Korean Peninsula*, 2013; Vol. IV, *Asian Diplomacy and Japan*, 2013 and Vol. V, *Eastern and Western Cultures and Diplomatic Strategies*, 2013), as well as numerous articles in both English and Chinese.

Peter Zabielskis received his doctorate from New York University and is currently assistant professor of anthropology at the University of Macau. His research interests include material culture, art, architecture, identity, religion, civil society, development and urban space in Macao and Southeast Asia, especially Malaysia, where he has conducted extensive field research. He recently published 'Towards a Moral Ecology of the City: A New Form of Place-Based Identity and Social Action in Penang, Malaysia' in *International Development Planning Review*.

Tianshu Zhu received her PhD in Buddhist art from Ohio State University, with specialization on Buddhist art in Central Asia, China and India. She is currently assistant professor of art history in the Department of History at the University of Macau. Her research addresses topics of Buddhist art in relation to religion, and the relationship between religious texts/doctrine and visual representations. Recently she has also started to explore Chinese popular religion.

Foreword

Roderich Ptak

Being invited to write a foreword is always a great honour, especially if the volume in question wishes to promote a fresh academic initiative. This is the case with the present collection. It presents a fine selection of articles related to the field of 'Macaologia', 'Macaology', or 'Aomenxue' (澳門學) – more simply put, to 'Macao studies'. Labels such as these are not entirely new, but for various reasons scholars and administrators have been reluctant to use them. In 2009, when the University of Macau hosted a major international conference, this barrier fell: the word 'Macaology' appeared in the title of the conference and, since then, the academic world has responded positively to the idea that studying Macao's past and present should be seen in its own light, almost like a special category in the vast field of social sciences and humanities.

One of the internationally known scholars interested in 'packaging' Macao studies anew, is Dr George Wei (魏楚雄), Professor at the University of Macau. After the conference he undertook efforts to collect a set of representative papers read to the meeting; these manuscripts provided the groundwork for the present collection edited by him – with expertise, dedication and much enthusiasm. The final product, I believe, gives the reader a good impression of what 'Macaology' is about, and which roads scholars may opt to take in order to find out more about Macao's uniqueness.

Macao, we all know, was Europe's first gate to China. As such it is a location, where different voices of the past and present have joined to form a very special chorus. That also applies to the perception of these tunes – to 'Macaology'. One may describe the latter as a flexible matrix combining trade and politics, religion, ethnic issues, social dimensions and a myriad of cultural entities in the broadest sense. Clearly, these elements and their imagery went through many stages, but certain ingredients have remained fairly constant over time, never loosing their original flavour, and some of them are even apt to replenish theories and models.

Old Macao, for example, has often been depicted as a 'diaspora'-like settlement, even as a variation of a Chinese *fanfang* (番坊), or foreign quarter. There can be no doubt, it was and still is a multicultural entity, a filter between civilizations. Some historians have stressed its role within the network of mini-possessions that once constituted Portuguese-Asia, others have characterized Macao as an autonomous or semi-autonomous urban area, with varying degrees of dependency on Portugal or China, or on both. Not too long ago, 'double loyalty' (雙重效忠), in the best sense of the term, became an academic slogan – to grasp the past and to explain, rather intuitively, how Macao was able to hold out for so long.

Certainly, many more ideas could be used – or invented – to sketch the extraordinary status of this city and to search for its *segredos de sobrevivência*, or 'secrets of survival', as one eminent scholar has put it. For the period during which the *Padroado* (Patronate) was reality, the general political constellation could be enlarged, for example, by introducing a 'triple loyalty' theorem, with the Church and Rome being the third entity, next to China and Portugal.

Macao was rarely disturbed by excessive violence. While the later imperial powers did injustice to China, there were long periods of silent understanding between Macao, Lisbon and Beijing. The famous wooden tablet with the two ambiguous characters *jing tian* (敬天), meaning something like 'respect heaven', which the Kangxi emperor presented to the Jesuits, may be seen as a token of this equilibrium. At that time diplomacy was still an art and all sides knew well how to employ signs of harmony and tolerance. Macaology will certainly show us that these good manners have not entirely disappeared in our days.

One important constituent of the complex matrix enriching Macao's urban panorama is the world of Chinese popular cults, through which readers will access this volume. In the eyes of many scholars, Macao belongs to the sphere of *haiyang wenhua* (海洋文化/ maritime culture), a term often encountered in modern Chinese writing; therefore such an arrangement was a natural choice. Put differently, Macaology is a flexible tool; to seek a new beginning in the arms of Mazu and other deities suggests that we may interpret the past and present in fresh ways.

Other approaches move ethnic and political groups to the foreground. When this touches the Dutch, British and Americans – and the dichotomy between peace and conflict – scholars remain divided in their opinions, while there is less or no mental stress at all when one switches to the history of Chinese merchants and entrepreneurs, fishermen and settlers moving to Macao from Fujian, central Guangdong, Southeast Asia and other distant locations. A related topic is the very elastic question of identities. These themes are not very well-known yet, partly because Macao has received new waves of migrants during the past three decades, whose roles still need to be explored. Here one may think of the Filipino community, to mention just one case. This is one area where I believe Macaology will achieve interesting results, inspired by existing modes and models.

In short, although Macao experts have disentangled many facets of the past and present, more efforts will be needed, especially in regard to the nineteenth century and the first half of the twentieth century, to unearth what still lies hidden beneath huge stacks of paper. Besides 'playing' with these data and reassembling little details, we may of course also use Macao as a platform for new intellectual experiments. The idea of transformation is a case in point. As was said, Macao can serve as a compass for the old and new alike. The ever-changing landscape of the city's past, its economy, its position within regional and global contexts – the 'iconography' created by Macaologists – all these dimensions and the qualitative alterations associated with them call for careful definitions that may, one day, become applicable to similar arenas in different parts of the world.

Some of these thoughts are addressed in recent scholarly writing, usually between the lines. But this is not the place to discuss them. What I may say, as a general footnote, concerns a different, yet related issue: China sees the twenty-first century as a new maritime age. There are good arguments for such a view, and there are many reasons to embed Macao in a complex 'oceanic mosaic', where it can remain 'online', in a leading position. It should be clear, then, that Macao will keep its VIP status at the methodological frontier – and elsewhere, in the 'real world', at many levels. Historians in particular may relax when this flash is on: the old Mediterranean model promoted by French scholarship has revealed a set of discernible *longue durée* phenomena applicable to Macao and some of the adjacent regions; these are likely to remain valid irrespective of the looking glass.

In terms of geography, the Macao specialist may see the object of his inquiry as part of the Nanhai world, or as part of a different entity, which is closely tied to China's coastal belt and the interior. The conventional view goes from land to sea, but there are also those who turn their eyes in the other direction. Be this as it may, Macao has always been a bridge between the dry and the wet element. In a world that gradually grows together, cities have become like junctions within a tightly-woven web of nerves. Macao is no exception to the rule. But, as was mentioned, its past has always remained exceptional. In spite of its physical smallness, it functioned like a knot between empires. Its potentials were held in high esteem, and it was and is a mental gate, to splendour and modesty alike. There is *poder e saber*, or 'power and knowledge', to use a recent formula. Metaphorically put, Macao may appear 'Confucian' at all times, a paradox, empty, yet full of splendid wine.

觚不觚, 觚哉觚哉… 'A wine cup that is not a wine cup, what cup is that?' – There are no static solutions to the riddle. The quasi-Mediterranean historian, residing in Beijing or elsewhere on the continent, with a direct line to the spiritual centres of the Latin world, secretly adores the enigma that is Macao. The model is being worked on, a new set of essays is out, the search for *zheng ming* (正名) – for 'correcting labels' – will go on. We shall need new symbioses, ad infinitum, the rest is of no concern…

Introduction

C.X. George Wei

Sonnet to Macao

Gem of the Orient Earth and open Sea,
Macao! That in thy lap and on thy breast
Hast Gathered beauties all the loveliest,
O'er which the sun smiles in his majesty!
Sir John Bowring[1]

Macao: A cosmopolitan/global city

Adjacent to its counterpart Hong Kong – which has been well-known as one of the major cosmopolitan cities in the world for long – Macao, a tiny mass of islands with a total land area of less than 30 square kilometres and a population of a little more than 550,000 people, has been much less widely noticed until its suddenly booming gambling industry recently thrust it into the spotlight. Despite this, Macao has been no less cosmopolitan and global than Hong Kong over the years, if not more so. It is no wonder that Sir John Bowring, governor of Hong Kong in the nineteenth century (1854–1859), who must have known his neighbouring city very well, called Macao the 'Germ of the Orient Earth' in the poem quoted above.

Jonathan Porter believed that Macao became a cosmopolitan city during its golden age of the early seventeenth century, though he did not clearly define what a cosmopolitan city should be like.[2] Cosmopolitanism is the main feature of a global city where, according to Kwame Anthony Appiah, individuals originating from various locations live together in a relationship of mutual respect despite their differing religious or political beliefs.[3] The term 'cosmopolitanism' was initially mentioned by the ancient Greek cynic philosopher Diogenes Laertius when he responded to the question 'where are you a countryman of?' with the answer, 'a citizen of the world [kosmopolitês]'.[4] In a broad sense, cosmopolitanism means that all human beings, regardless of their political affiliation and religious or cultural background, do (or at least can) belong to a single community, and that this community should be cultivated.[5] Cosmopolitanism, as Paul Gilroy pointed out, resulted from a 'process of exposure to otherness' and resulted in a consensus to foster 'the irreducible value of diversity within sameness'.[6] Yet, since it is impossible for all of humankind to closely live in one location, cosmopolitanism in a narrow sense means a global interaction and integration in a confined place, either a city or urban centre. A cosmopolitan centre or a global city is where local residents – bound together by common interests, shared values and morality and a political system that accepts, respects or tolerates different lifestyles, religious practices and cultures – are open to and interact with each other as well as external members and communities, while remaining their own autonomous space, culture and identity. Cosmopolitanism is a mechanism that runs a global city with the collective norms agreed upon by its local residents, despite these residents being mostly immigrants who have, to a greater or lesser degree, experienced identity confusion and the problem of transition.

The phenomenon and nature of cosmopolitanism can be largely seen through the history of Macao because Macao is a global city and its evolution has occurred in a global context. Since 1557 when the Portuguese established their settlement in Macao, the city has been inhabited by multiple nationalities that were drawn to move there by the promise of job opportunities or the attraction of the profits being made from maritime trade. The formation of Macao was, therefore, profoundly affected by its close ties with the maritime business and trade, as well as its intimate association with Western missionary activities and diverse Chinese and foreign elements and forces. Macao – where various imperial powers and cultures and immigrants from various countries and regions encountered, competed, mingled and made their mark – became a cosmopolitan hub and a cultural melting pot. The urbanization of Macao, which took place on a large scale after the breakdown of the city wall in the middle of the nineteenth century, took place along with the confluence of the continental and global forces.

Moreover, politically, Macao has been administrated by a type of 'world government' necessary for a cosmopolis, as a territory governed by the Portuguese from the middle of the sixteenth century up to 1999. (Indeed, even after 1999, Macao continued to enjoy its privileged political power with the rule of 'one country, two systems', under which the traditional administrative style and immigration policy have been largely followed and many foreigners moved into Macao due to the economic and job prospect there.) Despite its status as one of the earliest colonies, Macao enjoyed its uniquely democratic form of government in the past, in contrast with the despotic rule that prevailed in other Portuguese colonies (or in those under all other European powers for that matter). The free and peaceful status of Macao grew out of its dislocation from both China and Portugal, which rendered Macao free from a tight juridical control. As historian C.R. Boxer explained to the Portuguese, 'For fear of provoking a clash with the Chinese, no *auto da fe* was ever held at Macao' and 'the local ecclesiastical officials did not dare to interfere, in contrast to the rigour with which the Goanese Hindus were sometimes treated in Portuguese India'.[7]

With that kind of cosmopolitan governance, Macao was held together by racial accommodation and tolerance as well as active cultural interactions. Although there was a visible division between the Chinese and the Portuguese settings in Macao, there has been very few conflicts in the city's history. An overview of Macao's landscape and urban settings vividly reveals the cosmopolitan nature of the city. It was a forted city – and thus prepared for possible attacks and invasions – and yet its people were contented with their peaceful and harmonious lives. With its diverse human elements and marvellous people from different parts of the world who knew how to make life better, Macao's natural beauty and the city's architectural structures have been smoothly and elegantly blended together. The Westernized houses, religious buildings and fortification added a great deal of Western flavour to the city, yet the artistic harmony between Eastern and Western architectures and of cross-cultural interactions stands salient. Its cultural and environmental genre, as well as its architectural configuration that is a vibrant mixture of the East and the West, have made Macao a tourist attraction.

Scholars such as Saskia Sassen and Allen J. Scott introduced the concepts of the 'international city' and the 'international city-region'. They emphasized the role of the 'international city', such as New York, London and Tokyo, in the economic affairs of the world that has gone far beyond their traditional status in the national economy.[8] They also highlighted the impact of geopolitical relations and the complicated and conflicting historical conditions on urban development.[9] Particularly, they analysed the phenomenon of the 'international city-region' or new regionalism,[10] holding that the rise or fall of a city, a region or a country is really dependent on its position in the global economy. The fluctuation of the economic development in the world could lead to the decline of Asia and the rise of Europe and America, or vice versa.[11] These points and concepts could well apply to our understanding of the nature of Macao's cosmopolitanism and examination of its role to premodern/modern China.

Indeed, Macao's cosmopolitanism is characterized by its place but not geographically or territorially confined. All of the cosmopolitan cities in the world similarly hold a strategic location that makes them well-connected with the rest of the world, and Macao is no exception. Strategically located at the mouth of the Pearl River in South China, Macao, although small, had been extremely attractive to the merchants of Portugal, Netherlands, Britain, the United States, and even Japan during the maritime era. It served as a gateway and critical stepping-stone to Canton and then the huge market of mainland China and as a vital node for economic interactions between China and the West. Owing to the Canton trade system as well as the efforts by Western merchants, four major global trading routes starting from or via Canton/Macao were formed during the maritime era: 1) Canton-Macao-Goa-Lisbon; 2) Canton-Macao-Manila-Acapulco/Lima; 3) Canton-Macao-Nagasaki; 4) Canton-Macao-Markasar-Timor. All these enabled Macao/Canton to play a distinctive and key role in the trade of China, Asia and the world, as well as for China's commercialization and modernization before the First Opium War. Propelled by the global commercial force, Macao and its commercial affiliation/headquarter Canton flourished into a commercial centre in South China and made an enormous contribution to the eighteenth-century maritime trade, the national commercial integration, the development of merchant capitalism and proto-industrialization of China, and then ultimately, therefore, to the modernization of China and Asia.[12]

Neither is Macao's cosmopolitan nature and international role limited to trade and economy. As mentioned above, Macao has been the nexus between the East and the West and an epitome of China's cultural and religious interaction with the outside world since the sixteenth century. Macao had the first college in Far East that graduated several hundreds of Western missionaries who later became the first generation of sinologists and who built up a cultural bridge between Macao/China and the West. During the same period of time, many Westerners visited and lived in Macao, who left their footprints and images in Macao/China, for better or worse, and who made their impression on the city and the mainland as well. Macao was a station entrance closest to the vast country of China for, from where Western merchants and missionaries, whose legacies would be integrated into the history of China, introduced foreign religions, cultures, ideas and commercial patterns to the Chinese in Macao and then on the mainland. Macao was also a safe haven for reformers, revolutionaries and other dissidents and refugees from the mainland in different times, providing a place for people such as Zheng Guanying and Sun Yat-sen to hide while they studied and promoted Western and advanced ideas for the future of China. It was from Macao that Western cultures and influences entered into China. On the other hand, the images of Macao, China and the East were rooted in the mind of these Westerners coming to Macao, who then took with them views of Macao/China/the East back to their homelands in the forms of writings, publications, paintings, poems, etc., along with the trade items they brought from China.

As a typical cosmopolis, even the dark side of Macao's urban and economic development is internationalized. Since the First Opium War, Macao's importance in the world economy has gradually given way to Hong Kong. As a tiny economic entity that relied highly upon the world economy, Macao had no way to turn around but was forced to make various other desperate attempts to keep up. As a result, by the 1920s–1930s, Macao had become one of the world's notorious 'cities of sin', where gambling houses, brothels and opium houses flourished. Some Western writers called Macao 'the Far East's Las Vegas' or 'the Monaco of the East', and the Chinese 'the greatest gamblers on earth'.[13] Macao was also considered centre of piracy and an asylum for people who feared no law, human or divine. Historian Jonathan Porter called Macao a 'dangerous place, a refuge for the down-and-out and a haven for smugglers, spies, and other malevolent characters.'[14] Gaven Black described Macao as 'the Far East headquarters for American, Russian,

Chinese, Japanese, French, and British espionage services', and reported that it 'offers as well the world's most sophisticated and comprehensive networks dealing in commercial snooping'.[15] All those phenomena and activities may have been significantly reduced in the recent years, but to a certain extent they still remain today.

Thus, Macao has been a cosmopolis, an 'other place' for explorers of different nationalities, and a place where continental and overseas forces mesh, as do the past, the present and the future. We cannot separate Macao's development from its association with mainland China and the world, neither its present nor its past. Thus, a study of Macao's cosmopolitan development and its complex and multifaceted formation and transformation may render us a special angle to look at China's interaction with the outside world as well as the impact of global forces on China via Macao. Macao's history reflects the history of not only China but also the West and the rest of the world.

A study of the multiple aspects of Macao's cosmopolitanism

As described above, the formation of Macao and its cosmopolitanism is a very interesting but comprehensive phenomenon, which calls for an interdisciplinary study. It was with this kind of belief and interest that the contributors of this book, along with many other Western and Chinese scholars devoted to Macao studies, enthusiastically participated in the 'First International Interdisciplinary Conference on Macao Studies: Intercultural Exchanges between East and West' organized by Rogerio Puga, then a member of the History Department of the University of Macau (UM), and held at the UM on 25–27 May 2009. Afterward, thanks to the initial effort by Rogerio who collected the conference papers, as well as the firm support from the publisher's editor Peter Sowden and Professor Ming K. Chan who made valuable comments on and suggestions for the manuscript of this collection, the contributors of this book eventually began to develop their chapters from their conference papers in early 2012, which, with the assistance from PhD student Xiaoran Wang at the UM, eventually have been compiled into four parts for this publication.

In the first two parts 'Faith and the formation of Macao' and 'Western footprints', the contributors explored the relations of religions and the formation of Macao in different areas and from different angles. Cosmopolitanism has a multiple dimension, among which the interactions, confrontations and accommodations between different religions or between religious traditions and modernization are probably the most sensitive and the most uncompromising element standing in the process of urbanization. As all ancient cities, Macao is also famous for its religious traditions and features. How Macao people have culturally and religiously interacted, successfully or unsuccessfully dealing with the possible confrontation or hostility between different religious groups, between the lasting religious establishments and the new driving force for modernization, is an interesting but challenging subject to explore.

The first two chapters in Part I investigate the way in which the ancient religions in Macao have interacted with and accommodated the new driving force for urbanization and modernization. The issue regarding Chinese folk religion in relationship with the private ownership of temples in Macao is addressed by Peter Zabielskis in Chapter 1. Focusing on one small temple, the Kwan Tai – Tin Hau temple and one man's long and intimate involvement with it, Zabielskis explores from the anthropological perspective the survival issue of Chinese popular religion in face of rapid commercialization and urbanization within and without Macao, Macao's social conservatism, as well as the relationship and balance between the owner of a private temple and the Macao government and between the financial and spiritual needs. The Tin Hau temple, as many temples in cosmopolitan cities, was never simply an institution for serving only the local community; it, as Macao itself, has been a magnet attracting devotees from an entire transnational region. Thus, the fate of this temple was a regional and multiethnic phenomenon, subject to not only the need of the city's modernization and the official urban plan but also the changing demand due to the regional and continental, economic and political development. In other words, no matter how spiritual the owner of a private temple could be, Chinese folk religion is materialistic, not only because of its traditional popular practice that has always been quite materialistic but also because it is surrounded by the force of materialism, namely a rapidly developing consumer culture, in the name of tourism and world heritage protection, in addition to the increasing bureaucratization of previously informal local administrative powers.

In the next chapter, Tianshu Zhu examined the same issue on a communal level. She traced the layout and the transformation of communal earth god worship in Macao, trying to figure out the relationship of the communal worship of earth gods with the territory of a city, the residential expansion of kinship and the development of the urban social settings. Indeed, one of the salient phenomena of Macao's cosmopolitanism is that there are varying religious sites all over: the conspicuous churches and temples, and numerous shrines at the gate of households, in front of shops, at the corner of streets, and even in apartment doorways. Surprisingly, however, the continuing and omnipresent religious practice in Macao sat quite happily alongside the development of Macao's urbanism and cosmopolitanism. Zhu discovered that the collective worship at public earth god shrines in Macao can be roughly divided into three phases; each of them represents an evolving relationship between the worship of a territorial deity and the base unit of the community at a different stage: **She**, a community formed by the earliest residents – or the immigrants in a new place – through worshipping the same earth god together; **Paohui**, social organizations that emerged in Macao along with the process of urbanization through the incorporation of several earth god shrines for annual worship activity; and **earth god worship communities** affiliated to officially registered non-religious organizations. Eventually, the foundation of earth god worship communities has shifted from kinship to territory and human organization, and became less religious and less territorial. This study of worship of earth gods in Macao provides our fragmentary knowledge of the worship of the spirits of localities in urban and new settlements with a fresh look.

The origin of cosmopolitanism is almost inevitably associated with religious interactions as immigrants with different religious backgrounds and Western missionaries move into a new place. How Western missionaries and religious groups survived, grew and integrated into Macao is certainly another important aspect of Macao's cosmopolitan development, which is the central theme of Part II. In Chapter 3, Isabel Morais brings our attention to the way in which expatriates formed their communities and collective spirit in a location far away from their homelands. The chapter is concentrated on the unique works among pro-Darwinism publications by two elites of Macao, Lourenço Pereira Marques and Polycarpo da Costa from the expatriate Portuguese Eurasian community, an echo of the heated debate between supporters of Darwinism and religious fundamentalism in Europe in the 1880s. With an attempt to fight against obscurantism and discrimination within the colonial and ecclesiastical establishments and inspire their compatriots with the spirit of their 'indigenous cosmopolitanism' – a distinctly global but also regional perspective, the above two dilettanti analysed in detail and disseminated the issues related to identity, social awareness, education and modern scientific thought, using Darwinism and Freemasonry as ways to consolidate their social positions inside their community and to forge strong ties with the powerful local merchant elites. They dared to criticize the religious dogma followed by missionary works, and challenged the Catholic Church and conservative circles. They embraced atheism and anti-clericalism, promoted science and democracy as well as religious and intellectual tolerance, and tried to relate Chinese philosophy to the theory of evolution and Darwinism, the first Western sociological theory that had made significant impact on China. With the means and motives to contribute to forging the Portuguese 'imagined community' in the East based on a regional solid kinship and ethnic, commercial and social networks, they utilized the convergence of capitalism and print technology to link together not only readers of common origin and ancestry in Macao and Hong Kong but also those with the same kinship origin who had migrated to China's other treaty ports and Southeast and East Asian settlements, to assist the rise of the Macanese identity.

Focusing on the case of the Holy House of Mercy under the background of the wide movement of renovation of the European brotherhoods, Leonor Diaz de Seabra portrays in Chapter 4 the localization and expansion of this movement into Macao. She analyses the development, actions and financial management of the Mercy in relation to the local needs and situation, as well as the impact of the Mercy on the fate and role of Macao women. The great social malfunctions and problems in the social structures of Macao, Leonor argues, had their roots in the disequilibrium of the pyramid of ages. Women, mostly Asian women, were the most fragile sector of the historical population of Macao. They were mostly of low social classes or enslaved and deprived of any rights, yet they were expected to provide sexual services, do housework and raise the children. With charity as its aim, on the one hand, the Mercy was helpful to women and led these subaltern women to marriage by providing them with dowries, alms and other assistances. As a result, despite their weakness, women of Macao became vital in the formation of Euro-Asian kinships through interracial marriages. On the other hand, however, the Mercy was supporting and reinforcing the female dependency and social marginality.

Part III 'The impact of global forces' portrays the global context within which the city of Macao was evolved and Macao's cosmopolitan characteristics were formed. It is well-known that the relationship of the maritime imperial powers was very unstable and intricate, fraught with competitions and conflicts as well as cooperation, both between the powers themselves and between them and the local governments of their trade destinations. More often than not, the possibility of the presence and advance of a rising European power in an Asian country or location was decided not only by its mighty military power or alignment with another established or rising European power but also by its capability of making a good deal with the major regional power. In Chapter 5, André Murteira traces the Portuguese-Dutch conflict along the Goa-Macao-Japan shipping route, an economic line extremely important to Macao during the sixteenth and seventeenth centuries. The Dutch success in spreading their influence into the region of the Malacca and Singapore Straits, Murteira has discovered, hinged on the willingness of the regional government for collaboration. The capture of the Portuguese carrack *Santa Catarina* marked the beginning of Dutch-Johor cooperation against the Portuguese, which was further strengthened by an alliance between the sultanate and Dutch East India Company (VOC) sealed formally in 1606. However, the importance of the Malacca and Singapore Straits region to VOC declined later and VOC concentrated its still limited resources on the defence of its positions on Maluku, Ambon, Banda and northern Java. As a result, it was not able to effectively protect its ally, the Malacca and Singapore Straits region, from the Portuguese retaliation, and the two parties soon grew apart. Eventually in 1609 the sultan opted to make a peace with authorities at Malacca controlled by the Portuguese. Even the coming of a 'pro-Dutch' figure into power in Johor could not reverse this course. On the other hand, the reason for the Dutch success or failure in other regions is quite different. The Dutch-Portuguese military actions on the Goa-Macao-Japan route against each other mostly came from a desire either to open up contacts with some units of the Chinese government or to blockade the approach of the opponent to the Chinese authorities. Thus, which of the two European powers could win their battles over their relationship with China was not so much determined by their battles on seas but rather by the internal debate among the Chinese administration regarding the position to take on the Dutch. Finally, the Portuguese decision to replace great ships with squadrons of small ones that have much less cargo and therefore little capture value and that could easily escape from capture, significantly contributed to the cease of vessels being taken on the Goa-Macao-Japan shipping route.

Similarly, the Anglo-Portuguese maritime relations were closely connected to their association with China. In Chapter 6, through analysing and deconstructing the case of the *London*, the first Anglo-Portuguese voyage to Macao with much skill and nuances, Rogério Miguel Puga expounds the uneasy and sophisticated Anglo-Portuguese relations shifting from the former enmity to the new partners. The early British expeditions to distant Cathay under the 'dormant' Anglo-Portuguese alliance were unsuccessful. In the wake of the annexation of Portugal by Spain in 1580, England's respect for Portugal waned and the British intensified their attacks on Portuguese ships, aiming to weaken its Catholic Spanish enemy, demonstrate its naval superiority and put a foot in the lucrative Far Eastern market that had been dominated so far by the Portuguese. The Treaty of Defence between two Protestant enemies against the Catholics – the combined British and Dutch fleets –in 1619 made the Portuguese realize that they could no longer keep the British away from the Asian market and that they needed the British military assistance to resist Dutch attacks on them. Therefore, the Convention of Goa was signed in January 1635, under which the Portuguese began to trade through the East India Company's ships to avoid Dutch attacks. It was under these circumstances that the voyage of the *London*, a ship chartered by the Portuguese viceroy of Goa to the East India Company travelling to Macao, took place in 1635. The Portuguese, on the one hand, feared English competition from the moment the *London* had been sent to Macao. On the other hand, this had been their wish. Thus, the Portuguese had to operate a two-pronged strategy on two fronts to collaborate with the British while keeping all other European nations away from China as much as they could, through denigrating other European powers' image to the high-ranking Chinese officials and negating their efforts in approaching the higher echelons of China's provincial administration.

The Cushing mission to China has been a hot topic of the early Sino-American relations. It has been long-believed that due to the threat of British monopoly of the Pacific markets the mission marked the beginning of the US government's move from a passive to an active role in its interaction with China. With a critical review of historiography on the subject and a synthesis of biographical studies of Cushing, He Sibing re-examines in Chapter 7 the case within the Macao environment. He argues that there was little evidence indicating that the bitter rivalry and antagonism between the US and Britain in other parts of the world was carried over into China. In fact, it was Cushing that shrewdly played with his counterpart negotiator Qiying against his fear that Cushing might proceed north to Beijing with his naval squadron, which altered the traditional American diplomatic course based on the refined British political technique of imperial expansion and simply following the British lead in the past, by inventing a clause of extraterritoriality in the

Treaty of Wangxia to aggressively forge America's informal empire in Asia. Thus, this treaty created a new American diplomatic model in the Pacific, to be followed by European powers later. It signified that the US no longer fully respected the sovereign equality of the Asian nations and that the US was able not only to exercise its mighty military and economic power abroad but also to utilize international law for its overseas expansion. The formation of the Wangxia Treaty was perceivably influenced by the opinions and suggestions of American China traders and an American community in Macao. In that sense, Macao, where the Treaty of Wangxia was negotiated and signed, played a pivotal role in the evolution of early Sino-US relations. The origins of US policy toward China lay among the American residents in the Canton-Macao area. Ironically, it was through Macao that Cushing, who highly regarded the neatness, creativity, manners and work ethic of the Chinese people, developed a taste for Chinese art and language while holding contempt for the commercial community as well as the Protestant missionaries that fervently supported his mission.

When a place is being urbanized and cosmopolitanized, the local residents there inevitably face many challenges caused by the demographical, urban and economic movement, identity shift as well as intercultural encounters between races, genders and ages in their everyday lives and practices. To investigate how Macao government and residents met with these challenges to their community, identity and solidarity at several critical moments in history is the subject of Part IV 'Cosmopolitanism'. In Chapter 8, Iona Man-Cheong analysed the cosmopolitan development of Macao, characterizing Macao as a city of liminality, of transience and of drift. Although Macao's cosmopolis was geopolitically marginal, Man-Cheong points out, its very existence and cosmopolitanism challenged the already challenged nation-state discourse of the pure Han blood and race and the singularity of Han culture. Through demographical mobility, intermarriage of merchants, sailors, tavern keepers, store owners, missionaries, servants, slaves, prostitutes, and especially, women of different origins and ages who contributed significantly to the racial and cultural hybridization of Macao, as well as the actions of Chinese-Portuguese administrators who had the same class background, ideology and willingness for collaboration, Macao as a cosmopolis achieved its greatness and distinctive identity and acquired its vitality and vibrancy, with its unique way of intercultural and interracial exchanges and negotiations and creative hybridity.

In the next chapter, in echo to Man-Cheong's interpretation of Macao's cosmopolitanism, Paula Morais analyses the characteristics of Macao's cosmopolitanism in relation to space, power, urban development, globalization and identity. In Morais' view, Macao's main character is difference, which shall not be eliminated by ill managed urban development unless Macao is willing to suffer a loss of its identity. Macao, with a very polysemic and complex urban space, was indeed a unique urban interface for eastern and western civilizations. The production of urban space is not just architectural and urban designs and plans but also, more importantly, part of social production and a spatial political economy, which should be examined in the context of globalization and external influences. The fact that Macao was a 'Portuguese territory in Chinese land', Morais points out, had led to the situation of indetermination. In addition, the economic growth created by the booming gambling industry, the inexistence of a statutory planning system and effective development control, and the final withdrawal of the Portuguese administrative presence in 1999, all have contributed to situation that Macao's territorial formation and construction of urban identity have been constantly influenced by a request for flexibility, negotiation, reinvention and identity affirmation. Morais divides the development of urban space and identity of Macao into three main spatial order projects: 1) A territorialization under the Portuguese from its foundation in 1557 to 1987; 2) A deterritorialization led by capitalist project and globalization post-1987; 3) The call for a future urban-regional reterriorialization due to the pro-growth politics.. Currently, Morais concludes, in face of the mighty productive forces of the local, regional and world-scale capital and the state's strategic planning for rescaling, Macao is rapidly losing its unique traditional urban identity and diversity. Thus, Macao must have a new vision, effective leadership and strategic management, not just planning, in meeting the challenge.

In Chapter 10, Bill Chou also contours the interactions between state and market forces in shaping the identities in Macao during the colonial and post-colonial periods, with an emphasis on the period after the handovers (Hong Kong in 1997 and Macao in 1999 respectively) and a comparison with the situation in Hong Kong. National identity, Chou believes, is shaped by a confluent force combining elements such as education system, mass media, market forces, etc. Initially, conscious of the distinction between their mainland Chinese counterparts and themselves, the people in Macao and Hong Kong did not identify themselves with the mainland, but this situation began to change after the handovers. On the one hand, Chou states, the relatively different extents and strengths of local identities of the people in the two cities led to their different progresses in identifying themselves with the new sovereign states. Traditionally, the residents of Macao, where the former colonial ruler never seriously built national identities of any sort, had a weaker local identity than the Hong Kong residents who were held together by an identity contrasted considerably with the Chinese national identity due to their divergent views towards civil liberty, legal concepts and linguistic culture. On the other hand, however, although the state's efforts to promote national identities in the two cities pointed to the same direction, market forces in the two cities worked differently. In Macao, the market force built up by the government's economic rationality and policies promoting cultural tourism of the city had in fact fostered a distinctive identity centred on the city's historical and cultural heritages, both Eastern and Western. In Hong Kong, however, due to the vast business opportunity in and commercial connection with the mainland, the market force pushed the local identity toward converging with the national one, despite that the Hong Kong identity also became stronger at the same time in resistance against the increasing penetration of Beijing's influence.

A cosmopolis is usually governed with an international elite or rule, but how could a city like Macao be successfully managed by an 'international government' without challenging its Chinese sovereignty? The case of Macao has significant international implications. The sovereign status of Macao has been a polemic issue among the scholars of Macao studies, who mostly have been divided by two opposite views: either Macao was once a colony of Portugal, or Macao had been just a Chinese territory administrated by the Portuguese with the permission from Beijing.[16] Re-examining this issue within a global context and through comparisons, Carmen Amado Mendes argues that all the colonies in the world could be divided into two main types: the one of white settlement thoroughly controlled by colonizers that overwhelmed the indigenous peoples; and the dependent one where colonization was not complete. Macao and Hong Kong fall in the second group. After the Second World War, on the one hand, the international political trend was secession namely decolonization, when the decline of the European powers gave rise to the mass nationalism in colonial societies and the emergence of independent states. On the other hand, however, the trend was exactly the opposite in some cases, namely retrocession, through which small units rejoined bigger ones, such as Macao and Hong Kong returning to China in 1999 and 1997 respectively. Under the 'one country, two systems' formula the two dependencies did not achieve full independence but have been absorbed into a larger country. Thus, as there are still anomalous cases of colonial disputes far from being solved today, such as Gibraltar or the Falklands, the model of the Special Administrative Regions (SARs) of Macao and Hong Kong provides a case of success under international law that may inspire other anomalous cases of the international system to peacefully resolve territorial disputes. Today Macao continues to play a unique role in the international arena, serving as a bridge between different cultures and a Chinese platform to interact and cooperate with Portuguese-speaking countries and the European Union, while reinforcing its own identity by being acknowledged as a Chinese region with 'lusophone characteristics'. The dual political system and global function of Macao and Hong Kong may well represent a feature of the cosmopolis in the future.

Macao's cosmopolitanism and Macaology

From the above introduction of a collective effort in studying Macao's cosmopolitanism, one could see that the study of the formation of Macao and Macao's cosmopolitanism is a valuable but very challenging project, which actually requires a much broader and greater endeavour. The dimension of cosmopolitanism is so broad and multifaceted that it covers almost every aspect of Macao and beyond. That's why some local scholars of Macao began to initiate the term of 'Macaology' in the 1980s,[17] in order to promote the study of Macao to a level equivalent to the nature, substance and significance of Macao's cosmopolitanism. Yet, although scholars from Macao, China and other countries have produced valuable works on Macao history and culture in a good number, the scholarship on the subject has remained confined to a small academic circle and has not been very 'cosmopolitan' and global.

To fully explore and understand Macao's cosmopolitanism and the way in which Macao has evolved into a global city, we must investigate and examine all the aspects of Macao's past, namely all the elements of Macaology, and this is not an easy task. Scholars, who agreed that 'Macaology' is a phraseological term worth of exploration, have been divided due to their different concepts, definitions and views of Macaology.[18] To discuss the possibility of Macaology, at least we need to satisfactorily address the following questions: What is Macaology and how do we define it? What are the basics and foundation of Macaology? What are the main factors that could justify and qualify the study of Macao as Macaology? Are the historical status of Macao and the current historical source materials sufficient for Macaology? Will it be inappropriate or exaggerated to call Macao studies Macaology? If the term 'Macaology' is legitimate, what would be its paradigm, scope and theoretical framework? What will be the unique feature of Macaology that could qualify it as such yet distinguish it from other '-ologies' such as 'Sinology', 'Dunhuangology', 'Rediology', etc.? So far, all these key issues related to Macaology remain open, calling for a greater scholarly effort to deal with them.

Despite all that, I believe that there is sufficient evidence and a solid foundation to support the concept and development of Macaology, which can be illustrated with a comparison of that of Dunhuangology. The experts of Dunhuangology believed that Dunhuang studies became a hot academic subject across the world and therefore worthy of being named 'Dunhuangology' mainly because of the following conditions: 1) The long history of Dunhuang and its attachments for at least 1,000 years; 2) The Mogao Grottoes and the surrounding caves that contain and preserve many murals, sculptures and inscriptions; 3) The discovery of 40,000–50,000 items from and around Dunhuang, including ancient books, writings, calligraphies, paintings, artistic products and Buddhist objects made by people of more than ten different nations and ethnicities; 4) The archaeological discoveries in the Dunhuang region that include many valuable inscribed wooden slips with rich information regarding ancient China; 5) The location of Dunhuang as a key spot on the Silk Road connecting China with West Asia and the rest of the world. All these conditions have made Dunhuang a unique and historical place and have rendered Dunhuangology sufficient source materials and historical contents for extensive, in-depth yet subject focused research. Dunhuangology, therefore, combines multiple nations and ethnic peoples and their cultures and so became a worldwide academic project, joined by scholars from many different countries and regions.[19]

In comparison, Macaology enjoys similar conditions as Dunhuangology:
1) The 500-year history of Macao is not as long as that of Dunhuang,
but enough for a significant historical process and social development,
not mention that the history of Macao won't be limited to 500 years as
Macao is a living society and city, and so will continue to develop into the
future; 2) There is a lot of historical architecture containing valuable religious relics in Macao, 25 of which have been included in UNESCO's World
Heritage List; 3) The total accumulated historical files and documents written in more than ten different languages and related to Macao over the past
500 years are enormous. The total Portuguese documents on Macao just
reserved in Overseas Historical Archives, Lisbon, Portugal have reached
100,000 pieces, in addition to many other documents and source materials
scattered and preserved in many other archives, libraries and museums in
other locations of Portugal and across the world – such as in Macao, Taipei,
The Hague, London, India, Thailand, Japan, the Philippines, Spain, Italy,
Brazil, Vietnam – which cover areas including history, geography, religion,
literature, arts, education, economy, law, sciences, technology, etc.[20] 4) There
are certainly many unexcavated shipwrecks buried beneath the waters along
the maritime trade routes to and from Macao, as well as excavated archaeological items in association with Macao, collected and preserved in the
museums of Macao, China, Portugal, Italy, Spain, Netherlands, Britain,
etc.; 5) The location of Macao as a vital spot on the Maritime Silk Road
connecting China with the West, East Asia and South East Asia; 6) Macao
is a melting pot for various cultures of China, Portugal, Britain, America,
etc.; 7) The history and culture of Macao has attracted worldwide scholars
and has been studied by scholars from China, Macao, Japan, Singapore,
Portugal, France, Spain, the United States, Britain, Germany, Belgium and
many other places.

In contrast, what distinguishes Macaology from other '-ologies' is Macao's
uniqueness. This has been distinctly displayed in several aspects. First and the
foremost, the sites of other '-ologies' are either mountain caves or writings,
printed materials and items containing incomplete dead information from the
past and narrowly focusing on one or a few aspects of society and human
life. The embodiment of Dunhuangology, for example, is a series of decay-
ing caves preserved mainly for tourist and research purposes since the beginning of the twentieth century when the Dunhuang caves were discovered.
Differently, the location of Macaology – Macao – has been and continues
to be a place for living and human activities. Macao began as a small entrepôt, but it has developed into a modern cosmopolitan city and will continue
to grow in the future. Indeed, since the Portuguese government handed its
administrative power over Macao to China, Macao has achieved a spectacular economic growth through its booming gambling industry. In 2006, for
the first time in history, Macao's GDP per capita surpassed its neighbouring
global centre Hong Kong. Macao's past glory has certainly been restored,
which can be witnessed by the daily influx of hundreds and thousands of

visitors and also the city's dramatic economic, social and cultural transformation. Macao's landscape and configuration has been turned from a shabby fishing village into a modern urban city – with many newly arisen skyscrapers and brilliant and colourful neon lights – in just about one decade. Thus, Macao is a forever regenerated fossil that keeps changing all the time and accommodates all aspects of human life and society. The source materials of Macaology include not only the numberless dead items inherited from old Macao but also the entire living, transforming and continuing society of current and future Macao. Macaology is not a dead subject but an ongoing object whose past can be vividly seen through the its present and whose present can be better understood by researching its linkage with the past. The objects of Macaology are alive, omnipresent and timeless.

Macao's uniqueness also lies in its great strength and capability, which is accumulated from its past experience in dealing with its encounters with international forces and globalization. In the past, Macao was very successful in tactically tackling the threats from the Netherlands, Britain and Japan and maintaining its good relationship with the Chinese governments in Canton and Beijing. Since modern times, Macao has also demonstrated its elasticity and resilience in utilizing its strategic position and historical legacy and absorbing the cultural merits and fruits of both the East and the West for urban development and economic and political success. Thanks to its historical linkage with Europe and the former colonies of the European empires, Macao has developed its broad diplomatic relationship with many countries in the world, of which more than 60 countries have their consular offices in Macao and nearly 40 countries established their consulates-general for the region of Hong Kong/Macao today. Although not a country, Macao serves as a member of several major international organizations such as the World Trade Organization, UNESCO and the World Tourism Organization. Macao is persistently playing its traditional role in promoting economic and cultural exchanges and interactions between East and West. With the political and economic independence and power gained from the principle of 'one country, two systems', which is in fact a continuation of past practice, Macao continued to enjoy the privilege and flexibility that allowed it to design its own political, economic and cultural policies and pattern for urban development and interaction with other countries and regions. With that leverage, Macao has been turned into a world tourist, gambling and entertainment centre seemingly overnight.

In short, although Macao is just a tiny mass of islands, it is a cosmopolitan city through which we can well see the phenomenon of urbanism and cosmopolitanism. The formation of Macao into a global city has provided us with a unique case to explore the kaleidoscope and common feature of cosmopolitanism and urbanism. The evolution of Macao, especially after the handover, has its unique pattern and has been closely associated with the legacy of Western expansion and the new agenda of China's modernization. Therefore, Macao has to a great extent been a vanguard of Western forces, a Chinese door open to the world, and a nexus of the West and the East. It has revealed the dynamics of modernization and glocalization in the region of China and Asia. What Macao will become in future will be an interesting phenomenon to observe and study. Macao has been and will continue to be a unique place, a small city yet a cauldron for both West and East, traditional and modern, religious and impious, beautiful and ugly, good and evil, lasting and transient – the list is inexhaustible. That is what Macaology is all about.

Notes

1 See Christina Miu Bing Cheng, *Macau: A Cultural Janus*, Hong Kong: Hong Kong University Press, 1999, pp. 133–134.
2 Jonathan Porter, *Macau: The Imaginary City – Culture and Society, 1557 to the Present*, Boulder, CO: Westview Press, 1996, pp. 74–79.
3 Kwame Anthony Appiah, 'Cosmopolitan Patriots', *Critical Inquiry*, 23(3), 1997, pp. 617–639.
4 Diogenes Laërtius, *The Lives of Eminent Philosophers*, Book VI, *The Cynics*, p. 241.
5 *Stanford Encyclopedia of Philosophy*, http://plato.stanford.edu/entries/cosmopolitanism/ (accessed 14 July 2012).
6 Paul Gilroy, *After Empire: Multiculture or Postcolonial Melancholia*, New York: Columbia University Press, 2005, p. 67.
7 C.R. Boxer, 'A *Fidalgo* in the Far East, 1708–1726: Antonio de Albuquerque Coelho in Macao', *The Far Eastern Quarterly*, 1946, pp. 392–393.
8 Saskia Sassen, *The Global City: New York, London, Tokyo*, Princeton, NJ: Princeton University Press, 1991.
9 Ryan Bishop, John Phillips and Wei Wei Yeo (eds), *Postcolonial Urbanism: Southeast Asian Cities and Global Processes,* New York: Routledge, 2003.
10 Allen J. Scott (ed.), *Global City-Regions: Trends, Theory, Policy*, Oxford: Oxford University Press, 2001.
11 Andre Gunder Frank, *ReORIENT: Global Economy in the Asian Age,* Berkeley: CA: University of California Press, 1998.
12 For more detailed analysis of Macao/Canton's role to China's and Asia's modernization, please see my article 'Canton/Macau: The Key to Pre-Modern/Modern China', *The Journal of Asian Politics and History*, no. 1, Fall of 2013, pp. 1–28.
13 Gavin Black, *The Golden Cockatrice,* New York: Harper & Row, 1975, p. 12; Henry Norman, *The Peoples and Politics of the Far East*, London: T. Fisher Unwin, 1907, p. 190–191. See Cheng, *Macau: A Cultural Janus*, p. 136.
14 Jonathan Porter, *Macau: The Imaginary City – Culture and Society, 1557 to the Present*, Boulder, CO: Westview Press, 1996, p. 94.
15 Gavin Black, *The Golden Cockatrice*, New York: Harper & Row, 1975, p. 3.
16 Those who believed that China did never cede Macao to Portugal are mostly Chinese scholars, including, for example, Huang Hongzhao, *Aomenshi (The History of Macao)*, Hong Kong: Shangwu yinshuguan, 1987, pp. 65–66; Yuan Bangjian and Yuan Guixiu, *Aomen shilue (A Brief History of Macao)*, Hong Kong: Zhongliu chubanshe, 1988, p. 45; Tan Zhiqiang, see his *Aomen zhuquan wenti shimo (1553–1993)* (Camoes C.K. Tam, *Disputes Concerning Macao's Sovereignty between China and Portugal, 1553–1993*), Taipei, Taiwan: Yongye chubanshe, 1994, p. 149; Liang Jiabin, 'Lun Aomen zai lishishang tiaoyueshang de diwei' ('Macao's Position in History and Treaties') in Huang Qichen and Deng Kaisong (eds), *Zhongwai xuezhe lun Aomen lishi (Comments by Chinese and Foreign Scholars*

on the History of Macao), Macao: Macao Foundation, 1995, p. 362. Those who claimed that the Qing government did yield the sovereign right over Macao to Portugal, however, are mostly Western scholars such as Huang Hongzhao and Li Baoping (trans.), Montalto de Jesus, *Lishishang de Aomen* (*Historic Macao*), Macao: Macao Foundation, 2000, p. 23.

17 To name just a few, for example, see Huang Hanqiang, 'Guanyu jianli Aomenxue de yixie sikao' ('Some Reflections on the Establishment of Macaology'), *Gang Ao Jingji* (*The Economy of Hong Kong and Macao*), Canton, no. **2**, 1989; Chang Shaowen, 'Cong Aomen lishi wenhua de tedian luetan jianli "Aomenxue" wenti' ('A Brief Discussion on the Issue of Establishing "Macaology" from the Angle of the Characteristics of Macao's History and Culture'), *Wenhua zazhi* (*Review of Culture*), no. 19, 1994. Also, conferences on Macaology were respectively held by the Association for Social Sciences of Macao in November 1986 and the Institute of Macau Studies at the University of East Asia in February 1989.

18 See the articles by Xu Jialu, Zhao Wei, Jin Li, Wu Zhiliang, Hao Yufan, Zuo Xinping, Tang Kaijian, Chen Shurong, Zhang Xiping, Lin Guangzhi, Zhu Shoutong, Wang Jie, Ren Dayuan , Li Changsen, Huang Hanqiang, Yang Kaijing, Wu Hongqi, Zhao Chao, Hu Gen, Gong Gang, Geoffrey C. Gunn, Tereza Sena, etc. in Hao Yufan, Wu Zhiliang and Lin Guangzhi (eds), *Aomenxue yinlun: Shoujie Aomenxue guoji xueshu yantaohui lunwenji* (*The Introduction of Macaology: A Collection from the First International Academic Conference on Macaology*), Beijing: Social Sciences Academic Press, 2010; and articles by Huang Hanqiang and Wu Zhiliang in Wu Zhiliang and Chen Zhenyu (eds), *Aomen Renwen shehui kexue yanjiu wenxuan: Zhonghejuan* (*The Selection of Sutdies in Humanities and Social Sciences of Macau: Miscellaneous*), Beijing: Social Sciences Academic Press, 2009; as well as newspaper articles by Lin Guangzhi, Hao Yufan, Zhu Shoutong, Hao Zhidong, Gong Gang, Yang Kaijing, Guan Feng in *Aomen ribao*, 24 and 31 March 2010, 7, 14, 21 and 28 April 2010 and 5 May 2010.

19 Bai Huawen, 'Zhongguo Dunhuangxue mulu he mulu gongzuo de chuangli yu fazhan jianshu' ('A Briefing of the Establishment and Development of the Catalogue and Cataloguing of China's Dunhuangology'); Cai Jianhong, 'Dunhuangxue yu Dunhuang wenhua de sikao' ('Dunhuangology and Reflection on Dunhuang Culture'), in the Documentary and Research Center for Dunhuang and Tulufan Studies at the Special Section for Rare Books and Manuscripts of National Library (eds), *Dunhuang yu silu wenhua xueshu jiangzuo* (*Academic Lectures on Dunhuang and Silk Road Culture*), Beijing: Beijing Library Press, 2003, pp. 21–26; 38–57.

20 Tang Kaijian, '"Aomenxue" zouyi' ('An Argument for "Macaology"'), in Wu Zhiliang and Chen Zhenyu (eds), *Aomen renwen shehui kexue yanjiu wenxuan: Zhonghejuan* (*The Selection of Studies in Humanities and Social Sciences of Macau: Miscellaneous*), Beijing: Social Sciences Academic Press, 2009, p. 69.

Part I
Faith and the formation of Macao

Religions and urban development

1 Faith and property

Pressures of development and change on the Kwan Tai – Tin Hau temple in Cheok Ka Chun, Taipa, Macao

Peter Zabielskis

Prologue

If there is one simple thing that can be said about Macao, both past and present, it is that it is full of surprises. Everything else about it, or so it seems, is not so simple. For all its diminutive size geographically – it is one of the smallest separately administered civic regions in the world – there is always something about it that is difficult to figure out, still unknown or only partially known, more historical detail or nuance yet to be discussed, with likely new sources of information yet to be uncovered as new research methods develop and people go out into the street to find out what is going on. By some measures, Macao is the richest place in Asia per capita, the most densely populated urban area per square kilometre in the world, and the place with perhaps the largest amount of land claimed from the sea relative to its original size and extent anywhere, with plans for more underway.[1] It is now the venue for the largest amount of casino gambling anywhere in the world, visited, on average, by more than 1,000,000 tourists per month, primarily from mainland China but increasingly from other parts of Asia as well. Yet the people who make up Macao's current population of just over 550,000 do not necessarily see themselves as part of all these new developments, certainly not the glitzy symbolism of its recent, and massive, urban and economic transformation. Macao people are still known to be quite socially conservative, more easy-going, even 'laid back', perhaps even reluctant to entertain progressive new ideas in their approaches to life, when compared to their Cantonese-speaking counterparts in Hong Kong (who share with Macao the use of traditional Chinese characters) or in Guangzhou (Canton), the major city in the adjoining Guangdong province of China. Although booming now, it was not too long ago that Macao was a somewhat sleepy backwater, with a sluggish economy, appreciated for more for certain old-world, folksy and European ways of doing things rather than anything very modern or current or new. But that was prior to the administrative handover of Macao to the People's Republic of China in 1999. Many things have changed since that date, but many also seem to have stayed at least somewhat the same. People in Macao walk slower on the street than people in Hong Kong, apparently work fewer hours, and seem to experience less stress, so perhaps that which has remained or been resistant to change is for the good.

The surprising thing about the social and material transformations in Macao is that there is still so much that is 'old' in Macao in terms of genuine links to the past that still vibrate in people's lives. This should logically be most self-evident in the material heritage of what remains of Macao's old and historic built environment, a section of which was designated as a World Heritage site by UNESCO.[2] But the monuments and buildings that are listed in this programme cover only a narrow swatch of the city that most visitors, coming to Macao for an average of two days and mainly for the purpose of gambling, can easily avoid entirely. Widely touted by the government in its tourist promotions as a mark of Macao's brand identity, the sites in this protected area are nevertheless so often filled with crowds of transient visitors that many local people no longer use them or consider them their own. Sleepy no more, they now belong to the world. These beautiful old buildings may well be a source of history-based pride on the international scene, for those who care about such things, but there are many more locally significant connections to the past that are sometimes harder to see. Rooted in a reluctance to embrace newness for its own sake, and an understandable queasiness at the thought of identifying with casino culture or even the considerable economic benefits it has brought, these links to the past consist of certain ways of doing and thinking about things that continue to go their own way despite a sea of change and mountains of high-rises growing up around them. Some of these dynamics concern long-established Chinese values and social patterns that continue to be present and viable in social life: filial piety, pragmatism, the importance of *guanxi* or personal relationships and the informal but highly articulate art of 'gift giving' that keeps connections alive.[3] Others concern what may be the legacy of a culturally specific combination of Chinese and Portuguese ideas and procedures, such as a high value placed on the ease and casualness of interpersonal trust, based not on paper, law and regulation, but dinner, drinks and handshakes.[4] All of these can work to keep people's feet on the ground of the past and perhaps also to help keep heads above the water in the midst of rapid social and economic transformation. But perhaps another significant factor in connecting with the past is the value still found in 'traditional' Chinese religious beliefs and practices, which does not seem to have been impacted much by ideas of official communist atheism that could have travelled with new waves of immigrants from China in recent decades but apparently did not.[5]

Given this conservatism, one could easily assume that Macao society must also be very religious. It is religious but not very. Religious fervour is perhaps a defining feature of social conservatism in other places, such as the United States, but yet another surprising thing about Macao is that religious practice here is more of an understated or casual assumption of everyday life than a highly emotive and public symbol. To think that high emotion must be part of its religiosity is understandable since so many of the prominent monuments in the official heritage list are religious: churches, temples, shrines or religiously affiliated schools and cemeteries.[6] But actual religious practice is often more personal than monumental. In Chinese folk religion, it may be no more than a small plaque, barely three dimensional enough to be called a shrine, to Tu Di, the god of earth, or the quick burning, in a metal box on the sidewalk, of paper offerings to the spirits, quickly cleaned up and removed afterwards, or the smell every morning of joss sticks burning in the hallways of high-rise apartment complexes. Catholics may no longer go to mass regularly in any of Macao's spectacular historic churches, but some may still keep a crucifix or religious pictures and statues at home. Other Macanese, with ancestors both European and Asian, may have a keener interest in Feng-shui than in Christian saints and display images of Chinese deities at home.[7] The point is simply that whatever religiosity exists in Macao, its most significant extent is not necessarily seen or embodied in the great, architecturally and histori-cally significant, heritage-designated monuments for which Macao is known. These grand venues do still continue to enjoy a tradition of continuous use, and their fame is well deserved, but they are also subject to disruptive recent increases in the volume of activities unrelated to their original local function, such as tourism, and are therefore perhaps no longer completely indicative of local values, sentiments and practices.

Such intangibles of everyday life, tied of course to different sets of material practices, is the stuff of anthropology, and another surprising thing about Macao is that, despite its cultural richness, there has been so little anthropo-logical research done there. The number of full-length, interpretive, cultural anthropological monographs (in English) that immediately come to mind would require less than one hand to count.[8] These works concentrate largely on the political dimensions of life in Macao as the crossroads of history, cul-ture and people from different continents. The 'East meets West' theme of Macao as a former Portuguese colony in China has received obligatory men-tion by writers and researchers in many other disciplines, but there is still so much more that can be said and thought about this and many other topics from an anthropological point of view. Macao and its many surprises are long overdue for more contemporary ethnographic, and not just historical, inves-tigation. In shorter works, the all-important topic of religion in Macao has been covered from many angles, very often focused on Macao as the launch pad for the spread of Christianity in Asia, but there has been considerably less work done, in Western languages, on Chinese religious practice in Macao.[9] Several short works attempt interpretations of Chinese religion with data from both Hong Kong and Macao, but this is insufficiently local and specific for current anthropological tastes. When the two places are combined like this, it seems that the vast majority of materials and cases covered are from Hong Kong only.[10] Historians writing on Macao must invariably account for religion, but in one instance of an article specifically about Chinese religion in Macao, it is not clear that the author actually ever spoke with anyone about local points of view toward its history.[11] Therefore the contribution by Tianshu Zhu, the next chapter of this collection, combining as it does both historical and ethnographic methods in addressing current religious practice in the unique urban setting of Macao, is especially welcome.

The current chapter attempts a small contribution to the understanding of Chinese religion in Macao by presenting an 'ethnographic sketch' of one small temple and one man's intimate involvement with it throughout most of his life. In many ways, this is a subject beloved by anthropologists: listening hard to what the 'little guy' has to say, attempting to delineate how all this fits into a larger scheme of things, both past and present, and paying attention to what people in a given place find meaningful or significant things in their lives. 'Ethnographic' in this sense does not mean any comprehensive, 'objective' history. Historical background is provided, of course, but more attention is paid to those social or historical aspects or themes that local people themselves feel are important because these are what they have chosen to emphasize in open-ended interviews, which is the field research method used here. The temple in Cheok Ka Chun described here is very small and certainly not very prominent, in the larger, officially recorded scheme of things. There do not seem to be many printed materials about it that are readily available in any language, so this research approach seems to be appropriate.

This temple is thus a historical monument that is easily overlooked, both by scholars and any visitor to Macao. I venture to say that the vast majority of both have never heard of it. The man in question lives in the temple and has cared for it for more than 30 years, rarely venturing out nowadays except to visit his home village in China once a year during the Ching Ming festival. By looking at his situation closely, hopefully some wider relevance will be revealed: how social patterns and institutions, in the long run and changing over time, combined with more immediately dramatic changes of recent political and historical events, impact individual lives and sentiments, as well as spiritual outlooks and practices. Compared with other, major, 'world religions' (Buddhism, Christianity, Islam) that have strong textual traditions explicitly concerned with interior mental or emotional or spiritual states, this task of investigating lived histories and social patterns is perhaps most immediately pertinent to the study of Chinese folk religion, which, in some ways, can not easily be approached in any other way since, by contrast it is pragmatic, practical, action oriented, material minded, highly locally specific and without any common or widely accepted scriptural basis.[12]

Chinese popular or 'folk' religion is neither Taoism nor Buddhism but combines elements of both, along with ancestor worship and perhaps some influences from Confucianism; it has been practiced for thousands of years throughout the world, wherever there are Chinese people. It has been called a 'nameless' religion,[13] or 'shenism',[14] for want of an appropriate '-ism', because its focus is worship of 'shen' – spirits – of various sorts. Spirits may be ancestors, deified historical figures or heroes, spirits in control of various natural forces, or various combinations of these who visit, inhabit and fill the human world from a realm beyond death.[15] They offer people who attend to them solace, protection, hope, health and good luck. Religious practices anywhere variously mirror, support or challenge existing human social patterns and organizations, but in this case a hierarchy of spirits is thought to reflect and influence more or less closely the human social hierarchy of kings, ministers, servants and natural powers that make up actual mundane governments and lives. But the crucial difference between Chinese folk religion and other big name '-isms' is that in folk religious practice the gods and their worship often reflect and represent very unofficial structures of authority that may act to influence lives in ways alternative to any real worldly government. Some spirits and temples have been sanctioned by official elites and they have supported ruling administrative power structures in Chinese history, but this is not what we are talking about here. Spirits (or gods), the ways that people understand them, and the practices of the people who worship or attend to them are themselves forms of social organization that provide means for both community coherence and the creation and reproduction of social structures that are embedded in contemporary social and political realities.[16] The spiritual hierarchy is 'far less precisely defined and organized than the civil bureaucracy', works to provide definite and desirable, but ineffable, services such as ensuring fertility, male children and luck, and thus 'it fills the gaps left by the civil bureaucracy'.[17] It is not just a parallel alternative option but crucially a 'part of the order of life'.[18]

The plan for this chapter is as follows: a more or less 'objective' account of the temple, its history and its current status, based on a very limited number of available sources; followed by biographical details, past and present, of the man currently in charge of its upkeep; followed by a series of his actual statements about its origins, history, current situation, the meaning of all of the above, and his plans and fears about its future. Chinese folk religion is materialistic in that it involves concrete action more than interior mental states: the primary ritual action is the offering of material gifts, fruit, cooked food and paper offerings.[19] But in its current urban context, temples such as this one are surrounded by materialism of a different sort – a rapidly developing consumer culture, large-scale and massively transforming real estate development, land grabs and increasing rationalization and bureaucratization of previously informal local administrative powers that had allowed more local forms of organization to thrive. The question then becomes: how, and in what form, will this temple be able to survive? The bulk of the chapter will be spent interpreting what its very articulate spokesperson has to say. Some of what he has to say about the nature of value, land, religion, temples and society, is quite unexpected, even surprising, which is perhaps typical of Macao. His story is valuable in that it clearly shows how individual biographies, political realities and living histories all reflect, bounce off and impact each other in everyday life in the unique combination of forces and factors that is Macao and how all this plays out in the continued practice of a very ancient tradition.

Jumping ahead to what his story specifically reveals, there are perhaps three main points. First of all, the fortunes of his temple, in terms of numbers of visitors and their donations, has waned since the handover of Macao to mainland China in 1999. From his point of view, this is largely because many of the somewhat 'unsavoury' types of people who seem to have patronized the temple throughout its history – pirates, gangsters, thieves, triad members – found it more difficult to travel freely between mainland China, Macao and Hong Kong, following a stronger rationalization and enforcement of administrative control by the Chinese than by the Portuguese. His temple may have also been especially attractive as a venue for religious worship at a time when such practice was officially discouraged in China, and may now be less attractive since religion is once again permitted and many activities have been revived in the mainland, with some temples even built or rebuilt on very grand scales. Second, what is surprising is that he seems perfectly willing to move the temple if the government wants the land it sits on for development. This flies in the face of most standard principles of historical preservation, which insist on protecting original physical materials, in their original environmental contexts, as much as possible. Third, and perhaps most importantly, this individual reminds us of what is perhaps most important to consider in all of this: human social organizations and how they impact each other. If the outcomes of such impacts are not satisfactory, perhaps the ways people, and especially governments, organize things can and should be changed.

Despite the various, and sometimes conflicting types of material organization involved here – the materialism of ritual action in the form of tangible gifts to the gods; the historical material of the old temple itself; the economic value of the land it sits on; and the increasingly monetized, materialist ambitions of the high-rise, consumer society that now engulfs it – perhaps something less physically evident is more valuable and important to consider, such as belief in the value of individual passion, effort and initiative that marks the traditional Chinese religious concern to maintain harmonious, prosperous, and auspicious relationships between humans, administrative structures and hierarchies, and the world of spirits, gods and ancestors. These concerns are keys to understanding the essence of a local brand of social conservatism, Macao style.

History of the temple

Although there is no problem in finding it once you have been there, the Kwan Tai – Tin Hau temple is in the rather secluded and now sparsely populated village of Cheok Ka Chun, which can be translated as 'Village of the Zhuo families'. Both the village and the temple are not too distant from, but also not visible from, Avenida Dr Sun Yat-sen, a major artery on the island of Taipa, just off the Macao peninsula. This separation of the island of Taipa facilitated a slower incorporation of the area into the Portuguese administration centred on the Macao peninsula. Control of Taipa was one of the policies of the much-hated, and eventually assassinated, Governor Ferreira do Amaral (1803–1849) that was most strongly opposed by the Chinese.[20] Taipa as a separate island entity no longer exists but is now connected to the also once-separate island of Coloane due to reclamation named the 'Cotai Strip'. These islands were the last to be heavily populated and urbanized in Macao, so there is still some quiet and green, but the new strip between them is now home to possibly the world's largest concentration of high-rise resort-hotel casinos. The temple in the village – if it is still called that in any official records – is on a road, but barely. If you drive there it seems to be a place where real roads stop: some are so narrow and roughly pitted, and not even paved in some portions, that as you drive in you may begin to wonder if you've turned into a place not meant for cars at all. But this was not always the case. The quiet roadways wind through deserted empty lots marked by the ruined foundations and walls of what were once lively nightclubs and beer gardens. The temple, tucked off to the side of a cul-de-sac, is immaculately maintained and always open, lying just beyond a swinging metal gate that can be closed and locked but seemingly never is.

Kwan Tai and Tin Hau are two of the most popular deities in Macao, but this temple is too remote from the centre of things and too difficult to find to be on any heritage walking tour,[21] despite it likely being the oldest temple in Taipa. By one reckoning, two forms of traditional Chinese worship, each with a corresponding temple, have served historically as symbols of 'territorial unity in Chinese society':[22] the lineage or ancestral hall and the territorial temple.[23] This temple in Taipa is neither, or rather has elements of both, which may be an indication that 'territorial unity' was not of much concern in this case and that the temple represents a uniquely urban way of organizing both worship and territory that can accommodate a range of various devotees and concepts both near and far. There is no evidence that it was ever a lineage temple of the Zhuo family, for whom the village is named, and it does not have the architectural plan of such a temple. Very likely it did at one time serve a local village community who may have grown rice in the area, but due to its location, originally near the sea before extensive land reclamation, it also seems to have always attracted worshippers from throughout the region of the Pearl River Delta, which is also the recollection of its current caretaker.

The unsubstantiated date for its construction is 1684, during the early Qing dynasty. Tin Hau, known also to other ways of speaking and spelling as Mazu, Tian Hou, Tien Hau, or A-Ma, is the queen of heaven and goddess of the sea who lent her name to that of Macao itself. The famous A-Ma Temple in the Inner Harbour, facing China, is a must-see item on any list of heritage 'greatest hits' in Macao, but it is not clear if her temple in Cheok Ka Chun village is even listed in any official heritage register of protected sites. The origins of the Tin Hau or Mazu cult are not clear, but she seems to have been a historical figure, a maiden from the Lin family in either the Fujian or the Zhejiang province of China, who was born in the eighth, tenth or twelfth century.[24] Legend has it that she died very young, sacrificing her life to save seafarers. She was subsequently deified and her cult became widely popular among sailors and fishermen throughout maritime regions of China. Tin Hau/Mazu received imperial patronage in the early Ming dynasty and her temple in Fujian was restored by the great Chinese admiral Zheng Ho. She is associated with the earliest temples of Macao that predate the arrival of the Portuguese.[25] A favourite among overseas Chinese communities with any connection to the sea, she is present in numerous temples and shrines throughout Southeast Asia, is especially popular in Taiwan and is also found on many home altars in Macao.[26]

Many Chinese folk religion temples that take their name from the main or major deities in residence also provide space for other gods as well, which is obviously the case here. Tin Hau shares equal billing, architecturally and in terms of the temple's name, with Kwan Tai, also known as Guan Di, Kwan Kung, or Kwan Ti/Mou Tai. 'Di' means 'god'. Another deified human, Guan Di started out as Guan Yu, one of the greatest heroes in an age of heroism, the Three Kingdoms era of China in the third century; he was betrayed and executed by his enemies in 220 AD. Similar to the case of Mazu, a long process of apotheosis culminated, this time in the late Ming, with imperial conferral of the title 'Di'. During the Qing, he was awarded an even higher upgrade with the title 'Guan Dafuzi', 'Guan the Great Sage and Teacher', equivalent in rank to that of Confucius.[27] He is known as the god of war and business, and a fierce warrior who protects people who worship him from any kind of harm. He is often depicted with a red face and in an active pose and is a favourite among triad (gang) members. He is also present on altars inside many shops and businesses. At the temple here he is worshipped, as in other temples, along with his two attendants: his adopted son, Guan Ping or Kwan Ping, a young man often shown with a sack of money, and his bodyguard and arms-bearer, Zhou Cang or Jao Chong, a ferocious figure with a battleaxe. Other deities with presences in the Taipa temple are Tu Di or To Dei Kung, the earth god,[28] and the gate gods Chan Shuk Bo and Wat Chi King Tak.

The Kwan Tai – Tin Hau temple in Cheok Ka Chun is somewhat unusual in that there are two separate chambers, side by side, one for each of the main deities, female and male, and each with their own entrance, although there is a connecting passageway. Each room is roughly equivalent in size, but Kwan Tai's is slightly larger, perhaps because his room also holds several additional deities as well, or perhaps as an expression of gender difference, with the male given more space. This complex arrangement of places for multiple deities and a colourful range of furniture and equipment needed to serve them is typical of many temples of Chinese folk religion.[29] Some offerings, at the very least some burning joss sticks, should be offered to the gods at all times.

Inscriptions still extant inside the temple include lists of donors and the amounts they gave, some as small as one yuan, along with the names of their businesses or shops, at the time of repairs and restorations made in 1856, 1893, 1901 and 1917.[30] These personalize, in a permanent way, the widespread support the temple has received throughout its history, but little more than

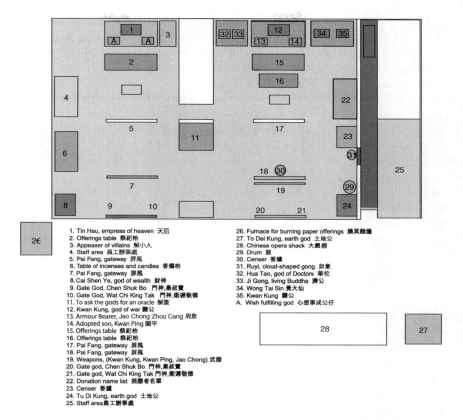

1. Tin Hau, empress of heaven 天后
2. Offerings table 祭祀枱
3. Appeaser of villains 解小人
4. Staff area 員工辦事處
5. Pai Fang, gateway 屏風
6. Table of incenses and candles 香燭枱
7. Pai Fang, gateway 屏風
8. Cai Shen Ye, god of wealth 財神
9. Gate God, Chen Shuk Bo 門神,秦叔寶
10. Gate God, Wat Chi King Tak 門神,衛遲敬德
11. To ask the gods for an oracle 解簽
12. Kwan Kung, god of war 關公
13. Armour Bearer, Jao Chong Zhou Cang 周倉
14. Adopted son, Kwan Ping 關平
15. Offerings table 祭祀枱
16. Offerings table 祭祀枱
17. Pai Fang, gateway 屏風
18. Pai Fang, gateway 屏風
19. Weapons, (Kwan Kung, Kwan Ping, Jao Chong) 武器
20. Gate god, Chen Shuk Bo 門神,秦叔寶
21. Gate god, Wat Chi King Tak 門神,衛遲敬德
22. Donation name list 捐獻者名單
23. Censer 香爐
24. Tu Di Kung, earth god 土地公
25. Staff area 員工辦事處

26. Furnace for burning paper offerings 燒冥鏹爐
27. To Dei Kung, earth god 土地公
28. Chinese opera shack 大戲棚
29. Drum 鼓
30. Censer 香爐
31. Ruyi, cloud-shaped gong 如意
32. Hua Tao, god of Doctors 華佗
33. Ji Gong, living Buddha 濟公
34. Wong Tai Sin 黃大仙
35. Kwan Kung 關公
A. Wish fulfilling god 心想事成公仔

Figure 1.1 Kwan Tai – Tin Hau temple in Cheok Ka Chun, Taipa, Macao: plan of the temple and its interior furnishings. Drawn by Leong Fong Hio, Leong Mei Ian, Lei Mei In and Kong Mio Si.

this simple fact about the temple's history can be gleaned from such inscriptions. More recent renovations and donations for them would not necessarily have been recorded in such lasting inscriptions, but the current practice of publically posting on paper strips inside the temple the names of donors and the amounts they gave during festivals for the gods' birthdays replicates these earlier, more permanent accounts.

Whether by oral tradition, unpublished inscription or artistic style and material, the current caretaker estimates that there are two items in the temple that may date from the time of its original construction: the statue of Tin Hau herself, which is unusual in that she holds a book and which he claims is older than the image in the main A-Ma Temple; and a stone candlestick. There is also a tablet from Fujian, 'because people from Fujian settled here', he says, which he claims is 200 years old. Due to the temple's now isolated location, far from the places many people live or regularly frequent, attendance at the temple has radically diminished in recent years, but has not dropped off entirely. There are still some loyal devotees, from Macao, Hong Kong and mainland China, who visit when they are in the area, and especially during festivals celebrating the gods' birthdays, which, according to the caretaker, has always been the case throughout the temple's history. Currently diminished numbers may represent increased rationalization of administrative controls at the border since the handover to China by the Portuguese, which prevents casual movement between the mainland, Hong Kong and Macao, increased competition from temples in the mainland, or perhaps a combination of both. Little has been written about the temple, and to the author's knowledge it has never been featured in any tourist brochure.

The above represents just about the full extent of the history of the temple that can be readily be ascertained from standard historical sources, such as inscriptions, together with the testimony of a living informant – its current caretaker – for whom the temple has been a major part of his life and that of his family for many years. It is to his story, and to his testimony, much richer than any written source, that we now turn.

Biography

When one looks at such a venerable structure, very likely the oldest temple in Taipa, one would think that every aspect or basic bit of information about it – pending further historical research, of course – should by now be perfectly clear and evident as a matter of public record. Such an important old building should already be registered with the government, perhaps listed as a heritage property, and likely subject to both government subsidies and preservation management plans. Certainly the ownership of both the structure and the land should be beyond question. But once again – surprise – this is not the case here, because this is Macao. Aren't such properties either owned or largely controlled and supported by the government? In Hong Kong, especially, and in many other places, one would expect that all such matters would have been firmly settled long ago, but this has not been the case in Macao. The Macao government had no registration requirement for temples until the era of heritage preservation, which dates only from the past few decades. Some temples in Macao are privately owned, and not always by corporate entities or boards of trustees but by individuals or individual families. The latter is the case here. My main informant for this project was Mr Wang, who lives in temple and claims to be its rightful owner just like two generations of his family before him. It is he who has provided me with a wealth of information about the temple's past, its current situation and its uncertain future. His life, intimately tied to the temple as a site of living history for himself and his family, represents a lot of what Macao religion and society, at least for Chinese people in Macao, is all about. His is a story of a specific kind of transnational outlook and regional mobility common to the life histories of many people in Macao – transnational because political, social and religious influences on individual lives in this region, the Pearl River Delta, come from three nation-states (China, Portugal and Britain) and, in the postcolonial era, three different Chinese political administrations (the People's Republic of China, and the Special Administrative Regions of Macao and Hong Kong). Mr Wang's life and movements span all these regions and eras.

Mr Wang was born in Shanshui, in Guandong province on the mainland, grew up in Hong Kong, and has lived in the Kwan Tai – Tin Hau Temple in Cheok Ka Chun village, Taipa, for the past 30 years as its caretaker and owner. He was 70 years old when I talked with him. Key events in his life have always revolved around the temple, which he says his great-uncle bought for 8,000 silver dollars, likely in the late 1940s:

> My great-uncle spent all the money he had to buy this temple... At that time, 8,000 silver dollars meant a lot of money. He could have bought all the shops in Rua do Cunha with 8,000 silver dollars ... With 300 silver dollars you could buy one shop. Some shops were only worth 200 or even less. So you can see how much money we spent on this temple.

Several things are worth noting in this statement. First of all, the amount of money involved is significant, as Mr Wang clearly indicates. It is not clear what kind of silver dollars are involved – the coins of which nation and at what comparable value? Yet Mr Wang immediately anticipates this question by citing an equivalent worth at the time. The price is much higher than that of a commercial shop, and the value paid is an amount of precious metal, rendering any particular nation's currency irrelevant. The amount represented a significant investment in a non-commercial, religious property and the magnitude of the commitment was made even more significant by current common knowledge that those same shops, in the centre of Taipa, are now worth many thousands of times more. So in telling me this, Mr Wang was reaffirming the values and strength of his family's commitment to serve the gods and a community of worshippers in ways less commercial or materialistic than current trends in Macao's currently high-priced property market would seem to indicate.

The strong subtext here is a firm commitment to Chinese folk religion, as a matter of both a continuous practice in this location for hundreds of years and an enduring family tradition spanning multiple generations. Mr Wang's story here is also significant, not just as an individual family history, but because it is highly indicative of Macao's unique historical position in the region's socio-economic-religious scheme of things. To put it shortly and bluntly, being in Macao gave him and his family the space, since they could afford it, to do their own thing, to follow their own sets of values, to be as 'traditional' as they liked, and to be Chinese in ways largely separate and distinct from the powers and controls of any political regime, especially the Portuguese administration of Macao, with its notoriously hands-off approach

toward the affairs of its local Chinese population. In terms of religious practice, such continuity would not have been possible amid the political turmoil
in the People's Republic; in terms of economic opportunity, it is also hard
to imagine a land purchase made in Hong Kong for similar spiritual reasons
given that territory's long-standing and current emphasis on profit-minded
production and materialist consumption. Much has been made of Macao
as a meeting point, a crossroads between East and West.[31] But apart from
the unique, and minority, case of a distinct blend of Chinese and European
created physically and culturally by the Macanese community, for most people in Macao this was a place marked by 'cultural duality',[32] and was never a
melting pot:

> Although the Portuguese presence in Macao had been colonial, the form
> it had taken, rather than creating a hybrid culture, had allowed 'tra-
> ditional' Chinese culture to develop more 'naturally', free from forcible
> intrusions by states (as in the PRC) or dilution by globalizing economic
> forces (as in Hong Kong).[33]

People came to Macao in search of opportunity: to trade, to make money, to
practice their faith and perhaps to create new believers (in approximately that
order of importance), and Macao afforded them relative freedom to do so.[34]
Mr Wang's family was no exception. They had bought a historic temple with
the hardest cash there is – precious metal – a unit of value well-understood by
anyone anywhere in that it is outside the purview or control of any national
currency, just as the temple's clientele were drawn to worship there from a
range of differently administered regions: China, Macao and Hong Kong.

The purchase may have been nobly religious-minded but the opportunity
it represented was also not completely divorced from a pragmatic eye toward
business. Mr Wang's great-uncle and his father and other uncles were all
Feng-shui masters who were well-known in Hong Kong for advising clients
about geomancy. Here was an opportunity to expand operations in a territory new to the family trade. Not only could some family members live in
the room adjoining the temple but their presence there would help establish
a new branch in Macao. A temple need not be exclusive in its religious function; it can also be a residence, a community centre and a for-profit enterprise.
Similar arrangements occur in at least one other privately owned temple in
Taipa, which does a thriving business as a venue for fortune-telling, especially
during Chinese New Year.

João de Pina-Cabral notes that, in some ways, everyone in Macao, as a
member of any group, continues to experience now as they did in the past,
a certain amount of disjuncture in terms of long-term political and social
identification, as well as a feeling of fluidity and geographical transience,
either potential or real.[35] Both Portuguese and Chinese, it seems, have felt
ready to leave Macao should conditions ever prove less than favourable for
their pursuits, and for both there is a disjuncture, conversely articulated for

each, between what he calls the 'rights of citizenship' versus the 'rights of sovereignty'.[36] During the Portuguese administration, the citizenship of the Portuguese was never in question, but Portuguese sovereignty over Macao was never certain or secure. For the Chinese it was the reverse. There was little question that the place was, after all, part of China, but the struggle to attain or maintain rights of citizenship for Chinese not holding Portuguese passports, such as the right of permanent abode, was often problematic. Such conflicts also characterize Mr Wang's family history.

If a date in the late 1940s for the sale of the temple to his great-uncle is correct,[37] Mr Wang would have been a child at the time of the purchase. Since his family was from China, such a large investment also meant a firm commitment by the family to Macao as a place to settle and also, perhaps, legal legitimation of their right to do so for generations to come. Albert Yee has identified what he calls the 'Chinese stepping-stone syndrome'.[38] Misruled, or at least denied economic opportunities and, later, freedom of religious expression in China, many mainland Chinese turned to Hong Kong and Macao as stepping stones toward better lives, with the ultimate goal being the transformation of transience into long-term, legal permanence. Mr Wang mentioned that he grew up as a child in Hong Kong and moved to Macao when his family bought the temple. Thus it must have seemed that either Hong Kong or Macao would do as a stepping stone for the family, with the ideal situation being easy mobility between the two, since the family business was already established in Hong Kong. But this was not as easy at mid-century as it might seem for someone from the mainland, despite somewhat lax border controls at the time, since there were three different administrative Chinas involved. Legal or not, the family would live in the temple and centre their business there, with similar stories holding true regarding the casual mobility of their clientele as well. Being Chinese in ways they saw fit and enjoying traditional Chinese pursuits could continue despite administrative complexity and without official sanction, which could perhaps be kept at arm's length as something not completely necessary. As it turns out, Mr Wang did not follow in his father's footsteps in becoming a Feng-shui expert, but perhaps he was considering it at the time when his application for residency in Hong Kong was denied in 1956, when he must have been a young man. If he was uncertain then about his path in life, or where he would finally settle, this is something that now, at age 70, has long been resolved:

I treat this temple and this place as my home.

Legitimizing residency in this home was never easy, and it still is not, for a new set of legal administrative reasons, as seen below. Movement between Hong Kong and Macao, for both his family and their clients, may have been casual and largely uncontrolled in some ways at mid-century and even later, but it was perhaps somewhat more difficult for mainlanders. Legal residency in either Hong Kong or Macao would have facilitated Mr Wang's role in helping to run the temple, even if he was never to become a Feng-shui expert. Mr Wang applied again for Hong Kong residency in the 1970s, this time likely due to feeling pressure to fulfil his duties of filial piety. This was around the time that both parents, first his father then his mother, were urging him to keep and maintain the temple after they died.

> [When] my father was in the hospital, and asked to see me he said to me: 'Your younger brother isn't interested in watching out for this temple, but you should keep it as your job.' He also said, 'whoever knows you will come'!

Similarly, before his mother died

> ... she said, 'no matter how difficult it will be, you have to keep this temple as a way to make a living, as a family heritage'. So I had no choice but to listen.

With loyalty toward a family tradition that was tied to a material monument with staying power beyond any individual family member's death, Mr Wang felt compelled to keep and maintain the temple no matter what. But legal administrative support in terms of official residency outside the mainland was slow in coming. His application for Hong Kong residency was again denied in the 1970s, which he now blames on political reasons:

> At the time I really didn't know much about the Communist Party and their policy ... [but] after the liberation of China in 1949, it was difficult for people to go and live in Hong Kong ... During the reign of Mao Zedong anyone who mentioned Hong Kong and Macao should be opposed because Hong Kong was a capitalist society.

It was only later, under a different state ideology, that his residency outside the mainland was legitimized:

> After Deng Xiaoping came to power, the controlling was deregulated. Based on the rule of 'you belong to where you come from', people from Hong Kong and Macao could return to Hong Kong and Macao.

These are simple statements of a political reality but they express Mr Wang's confusion as to what administrative power he fits into or has a claim on him. Which of the three Chinas is pushing and pulling and in what ways? Was the mainland preventing him from becoming a capitalist, or Hong Kong and Macao refusing him because he was born and grew up in a communist region? The Portuguese administration of Macao was notoriously lax in certain aspects of its governance, but more mainland friendly – a 'chaotic jumble ...

that reflected the shortcomings of Portuguese colonialism' with 'no clearly identifiable system'[39] in comparison to the British administration of Hong Kong. This was the tangle of an inconsistent disjuncture between rights of sovereignty and rights of citizenship that Mr Wang found himself in the midst of,[40] simply by acting on his family's desire to keep up certain Chinese traditions much older than any of these political administrations, such as the expression of filial piety through continuity of worship in the family's temple. In his case this meant a fair amount of regional travel and cross-administration movement and manoeuvre. Although I did not press him as to which ID card, Macao or Hong Kong, he ultimately received (perhaps both), presumably Mr Wang was able to demonstrate sufficient family residential history outside the mainland to have his application for permanent residency approved, hence his citation of the idea that the new openness of mainland political reform included the 'rule of "you belong where you come from"'. His use of the word 'rule' is significant here. Places have authority, both personally, over emotions, and politically. They are not matters to be taken lightly. Hong Kong and Macao as 'Chinese stepping stones' is an interpretation of the effort involved in settling in these places which,[41] once achieved and established, can be considered 'new' places to come from. Through effort, Mr Wang and his family have created a new home: 'I treat this temple and this place as my home.' Creating a new home is possible. This is a different sentiment than loyalties of blood and birth, which can also remain significant at the same time, even in very traditional ways, but with a shift in emphasis required by new territorial contexts. Now limited in his movements by his age, Mr Wang leaves Taipa and the temple only once a year, to go to his ancestral village in Shanshui, in Guandong province on the mainland, during the Ching Ming festival. Questions of his legal residency are now resolved but, as will later be seen, tensions remain between the personal, individual energy of self-created effort and entrepreneurship he and his family have demonstrated, and the public or impersonal constraints exerted by larger political and social structures and administrative requirements.[42] As far as Mr Wang's life history and social milieu are concerned, the less external sources of regulation the better.

The clientele of the temple

When Mr Wang finally inherited the temple from his father in 1979, he inherited an entire social system as well. Without his asking them to, a Chinese opera troupe still appeared to perform for the gods on their birthdays in front of the temple, collecting enough donations from visitors to support their performances. Before he died his father had told him 'whoever knows you will come'. But unlike his father, he was not a Feng-shui expert and fewer people knew him, resulting in fewer numbers visiting the temple. Until such time that the temple business picked up, and still with no legal local residency, like so many others at the time, he took advantage of relatively easy transit between Macao and the mainland to make ends meet by engaging in small-scale, cross-border trade:

> It was not until eight years after my father passed away that people came to the temple. Because no one knew me at the time the only thing I could do was to go to the Mercado do S. Domingo to sell clothes. At that time I went to Gongbei to sell clothes at night and to the Mercado do S. Domingo during the day in order to make a living. And I also helped others transfer things between Zhuhai and Macao. Sometimes I went to Jiangmen [a city in Guandong province] to sell clothes. People [worshippers] didn't believe in me because they didn't know me, so they didn't come to the temple after the death of my father.

The small amount of income he received from a small number of still regular worshippers was not enough to support either himself of the temple immediately after his father's death. But *guanxi* – personal connections or relationships, also likely inherited from his father – was something he could rely on to tide him over in times of trouble, even if the help came from friends of his father that some would consider less than savoury:

> Some [big men] said 'don't worry. We will take the responsibility to protect you. We will help you if you meet troubles.' I was very afraid at that moment because I was like a stranger to this place and I was afraid of saying something wrong and somebody would beat me!

It seems that the social system that Mr Wang inherited with the temple included both the need to pay protection money, and a clientele for the temple that included people from all walks of life, including some with involvement in illicit trades. His perception was that such was also the case in the past:

> There were many pirates in Taipa and Coloane … They believed in Kwan Tai. It was a long, long story! There were many pirates here and they would charge us with a 'protection fee'. I had to give it to them too! If something bad happened to me or my temple, they would protect me.

Kwan Tai/Mou Tai, as a fierce warrior god who offers his worshippers protection, is a favourite deity for worship by secret societies, or organized crime gangs known as triads, whose members are commonly sworn into the brotherhood in temple rituals. The association of triads with certain temples is an old tradition in China, and it seems to have also been part of the history of Mr Wang's temple. When asked about this he replied:

> Yes, in the old days, many people came here to be sworn brothers. They kneeled down before the statue of Kwan Tai, they worshipped Kwan Tai, and then they became sworn brothers. And also, people who did

loan-sharking in the casinos, people who committed murder and arson also came here to worship. But now, they have already stopped their 'business'. Good people and bad people ALL came here!

It is not surprising that Mr Wang speaks of 'all' people in the same breath as the idea of 'brotherhood'. Good and bad exists on a sliding scale within what has been called this 'ideal of brotherhood', a concept central to Confucianism as well as traditional Chinese social structure in general:

[T]he concept of 'fraternal submission'[43] functions as a major structuring metaphor of modern everyday life, performing a central role in the attribution of meaning to the interpersonal relations of subjection and mutual support that are the very stuff of young male association – both in entrepreneurship and in youth gangs.[44]

Mr Wang was not a member of any gang himself, but the fact that he felt compelled to pay protection money to certain big men is part and parcel of this system of submission and mutual loyalty that exists alongside, or outside, any official administrative system.

Mr Wang's efforts to ensure sufficient outside income during the early years of his ownership of the temple also demonstrate an involvement with less-than-official procedures, politics and economic structures, which, in turn, also reflects the activities and interests of the old-time clientele of the temple. This time period, from approximately mid-century to the return of Macao to China in 1999, was marked by an easy flow across political borders into and out of Macao for various purposes, both legitimate and illegitimate, by people with multiple possible affiliations such as himself.[45] In his case, the purpose was petty trade: he sold clothes between and across both China and Macao. Movement through this easily permeable region, which included Hong Kong, replicated the movements of the temple's clientele as well, who were also from all three jurisdictions – China, Macao and Hong Kong. But this administrative ease also meant a freer flow of unsavoury individuals, such as triad members and thieves, who had also patronized the temple, both during Mr Wang's time and before. The Portuguese administration did not seem interested in stopping or able to stop this flow, but once they left the new Chinese administration that took over effected quite a different stance that has affected the fortunes of the temple ever since:

To be honest, in the old days, when Macao was under the rule of the Portuguese government, there were many, many 'bad' people. For example, those who did smuggling business, the bullies, those who cheated people. Some people from outside Macao also came to Macao because it was easy to come here. They believed in Kwan Tai. They all came here to worship ... People from Hong Kong came to worship. And other 'bad' guys from other places also came to Macao. Some were gang members.

But after the handover, the laws and regulations were much stricter than before. So fewer bad people came here to worship.

To put it briefly and bluntly, as far as colonial administrative regimes go, the Portuguese in Macao had demonstrated an extremely light touch. There is even one strain of historical discourse that has it that Macao was never even a proper colony at all given the fact that a Portuguese presence in Macao was well-established long before strong-arm colonialism made a name for itself and peaked in the nineteenth century.[46] Macao was never a product of 'political strategies drawn up in Lisbon, but instead sprang from the determination of private individuals' who enjoyed considerable freedom in their pursuit of trade.[47] Ever since its establishment at the end of the sixteenth century its political and administrative status 'was never too clear' and 'considerable clandestine and semi-clandestine interests' had permeated the territory throughout its history.[48] By the late twentieth century, China appeared to exert more under-the-table control over Macao than Portugal and there was a widespread sense among the public that 'the local government lacked any real economic or political autonomy'.[49] The handover of Macao to China was thus a crucial moment for both countries. For China it meant 'formal inclusion in the outwardly legitimate system of government' and consolidation of its national integrity in terms of sovereign territory,[50] and for Portugal it was an opportunity to leave a 'cultural legacy' because, as some residents, both Chinese and Portuguese, suggested, 'they had left nothing else – not a robust economy, not a flourishing democracy, not a well-ordered society, not a well-educated populace'.[51] The handover was a time to clean things up and Mr Wang could see the effects of this macro-level policy in terms of a sharp decrease in the numbers of visitors to his temple.

What has been called the 'socio-political instability', the 'fragility of the Portuguese position', its 'precarious context',[52] and its 'blatant corruption and lack of efficiency' was brought to dramatic climax,[53] and public media attention, during a number of triad shoot-out murders of members of rival factions that began in 1997, the year of Hong Kong's return to China, and ended just weeks before Macao's return in December 1999. Bikers would pull up to their victims, fire point blank, and disappear across the border into the mainland. A key protagonist, triad boss Wan Kuok-koi, aka Broken Tooth Koi, told *Time* magazine later from jail that it was all part of a 'beautiful war' in which the victors are chosen by Kuan Tai, the Chinese god of war, to whom every true triad member prays for guidance: 'I'm a very old fashioned guy … that means to defend the interests of the society, to fight for your brothers and to uphold the codes of the brotherhood.'[54] Mr Wang's temple may have played a small part in this kind of shadow society, also a long-standing tradition in Macao,[55] but it was not anything the People's Republic wanted to see promoted as any business plan for the future of Macao, despite Deng Xiaoping's comment, at the time of Hong Kong's return, that secret societies in Hong Kong were also 'patriotic'.[56] As part of the terms negotiated between

China and Portugal, it had been agreed that no Chinese troops would be stationed in Macao. This policy was changed in the aftermath of the murders and there is currently a prominent headquarters of the People's Liberation Army (PLA) in Cotai, the new casino strip, in front of which two guards are permanent duty. Reforms strengthening a wide range of administrative regulations and controls in Macao, including law enforcement, border crossings and the issuance of visas, were put in place under the Chinese and these have now rationalized procedures in the direction of greater efficiency and effectiveness. The expectation is that both outbursts of public violence and the casual movement of undocumented visitors between political jurisdictions are now largely things of the past. An earlier informality seems to have been a defining motif in both Mr Wang's life and the ability of his temple to attract worshippers. But times change, and with them new constraints arise. As will be seen in a later section, Macao now has a highly regulated, profitable, and some would say 'overheated' property market; it is this latest development that is presenting Mr Wang and his temple with their newest challenge.

It would be wrong to characterize Mr Wang's temple as in any way a triad hangout, or its current lack of worshippers as simply due to stronger border and law enforcement controls. In fact, Mr Wang also mentioned that among the temple's current regulars are a number of civil servants and even police officers themselves. Inclusiveness of all types of people under an umbrella of worship is the idea that he was expressing. Among the ostensibly good people he mentioned as having come to the temple are, or were, family members of some famous people, such as actors and high-level government officials from both Macao and Hong Kong. By the time I spoke with him, however, visitor activity at the temple was much less vibrant and diverse than he said it had been in the past. Perhaps the temple had attracted more mainland worshippers during the period when religious activities were suppressed in the People's Republic, which only changed during the reforms of the 1980s. The unavailability of venues for traditional religious expression in China combined with rather lax border controls may have been a winning combination in attracting people to the small temple in Taipa. But since then, not only have many old temples been reconstructed on the mainland, but new ones have also been built, and such venues mark a great revival of traditional religious practice throughout all regions of China that has been much commented on by scholars.[57] Many of these temples were constructed, or their religious activities financed, 'as a result of a transnational … concern with cultural heritage, the local economy, and tourism',[58] often by 'overseas Chinese' migrants to Hong Kong, Taiwan or Southeast Asia who seek both to invest in and morally support their original ancestral villages in China. Mr Wang's long-term transnational clientele may thus have shifted their religious financial support more directly toward their own ancestral centres, which would have also been seen as being in greater need following the years of suppression. In any case, casual visits to the temple in Taipa, as well as attendance at the deities' annual birthday festivals have been down considerably in recent years, concurrent also with the dissolution of Cheok Ka Chun village as an entertainment and residential centre. The rise in prominence of the 'heritage' industry, the preservation of many other higher-profile monuments, and government promotion of heritage tourism in the core of the old city may also have had an effect: the temple in Taipa never appeared on any government list of places to visit, while at the same time tourists became more involved primarily in only a small number of mainstream venues. As far as local visits are concerned, apart from a small number of people still living in several remaining single-unit houses and a few scattered but small-scale multi-storey apartment units in the immediate area, few worshippers have much reason – or easy incentive – to come to his temple anymore. Like many urban temples, this was never simply a community temple in the sense of serving only those who lived or worked in the immediate vicinity. Like Macao itself, the temple had once been a sort of magnet that drew devotees from an entire transnational, but still locally accessible, region. But as popular trends, political jurisdictions and regulations – controlling or not controlling movement, or controlling or not controlling religion – changed, so too did this easy power of attraction.

Mr Wang said that there are still some regulars from China and Hong Kong that he sees every year during the gods' birthday festivals. These are also the times at which he thoroughly cleans the temple inside and out and all of the associated equipment. There seem to be only one or two regular worshippers left from the immediate area, but his temple remains a favourite for drop-in visits by policemen and other government service workers. In a new trend, there are also visits by young casino workers, college graduates, and others of a new generation who seek the same things that people ever did: health, wealth and luck. However he mentioned that whenever new, young faces appear, it is usually only because someone who already knows the place has brought them there, because it is unlikely that people would ever stumble upon the place on their own. Like any other business, it seems, even temples depend at least in part on word-of-mouth promotion, personal knowledge or *guanxi* networks of personal connection.

According to Mr Wang, average donations per drop-in visitor had been five to ten Macao patacas in the 1980s.[59] This has since doubled – a small reflection, perhaps, of greater individual wealth in Macao, or perhaps just a high rate of inflation. Such donations, however, are still not enough to meet the temple's monthly expenses of 2,000–3,000 patacas,[60] which primarily covers the utilities. Although Mr Wang eventually found enough outside work – primarily as a security guard – to keep the temple and his family going, he is now retired from any salaried position and lives with his wife in a side room of the temple, with only very basic amenities. He has three sons, a daughter, and eight grandchildren, all or most of whom have higher levels of education than he does. One son is a lawyer. They are all interested in the temple and help out however they can, especially during festival times, but their interests do not extend to working in the temple full-time, which Mr Wang continues to see as his duty and his life's work.

An origin myth

Mr Wang also had things to say about the early days of the temple, which, like most oral histories that extend further back than an individual's life or the memories of people that person knew, must be taken with a grain of salt as far as absolute historical accuracy is concerned. The point is that knowledge or memories or narratives passed down orally constitute embodied and lived forms of history regardless of their objective truth value as facts. Most cities have 'foundation legends' that embellish their histories,[61] so too do many temples and other religious venues. There is usually a very good reason in people's minds why religious structures are located where they are. Such accounts may be more interesting and evocative than the standard histories of origins put together by outsiders. Many popularly recounted narratives explaining the origins or early days of Chinese temples are colourful enough to join the ranks of myth, and this is the case here. Mr Wang was very articulate about the origins of his temple:

> At the very beginning there weren't any temples here. There was a big stone here in this hill. A turtle was lying on it and it seemed to worship the big stone. This place used to be a large field of rice. People worked on farms and grew vegetables. There were a lot of fishermen as well. Sometime [after a pestilence] people came up with an idea that they should build a temple where the sacred stone was located and that they should worship the gods so they could be blessed and protected. Thus, villagers, fisher-men and other businessmen collected money and they built this temple.

Whatever its ultimate source, this story was apparently what had attracted Mr Wang's great-uncle to purchase the temple in the first place. The area was originally quite close to the sea, and the turtle was behaving as if it were worshipping a stone marking an apparently sacred place. Having barely survived some kind of contagious disease at the time, the behaviour of the creature seemed to be a sign that the spirits were demarcating a place to build a temple to ensure the area's continued protection. As a family of Feng-shui geomancers, Mr Wang's uncles would have understood the symbolism of the event: the auspicious power of the turtle and the stone and the land in the immediate vicinity, which Mr Wang also called 'turtle-shape'. This was how the temple got built in that particular location. 'Turtle-shape' is a geomantic concept similar to the more widely known 'dragon features' of landscapes, which are thought to produce powerful Feng-shui benefits. This story also explains the rather unusual feature of the temple having exterior walls that are painted green rather than the more common red:

> The colour of the turtle is green. Red means the death of the turtle. When you boil the turtle, its colour becomes close to red. If this temple is painted red, then these gods will not be efficacious. The gods' powers will not work.

Asked where the stone is now or where it originally was Mr Wang said that it was 'broken up', but since it was so sacred it was the material used to build the temple. He thought that the original location of the stone would have likely been directly behind the statue of Kwan Tai, forming a type of foil or halo for the power of the god. Both of the use of the stone as building material and the exact siting of the temple to line the god up with the original location of the stone would have locked in the pre-existing power of the place with structures built or arranged through human intervention – precisely the job of a Feng-shui master. In this case, myth, memory, spiritual efficacy, human agency and the power of place and materiality are all closely intertwined.[62]

Conflict, change and an uncertain future

In the midst of a decline in visitors, especially since the handover of Macao to China, and a continuing struggle to generate enough funds for the temple's upkeep, Mr Wang and his temple faced an even larger problem: no written deed to the property of even bill of sale was ever issued to his great-uncle when he purchased the temple. That was just the way things were done at the time. All that was needed for such a transaction was trust, a handshake and some witnesses, which is what Mr Wang called a 'sand paper deed':

> In the old days, a promise would always be kept. It didn't need any written things. Everyone knew that. The only thing needed is the eyewitness. It wasn't too complex … but now everyone [who witnessed it] has died.

This is an example of a very old tradition regarding how a society keeps track of who owns what. Since ownership was most often local, publicly acknowledged and defined by use and custom, paper records were not always necessary. Jorge Flores notes that Macao, like many Chinese urban systems and other places throughout Southeast Asia where there were large Chinese communities, developed a system of local neighbourhood organization, headed sometimes on a street-by-street level, by what was known in Portuguese as *cabeças de ruas* (street-heads).[63] These would have been prominent men who served as go-betweens, if necessary, between local residents and a larger, but also local, governing administration, very often itself informally organized. This is likely to have been the case here. Mr Wang's great-uncle had not pursued getting a written deed for the temple because everyone knew he had purchased it and likely also knew from whom he had purchased it. This local acknowledgement, combined with confirmation of the purchase by local leaders, who were perhaps the street-heads and also perhaps the witnesses, would have been enough to establish ownership at the time. Similar practices regarding leases or ownership of structures rather than land continue today among undocumented, 'floating population', urban immigrant populations, even in present-day Beijing. Such a system is 'largely based on mutual trust and word of mouth among a group of relatives and close friends … with little legal paperwork involved ... [which is] deemed more accountable than formal, impersonal legal procedures'.[64]

Such informality would have perfectly suited the needs of the Wang family at the time of the purchase. They were not yet legally documented as residents of Macao, likely also not of Hong Kong, which may have made more formal documentation difficult, perhaps impossible, or at least more expensive. Mr Wang's father had also not pursued it because he did not think it was necessary since it was not clear to him until just before he died whether his sons were even interested in continuing to maintain the temple. Upon the departure of the Portuguese and under public media pressure to clean up all aspects of governance under the Chinese, an increasingly rule-driven rationalization of Macao SAR government bureaucracy meant that it was perhaps now too late for the third and fourth generations – Mr Wang and his children – to do anything else to prove the family's purchase and ownership. The Macao SAR government was taking steps to retrieve for itself many such dubiously held lands for which there was no clear title. Some of these properties had been occupied for many decades on the basis such 'sand paper' or 'rice paper' transactions, i.e., non-registered or non-written agreements. Some landholders maintained that these informal land titles had been held by their families since the Qing dynasty. Given the extreme value of any and all land in Macao, one of the densest urban areas on earth, recovering such lands was now a high-stake matter for the new government.

Mr Wang could only vent his wrath when talking about what he felt was a betrayal. For 30 years he had struggled to preserve and protect what was not only his own family's legacy but what should also be recognized as a significant part of Macao's historical and religious heritage. Part of the problem was generational, and a change in values and ways of doing things over time:

> The young people are all eager for this place! Only the old people knew the verbal contract but not the younger ones. So now they claim that I have occupied this temple as a squatter! You never know what kind of people there can be in this world! ... The Cultural Affairs Bureau, the Municipal Council of Macao, want this land. The Taipa Neighbourhood Committee also wants it. It is just like a world war! ... How can they claim this land? Did any of them pay any money to fix things that were blown down by the typhoon? Did anyone of them clean the street for me? ... You cannot receive a reward without making a merit. My great-uncle died but I still stay here. Your words do not count. I will not give it to you.

A new generation of bureaucrats was not to be trusted in the way that people had trusted each other in the old days. Values had changed and people were more materialistic and money-conscious, but not in any sensible spiritual or moral way. People now expected rewards without earning the merit required to deserve them. What Mr Wang has done for 30 years – cleaning and maintaining the temple and at the very least making sure a joss stick was constantly burning at all times – he has done, not out of simple self-interest but also and especially for a greater public good. This is what the temple has always stood for – the safety and spiritual protection of all – and as such it embodieds a different system of value and meaning than the simple economic exchange value of a piece of land:

> They should mend the temple, but if they want the land they should compensate us for it. … They can compensate me with a house, with shops in which we can do business, or simply just money! We have to negotiate … because this land was bought by my family. If both of us can be satisfied, I will give this land back to the government.

But then, in a surprising non-standard interpretation of the material rights he really seeks to claim, and in spite of the beautiful story of the turtle defining a very specific sacred place down to the material level of the stone itself, he insists that the temple and the land should be kept conceptually distinct. The temple is 'intangible' heritage, a social-religious institution, that includes significant elements which may not be easily seen and need not necessarily be tied to specific piles of bricks and mortar in a particular place:

> The temple is different from the land! They should be distinct. … This is my heritage! Even though no one comes to visit the temple, I have to stay in this temple, I have to burn the incense as usual … from 1979 to 2009 – 30 years! And my father worked at this temple since the 1950s. Altogether there are 60 years.

He is making a moral claim here based on several ideas. 'We really did pay for this land', he said, so there is nothing wrong or contradictory about seeking financial compensation for giving it up. 'We have been in charge of this place' for 60 years, making sure that the value of the land has been maintained by doing things that the government should have been doing, such as killing insects, pulling weeds and removing fallen trees from the road. But the temple is more than all of this. It is separable from the land that has commercial monetary value, and it is the temple's value as an institution that he feels is most important.

What is his proposed solution? Move the temple to a place where there are 'more people … because few people know that a temple is here'. Here his thinking, like that of his great-uncle, is not too far from sounding like a pragmatic business decision, but it cannot be equated with simple or crass commercialism. His concern here is social and religious – people and the meaningful places and things they need to protect and guide their lives. He said he proposed moving the temple to a location near the Sam Po temple in Taipa, but that 'the Cultural Affairs Bureau said this temple was a cultural relic so it could not be moved'. He meant moving the social institution that is the temple, not its material structure, which, without people power and their active spiritual actions played out in tandem with the gods, would be condemned to a lifeless museum tourist attraction, which is perhaps what the Cultural Affairs Bureau had in mind in calling it a 'cultural relic' rather than a 'living tradition'. The latter, as I see it, is what he is accusing the bureau of not understanding.

Competing conceptions of both heritage and the value of historical materiality are at work here – playing out against a backdrop of a highly monetized and overheated land and property market. In terms of standard heritage protection practice, moving the temple would radically compromise the historic fabric of the material building itself, which somehow *is* intimately tied both to its bricks and mortar as well as its original specific location. This is a basic principle of what is widely accepted as the most desirable form of historic architectural preservation, but it is something that Mr Wang denied as being the most socially or culturally important.

I do not know the current status of the temple or the nature of Mr Wang's continued involvement in it, if any. But I see that the temple still looks much the same, and its doors remain open to all comers. Perhaps the peace and quiet of its little-known location is a blessing in disguise in that it prevents any facile resignification into a largely commercial tourist commodity, snatched from local meaning and use by a well-intentioned government and transformed into a quick and easy 'heritage' experience for mass consumption by disengaged and perhaps indifferent outsiders. As previously discussed, the return of Macao to China by Portugal had high-profile significance for both nations in that, for each, their national agendas required that Macao's past needed to be realigned to provide an appropriate transition to and vision for the future. Then and now, with the world still watching, the idea is that Macao should exemplify the new China, prosperous and efficient, but also the unique product of a long history, an enduring cultural, if not necessarily administrative, legacy bequeathed by Portugal. But what about the little guy? Who is watching or watching out for him? As we have seen, increased regulatory efficiency in such matters as border controls left its mark on attendance at Mr Wang's temple, and newly prosperous donors apparently took their religious financial contributions elsewhere. On the other side of the coin – cultural heritage – government-sponsored preservation of historic architecture in Macao, both Chinese and Portuguese, both before and after the handover to China, has been accused of both going too far and not far enough, cleaning up too much, distancing structures away from local meaning and use toward oversimplified and commodified mainstream monumentality, such that it becomes fair to speak of 'staged authenticity',[65] 'fabricated heritage',[66] or the outright invention or reinvention of history and cultural identities.[67] Within such a condition '"living memory" ... ceases to have a significant role'.[68] In the midst of such trends, Mr Wang continues to remember and assert a different but not completely incompatible set of values: the value of community, of social continuity of meaning not necessarily or completely tied to specific objects, and of moral recognition of the public relevance of individual action and responsibility. Thank you, Mr Wang, for reminding us of what is perhaps most important and alive about history and heritage.

Notes

1 By 1999, the year of Macao's return to China, land reclamation projects had more than doubled the original size of the territory. See Jon Prescott (ed.), *Macaensis Momentum – A Fragment of Architecture: A Moment in the History of the Development of Macau*, Macao: Hewell Publications, 1993; Bruce Taylor, 'Planning for High-Concentration Development: Reclamation Areas in Macau', in D.Y. Yuan et al (eds), *Population and Development in Macau*, Macao: University of Macau, 1994; Cathryn H. Clayton, 'Discourse on the City: Identity Formation and Urban Change in Contemporary Macao', *Review of Culture*, 3, 2002, pp. 59–81.

2 Arthur H. Chen (ed.), *Culture of Metropolis in Macau: An International Symposium on Cultural Heritage – Strategies for the Twenty-First Century*, Macao: Cultural Institute of the Macao SAR, 2001. For a complete listing of the protected structures in the core zone, see *Supplementary Document: The Historic Monuments of Macao*, 2004, pp. 6–14; Thomas Chung, 'Valuing Heritage in Macau: On Contexts and Processes of Urban Conservation', *Journal of Current Chinese Affairs*, 38(1), 2009, pp. 129–160.

3 Mayfair Mei-hui Yang, *Favors, Gifts & Banquets: The Art of Social Relationships in China*, New York: Cornell University Press, 1994.

4 Wang Wuyi and Peter Zabielskis, 'Making Friends, Making Money: Macao's Traditional VIP Casino System', in Sytze F. Kingma (ed.), *Global Gambling, Cultural Perspectives on Gambling*, London: Routledge, 2010.

5 Rui Brito Peixoto, 'Arte, lenda e ritual: elementos da identidade dois Pescadores Chineses do sul da China' (Art, Legend and Ritual: Elements of identity of Chinese fishermen in the South of China), *Revista de Cultura* (*Review of Culture*), 5, 1988, pp. 7–24; Graeme Lang and Lars Ragvald, *The Rise of a Refugee God*, Hong Kong and New York: Oxford University Press, 1993; Ana Brito, 'Religion, Politics and the Construction of Ethnic Identity in Macao', M. Phil Dissertation, Department of Anthropology, Hong Kong: Chinese University of Hong Kong, 1994.

6 Carlos Marreiros, 'Traces of Chinese and Portuguese Architecture', in Rolf D. Cremer (ed.), *Macao: City of Commerce and Culture* (2nd edition), Hong Kong: API Press, 1991, pp. 101–116; Carlos Baracho, 'The Churches of Macau and their Placement in Urban Space and within the City's Architectonic Context', *Macau Focus*, 1(3), 2001, pp. 29–45.

7 Carlos Marreiros, 'Alliances for the Future', *Review of Culture*, 1994, p. 170.

8 Cathryn H. Clayton, *Sovereignty at the Edge: Macau & the Question of Chineseness*, Cambridge: Harvard University Asia Center, 2009; João de Pina-Cabral, *Between China and Europe: Person, Culture and Emotion in Macao*, London and New York: Continuum, 2002.

9 Padre Manuel Teixeira, *Templo Chinês da Barra, Ma-Kok-Miu* (*Ma-Kok-Miu: Chinese Temple of Barra*), Macao: Centro de Informação e Turismo de Macau (Center of Tourism Information of Macau), 1979; Padre Manuel Teixeira, *Pagodes de Macau* (*Pagodas of Macao*), Macao: DSEC, 1982; Leonel Barros, *Templos Lendas e Rituais, Macau* (*Temples, Legends and Rituals, Macao*). Macao: APIM, 2003.

10 Keith G. Stevens, 'Chinese Monasteries, Temples, Shrines and Altars in Hong Kong and Macau', *Journal of the Hong Kong Branch of the Royal Asiatic Society*, 20, 1980, pp. 1–33.

11 Jonathan Porter, 'Chinese Popular Religion and the Settlement of Macau', *Review of Culture*, 1990, pp. 51–66.

12 C.K. Yang, *Religion in Chinese Society: A Study of Contemporary Social Functions of Religion and Some of Their Historical Factors*, Berkeley: University of California Press, 1970.

13 Tik-sang Liu, 'A Nameless but Active Religion: An Anthropologist's View of Local Religion in Hong Kong and Macau', *The China Quarterly*, 2003, pp. 373–394.

14 Alan J.A. Elliott, *Chinese Spirit-Medium Cults in Singapore*, London: London School of Economics and Political Science, 1955.

15 One of the distinctions of 'Chinese folk religion' is that it embraces the worship of historical heroes or persons who were subsequently deified. Taoist gods are immortals or personified embodiments of astral forces but they are not deified human beings popularly worshipped in temples such as this one. See Daniel L. Overmyer, 'Religion in China Today: Introduction', *The China Quarterly*, 174, 2003, pp. 307–316.

16 Yang, *Religion in Chinese Society : A Study of Contemporary Social Functions of Religion and Some of Their Historical Factors*, Berkeley: University of California Press; Emily Martin Ahern, *Chinese Ritual and Politics*, Cambridge and New York: Cambridge University Press, 1981; Jean DeBernardi, *Rites of Belonging: Memory, Modernity and Identity in a Malaysian Chinese Community*, Stanford: Stanford University Press, 2004; Jean DeBernardi, *The Way That Lives in the Heart: Chinese Popular Religion and Spirit Mediums in Penang, Malaysia*, Stanford: Stanford University Press, 2006; John Lagerwey, *Religion and Chinese Society*, Hong Kong and Paris: Chinese University Press and Ecole francaise d' Extreme-Orient, 2004.

17 Porter, 'Chinese Popular Religion and the Settlement of Macau', pp. 59–60.

18 Ibid., p. 60.

19 Janet Lee Scott, *For Gods, Ghosts and Ancestors*, Hong Kong: Hong Kong University Press, 2007.

20 De Pina-Cabral, *Between China and Europe*, p. 69.

21 Jeremy Tambling and Louis Lo, *Walking Macao, Reading the Baroque*, Hong Kong: Hong Kong University Press, 2009.

22 Tam Wai-lin, 'The Worship of Local Gods and Traditional Chinese Society', *Ching Feng*, 3(1–2), 2002, pp. 177–190.

23 David Faure, 'Religion and the Representation of Territory', in *The Structure of Chinese Rural Society: Lineage and Villages in the Eastern New Territories, Hong Kong,* Hong Kong: Oxford University Press, 1986, pp. 70–99.

24 Porter, 'Chinese Popular Religion and the Settlement of Macau', p. 51.

25 Padre Manuel Teixeira, *The Story of Ma-Kok-Miu*, Macao: Information and Tourism Department, 1979; Yin Guangren and Zhang Rulin (eds), *Aomen Jilue*, Taipei: Ch'eng-wen Publishing, reprint, 1968, pp. 73–74.

26 For the Mazu cult in Taiwan see P. Steven Sangren, *History and Magical Power in a Chinese Community*, Stanford: Stanford University Press; P. Steven Sangren, 'History and the Rhetorica of Legitimacy: The Ma Tsu Cult of Taiwan', *Comparative Studies in Society and History*, 30, 1988, pp. 674–697; P. Steven Sangren, 'Power and Transcendence in the Ma Tsu Pilgrimages of Taiwan', *American Ethnologist*, 20(3), 1993, pp. 564–582. For Admiral Zheng Ho's worship of Mazu see J.J.L. Duyvendak, *China's Discovery of Africa*, London: Arthur Probsthain, 1949, pp. 28–30. For Mazu temples see Joseph Bosco and Ho Puay-peng, *Temples of the Empress of Heaven*, Hong Kong: Oxford University Press, 1999, and Ho Puay-peng and Joseph Bosco, *Tianhou Temple: Ritual and Architecture* (CD-ROM), Hong Kong: The Chinese University of Hong Kong, 2001. In 1998 an immense stone statue of Mazu/Tin Hau was erected on the highest point of Coloane, facing the city. See Jonathan Porter, '"The Past is Present": The Construction of Macau's Historical Legacy', *History & Memory*, 21(1), 2009, pp. 63–100.

27 Porter, 'Chinese Popular Religion and the Settlement of Macau', p. 57.
28 See Chapter 2 in this volume.
29 See Figure 1.1.
30 Zheng Weiming, *Puzhan Dan zai Luhuan beiming yingbian huibian (Compilation of Inscriptions, Couplets, and Plaques in Taipa and Coloane)*, Hong Kong: Company of Jialue shangfang, 1933.
31 Clayton, *Sovereignty at the Edge*, pp. 59–81; Porter, '"The Past Is Present"', pp. 63–100.
32 Porter, '"The Past Is Present"', pp. 63–100
33 Clayton, *Sovereignty at the Edge*, p. 15.
34 According to one historian, trade has been the primary defining identity of Macao since the sixteenth century: 'Macao lived from and for trade, and its administrative form, defense structures, its "foreign policy" and its social fabric must all be considered in the light of that fundamental principle.' See Jorge Manuel Flores, 'The Portuguese Chromosome: Reflections on the Formation of Macao's Identity in the Sixteenth and Seventeenth Centuries', *Review of Culture*, 3, 2002, p. 88.
35 De Pina-Cabral, *Between China and Europe*.
36 Ibid., p. 8.
37 I could not pin it down with him exactly.
38 Albert Yee, *A People Misruled: Hong Kong and the Chinese Stepping Stone Syndrome*, Hong Kong: API Press/UEA, 1989.
39 Clayton, *Sovereignty at the Edge*, p. 27.
40 De Pina-Cabral, *Between China and Europe*, p. 8.
41 Yee, *A People Misruled*, 1989.
42 This is the subject matter of what Catheryn Clayton calls 'a revitalized political anthropology [that] has addressed the socio cultural impact that various (and variously changing) practices of sovereign power have, especially on the lives of those whom they marginalize or exclude'. See Clayton, *Sovereignty at the Edge*, p. 8.
43 Yu-Wei Hsieh, 'Filial Piety and Chinese society', in Charles A. Moore (ed.), *The Chinese Mind: Essentials of Chinese Philosophy and Culture*, Honolulu: University of Hawaii Press, 1967, pp. 167–187.
44 João de Pina-Cabral, 'New Age Warriors: Negotiating the Handover on the Streets of Macao', *Institute of Germanic & Romance Studies*, 5(1), 2005, pp. 9–22.
45 The history of this flow of people is beyond the scope of this chapter. Catheryn Clayton notes that Macao's population statistics are notoriously unreliable, but that in a single decade – between 1981 and 1991 – 100,000 'new immigrants' arrived from China, which led to a 50 per cent increase in population. See Clayton, 'Discourse on the City: Identity Formation and Urban Change in Contemporary Macao', pp. 59–81: 'Thanks to China's looser emigration policies after 1978, and to Macao's growing demand for cheap labour, the number of Chinese immigrants arriving in Macao, both legally and illegally, skyrocketed during the 1980s; on three occasions between 1982 and 1990, the Macao government granted amnesty to a total of more than 70,000 illegal Chinese immigrants. In addition to these, the number of immigrants from mainland China living in Macao illegally was estimated, in 1994, to be from 47,000 to 100,000.' If some of these were the people who patronized Mr Wang's temple, it would have been ordinary or typical for them to be undocumented mainlanders.
46 De Pina-Cabral, 'New Age Warriors', pp. 21–22; Clayton, *Sovereignty at the Edge*, pp. 1–32.
47 Flores, 'The Portuguese Chromosome', p. 92.
48 De Pina-Cabral, 'New Age Warriors', pp. 12, 16.
49 Clayton, *Sovereignty at the Edge*, p. 26.
50 De Pina-Cabral, 'New Age Warriors', p. 21.

51 Clayton, *Sovereignty at the Edge*, p. 4.
52 Carlos Marreiros, 'Alliances for the Future', p. 164.
53 De Pina- Cabral, 'New Age Warriors', p. 16.
54 Ibid., p. 17.
55 João Guedes, *As Seitas: Histórias do Crime e da Política em Macau* (*Secret Societies: Histories of Crime and Politics in Macao*), Macao: Livros do Oriente, 1991.
56 Deng Xiaoping was quoted as saying that secret societies in Hong Kong were also 'patriotic' by the *Sunday Times* of Hong Kong on 30 August 1997. See de Pina-Cabral, *Between China and Europe*, p. 211.
57 Overmyer, 'Religion in China Today: Introduction', *The China Quarterly*, 174(6). 2003, pp. 307–316; Selina Ching Chan, 'Temple-Building and Heritage in China', *Ethnology*, 44(1), 2005, pp. 65–79; Adam Yuet Chau, 'The Politics of Legitimation and the Revival of Popular Religion in Shaanbei, North-Central China', *Modern China*, 31(2), 2005, pp. 236–278; Mayfair Mei-hui Yang, 'Putting Global Capitalism in Its Place', *Current Anthropology*, 41(4), 2000, pp. 477–495; Mayfair Mei-hui Yang (ed.), *Chinese Religiosities: Afflictions of Modernity and State Formation*, Berkeley: University of California Press, 2008.
58 Chan, 'Temple-Building and Heritage in China', pp. 65–79.
59 About US$0.60–1.20.
60 US$240–360.
61 Flores, 'The Portuguese Chromosome', p. 94.
62 Paul Christopher Johnson and Mary Keller, 'The Work of Possession(s)' *Culture and Religion*, 7(2), 2006, pp. 111–122; Oren Baruch Stier and J. Shawn (eds), *Religion, Violence, Memory, and Place*, Bloomington: Indiana University Press, 2006.
63 Flores, 'The Portuguese Chromosome', p. 86.
64 Li Zhang, 'Migration and Privatization of Space and Power in Late Socialist China', *American Ethnologist*, 28(1), 2001, p. 185.
65 Porter, '"The Past Is Present"', p. 94.
66 Chung, 'Valuing Heritage in Macau', pp. 136–138.
67 Clayton, 'Discourse on the City', pp. 68–75.
68 Porter, '"The Past Is Present"', p. 94.

2 Earth god worship in Macao

The transformation of communal earth god worship in an urban setting

Tianshu Zhu

In Chinese indigenous religion, the earth god is perhaps the most enduring and popular deity. Although the cult of earth is derived from the worship of nature, which can be traced back to the prehistorical period – a unique phenomenon in China, the earth god became a territorial deity bonded to the hierarchical structure of Chinese bureaucratic system since the very early stage of the dynastic periods.[1] The representation and worship of the earth gods have taken different forms during such a long period of time.[2] In Chinese popular religion the earth god as a territorial deity still receives wide veneration today. Macao is a place in which Chinese popular religion has survived as a living tradition and worship of the earth god in Macanese religious practice is particularly prominent. There are earth god shines in virtually every corner: independent earth god altars on the streets, attendant shrines inside temples, stores and households, and even in cemeteries along with the tomb mounts. Recently, various forms of these earth god shrines in Macao and the religious festivals associated with the earth gods have started to attract people's attention, both scholarly and non-scholarly.[3] However, it is still not entirely clear how the practice in Macao is related to or different from the worship of the earth god in other parts of China and during other periods in history.

Before land reclamation, the shape of the Macao peninsular looked like a lotus flower. Therefore, in the perspective of Feng-shui theory,[4] Macao is called *Lianhua Baodi*, or 'the precious land of a lotus flower', meaning an auspicious place of peace. Compared to other parts of China, Macao has been relatively free from large-scale social turmoil and warfare throughout 500 years of its history and, as a result, popular religion in Macao has survived as a living practice although it has certainly declined in the modern era. Thus, the practice of earth god worship in Macao preserves valuable information that is often missing in the written history of Chinese religion, or has been long forgotten in other areas where such worship has stopped or been interrupted. In addition, Macao was developed by immigrants over time in a continuous process of urbanization and commercialization. What we know about earth god worship has primarily referred to rural areas, and our knowledge of religious practice in cities and new settlements is fragmentary. In this respect, the history of earth god worship in Macao within the context of its urban development is particularly significant.

The earth god shrines in Macao can be divided into two groups, the earth god altars (or temples) for the community and earth god shrines for individual households, stores, tomb mounts or temples. In different locations, the earth god may assume different titles and function differently. In this chapter, I study the first group – the communal earth god shrines on streets, with the focus on the function of the earth god and community worship. Ultimately, the goal of this study is to understand earth god worship in the urban social history of Macao.

In a traditional Chinese society, collective worship serves as a symbol of territorial unity whether it is centred on earth god shrines, ancestral halls or temples. The earth god and temple god reflect a different aspect in the relationship between human society and the territory/gods.[5] The earth gods are considered to be the spirits of the localities in which they stand. In general, each distinct locality can be recognized as a unit, and in rural China and in old tradition, such a unit would be a village. In a village, the earth god shrines are set up to guard the entrances to the village, and sometimes wells and fields as well. In contrast to this, the temple gods are derived from a much wider culture than that of a single village, and they offer protection to people regardless of where they reside. The establishment of a temple in a village sets up a bond between the villagers and the deities, who are thought of as being invited to the local temple from the original temple. The temple gods are therefore both omnipotent and specific to a locality. Community worship is centred on temple gods, although earth gods are also invited and venerated.[6]

On the Macao peninsular, there are places that used to be villages but they are now incorporated into the modern urban fabric. At least one example, the earth god temple of Longtian (Long Tin/龍田) village, represents the typical earth god shrine found in a village. Longtian used to be a village near Wangxia (Mong Ha/望夏) village and was transformed during the Ming dynasty (1368–1644).[7] The village had two temples in total with one dedicated to Guandi inside the village and the other called Fude Ci (Fok Tac Chi/福德祠) dedicated to the earth god at the entrance of the village. In addition, the village also has two earth god altars, called Yongxingshe (Weng Heng Se/永興社) and Jianlongshe (Kin Long Se/建隆社) located in the north and south of the village respectively. In this case, the earth god would be the deity who oversees the territory of the village; whereas Guandi, the war lord and wealth god popular in China, would be the actual temple god for the villagers. The two temples and two altars were all relocated to Wangxia village in 1908 (the year that saw the end of Guangxu's 33-year reign) after Longtian was taken over by the Portuguese and villagers evacuated from their homes.[8]

Nowadays, the entire Macao peninsular has been urbanized. How does the earth god relate to the territory of a city? My finding is that the establishment of those earth god shrines in Macao echoes the history of the city's expansion, and the collective worship of the earth god reflects aspects of the social changes of local Chinese religious practice. To elaborate these phenomena, I first start with examining the layout of earth god shrines in the city and follow up with the study of the activities of collective worship.

The layout of the earth god shrines

There are more than 100 community earth god shrines scattered in the alleys of Macao and they have never been systematically studied. In previous studies, Tong Qiaohui conducted the most comprehensive survey of the communal earth god shrines in Macao and found around 90 of them[9] – I have found 118, which is likely close to the total number of earth god shrines in Macao. Most of these shrines are small scale, open-air altars and roofed shrines, and only several of them are in the format of a complete house such as an independent temple. These 118 earth god shrines are not evenly distributed across the territory of Macao. In the expansion of the city and process of modernization, the domain of an earth god also expanded and became unclear.

Map 2.1 shows Macao in 1800 and Map 2.2 in 1899. The black outlines in the centre mark the original coastline of the Macao peninsula before the land was reclaimed. The area marked '1' (light grey shading) confined in the south indicates urban areas; the area marked '2' (darker grey) is uninhabited hills, and the area marked '3' (with hatching) in the north maps out the farmland. Area 1 in Map 2.1 is basically the area of the old city. Large scale urbanization did not occur in Macao until the destruction of most of the city wall in the middle of the nineteenth century. Before the end of the nineteenth century, the urban areas expanded slowly, street by street, in an organic manner. The urbanization in the north and east on the farmland and reclaimed land in the twentieth century took place on a large scale, area by area/district by district basis.

In the old part of the city, especially the Chinese residential area within the old city walls, almost every small alley has an earth god altar. These small alleys are often named such-and-such Wei (圍) or such-and-such Li (里), the terms for enclosed space. They are usually short dead-ended small alleys with one entrance, which are sometimes marked with gate-like structures. In my survey, I found around 56 earth god shrines, nearly half the total number, in such streets, 47 of which have Wei or Li in the street name. Old people still remember that in the past door guardians were also worshipped at the door-ways of such old alleys.[10] The earth god altar usually guards the entrance or the end of an alley, or is located at the turn of a street so that the earth god can watch out toward both ends. The territories of the earth gods in these areas are quite small and clearly defined.

Although no new major temples of popular religion were built after the Republic Period (1911) in Macao, people still occasionally build new earth god shrines in newly developed areas in the present days and refurbish/enlarge old earth god shrines. In the north and the east, the areas developed in the twentieth century and later, the earth god shrines are much more scattered, with very often only a few shrines in one area. And the boundaries of these earth

Map 2.1 Macao in 1800. Courtesy of Xing Rongfa 邢榮發.

gods' domains are usually vague. For example, the Taishan (臺山) area in the north of the Macao peninsula, is on reclaimed land that did not exist until the 1920s. At the end of the 1980s, apartment buildings were constructed in the area to replace the old houses. Two half-house-sized roofed earth god shrines decorated with glazed tiles were built in the 1990s on the main street near each

Map 2.2 Macao in 1899. Courtesy of Xing Rongfa 邢榮發.

other.[11] People living nearby burn incense at one of these shrines on a regular basis. They know which earth god shrine they should go to. However, when I asked how to draw the boundary of the territories of these two earth gods, no one seemed to know how to respond to the question. Old small steles inscribed with 'the gods of She and Ji of Lianhuan' ('Lin Wan/蓮環') and 'the gods of

She and Ji of Longhuan' ('Long Wan/龍環') are present in these two shrines respectively. 'She' is an archaic term referring to the god of soil, while 'Ji' ('稷') refers to the god of the grain.[12] The two usually appear together. These small steles must have come from old altars before the reconstruction, and the terms of Lianhuan and Longhuan are probably the names of places or communities in the area to which the earth god shrines originally belonged. Both Lianhuan and Longhuan have no trace in the current map of Macao. When I interviewed the people living near to these two earth god shrines, they were not even aware the inscriptions of 'Longhuan' and 'Lianhuan'. So how do people choose which shrine to go to? In answering my question, a local worshipper in that area replied: 'You go to the one which you feel is effective.'[13]

Actually, Longhuan used to be a small village in the area and was recorded in both the *Guangdong Tushuo* (廣東圖說/*Illustrated Gazetteer of Canton*) and the *Xiangshan Xianzhi* (香山縣誌/*Gazetteer of Xiangshan County*).[14] The village had more than 20 families. After the Portuguese built a road across the area in 1849, the village soon vanished.[15] Lianhuan must have a similar history. In the expansion of the Taishan area, the earth god altars of Lianhuan and Longhuan were reconstructed and many more people living nearby could come to worship the earth gods than the original 20-plus families. As a result, the domains of the two earth gods have been changed and enlarged, but their boundaries are also unclear. People who relate themselves with the earth god do so not because they are in the territory of this earth god but because they feel the deity is effective.

Another example is the earth god shrine at the Fifth Street of Heishawan (Hak Sa Wan/黑沙灣) built in 2006, probably the most recently constructed community earth god shrine in Macao. The earth god here is inscribed as 'The Gods She and Ji of the District of Heishawan' ('黑沙灣區社稷之神'). It looks like this earth god is meant to be in charge of the whole area of Heishawan district. Heishawan is also a large new residential area on reclaimed land, now occupied by towering business and apartment buildings. When I asked people living in this district, not all of them were aware of the presence of this earth god or its effect on them. Unlike a traditional village or a Wei/Li in old Macao city, a district in a modern city is an open space connected with neighbouring districts in all directions. In such new districts, the domain of the earth god is also an open diffused space.

As revealed in their history mentioned above, some of the earth god shrines have been relocated and therefore detached from their original territory. The change of the landscape in Macao, mainly from village into city, also marked the decline of some earth god shrines. The two earth god altars in front of Guanyin Tang (Kun Iam Tong/觀音堂), the two in front of Guanyin Gumiao (Kun Iam Tchai/觀音古廟), and one of the altars at Chaichuanwei Jie (Chai Sun Mei Kai/柴船尾街/Rua da Barca da Lenha) have all been relocated there from other places. The earth god temple in Wangxia was removed from Longtian village, which no longer exists. These are all the earth gods who have lost their original territories. As far as an earth god shrine is still in a public area not too far from residential areas, especially if it is near a temple, there will be people go there and burn incense. In my investigation, I only found one abandoned earth god shrine in Zhuojia Cun (CheokKa Chun/卓家村/Povoação de Cheok Ká), Taipa. This is because the earth god altar is located in a wasteland enclosed within a fence, not easily accessible to the public.

Compared to what we know about earth god worship in other cities in China, the spatial distribution of community earth god shrines is extremely uneven in Macao. It is a changing history that mirrors the rise and fall of different areas in Macao. In general, the shrines are dense in the old part of the city and sparse in the newly developed areas. Like the villages, Chinese cities of the Ming, Qing and Republic periods also have temple gods and earth gods at least at two levels, with the former for large communities and the latter as the base territorial units of the city. For example, in the Chenghuang (城隍/the god of the city wall) temple in Pingyao city, 40 earth gods, who represent the 40 districts (consisting of eight Fang 坊 and 32 Li) of Pingyao city, were worshipped in the western hall. On the back wall, each earth god statue is inscribed as 'such-and-such Li Tudi Shenwei' ('某某里土地神位'), or 'the earth god of such-and-such Li'. This setup of the god Chenghuang together with the earth gods mirrors the Chinese bureaucratic system with the earth gods appearing to be subordinate officers under the command of the god Chenghuang who is responsible for the whole city. Gu Jigang, a renowned scholar of Chinese history, conducted an investigation of the earth god shrines in Quanzhou city in the 1920s and found that Quanzhou was divided into 36 Pu (鋪) including both the down town areas and suburbs, with each Pu, according to its size, further divided into two or three Jing (境). Every Jing has its own earth god. Instead of using the street names, Quanzhou citizens actually used Pu and Jing for their address, although Jing does not appear in the bureaucratic system of Quanzhou.[16] In the eyes of Quanzhou people, it is the Jing, the base unit of the earth god, to which they belong. In Quanzhou the domain of an earth god also defines the communities in the city.

Setting up earth god shrines in Macao reflects the Chinese tradition of worshipping the earth god as a territorial deity in cities. The difference between Macao and the aforementioned examples is that Macao developed organically. The uneven distribution of earth god shrines on the street in Macao ultimately demonstrates the history of the city – how the urban area developed slowly street by street in the old part of the city and then extended rapidly, district by district, in the new areas. In the Pearl River Delta region, earth god altars on every street also appear in other cities, such as the commercial area on Cheung Chau Island of Hong Kong, which was gradually developed from a market in an organic manner similar to that of Macao.[17]

Collective worship and communities

The development of the collective worship at public earth god shrines in Macao can be roughly divided into three phases, which represent three different staged relationships between the worship of a territorial deity and the base unit of the community. The earliest new residents in a new place form a community by worshipping the same earth god together. In the process of urbanization, several earth god shrines were developed into temples that are recognized throughout Macao. Large numbers of social organizations affiliate to one of these earth god temples by annually inviting a statue of a god from the temple to reside in the organization for a year. Finally the earth god worship community (Tudihui 土地會) became affiliated to officially registered non-religious organizations of the neighbourhood (Jiefanghui 街坊會). The chronology of these three phases is only in a relative sense. Different areas are evolved at different times. There is no clear timeline between the three phases. And most of the small worship communities did not develop into the second and the third phases.

Forming 'She' ('社') – community worship of the same earth god

For the first generation of immigrants in a new place in Macao, residents in the same area would work together to organize and set up an altar for the earth god before any other deity was worshipped. Such organization is often called 'such-and-such She (社)', meaning 'such-and-such society'. The territorial deity of a new land is the first god that is recognized and worshipped as the protector of the community. After the community developed, other gods may be invited and a temple may be built near the earth god altar, which has been a public centre in the community.

This phase of history is absent in textual history and has been largely forgotten in the collective memory of younger generations. However, abundant earth god altars with inscriptions survived to the present day. Among the total of 118 earth god shrines that I found, 35 of them record the names of the original society who set up the altar. Those names are not names of places (only a few shrines are inscribed with street names). For instance, the earth god shrine at Shalitou (Sa Lei Tau/沙梨頭) was originally worshipped by the Yongfu Society (Weng Fok Se/永福社). Yongfu is not the name of the area or any street in the area. The oldest inscription at the site is carved on the cliff – 'Yongfu Gushe: Benfang Sheji Tudi Fushen' ('永福古社: 本坊社稷土地 福神/'The ancient society of Yongfu: the gods of She Ji and the earth god of good fortune of this Fang'). It typifies most of the inscriptions of these early organizations in the way that both She (society) and Fang (block) are mentioned. Fang, referring to a block confined by four main streets on four sides, is an archaic term for the district (or base unit) in the city in ancient China. This feature demonstrates that the earth god assumes dual roles – a god worshipped by an organization who is also recognized as the lord in charge of a territory, on which there could be inhabitants not included in the organization. The earth god shrine was set up for some people in his territorial domain who joined this She. Members in such type of She may live close by but are not necessarily related by blood, or linked by career. Neither do all residents in the neighbourhood have to be included in the She organization.

The earth god altar on Julong Jie (Tjoi Long/聚龍街/Rua de Choi Long) street in Taipa is a newly established shrine, whose history can shed light on how an earth god altar might have been erected in the past. Julong Jie used to be the coastline of the Taipa Island near a wasteland for burying homeless poor people. Mr C became the first resident here after immigrating from Fujian province in 1982. Once he settled down, he decided to set up an earth god altar. In his words, he built the altar with his Jiefang (neighbours). Actually, they were just a few of his friends. Mr C brought up this sugges-tion one day when he was drinking with his friends, they all supported his idea and wanted to donate money. Mr C didn't take all the money offered. In his words: 'I did not accept some people's money because their money was not clean.' Mr C paid most of the cost, as well as selecting the location and inviting a priest to consecrate the altar. The project of reclaiming the land in the area started in 1984. The place did not have the official street name of Julong Jie until 1985. Later on, without informing Mr C, someone put three porcelain statues of the gods of good fortune, wealth and longevity (Fu Lu Shou/福祿壽) on the altar, which now have become the main deities receiving veneration. One of Mr C's friends donated two large stone lions to be put in front of the altar. Mr C also keeps refurnishing the altar, including adding an altar for the god of heaven next to one of the stone lions. In recent years, more new streets and gigantic apartment buildings have been built up on the reclaimed land nearby. So far, this remains the only earth god altar in the area. A number of residents in those apartment buildings come to worship this earth god every day. Mr C is a pious Buddhist. During the interview, he expressed his wish to build a beautiful temple at this location. The problem is not money, but the land. Officially, the government owns the land, Mr C does not. Anything he constructed here could be pulled down by the government as illegal construction. Therefore, he gave up this idea.[18]

A couple of points in Mr C's story are likely to be common to the establish-ment of earth god shrines in Macao in general. The first group of residents settled down in a place before the area is assigned an official street name by the government. Therefore the names inscribed on those earth god altars are meant to be the name of the community or the Fang, instead of a formal street name. Unlike in a traditional village, where every villager is naturally a mem-ber of the community, membership in communities of immigrants in Macao can be selective and voluntary. This is not surprising because the immigrants come from various backgrounds and nothing binds them together except that they are neighbours. In the expansion into nearby areas, especially after more people moved in at later times, both the geographic domain and the com-munity in the domain of an earth god are enlarged. Once a public earth god shrine is erected, it is no longer restricted to the members of the original orga-nization. People in the neighbourhood are allowed to make offerings.

Scholars on Chinese popular religion suspected that a new settlement or village was a territorial society formed by immigrants centred on an earth god shrine, and that establishing and relocating the earth god shrine is ultimately a reflection of expansion of a residential area.[19] This is a long-standing tra-dition in China. The term 'She' originally refers to the god of soil but also means society – it is the organization of worshipping the same She (earth god) that constitutes the base unit of Chinese society. In Macao, the communities of the first residents of a new land originally also established themselves centred on the earth god worship. This kind of community is still territorial but not identical with the territory. In addition, the history of Macao is an example that demonstrates how the tradition of earth god worship also plays an important role in forming communities in the expansion of an urban city.

'Paohui' ('炮會') affiliated to the earth god temple

After the inception phase, in the city area of Macao the earth god shrines roughly corresponded to streets, blocks or districts in Macao. Special community worship takes place on the earth god's birthday just like those for temple gods, not the spring and autumn rituals as the tradition for She gods. On the earth god's birthday, 2 February in the lunar calendar, local communities in Macao would go to their earth god shrine to make offerings, the highlight of which is a whole roasted pig.[20] Recorded in newspapers in 1960s, the communities of Shalitou, Queziyuan (Cheok Chai Un/雀仔園/Avenida Conselheiro Ferreira de Almeida e Rua da Mitra), Xiahuan (Ha Wan/下環/Rua da Praia do Manduco), Guolan Jie (Kuo Lan Kai/果欄街/Rua da Tercena), Caodui Hengxiang (Chou Toi Wang Hong/草堆橫巷/Travessa das Janelas Verdes) and Sanjie Huiguan (Sam Kai Wui Kun/三街會館/Templo de Sam Kai Vui Kun) would organize Cantonese operas or puppet shows to entertain the earth god as communal celebrations.[21] Given the leading role that collective worship of the earth god plays in some communities, the earth god has been transformed into a temple god.

To the earth gods at Shalitou, Quiziyuan, Sanjie Huiguan and Xiahuan, the communities under one and the same earth god are not unified. Multiple organizations, called Paohui (炮會/firecracker societies), are affiliated to one earth god. Annually on the earth god's birthday, a Paohui invites a statue of a deity, called Pao (炮/firecracker), from the temple it belongs to and returns the statue next year, this being the reason for the name 'Paohui'. A Paohui can be an individual, a store or a factory, however most of them are organizations called She (society), Tang (堂/Hall), or (Tiyu) Hui ((體育)會/(martial art) association),[22] which are small-scaled non-government mutual aid organizations. These organizations range from about 20 people to more than 300 people. Members might be connected by locality, occupation or other backgrounds but they are certainly not restricted by any of these connections. People form Paohui together voluntarily mainly for the purpose of helping each other to make a living, and for covering wedding and funeral costs. A small fee as low as MOP$1 per month in the 1960s was required to maintain the membership. Every year on the deity's birthday, members celebrate together with a feast, and receive a portion of the food offerings to take home such as roast pork, cookies and fruits, and sometime they even receive other things for daily use.[23]

Lower class labourers forming non-government mutual aid societies have a long tradition in China, and they often overlap with the community of the same ritual space or cemetery.[24] Nevertheless, such organizations seem to have been extremely popular in Macao, as well as in Hong Kong, and Paohui is a notable phenomenon. Paohui is attached to a temple in general, not exclusively to an earth god temple. However, in Macao a large number of the Paohui celebrated the earth god's birthday. The numbers of these Paohui were increasing up until the mid-1960s, when large-scale celebration of temple festivals stopped. According to reports in Macao's daily newspaper *Aomen ribao*, in 1962, 84 Paohui belong to the Shalitou earth god temple, 61 to Queziyuan,[25] and at least 17 to Sanjie Huiguan.[26] These are extraordinarily large numbers jumping from one earth god to forming one society. Since these organizations are not officially registered and recorded in any textual references, they are like a missing page in the social history of the formal written history of Macao.

The earliest evidence of the presence of Paohui in Macao that I could find is on the stele in the earth god temple of Zhongheshe (Chung Wo Se/中和社) near Mage temple (Ma Kok Mio/媽閣廟/Templo de A-Má), the temple of Mazu. On this stele, the name 'Fudetang Paohui' ('福德堂炮會') is listed on the very top of donors who contributed for the reconstruction of this temple in 1904.[27] I propose that Paohui emerged in Macao in the late nineteenth century when the city expanded rapidly and became active in the twentieth century until 1966 when temple festivals were abruptly stopped under the influence of the Cultural Revolution in mainland China.[28] Although scholars noticed the presence of Paohui,[29] the significance of Paohui in the history of the relationship between Chinese popular religion and local communities is still not fully understood. A detailed study on Paohui has to be reserved for a future time, here I can only make a few comments on the changes of the nature of the earth god.

First, the gods invited to the Paohui are not the earth gods, but a wide variety of gods, such as Beidi (北帝), Nezha (哪吒) and Dashenggong (大聖公).[30] These are the popular gods in Macao. Statues of these gods still can be seen in the temples. In the pantheon of Chinese popular religion, there is no dominance-subordiance relationship between the earth god (or a temple god in Macao) and those Paohui gods. In the case of the earth god temple, the earth god in these locations used to represent the base unit of a territory, of a social structure and of the domain of deities. The elevation of the earth god here is not the rise of his rank in the pantheon of Chinese gods, but because he serves as the medium between the worlds of humans and gods, and between communities who worship different gods.

Each temple would prepare enough statues to be distributed to those Paohuis.[31] However some statues, particularly of the wealth god, are so popular that different Paohuis have to openly compete to be able to take it home. This is the so-called Qiangpao (搶炮/grabbing the fireworks), an activity notorious for its violent nature which was therefore banned in Macao in the 1950s.[32] Participants jostled to catch a short numbered stick shot out of a mini rocket. Whoever grabbed the stick could win the statue of the match-ing number. Both Shalitou and Queziyuan had about 20 to 30 such Pao, or statues of gods for people to fight for. The sixth Pao, Caibo Xingjun (財帛星君/god of wealth), had been the most desirable one at Queziyuan and conse-quently also most expensive. A Paohui needed to pay MOP$200 as the charge (called Paojin/炮金) to obtain this statue in 1960s. In the 1960s, most of the Paohui did not actually return their statues to the temple. They brought the statue to the temple on the earth god's birthday and immediately took it back with them to Paohui.[33] Among the Paohui's statues now displayed at the tem-ple in Shalitou, two of them – Hongsheng Dawang (洪聖大王) and Beidi – are inscribed with the names of the Paohui Lianluoshe (聯絡社) and Xinglongshe (興隆社) respectively.[34] It looks like that these two statues have a stable rela-tionship with these organizations. The shrine of Lianluoshe is also inscribed the name of Shalitou, indicating that Lianluoshe is affiliated to Shalitou.

A Paohui's annual payment to the temple of around MOP$200 would be more than enough for the organization to get a statue of its own. If the god of wealth is so desirable, why not make a statue of this god for every Paohui? If a Paohui no longer returns its statue of god to the temple for redistribution, why bother carrying it to the temple every year? These seemingly unneces-sary religious acts were logical to people at that time because they mirrored the power balance and power struggle in the social structure. Detached from their big family or clan and the domain of their village gods at home town, the immigrants in Macao formed various mutual-aid societies for survival. In the environment of commercial city, these mutual-aid societies, or Paohui, are less independent than in a village. In the city, people share resources, compete for business and job opportunities. In this competitive society, a small organiza-tion craves for the reorganization in the larger community. To get a 'Pao' from a local temple is to be legitimized in the local community. Not every Paohui had a headquarters. The local temples had been a public place of social gath-erings of these Paohuis.[35] Some of the temples, such as the earth god temple at Queziyuan and Xiahuan, also serve as the Gongsuo (公所/non-government court), from which justice was sought when conflicts arose in the neighbour-hood of the local community in the past. The temple at Queziyuan consists of two rooms, one dedicated to the earth god, and the other serves as Gongsuo, the inscription of which is still present above the door today. The presence of Gongsuo at Xiahuan is recorded on the stele of the temple.[36] Gongsuo is also present at a number of temples dedicated to other deities in Macao. Similar practices that incorporate religious worship into local community social organization occur in overseas Chinese communities elsewhere, especially in Southeast Asia.[37]

Parade or procession is an important activity in traditional communal worship on a major deity's birthday. Usually the statue of the deity, preceded by dancing dragons, lions and other performance, is carried out to circulate and/or walk through the major streets of the territory. It is a symbolic act to reinforce the power of the god in his domain and protect it from evil spirits and disease. Such a form of parade is present in Macao. In the past, the earth god of Shalitou was carried out and paraded on the four major streets in this area.[38] However altered forms of activities organized by Paohui also appeared. One of the highlights of the celebration of the earth god's birthday in Macao was the parade of the large Paohui with the statue of the god together with banners, Piaose (飄色/moving stage featuring characters from popular dramas), dancing lions, and offerings such as a whole roasted pig, marching from the headquarters of the Paohui to the earth god temple and then coming back. It was a pilgrimage of members of Paohui and the Paohui's god to the earth god. It was also a public display of each Paohui's power, wealth and piety to the god. The parade was so eye-catching that it was often mentioned in the news as one of the major events of the festival.[39]

Interestingly, the lion dance became independent from the parade of the gods. Some Paohui sent their young men to perform lion dances, street by street in their territories. Each store would give red packets of money to the dancers. In the past, the red packet could be considered a form of a protection fee to that particular organization. It is also an act that enforces the relationship between the organization and its members. Without the god, the parade of lion dancers symbolizes that the human organization is protecting members in the community, in addition to the protection of the gods.

The earth god worship society affiliated to the secular organization

After the late-nineteenth century, with the large-scale expansion of the city, large numbers of non-religious organizations emerged in Macao, especially during the periods 1912–1937 (the Republic time before the Japanese War),[40] 1950–1966 and the mid-1970s–1999.[41] Detaching from religion is one of the most remarkable characteristics of social organizations in Chinese modern society, i.e., religious organizations and non-religious organizations eventually become independent from each other. In Macao, the organization similar to the ancient She as base unit of the society is the Jiefanghui (街坊會), which literally means the 'Association of Streets and Blocks', or the community of local neighbourhood. It is called Aomen Jiefang Lianhe Zonghui (澳門街坊 會聯合總會/Uni o Geral das Associa es dos Moradores de Macau/The Union of Neighbourhood Community in Macao), a non-governmental organization officially registered at the end of 1983. Now it consists of 26 regional Jiefanghui covering most of the residential areas, as well as more than 30 various service centres, three schools, two kindergartens and three clinics.[42] As one of the major parties with a large number of members in Macao, it participates in the election for legislative council and has maintained at least one seat for many years. As a result, the Jiefanghui can receive large amounts of funding from the government to improve the environment and quality of life for residents through charity-like works.

After the Cultural Revolution, the practice of popular religion had a major comeback in mainland China, especially in rural areas. Following this trend, activities of community worship also gradually recovered in Macao. The collective earth god birthday celebration appeared again in the community at Shalitou, Queziyuan, Sanjie Huiguan, Xiahuan, Taishan (Toi San/臺山), Kuaiziji (Fai Chi Kei/筷子基), Qingzhou (Cheng Chao/青洲), Banying Fang (Pan Ieng Fong/板營坊)[43] and six streets at Caodui (Chou Toi/草堆/Rua das Estalagens) in the 1980s and 1990s. Most of these collective activities, except that in Queziyuan, are organized with the support and collaboration of the Jiefanghui. Among these communities, the earth god society (Tudihui/土地會) at Qingzhou called Aomen Qingzhoushan Tudi Miaohui (澳門青洲山土地廟會/Associação de Cheng Chao San Tou Tei Mio de Macau) formally declares in its regulation that it is a sub-organization of the local Jiefanghui, the Aomen Qingzhou Fangzhong Huzhuhui (澳門青洲坊眾互助會/Associação de Beneficência e Assistência Mútua dos Moradores do Bairro da Ilha Verde/The Mutual Aid Society of Qingzhou Fang).[44] In terms of finances, human resources and connection with the government, the Jiefanghui is definitely more powerful than the loosely organized traditional She (or Tudihui/土地會).

The collaboration between the earth god society (Tudihui/土地會) and Jiefanghui can be traced back to the 1960s. The earliest written record is a news report in *Aomen ribao* in 1965. According to this article, Wangxia Fangzhong Huzhuhui (望夏坊眾互助會/Associação de Mútuo Auxílio dos Moradores de Mong-Há), or 'The Mutual Aid Society of Wangxia Fang' revived the Fuhe She (Fok Wo Se/福和社/Fuhe earth god society) in 1960. The membership of the earth god society increased rapidly from 73 people in 1960 to 270 in 1965. The monthly membership fee was one MOP only. The two organizations celebrate the earth god's birthday together every year. On the earth god's birthday in 1965, members of the Fuhe She gathered at the earth god altar and worshipped the god together at 10am. In the afternoon, at 2:30pm, they distributed the offerings. Every member could get 750g of roasted pork, a tin basin, some tea, fruits, red-coloured steamed buns called Hongbao (紅包)and some particular types of traditional Chinese cookies and sweets for offering called Guangsubing (光蘇餅/20 pieces) and Jiandui (煎堆). A feast started at 6pm. Music or opera performances then lasted for two nights.[45]

The Kuaiziji Fangzhong Huzhuhui (筷子基坊眾互助會/Associação de Beneficência e Assistência Mútua dos Moradores do Bairro Fai Chi Kei/The Neighbourhood Mutual Aid Association of Kuaiziji), a branch of the Aomen Jiefang Lianhe Zonghui (澳門街坊會聯合總會/União Geral das Associações dos Moradores de Macau), now consists of four departments – the Yonghetang Huapaohui (永和堂花炮會/a Tudihui and Paohui), a clinic, a senior department and a youth department. The Yonghetang Huapaohui (永和堂花炮會) is a Tudihui and Paohui that is older than the Kuaiziji Fangzhong Huzhuhui, but has never been formally registered as an official organization. In the words of Ms CH, one of the organizers of the Kuaiziji Fangzhong Huzhuhui, the two organizations, the mutual-aid association and the Paohui, are like father and son, or no different from each other because it is the same group of people in the committees.[46] The Yonghetang Huapaohui has an earth god shrine, where the regulation of this organization was publically posted in 2001. According to the regulation, the activities and membership benefits are similar to the aforementioned Fuhe She. Sending eggs to members who have a newborn child is mentioned. This is a typical activity in traditional mutual-aid organizations. This Paohui has a statue of the wealth god, Caiboxingjun, circulated among members who gain temporary possession of it by throwing the divination wood blocks. On the earth god's birthday, Paohui members go to venerate at the earth god temple at Queziyuan together. They carry their statue of Caiboxingjun and pay Paojin to Queziyuan – the old tradition of Paohui. Actually, Shalitou is closer to this area than Queziyuan. Located at the northwest of Macao, Kuaiziji is far beyond the domain of the earth god at Queziyuan. This is the evidence that the power of an earth god went beyond its original territory. Overall, in the relationship of gods, being a pao of the Quziyuang earth god temple, the Caiboxingjun is of the subordinate to the earth god at Quziyuang; however in the relationship of organizations, instead of the community of Queziyuan, Yonghetang is subordinate to Kuaiziji Fangzhong Huzhuhui only.

The old She and Paohui did not have written regulations, which are now required for a registered organization in Macao. From these formal regulations and the current practice, the earth god communities appear to be further detached from territory and religion, as well as the aspect of mutual aid. Now they are more like charities, mainly social activities for senior citizens, a way of maintaining friendships. Almost the only requirement to be a member of such kind of societies is the monthly fee, which is currently about MOP$20, still very low. The Qingzhou Tudihui is open to any Macao citizen over 18 years old, regardless of gender. In principle, a person from other districts, or the domains of other earth gods, can also join the Tudihui in Qingzhou. In the society of a traditional of Chinese village, the base unit is the family and males play dominant roles. In Macao, the emphasis on individuals regardless of gender reflects a more modern concept.

Another innovation is that priests are not invited nowadays to the collective worship of the earth god. The parade of the statue of gods is also largely absent. The Tudihui at Qingzhou organizes a feast twice a year, one on the earth god's birthday, and the other on 1 October, National Day.[47] In the aforementioned article on Wangxia Jiefanghui, the author reported that this Jiefanghui was also prepared to organize similar types of activities for the forthcoming Women's Day on 8 March, after the earth god's birthday.[48] To the Tudihui and Jiefanghui, there is not much difference between the celebration of a religious festival and a non-religious holiday, as both are about the welfare of the community.

For people in poverty in the past, to pay a small amount of dues in exchange for things such as a piece of roasted pork and one or two feasts a year would be worth the financial outlay. Nowadays, people are largely freed from poverty. The material benefit from joining the organizations became much less significant than the desire to keep contact with old neighbours. At Shalitou, the feasts are free for elders over the age of 65. The earth god birthday celebration committee will also send the red packets, gifts and roasted pork to seniors in this district.[49] Taking care of seniors became one of the new missions that appeared in this phase.

Concluding remarks

In Chinese religion, the earth god is special. He is not just one of many gods. He is the territorial deity. In comparison to most parts of China, Macao as a place developed relatively late but went through the whole process from uninhabited land to modern city in a short period of time. What is preserved in Macao reflects traditions of worshipping the territorial deity of different periods of time in Chinese history. Some these traditions are specific to the regional culture of the Pearl River Delta. More importantly, they reflect the changes in the nature of the earth god and the practice of earth god worship as a result of urbanization.

In a traditional village in China such as those in the Pearl River Delta or the Canton region, human organization, kinship and territory are closely related with each other, almost like a trinity. Within the territory of one earth god, all the villagers are organized together in community worship. Thus community does not need an additional name other than the name of the place; and certainly no membership fees are required, although every family must make a contribution for the periodical ritual of the whole community. The three phases in the history of collective worship of the earth god represents the gradual breakup of such a trinity. Eventually, the earth god worship organizations became less religious and less territorial and more socially and bureaucratically organized with such things as official regulations, perhaps under government regulatory influence.

In a modern city, worshipping deities tends to be invoked almost exclusively on behalf of the individual and his/her household.[50] This is also true to the earth god worship at community shrines in Macao. It has to be said that even though the earth god worship organization no longer serves as the base unit of the society, worshipping the earth god is still active at an individual/family level to the present day.

Notes

1 For a recent comprehensive study of the earth god worship of the early periods before the Qin Dynasty, see Wei Jianzhen (魏建震), *Xian Qin she si yanjiu* (*The Studies of She Worship before the Qin Dynasty*), Beijing: Renmin chubanshe, 2008.
2 For comprehensive study on the overall history of the earth god in ancient China, see Du Zhengqian (杜正乾), *Zhongguo gudai tudi xinyang yanjiu* (*The Earth God Worship in Ancient China*), PhD dissertation, Sichuan University, 2005; John H. Chamberlayne and Kent Petts Wood, 'The Chinese Earth-Shrine', *Numen,* 13, 1966, pp. 164–182. For earth god worship in Taiwan, see Alessandro Dell'Orto,

Place and Spirit in Taiwan: Tudi Gong in the Stories, Strategies, and Memories of Everyday Life, New York: Routledge Curzon, 2002. For Hong Kong, see Carole Morgan, 'Notes and Queries: Traces of Houtu's (后土) Cult in Hong Kong', *Journal of the Hong Kong Branch of the Royal Asiatic Society*, 36, 1996, pp. 223–230; Richard Webb, 'Earth God and Village Shrines in the New Territories of Hong Kong', *Journal of the Hong Kong Branch of the Royal Asiatic Society*, 34, 1994, pp. 183–193.

3 José Simões Morais, 'The Earth God: A Deeply Rooted Macau Tradition Since the Eighteenth Century', *Macao*, April 2012, pp. 101–106; Tong Qiaohui (童喬慧), *Aomen tudi shenmiao yanjiu* (*The Study of the Earth God Temples in Macau*), Guangzhou: Guangdong renmin chubanshe, 2010; Tong Qiaohui (童喬慧), 'Aomen tudi shenmiao chukao' ('A preliminary study on Macau Earth God Temples'), *Huazhong Jianzhu* (*Huanzhong Architecture*), 25, 2007, pp. 150–153; Wu Bingzhi (吳炳銤), 'Aomen de tudimiao he fude zheng shen baodan jiqu' ('Anecdotes of Macau Earth God and the Earth God's Birthday'), *Zhongguo Daojiao* (*Chinese Daoismi*), May 2002, p. 35.

4 Cantonese is the local language in Macao. To be consistent, in this chapter I use pinyin to romanize Chinese characters for both names of places in Macao and more generic Chinese terms such as 'Feng-shui'. However, for the names of local place and organizations, I provide the official Portuguese name or the Cantonese, if not both, in parentheses.

5 Marjorie Topley, 'Chinese Religion and Rural Cohesion in the Nineteenth Century', *Journal of Hong Kong Branch of the Royal Asiatic Society*, 8, 1968, pp. 9–43; Hugh Baker, *A Chinese Lineage Village: Sheung Shui*, London: Frank Cass, 1968.

6 David Faure, 'Religion and the Representation of Territory', in *The Structure of Chinese Rural Society: Lineage and Village in the Eastern new Territories, Hong Kong*, Oxford: Oxford University Press, 1986, pp. 70–71.

7 Tang Kaijian (湯開建), *Aomen kaibu chuqi shi yanjiu* (*The Study of the Early History of Macao*), Beijing: Zhonghua shuju, 1999, pp. 254–277.

8 Wang Wenda (王文達), *Aomen Zhanggu* (*Anecdotes of Macau*), Macao: Aomen jiaoyu chubanshe, 1999, second edition 2003, pp. 139–143.

9 Tong Qiaohui, *Aomen tudi shenmiao yanjiu*, p. 74.

10 Interview with Ms O conducted in May, 2012.

11 Chan Wai Hang (陈煒恒) et al, *Aomen miaoyu* (*Macau Temples*), Macao: Cultural and Recreation Service of the Civic and Municipal Affairs Bureau, 2002, pp. 413–415.

12 For classic study on *She*, see: Édouard Chavannes, 'Le dieu du sol dans la Chine antique', *Le T'ai Chan*, Paris: E. Leroux, 1910, pp. 437–525 ; C.K. Yang, *Religion in Chinese Society*, Berkeley: University of California Press, 1961, pp. 81–99.

13 Interview with Mr C, a resident in the Taishan area, in 2012.

14 Wang Wenda, *Aomen zhanggu*, p. 161.

15 Ibid.

16 Gu Jigang (顾颉刚), 'Quanzhou de tudishen' ('The Earth God of Quanzhou'), *Minsu Zhoukan* (*Folk Culture Weekly*), 2, 1928, pp. 1–8; 3, 1928, pp. 8–12.

17 For information on Cheung Chau, see Choi Chi Cheung, 'Reinforcing Ethnicity: The Jiao Festival in Cheung Chau', in David Faure and Helen F. Siu (eds), *Down to Earth: The Territorial Bond in South China*, Stanford: Standford University Press, 1995, pp. 104–122.

18 Interview with Mr C conducted in May 2012.

19 For example, Zhu Haibin (朱海濱) (trans.), Hamashima Atsutoshi (濱島敦俊), *Ming Qing jiangnan nongcun shehui yu minjian xinyang* (*Society and Popular Religion in Rural Areas in Jiangnan of the Ming and Qing Dynasties*), Xiamen: Xiamen daxue chubanshe, 2008, p. 140; Lin Meirong (林美容), 'Tudi gongmiao – juluo de zhibiao' ('Earth God Temple – Sign of a Settlement'), *Taiwan fengwu* (*Taiwan Folk Culture*), 37, 1987, pp. 53–81.

20 'Tudidan dailai renao, jinxiangdui luoyi tuzhong' ('The Earth God Birthday Bringing Excitement'), *Huaqiao bao* (*Journal Va Kio/Va Kio Daily*), 29 February 1960, p. 3.

21 'Paohui choushen jinxiang mang' ('Paohui is busy visiting temples'), *Aomen ribao* (*Macao Daily News*), 19 March 1961, p. 4.

22 For lists of names of these *Paohui*, see 'Qing tudidan yipain renao, jinxiang choupao yanxi xucan' ('Excitement of the Earth God's Birthday Celebration'), *Aomen ribao*, 17 March 1962, p. 4.

23 Hechi (荷池), 'Cong wangtian dagua dao huzu huji – mantan Aomen paohui jinnian lai de bianhua' ('From fooling around to helping each other – changes of *paohui* in recent years'), *Aomen ribao*, 28 February 1960, p. 4.

24 Chen Baoliang (陳寶良), *Zhongguo de she yu hui* (*The Earth God and Society in China*), Beijing: Zhongguo renmin daxue chubanshe, 2011, p. 156.

25 Ma Chen (馬辰), 'Cong tudidan tan dao paohui' ('From the Earth God's Birthday to Paohui'), *Aomen ribao*, 17 March 1962, p. 4.

26 'Qing tudidan yipain ronao, jinxiang choupao yanxi xucan', p. 4.

27 Tan Shibao (譚世寶), *Jinshi mingke de Aomenshi* (*The History of Macau in Stone and Metal Inscriptions*), Guangzhou: Guangdou renmin chumanshe. 2006, p. 380.

28 Lou Shenghua believes that Paohui appeared in Macao in 1930s. Lou Shenghua (婁勝華), *Zhuanxing shiqi Aomen shetuan yanjiu* (*The study of societies in Macau of the transitional period*), Guangzhou: Guangdong renmen chubanshe, 2004, p. 66.

29 Tik-sang Liu, 'A Nameless But Active Religion: An Anthropologist's View of Local Religion in Hong Kong and Macau', *The China Quarterly*, June 2003, p. 381; James L. Watson, 'Fighting with Operas: Processional, Politics, and the Spectre of Violence in Rural Hong Kong', in David Parkin, et al (eds), *The Politics of Cultural Performance: Essays in Honour of Abner Cohen*, London: Berghahn Books, 1996, pp. 153–154; L. David Faure, 'Religion and the Representation of Territory', in *The Structure of Chinese Rural Society: Lineage and Village in the Eastern New Territories, Hong Kong*, Oxford: Oxford University Press, 1986, p. 204, ft. 28.

30 Cai Peiling (蔡佩玲), *Koushu lishi – Shengongxi yu Aomen shequ*, p. 31.

31 Ma Chen, 'Cong tudidan tan dao paohui', p. 4.

32 Cai Peiling, *Koushu lishi – Shengongxi yu Aomen shequ* (*Oral History – Operas and Communities in Macau*), Macau: Cultural and Recreation Service of the Civic and Municipal Affairs Bureau, 2010, p. 46.

33 Ma Chen, 'Cong tudidan tan dao paohui', p. 4.

34 These two statues are displayed in the Yiling Dian, the Hall of the Medicine Master, nearby the earth god temple at Shalitou.

35 *Aomen gongshang lianhe zonghui chengli sishi zhounian jinian tekan (1950–1990)* (*Special Issue of the 40th Anniversary of the Industry and Commerce Union of Macau*), Macao: Aomen Gonghui Lianhe Zonghui, 1990, p. 40.

36 Tong Qiaohui, *Aomen tudi shenmiao yanjiu*, p. 108

37 For example, Peter Thomas Zabielskis, 'House, Self, and Society: The Cultural Space of Identity in a Multi- Ethnic Southeast Asian City', PhD dissertation, New York University, Department of Anthropology, 2003.

38 Chen Guocheng (陳國成) (2005), 'He dan: jin yu xi' ('Celebrating Gods' Birthdays: past and present'), www.cciv.cityu.edu.hk/website/?redirect=/macau/1/1.php (accessed May 2012).

39 For examples: 'Qingzhu tudi dan yipian renao, xingshi chengche shimian xunyou' (The Excitement of Celebrating the Earth God's Birthday), *Huaqiao bao*, 19 March 1961, p. 3; 'Tudidan renao shengqian' (Unprecedented Excitement of the Earth God's Birthday), *Aomen ribao* 26 February 1963, p. 4; 'Jinri chuer tudidan, hedan huodong duo' (Today the Earth God's Birthday, many activities of celebration), *Aomen ribao* 15 March 1964, p. 4.

40 Lou Shenghua, *Zhuanxing shiqi Aomen shetuan yanjiu*, p. 63.
41 Ibid., p. 344
42 http://news.ugamm.org.mo/CN/?action-aboutus (accessed May 2012).
43 This refers to Banzhang Tang Yindi Jiequ Fangzhong Huzhuhui (板樟堂、營地街區坊眾互助會) or the Associação de Mútuo Auxílio dos Moradores das Ruas de S. Domingos, dos Mercadores e Vias Circundantes.
44 'Aomen Qingzhoushan Tudi Miaohui zhangcheng' (The Regulation of Macau Qingzhoushan Earth God Society), *Aomen Tebie Xingzhengqu gongbao*, 16 January 2008, Macao: Aomen yinwu ju, 2008
45 'Wangxia Fangzhong Huzhuhui ding si ri he tudidan, qi ri qingzhu sanbajie' (The Wangxia Neighborhood Mutual Aid Society will celebrate the Earth God's birthday on 4th and Women's Day on 7th), *Aomen ribao*, 2 March 1965, p. 4.
46 Interview with Ms CH conducted in May 2012.
47 Aomen Qingzhoushan Tudi Miaohui Zhangcheng.
48 'Wangxia Fangzhong Huzhuhui ding si ri he tudidan, qi ri qingzhu sanbajie', p. 4.
49 Tong Qiaohui, *Aomen tudi shenmiao yanjiu*, p. 61.
50 John T. Mayers, 'Traditional Chinese Religious Practices in an Urban-Industrial Setting: The Example of Kwun Tong', in Ambrose Y.C. King and Rance P.L. Le (eds), *Social Life and Development in Hong Kong*, Hong Kong: The Chinese University Press, 1984, pp. 275–284.

Part II
Western footprints
The missionaries in Macao and their contributions to the formation of Macao

3 Darwinism, Freemasonry and print culture

The construction of identity of the Macanese colonial elites in the late nineteenth century

Isabel Morais

Introduction

In his most quoted study *Imagined Communities*, Benedict Anderson argues that the invention of the printing press and the rise of print media contributed to a textual representation of the concept of the nation and nationalism. He states that 'popular' print culture was also crucial in its contribution to a global exchange that would have reinforced the idea of an 'imagined community'.[1] Anderson further explains that before the eighteenth century, the concept of nation was extensive, as Latin was the language of a broad, vast, imagined community called 'Christendom', but as there were changes in the religious communities, such a concept began to be replaced by French and English as vernacular languages of administrative centralization.[2] Thus, print capitalism allied to the book market supported by the improvement of communications and the emergence of new and diverse forms of national languages, originated the creation of clusters of small creole 'imagined political communities' that were eager to promote new forms of national and cultural consciousness, aimed at widespread literacy through liens of kinship, ethnicity, fraternity, and power loyalties.[3] This chapter posits that Anderson's arguments regarding creole nationalism in the new world, fit the particular case of the emergence of the printing, publishing and book-selling culture among a Euro-creole bourgeoisie from Macao with solid kinship, ethnic, commercial and social connections in Hong Kong, Canton, Shanghai and other littoral spaces in the treaty ports in East Asia, and takes these developments as a necessary point of departure. I argue that they used the widespread nature of print media to empower themselves and other community members with the progressive eighteenth-century Enlightenment ideas on rational scientific knowledge. They embraced atheism and anti-clericalism as important elements of enlightenment, thus promoting scientific culture, constitutional monarchy or republican forms of government, social mobility for ethnic minorities, and religious and intellectual tolerance that to a certain extent challenged the Catholic Church and conservative circles.

These people (many of them leaders of their community), were more favourably situated, and also possessed the means and motives to contribute to forging one 'imagined community' of Portuguese in the East within a regional kinship network and other dispersed vernacular readers. Newspapers, journals, essays, pamphlets and books on variety of subjects (either in Portuguese or English), printed and circulated widely – facilitated by an efficient postal system in the latter part of the nineteenth century – provided the technical and cultural means to link together not only readers of common origin and ancestry in Macao and Hong Kong but also those who had migrated to the China's treaty ports and other Southeast and East Asian settlements. This aspect strongly testifies to the intentions of these men to empower a new sense of community and cohesion through a shared national print media valuing social and linguistic culture. The relevance of this extensive kinship and ethnic network is exemplified by the fact that in Hong Kong as well as throughout other treaty ports in Canton, Shanghai, Kobe and Singapore, the cluster of family-run printing companies and the staff of the major printing companies and newspaper offices were Portuguese Eurasian originally from Macao, as were their succeeding generations.[4] After the maritime trade lost its significance in Macao following the Opium Wars and the foundation of Hong Kong, facilitated by the publication of foreign newspapers in China, many Macanese youngsters who received training classes as composite or printers at the St. Joseph College in Macao sought better employment opportunities in China's treaty ports and in Hong Kong.

However, my argument tries to extend beyond the importance of printing and publishing, since these pioneer creoles used other important modes in which their idea of a more liberal and civilized nation was constantly reimagined, shared and reinforced. Believing that science, reason and education would invariably lead to more advance and autonomy, they absorbed progressive ideas of influential European thinkers deeply influenced by European agnosticism in the age of Darwinism. They also established contacts and affiliated with important academies of modern scientific thought, embracing an ideal quest for the Enlightenment's rational scientific knowledge and diffusion. Besides the development of a national print culture that was crucial to their interests, these men who owned (or had connections to) the most prominent of Macao and Hong Kong's trade book publishers and entrepreneurs, also created and integrated local, metropolitan and international circles of scientific investigation aimed at disseminating and promoting the most advanced scientific information and higher education. Through their participation in institutions of print and society (medical and scientific societies, universities, social clubs, spaces of recreation and congregation from social clubs to Freemasonry lodges) many of which they founded and made more dynamic, they became involved in the organization of a wide range of related events such as historical commemorations, cultural festivities, performances, sporting and horticulture events, which would help communities imagine themselves united to a transnational community, as well as committed to perpetuating its historical origins. They contributed to the development of sworn brotherhoods of Freemasonry in Asia, promoted Masonic values of individual liberty, equality and fraternity among all men, including religious tolerance, separation of Church and state, freedom of the press and of speech mediated by a complex set of symbols and initiation rituals, and also exerted a strong appeal on these multifaceted men.

The aims and scope of this chapter is twofold. First, an attempt will be made to approach the printing culture in Macao and Hong Kong by returning to a transnational framework of space and time in an attempt to assemble scattered pieces of the history of the two colonies in the hope of unveiling a new global perspective of the late nineteenth century, which has so far remained relatively disregarded. I will also address questions of discourse and readership in an attempt to reassert the importance of a thriving print culture to the rise of the Macanese identity. Second, this chapter addresses the production of printed material around the debate on Darwinism through a study that includes analysing the interrelationship between the life trajectories and works of two members from the expatriate community of the Portuguese Eurasian community (Lourenço Pereira Marques and Polycarpo da Costa) within the historical context of both Portuguese Macao and British colonial Hong Kong. Finally, this study also focuses on how the emergence of printing or a capitalist printing trade in Macao with its ramifications to Hong Kong from 1871 onwards, provided a critical means for constructing an 'imaginary identity' enabled by writing, distribution and circulation of print products through a transnational communications network of scattered communities of subscribers and collaborators involved in participatory politics.

Unveiling untold stories of the Macanese in Macao and elsewhere

In the main alley cemetery of Macao's Catholic Cemitério de S. Miguel (Cemetery of St. Michael), the grandiosity of the old gravestones belonging to the family Pereira Marques still attracts attention. In particular, the human size statue of Lourenço Pereira Marques resembles no other funerary memorials in the cemetery, due to a total absence of any overtly Christian symbols and to its provocative epitaph. Indeed the base of the statue bears an epitaph, composed by his brother, praising the deceased's atheism, together with verses from *Odes et Ballades* by French atheist poet Victor Hugo, engraved on its northern side.[5]

L.P. Marques, like Victor Hugo, was raised as a Catholic, but both became atheists and republican supporters in adulthood. Marques (1852–1911) was born in Macao into a prestigious Macanese family who owned the property where one of Macao's legendary landmarks was located – the Camões grotto.[6] Marques studied in the Seminary of St. Joseph in Macao and later pursued his studies in Lisbon and in Dublin where he graduated in medicine in 1877. In the same year, he acquired British nationality, which would allow him to access positions in the civil service of Hong Kong, where he became acting director of the Government Civil Hospital and director of the Lock Hospital while he also worked for the British colony's Victory Gaol.[7] Marques befriended the Filipino revolutionary and notorious Freemason José Rizal and helped him settle down in Hong Kong and benefited from his connections with Freemason circles, especially with the Masons on the medical board who helped him get the medical licence to open an eye clinic.[8]

Marques was an acting member of the Lusitano Club, some of whose members were prominent Portuguese Eurasian figures in Hong Kong and Macao and, like Polycarpo da Costa, were Masons or had strong connections to Freemasonry, which persisted until the late twentieth century.[9] A writer, polyglot, collector and bibliophile, Marques donated part of his private 'transnational library' to the Club of Macau, but this library later disappeared. The surviving catalogue of the library confirms that he was acquainted with the most influential thinkers and currents of thought of his time, including representative works on Darwinism and Freemasonry, such as *A Concise History of Freemasonry*, dated 1903.[10] He also donated part of his private art collection on the Far East to the Sociedade de Geografia (Royal Geographical Society) in Lisbon, where he was also a fellow with his friend Polycarpo da Costa.

Although so far, there is no concrete proof that Marques was affiliated with Freemasonry, he might have been initiated when he was a medical student in Ireland, where exists the oldest grand lodge in world, or he might even have had contacts with the Irish Provincial Grande Lodge of Portugal created in 1872, which joined the United Grand Orient of Portugal formed in 1869.[11] He, his family and closest friends were not only friends or relatives of the founders of printers and progressive newspapers, but they were also close to the Freemasonry circles. He also had professional contacts and associated with senior medical and government health officers who were renowned Freemasons. As professor of medical jurisprudence at the Hong Kong College of Medicine, Marques worked and became friendly with other prominent doctors and Freemasons such as Dr Gregory Paul Jordan (an Armenian nephew of Sir Paul Chater, who was himself a Freemason), Sir Dr Kai Hoi Kai and Dr James Cantlie.[12] Like them, Marques was a member of the Hong Kong Medical Society created in 1886, which was part of the Medical Society Committee that established the Hong Kong College of Medicine for Chinese, the first Western medicine college in Hong Kong in 1887 where Sun Yat-sen studied.[13] Thus, a connection between Marques and Sun Yat-sen seems likely to have existed. Marques was a polyglot who wrote in English with the objective of promoting Camões' poetry, as in his family there was a cult of the Portuguese poet. His writings on Darwinism are full of quotations in French, Spanish and German, attesting to his cosmopolitan culture.[14] In 1890 he retired and returned to Macao in 1895, where he dedicated himself to pro bono medicine until his death in 1911 and he graciously continued to assist the Hong Kong government when necessary, such as during the 1898 bubonic plague epidemic.[15]

Unfortunately, unlike the case of Marques, regarding his friend Polycarpo da Costa (1837–1884) there is scarce bibliographical information available although there is concrete proof about his Freemason affiliation. In fact, the 1884 edition of *China Overland Trade* described in detail Polycarpo da Costa's Masonic funeral service held in the cemetery, which also became known as the Protestant Cemetery in Hong Kong.[16] According to the description, as part of his burial service, a procession was formed and the coffin, covered with his badge of the office as past district grand secretary and other Masonic regalia of the deceased, was conveyed to the cemetery.[17] Da Costa, then secretary of the Hong Kong & Macao Steamboat Company, died together with other Freemasons, including the captain, officers and some passengers of the company's steamer *Yotsai*, in a tragic accident on 24 February 1884 caused by a boiler explosion onboard during a voyage between Hong Kong and Macao. A funerary monument was built in their honour and their graves are among around 80 others adorned with the Freemason symbols found in the cemetery.

Such a significant number of Masonic graveyards attests to the fact that the Freemasonry brotherhood was not only becoming an increasingly important social network in Southern China in the late nineteenth century, but also that Masonic lodges were welcoming ethnic minorities such as the Portuguese Eurasians as well as Armenians, Parsees and Jews into their ranks, a fact that might have contributed to their social ascension and promotion to higher positions in business and civil service jobs in the British colony.

Yet, an earlier controversy was related to da Costa's burial, as the Catholic Church refused permission for him to be buried at the nearby Hong Kong Roman Catholic Cemetery – which was reserved for the Portuguese, Chinese and British Catholics – on the grounds that he was a Freemason. Protests and strong objections were raised in the local legislative council to the point of it being alleged by some of the legislators that the Roman Catholic schools in the British colony did not deserve to continue to receive government subsidies.[18]

Although there are no written records of its activities to show that Freemasonry existed in Macao before the first registered formation in 1906, it seems likely that Freemasons should have conducted their secret activities in the Portuguese colony, as the Chinese restriction to the presence of Europeans in China at this time forced them to stay in Macao for long periods of time. The first recorded activities of Freemasons in the Far East can also be drawn from the Portuguese and Spanish Inquisition records dating back to the eighteenth century. In fact, the earliest information about Freemasonry in the Far East can be traced back to 1756 when two Irish Masons were released after the Inquisition's trial in Manila because they enjoyed British protection.[19] Although sparse, there is also valuable information on the Goa Inquisition records revealing that Freemasonry under the charters granted by Portuguese lodges might have been secretly introduced earlier under the auspices of members of the armed or naval forces and mercantile elite in the Portuguese settlements, despite the prohibition.

Freemasonry was introduced in Canton in 1759 through the auspices of Swedish Freemason naval officers of the Swedish East India Company who created the 'Prince Carl's Lodge' after the name of their ship.[20] The first British Lodge of Amity no. 407 created in 1767 was warranted by the Grand Lodge of England and may well have met in the buildings housing the Swedish company.[21] Senior officers of army regiments or naval ships were granted 'travelling warrants', which allowed them to hold lodge meetings wherever the unit or ship might be during their overseas voyages.[22] During the eighteenth and nineteenth centuries, the British and the Dutch East India Companies' members and army officers created a complex transnational web of Masonic jurisdictions that became prominent in a myriad of settlements in India, Ceylon, Straits Settlements, the Indonesian archipelago and, ultimately, China.

The Lodge Royal Sussex was the first Masonic lodge created in Hong Kong in 1844, followed by the Lodge Zetland in 1846.[23] The former moved to Guangzhou and then to Shanghai in 1846. Masonic lodges were less numerous in China than in India, and subsequently there was a significant expansion of the fraternal order to the littoral areas of Shanghai, Guangzhou, Xiamen, Fuzhou, Tianjin, as well as to the inland cities of Nanjing, Beijing, Harbin and Chengdu, together with Macao, the Philippines and Batavia, with close connections to their counterparts in Portugal, England, Scotland, Ireland, Massachusetts and the Philippines in the 1880s. For instance, the first Masonic lodges created in the Philippines in 1856 were affiliated to the Lodge Grand Oriente founded in Portugal in 1804 due to its prohibition in Spain.[24]

The establishment of foreign concessions in the main port cities of Canton, Amoy, Fuchou, Ningpo and Shanghai in China after the Opium Wars (1842), led to the recruitment of European staff for Western commercial institutions and companies. Many of them were members of the Portuguese and Eurasian communities from Macao who had studied in Macao or overseas and settled with their families in China's treaty ports, and in the new British free port of Hong Kong since its foundation in 1841.[25] Over the succeeding years and decades, subsequent events – such as the abolition of the coolie trade in 1873 and consequent new economic crises allied to natural disasters such as typhoons and fires, which seriously damaged many properties of Macanese elite communities in Macao – originated several dispersions of the Macanese.

On the other hand, one of the contributions of the Liberal Revolution in Portugal in 1820 was the abolition of censorship, so that newspapers reappeared in every overseas Portuguese possession.[26] People of Portuguese origin, mostly Macanese, published the first newspapers in Macao, Hong Kong, Shanghai, Japan and Singapore and they even wrote works on the history of the publishing industry and on the Portuguese presence in the East.[27] Consequently, Macao's Portuguese periodicals and books flourished and expanded their circulation to subscribers of other Macanese diasporic communities in Southeast Asia. Many of them were aiming to serve a polemical cause and were highly critical, thus contributing to a sustained democratic debate.

'Indigenous cosmopolitanism' and Darwinism

In the last quarter of the nineteenth century, some influential Macanese men such as L. P. Marques and Polycarpo da Costa were sympathetic to the idea of evolution, and enlisted Darwin's sociological theory in their plight against conservatism and traditional forces, taking advantage of Hong Kong's open and free intellectual climate and of the wide availability of the means for all printed matter. The appeal that Charles Darwin's theories exerted in certain intellectual and academic circles in Hong Kong might be viewed in the light of being considered a universally applicable explanation to the social phenomena. Darwin's works were among those that were studied as part of the Western science curriculum taught at the college that influenced Sun Yat-sen's thoughts while he was a medical student in Hong Kong. During the same period (1887–1892) he was probably inspired by his direct mentor, the British specialist Dr James Cantlie (1851–1926) who precisely evoked Darwin in his speech at Sun Yat-sen's graduation ceremony in 1892.[28] The writings of these two Macanese may be considered unique among pro-Darwinism published works in the 1880s in the region, as they were the first attempt to analyse in detail and disseminate the theory of evolution. One of the reasons that they did not receive wider recognition might be that they were written in Portuguese. Another interesting aspect is that for the very first time there was also an attempt to relate evolutionism to Chinese philosophy. This aspect is even more impressive when bearing in mind that Darwinism was the first Western sociological theory to make an impact on China.[29] In fact, their writings anticipated the interest and influence that Darwinism would have more than a decade later from 1895 onwards, on the most famous intellectuals and revolutionaries of modern Chinese history in the late Qing and early republican periods in China, including Sun Yat-sen, when was introduced by Yen Fu.[30] Recent studies reveal that, in fact, Darwinism influenced the modern history of China and its great changes were attributed to acceptance of Western social theories, in particular Marxism, until the advent of Maoism.[31] Therefore, it is relevant to note that two pioneers' works dedicated to the theory of evolution were written in Portuguese and published in Hong Kong in the 1880s for diffusion among the Macanese and Portuguese communities in southern China – a fact that it has been neglected in the commemorative events and works dedicated to the impact of Darwinism in Portugal or in the region.

Marques and da Costa are true representatives of those individuals that, according to Frank Karpiel, shared a sort of 'indigenous cosmopolitanism', as they possessed a distinctly global but also regional perspective in their understanding of different cultures as they were deeply interested in the world beyond their community.[32] Marques' friendship with da Costa, a deeply committed Freemason, was especially productive as they were outspoken advocates of evolutionary ideas. Their works in defence of Darwin's modern theory caused quite a scandal among the Portuguese-speaking communities in Macao and Hong Kong, as they stirred up unprecedented rage in the most conservative and Roman Catholic dominated circles. Marques produced his first study titled *A Validade do Darwinism* (*The Validity of Darwinism*) in 1882, in an obvious homage to Darwin, whose death occurred that same year. In this work, relying on his professional expertise as a doctor, Marques gave a succinct summary of the principles of Darwinism and joined in the debate over *On the Origin of Species*.[33] He also co-authored the essay 'Defeza do Darwinism' ('Defence of Darwinism') with da Costa.[34] These and other works were the highlight of the reaction to Darwin's theory in Macao and Hong Kong as they sparked almost a decade of increasingly polarized debate between 1881 and 1889, through the publication of a sermon delivered at Macao Cathedral, as well as books, pamphlets and newspaper articles either supporting or contesting Darwin's theory of evolution. The debate was between conservative clergymen and laymen, and those liberal-minded Macanese for whom an absolute monarchy had become obsolete and who wanted science to be secular and independent from religious constraints. They admired Darwin and simultaneously aimed to be active in educating their fellow countrymen through their publications on modern Western science.

What is clear is that studies on Darwinian evolution that Marques wrote and co-authored with da Costa were associated with a controversy, which originated in an event held at the Clube Lusitano in Hong Kong in 1880. These works deserve careful scholarly attention because they echo the polemical debate between supporters of Darwinian science and religious fundamentalism in the main European literary and scientific circles during that same period, which continued into the twentieth century. Contextually, the works were written during the reign of King Luís I (1861–1889) in Portugal, and at the time of European imperial expansion into Africa, the Far East and Oceania. Macao, together with other undeveloped colonies in Africa, was all that was left of the once-vast Portuguese empire in the 1880s, after Brazil gained its independence in 1822, and the scramble for Africa by the imperial powers in 1878 was determined in Berlin, and thus in a way determined Portugal's political and cultural decay. After decades of ostracism, the Portuguese Catholic Church, especially the Patronage of the East, re-emerged, paving the way for the government's authorization of the return of religious congregations to every Portuguese possession.[35] In the same period, in the neglected colony of Macao, many clerics felt largely empowered. Far from the metropole and through their religious orders in Asia, they were persistently opposed to the spread of new European ideas originating from those Macanese who experienced the British and Portuguese liberalism, especially those who had embraced Freemasonry, republicanism and other new intellectual trends. The religious orders, in particular the Jesuits, through their control of seminaries and schools since the sixteenth century, possessed what Benedict Anderson calls the 'monopoly on linguistic access.'[36] For centuries, they controlled the knowledge and educational system and thus played a primordial role in the exclusive diffusion of culture among the natives and upbringing of local well-off elites in the colonies.

Despite the 1759 and 1834 decrees that successively expelled and extinguished the Jesuit congregation, the enormous power of the Church was not totally undermined in Macao. On the contrary, in 1862, the Jesuit orders returned to Macao to pursue their mission and even reacquired the Seminary of St. Joseph. In Portugal, the Freemasons opposed the reintroduction of the religious orders, such as at the Lodge Perseverance in Coimbra (1873–1876) which curiously had the same name as one of the long-lasting lodges in Hong Kong.[37] In 1884, as a consequence of the promulgation of the encyclical *Humamun Genus*, the Jesuits made an appeal to prevent the spread of Freemasonry, mainly among the young.[38] Some Macanese became involved with several initiatives aimed at lay teaching through free schools, for the instruction of their unprivileged fellow citizens' children, like the creation of the 'Associação para a Promoção da Instrução dos Macaenses' ('Association for the Promotion of the Instruction of Macanese') in 1871.[39]

However, for the purpose of this chapter, the most significant event occurred at the commemoration of tercentenary of the death of the Portuguese poet Luís Camões, a literary and musical event organized by an 'ad hoc' commission comprising L. P. Marques, Polycarpo da Costa, and other members from the Clube Lusitano at its headquarters in Hong Kong in 1880.[40] On the festive occasion, Marques, following his family's long-standing admiration for Camões (there was an authentic shrine to the poet in the grotto in the garden of their property in Macao) offered and unveiled a statue of Camões which stood by a silver statue of Pedro IV (1798–1834), the emperor of Brazil (1822–1831) and king of Portugal (1826), offered by another Macanese.[41] The choice of these statues of prominent Portuguese figures was a symbolic sign of national pride and exaltation of enlightenment as Camões is the most famous Portuguese poet and Pedro IV was associated with Freemasonry and freedom ideals.[42] On the other hand, it became customary to attribute the name of Camões to Portuguese lodges, as the two lodges named after the poet were established in Macao, respectively in 1909 and 1915.[43] As a matter of fact, both the statues of Camões in the grotto of the Marques' family property and the one offered to the Clube Lusitano had been commissioned to Bordalo Pinheiro, a famous sculptor and close friend of the Marques family, and a Freemason himself.[44]

As both L.P. Marques and Polycarpo da Costa were sympathizers of the republican cause in Portugal, they emulated similar Camões commemorations held in Portugal, in particular the one organized by members of the Republican Party in 1880, in order to gain popularity and to pave the way for the establishment of the Portuguese Republic, which was established in 1910. Besides the musical and literary program held at the Clube Lusitano, the group's promoters – which included Marques and da Costa – published an apparently innocuous pamphlet, the so-called *Memória das Festividades* (*Memory of the Festivities*), a bilingual literary publication (Portuguese and English) in 1880.[45] According to the organizer's intentions, that type of commemorative printed material was expected to have a great diffusion and was intended to be widely distributed, fulfilling the function of the absent public libraries and public schools in Macao.

One of the *Memória*'s literary contributions – written in Spanish and signed by an admirer who in subsequent writings was identified as Father Joaquin Fonseca, the rector of the University of Saint Thomas in Manila – was a polemic that propagated from Hong Kong to Macao. Indeed, the Spanish cleric criticized Darwinism in his literary contribution, considering it an 'affront' to God.[46] Notwithstanding this, the compilers of the *Memoria* published the cleric's opinion, together with a note signed by the compiler asserting their total discordance and their unequivocal support of Darwin's theory.[47] In the British colony it inspired enraged editorials in the English weekly *The Hong Kong Catholic Register*, the first Catholic publication published under the direction of A. Machado between 1878 and 1880, and Polycarpo da Costa's letters were published in the *China Mail*.[48] In Macao, António Joaquim Bastos (1848–1912), a lawyer and journalist at the newspaper *O Macaense* wrote a pamphlet criticizing the promoters, not only for the organization of the event but also for implicitly advocating Darwinism and emphasizing that the defence of such ideas was due to the wealth and social differences between the Macanese from Hong Kong and Macao.[49]

Criticism and defence of Darwinism

At that time, there was another related event that is worth discussing. Darwinism was also the topic of a condemnation in the sermon of Canon António Vaconcellos, which he delivered at the Cathedral of Macao during Easter on 6 March 1881, and which came to be published in Macao under a title that expressly stated that the '[sermon] refuted some of the arguments of the Darwinian system with reference to the man and to the Catholic religion'.[50] Above all, this publication criticized what the author called 'impious press' for its heresy in propagating anti-Catholic doctrines and besmirching Portuguese history and culture.[51] Polycarpo da Costa immediately published a response to the sermon in Hong Kong in the same year entitled *Análise do Sermão* (*Analysis of Sermon*) and dedicated it to the 'lovers of progress' who agreed that no change of the political order could be achieved unless religious beliefs were first totally transformed.[52] It was a blistering attack on clerical obscurantism and an aggressive defence of press freedom, claiming that printing could be an important tool not only for contributing to the advancement of the sciences, but also for the dissemination of anti-scientific sciences and the 'slavery of mind' comparable to the Inquisition's persecution against Galileo's scientific contributions.[53]

Polycarpo da Costa and L.P. Marques then went on to again defend Darwinism, and in response to their detractors they authored *Defeza do*

Darwinismo (Defence of Darwinism) published after da Costa's death in Hong Kong and on a date timed to coincide with the commemoration of Darwin's birth in 1889. In the preambles of both *A Validade* and *Defeza,* they purposefully introduced the main ideas of Darwinism, presented a theoretical basis and ideological content to their concept of progress, and assumed the mission of carrying out the debates over Darwin's theories in the public sphere. After recalling the incident related to Father Fonseca, the rector of the University of Manila, whom they refer to as 'orador sagrado' ('sacred orator'), both authors courageously identified themselves as 'liberal republicans', at a time when Portugal was still governed by the Portuguese Crown. Above all, they intended to de-emphasize the role of religion in favour of the primacy of reason, science and technology in society.

In the preface Marques wrote for *A Validade,* he announced a didactic and scientific intention in accordance with the growth in importance of public libraries and the spread of encyclopaedias aimed at the general public in Europe in the nineteenth century, as part of the ideals of Enlightenment thought.[54] He began by lamenting the lack of a public library in Macao and comparing the situation to that in Goa, which he considered the 'Athena of the Portuguese colonies', where he said inhabitants were happier than in Macao because, unlike in Macao, its citizens could benefit from the existence in that city of scientific and literary institutions.[55] He said that he also regretted that Portugal and Spain were the only European countries where there was not a single translation of Darwin's seminal work.[56] In fact, comparative to other European countries, the impact of Darwinism came much later in Portugal, bearing in mind that *On the Origin of Species* was published in England in 1859 and was immediately translated into several languages, while its Portuguese version was published more than five decades later in 1913.[57] Evolutionism was instrumental for Marques and da Costa's criticism of Portugal and Macao as profoundly backward in terms of science, education and culture, a situation that they were determined to remedy. Their solution to the problems of political inefficiency and social decadence was a general overhaul of the quality of education of Macanese society.

In fact, during the celebrations held at the Clube Lusitano, in his inaugural and opening address, da Costa had already made a speech on the importance of the study of the mother-tongue, and on that same occasion he even made an appeal to the governor of Hong Kong, Sir John Pope Hennessy who was the guest of honour. He asked for the governor's support in creating Portuguese schools for Macanese annexed to the existing educational establishments in Hong Kong.[58] Focusing on the total absence of a single Portuguese educational establishment in Hong Kong and the change of the Royal College of Saint Joseph in Macao into an ecclesiastical seminary, he blamed the Portuguese government for the omission and expressed regret that only those children from wealthy families could be sent to Europe to pursue their studies.[59] Da Costa also spoke of the creation of the commercial school in Macao where there was only one teacher unable to teach in both colonies.[60] He acknowledged the relevance of the acquisition of English:

> [F]ar from depreciating the acquisition of English, that language is indispensable to you for earning a living – to this supreme reason is added another important one, namely that it is the vehicle through which the scientific and industrial discoveries and the agitations of the political world reach us more quickly.[61]

In the nineteenth century, this liberal class of Macanese was well-aware of the real status of their compatriots' educational background. In fact, during that period, it is estimated that only a minority of the population of Macao had any command of the metropolitan language. He appealed to the young generation not to rely on the nation's past glories: 'I recommend … to you, because people do not progress by the contemplation of what they have been, but by force of will, by enlightenment and by industry'.[62]

In the work *Defeza*, Marques elaborated on the theory of evolution and used Darwinism to engage in a dialogue about science, faith and history. He also argued that, although he was not a Christian believer, he wrote his study not merely to contest the Catholic Church, but to support the thesis of natural sciences and advocate that 'work and knowledge of one's work are Christian as well those of the Sciences'.[63] Trying to articulate Christianity and Darwinism, Marques neither rejected the Christian religion nor disowned scientific theories. He stated that his purpose was to support a thesis of natural science following the English philosopher and Franciscan friar Roger Bacon: 'The saints would not condemn many opinions that the modern people think should be condemned.'[64] He compared important theorists (Kepler, Descartes and Aristotle, among others) whose theories were also condemned and were targets of persecution, to modern thinkers of the various European schools, which he studied in defence of complete liberty of discussion and impartiality.[65] Following da Costa's earlier arguments in the same work, Marques considered Charles Darwin much more fortunate than his predecessors, who had been condemned by the Inquisition, emphasizing the importance of the new forms of communication of his time, and reaffirming that the promotion of education in the nineteenth century contributed to the tolerance of all doctrines.[66]

Both da Costa and Marques reveal profound erudition and knowledge not only of all the works on Darwinism, that had been written at this time in English, French, Spanish and German or translated into Portuguese, but also of other relevant authors and their scientific theories. Marques went further to comment on the anti-Darwin Christians who defended the incompatibility of Christianity and Darwinism, and the scientists and theologians who demonstrated that evolution was in concordance with Church principles.[67] He questioned why religion feared science and he concluded that those who fight against science were damaging society's well-being and prosperity, as society's interests are intimately linked to science.[68] In essence, these studies on the different dimensions of Darwinism were concerned with social change as they viewed it as a truth.

Finally, one of the extremely interesting features of *Defeza* is the fact that Marques dedicated several pages of his study to trying to discuss the relationship between classic Chinese philosophy and evolutionary theory. He quotes Ernst Teil's 1873 classic work *Feng-shui: A Branch of Natural Science in China* on Feng-shui and its philosophical roots, to support two conclusions.[69] First, he used specific ideas such as the dual notions of female and male in the Chinese philosophy, to show similarities with the old Egyptian belief of female principle and the interruption or imperfection in the development of the male principle.[70] Then, Marques evoked the resurgence of Confucianism in China, which came to be called New Confucianism, in particular the Chinese thinker Chu Hsi (1130–1200),[71] He claimed that these Chinese 'literati' defended a humanist vision in which the cultivation of the self was integrated with social ethics and moral metaphysics adapted to their contemporaneity. Chu Hsi claimed that the there was a fixed cosmic order in the world (ch'i) from which man originated and that this consisted of two realms: the realm of the principle or concept of essence (Li) (or 'natural law'), permanent and eternally changeless, which did not exist either in space nor time, comparable to the platonic 'good'; and the realm of material force (ch'i).[72]

However, for the School of Principle, this immaterial and immutable principle law was innate in all created things in the universe, attributing to them form, motion and change. They assumed that the human mind was in its essence identical to the universe's vital energy, thus, the human mind could achieve perfection through meditation. This notion led to the belief that the study of the heavens or even of animals, would lead to the same principle common to the human mind and the universal mind called the Great Ultimate (taoch'i), which emanates from heaven. As the new-Confucian thinkers valued inwardness, the 'study of things' and empirical investigation was undertaken as they aimed to search for the principle of any material process, in order to ultimately find the principle innate in both material and intellectual processes. Despite certain inconsistencies in his interpretation of Chinese philosophy, Marques contended that the ideas of universal evolution, change and pantheism are important elements present in Chinese philosophy and these aspects would be precisely the starting points of discussions of the theory held by Chinese intellectuals over the following decades.[73]

Another important key factor to Marques' intellectual and humanist vision is undoubtedly found on the *Defeza*'s final page. The work concludes with a quote from Goethe's poem 'Epirrhema' without explicitly naming the author: 'You must, in studying Nature, /Always consider both each single thing and the whole; nothing is inside and nothing is outside, for what is within is without.'[74]

Like Goethe and Darwin, who had discovered the law of evolution in nature, throughout his work, Marques emphasized the study of natural science and the analysis of phenomena of nature applicable to heaven, earth and humankind. In the poem, the sublime idea of nature as a supreme being, a cosmic force and the interdependence of what is 'Innen' ('inside') and 'Aussen' ('outside') in the contemplation of nature, allows one to discover the harmony of the 'whole', the so-called 'open secret' of the Masonic initiation. This inclusion of Goethe's poem published in 1819 leads ultimately to the mystery religion of Freemasonry, a truth that is only available to the senses, a sort of nameless god, which is a concept common in many writings of notorious Freemasons such as Goethe himself.[75] This idea of a 'nameless one' appeared frequently in literary and musical works, and it was associated with the concept of 'translatability of religion' or 'cosmotheism', or worship of the world as the God of old Egyptian traditions, which flourished in the discourse of Enlightenment and in eighteenth-century Freemasonry circles.[76] This idea was also closely connected to Goethe's interest in the sciences and his own conception of evolution was achieved through the adaptation to the environment that anticipated Darwin's theory decades later.

In fact, the defence of Darwin's theory of evolution would have been a great challenge to the Catholic Church and community in both Macao and Hong Kong, with their close religious and political connections to the Philippines. In one of the rare references to Marques, Monsignor Manuel Teixeira, the famous author of the *History of Macau*, in one of his works accused L.P. Marques and his brother of deviating from the 'teachings of the Church' in a clear allusion to their open atheism.[76] Marques and da Costa dared to expose the intransigence of the Catholic Church and proclaim Darwin's indisputable contribution, as the concepts of struggle and survival were crucial for the Macanese community on the verge of extinction due to the neglected politics towards the colony of Macao and an unfair Portuguese educational system rooted in Church indoctrination. Without cutting across their admiration for the Portuguese historical legacy in its overseas colonies, where they were born and would eventually end their days, at times they criticized missionary works on religious dogma through the exposition of Darwinism, a theory that encouraged agnosticism and atheism. In fact, through the promotion and publication of works on the history of Portugal and Darwinism, they sought to awaken in their compatriots a consciousness of their past but also an interest in the progress for modern science and change.

Conclusion

This study analyses the works of two men, L.P. Marques and Polycarpo da Costa, who highlighted some significant aspects of the impact that Freemasonry and Darwinism, allied to the use of printing, exerted on many aspects of thought. It also reveals the active mode with which they used novel ideas of progress to justify social reforms. They fulfilled their pioneer function in anticipating and paving the way for the reception of Darwinism as the first Western social theory ever to have an impact on the political and intellectual development of twentieth-century China.

The cultural activities and published works on Darwinism discussed in this chapter illustrate how in the late nineteenth century, these Macanese educated elites committed themselves to enlightenment, Freemasonry, liberal ideas and philosophies through the printing press. Above all it was concomitant to the idea of achieving the progress and advancement of their compatriots through the promotion of science and education, and the creation of free institutions. Their starting point was the contestation that their dispersed community was threatened in its struggle for survival, and Portugal was unable to fulfil its obligation to help it survive. Moreover, they believed that human evolution was a process of increasing individual and communal liberties with more democratic and representative forms of government. It may not be surprising that these elites, themselves connected by their common European ancestry as well by their own diversity and instability as a social network, were also predominantly interested in a more universal and fraternal sense of community, which shared a common-denominator set of ideational and solidarity ties, rooted to an idealized Enlightenment based on kinship networks and sworn brotherhood institutions. On the other hand, they contributed to the fact that Freemasonry has always been present in the most important historical events of this region, particularly in Macao until the present day, in an intricate and persistent network involving the Portuguese, the British and other colonial subjects through their colonial possessions in India, China, Macao, Hong Kong, the Philippines and elsewhere in Brazil, and other influential Asian business elites such as the Parsees, Armenians and Jews. In fact, worldwide colonial expansion and trade favoured the flourishing of a solid and effective network of Masonic lodges from the eighteenth to the early twentieth centuries throughout the world. Freemasonry was present in a large spectrum of colonial ports and trading centres as the army and naval regiments as well as mercantile networks spread with from Europe, in particular Portugal, Spain, England, France and Holland, to the farthest places on the globe such as South America, India and China. For the local Eurasian and Asian elites, affiliation with Masonic lodges meant not only diverse forms of socialization but in many cases social and professional promotion that they would not otherwise have had access to. Freemasonic affiliation allowed them to freely interact, for example, with foreign royal visitors, colonial governors, East and Dutch East India Company officials, politicians and other influential Westerners at their clubs as if on an equal basis, taking advantage of their mutual assistance to better their own prospects in business, politics and colonial government positions at all levels, thus ensuring their visibility and respectability. Another worthwhile aspect was the opportunity to share in the prestige and opulence of the public and private Freemasonry ceremonial garb, lore and symbolic rituals ranging from balls, banquets and parades to burial processions in regalia. Moreover, Freemasonry's hierarchical structure and links to Grand Lodges all owed local leaders the rare opportunity to develop relationships with distant government officials and business people within a fraternal and global context. Similarly, Macao and Hong Kong's nineteenth-century Portuguese

Eurasian elites are an excellent illustration of these intertwining themes, and it is believed that a growing number of Portuguese Eurasians expressed an active interest in joining lodges and actively participated in Freemasonry either in the East or in Europe. Masonic lodges in Macao and in Hong Kong, like those in other parts of Asia, reflected the power relations of different sectors of the foreign community as well as the arrangement of social values. In the particular case of the Macanese, they may have found that Freemasonry's egalitarian ideals served to bridge the widening political and racial gap dividing Eurasians and Westerners.

This group of liberal-minded Macanese creoles in Macao and in Hong Kong fell under the sway of some ultra-conservative clerics and laymen. Yet they were men with broader views and more settled opinions than the traditional circle of society in Macao, with whom the Macanese were accustomed to associating.

The Portuguese Eurasians who were well-travelled found a different world in Hong Kong – a place where free thinkers and atheists spoke freely and disparagingly of their beliefs against the Catholic Church and the decadent monarchy. The writings and activities led by L.P. Marques and Polycarpo da Costa highlight three important themes in the late colonial debate among these creoles at the end of the nineteenth century: the progress of the sciences; the rights of the colonized native elites against the conservative and subservient mentality; and Freemasonry egalitarian principles embodied in their activities, writings, interests and alliances.

After the dictatorship was imposed in Portugal in the 1930s, the Macanese Freemasons continued to meet secretly in Macao or at the lodges in Hong Kong. Several of the Hong Kong lodges met informally and under very dangerous conditions in the internment camps. Perseverance Lodge no. 1165 EC, which met in Stanley Prison, even kept a minute book.[77] Throughout the twentieth century, some continued to play an important role in the Clube Lusitano and in the local lodges.

In summary, in the late nineteenth century these Macanese used printed publications to reach a significant portion of the population and create an avid readership, thus contributing to the development of a strong sense of community among the diverse and scattered Macanese populace in China, Asia and Europe. The emergent common sense of the Macanese community and the identity that started to be forged in that period is still quite significant today. Committed to their ideals, these dilettanti fought obscurantism and discrimination within the colonial and ecclesiastical bureaucracy, and reinforced a sense of difference through the mutual interaction of the Eurasian groups and foreigners in colonial port cities. This in turn was instrumental in forging a modern identity consciousness leading to the creation of self-imagined communities still dominant in modern Macao under the Chinese administration, through the organization of community meetings in Macao and elsewhere in the diaspora through their clubs, newsletters and internet websites of their members.[78]

Notes

1 Benedict Anderson, *Imagined Communities: Reflections on the Origin and Spread of Nationalism*, London: Verso, 1983, p. 28.
2 Ibid., p. 41.
3 Ibid., pp. 9–68.
4 J.P. Braga, *Portuguese Pioneering: A Hundred Years of Hong Kong*, Hong Kong: Ye Olde Printerie, Ltd., 1941.
5 *Odes et Ballades* is a collection of poems written between 1822 and 1828. Victor Hugo, *Odes et Ballades, Les Orientales* (*Odes and Ballads, The Oriental*), Paris: Flammarion, n.d.
6 Jorge Forjaz, *Famílias Macaenses* (*Macanese Families*), Macao: Instituto Cultural de Macau/Instituto Portuguese do Oriente, II, 1996, pp. 564–565.
7 Ibid., p. 566.
8 Reynaldo S. Fajardo, *Dimasalang: The Masonic Life of D. Jose Rizal*, Calasiao, Pangasinan: CMN Printing Co., Inc., 1999, p. 24.
9 Ibid.
10 Forjaz, *Famílias Macaenses*, p. 566.
11 Christopher Haffner, *The Craft in the East*, Hong Kong: District Grand Lodge of Hong Kong and the Far East, 1977, p. 52.
12 Ibid.
13 Hong Kong Medical Society, 'Minutes of Meetings, 1886–1912', Primary Source Microfilm, Special Collection, University of Hong Kong Library.
14 L.P. Marques, 'Louis de Camoens: A Discourse Delivered by Dr L.P. Marques at the *Clube Lusitano* on the Occasion of the Celebration of the Tercentenary of Louis de Camoens, the Prince of Portuguese Poets', *China Review*, ix, China Mail Office Shanghai: Kelly and Walsh/London, Trubner & Co.
15 E.V. Lucas, *Who's Who in the Far East, 1906–07*, Hong Kong: China Mail, 1906, p. 215.
16 *China Overland Trade Report*, Hong Kong: Y.J. Murrow, Vol. xxviii, no. 5, 4 March 1884, p. 2.
17 Ibid.
18 Patricia Lim, *Forgotten Souls, A Social History of the Hong Kong Cemetery*, Hong Kong: Hong Kong University Press, 2011, p. 493.
19 Haffner, *The Craft in the East*, p. 5.
20 Ibid., p. 18.
21 Henry Wilson Coil, *Coil's Masonic Encyclopedia*, New York: Macoy Publishing, 1961, p. 76.
22 J.M. McDonald, 'Military Travelling Lodges', *The Pentagram*, 30, 1940, p. 182.
23 Haffner, *The Craft in the East*, p. 18.
24 Ibid., p. 52.
25 *Eco Macaense* (*Echo Macanese*), Macao, 21 March 1897, p. 2.
26 The first law on the freedom of press dates back to 1821. M. Teixeira, *A Imprensa, Periódica Portuguese no Extremo-Oriente* (*Portuguese Periodical Press in the Far East*) Macao: Notícias de Macau, 1965, pp. 70–72.
27 There were 25 Portuguese newspapers registered in Hong Kong, five in Shanghai and one in Canton as well in Singapore and Japan. The first Chinese newspaper was also published by a Macanese with the title *Jinghai Congbao* (*Echo Macaense*) in 1893, in Portuguese and Chinese versions and was used as a propaganda vehicle for the revolutionary doctrines of the historic leader Sun Yat-sen. See *Echo Macaense*, p. 2.
28 L. Fu, 'From Surgeon-Apothecary to Statesman: Sun Yat-sen at the Hong Kong College of Medicine', *JR Coll Physicians Edinb*, 30, 2009; pp. 166–172, www.rcpe.ac.uk/journal/issue/journal_39_2/fu.pdf (accessed 3 May 2010).

29 Elisabeth Sinn, *A Study of the Influence of Social Darwinism on the Ideas of History in China (1895–1906)*, unpublished thesis, University of Hong Kong, March 1979.
30 Ibid.
31 For a study on the impact of Darwinism in China, see also Benjamin Schwartz, *In Search of Wealth and Power: Yen Fu and the West*, New York: Harper Torch Books, 1969 (first published 1964); James Reeve Pusey, *China and Charles Darwin*, Cambridge, MA: Council of East Asian Studies, Harvard University, 1983.
32 Frank Karpiel, 'Freemasonry, Colonialism, and Indigenous Elites', *Interactions: Regional Studies, Global Processes, and Historical Analysis*, 28 February–3 March 2001, Library of Congress, Washington, DC, www.historycooperative.org/proceedings/interactions/karpiel.html (accessed 3 May 2010).
33 L.P. Marques, *Validade (A) do Darwinismo* (*Validity of Darwinism*), Hong Kong: International Printing Office, 1882.
34 L.P. Marques, *Defenza do darwinism: reputação d'um artigo do jornal 'Catholic Register'* (*Defence of Darwinism: refutation of a journal article of 'Catholic Register'*), Hong Kong, Typ. de Noromha & Ca., 1889.
35 Catholic Encyclopedia Portugal, www.newadvent.org/cathen/12297a.htm (accessed 3 May 2010).
36 Anderson, *Imagined Communities*, pp. 42–43.
37 Lodge Perseverance was created in Hong Kong in 1867 and it is still active nowadays. See Haffner, *The Craft in the East*.
38 J. Ernst, *Masonic Voice Review*, Chicago: J.W. Brown, 1889, p. 133.
39 Associação Promotora da Instrução dos Macaenses (Association of Promoting Macanese Education), www.apim.org.mo/pt/ (accessed 5 June 2010).
40 Other members were José Luís de Selavisa Alves, João Miguel Sebastião Alves, Luciano Fortunato de Carvalho, Marcos António de Carvalho, José Philippe da Costa, Carlos Danenberg, José António dos Remédios, Jerónimo Miguel Dos Remédios, and Marcos Calixto de Rozario. Comisão do Tricentenãrio de Camões, *Memória dos Festejos celebrados em Hong Kong por ocasião do tricentenário do Príncipe dos Poetas Portugueses Luís de Camões* (Commission of the Tercentenary Celebrations of Camões, *Memory of the festivities celebrated in Hong Kong for the occasion of the tercentenary celebrations of the prince of Portuguese poets, Luis de Camões*), Hong Kong: Typografia De Souza & Ca., 1880, p. 1.
41 Ibid.
42 His son, Pedro II of Brazil, belonged to the Lodge Grande Oriente do Brasil.
43 Lodge Luis de Camões (The Ancient and Accepted Scottish Rite of Freemasonry) no. 309 was installed in Macao in 1909 and was active until 1914. It was followed by Lodge Luís de Camões no. 383 created in 1915 and which lasted until 1930. António de Oliveira Marques, *Dicionário de Maçonaria Portuguesa* (*Portuguese Freemasonry Dictionary*), Lisbon: Editorial Delta, Vol. II, 1986, p. 904.
44 Oliveira Marques, *Dicionário de Maçonaria Portuguesa*, p. 1122–1123.
45 Comisão do Tricentenãrio de Camões, *Memória*, p. 1.
46 Original in Spanish, Comisão do Tricentenãrio de Camões, *Memória*, p. 84. Father Joaqin Fonseca was a Dominican and the Rector of the University from 1878 to 1880.
47 Comisão do Tricentenãrio de Camões, *Memória*, p. 94; Marques, *O Darwinismo*, p. 5.
48 *Catholic Register*, Hong Kong, 14 September 1880; *Catholic Register*, Hong Kong, 16 October 1880; *China Mail*, Hong Kong, 13 September 1880.
49 António Joaquim Bastos, *A inépcia de uma acção ou uma página para a história dos festejos promovidos em Hong Kong pela Comissão do Tricentenário de Camões* (*The ineptitude of an action or a page in the history of the festivities promoted in Hong Kong by the Commission of Tercentenary Camões*), Macao: Tip. Mercantil, 1880. Forjaz, *Famílias Macaenses*, pp. 475–476.

50 António Maria Augusto de Vasconcellos, *Sermão pregado na sé Cathedral de Macau no primeira domingo de quaresma, 6 de março de 1881, no qual sam refutados alguns pontos do systema darwiniano, com referencia ao homem e á religião catholica* (*Sermon preached in the Cathedral of Macau on the first Sunday of Lent, 6 March 1881, in which Sam refuted some points of the Darwinian system, with reference to man and the Catholic religion*), Macao: Typographia Mercantil, 1881. Father A.A.M. De Vasconcelos came to Macao in 1862 as teacher in the *Escola Macaense* (Macanese School). Manuel Teixeira, *Toponímia de Macau* (*Macau's Toponym*), Macao: Instituto Cultural de Macau, 1997, p. 20.
51 Vasconcelos, *Sermão pregado na sé Cathedral de Macau no primeira domingo de quaresma*, p. 17.
52 Polycarpo A. Da Costa, *Análise do Sermão pregado pelo Reverendíssimo Senhor António Maria Augusto de Vasconcelos, Bacharel Formado em Theologia pela Universidade de Coimbra,, etc., na Sé Cathedral de Macau em 6 de Março de 1881* (*Analysis of the sermon preached by Reverend Mr Antonio Maria Augusto de Vasconcedos, Bachelor degree in Theology from the University of Coimbra, etc. in the Cathedral of Macau, on March 6, 1881*), Hong Kong: Typographia de Noronha & Ca, 1881.
53 Da Costa, *Análise*, pp. 5, 18.
54 Marques, *A Validade*, p. v.
55 Ibid.
56 Ibid. p. 24.
57 For more detailed information see de Ana Leonor Pereira, *Darwin em Portugal*, Coimbra: Almedina, 2001.
58 Comisão do Tricentenário de Camões, *Memória*, p. 89.
59 Ibid., p. 90.
60 Ibid., p. 91.
61 Original in English. Comisão do Tricentenário de Camões, *Memória*, p. 93.
62 Ibid., p. 93.
63 Author's translation from the original in Portuguese ('O trabalho e o conhecimento são tão cristãos como as ciências'). Marques, *A Defeza*, p. 57.
64 Author's translation from the original in Portuguese ('Os santos nao condenariam muitas das opinioes que os modernos julgam que devem ser condenadas'). Marques, *A Defeza*, p. 55.
65 Ibid., p. 19.
66 Da Costa, *Análise*, p. 15. Marques, *A Defeza*, pp. I–III.
67 Marques, *A Defeza*, pp. 5, 57–58.
68 Ibid., p. 58.
69 Ibid., pp. 61–63.
70 Ibid.
71 Ibid.
72 Sinn, *A Study of the Influence of Social Darwinism on the Ideas of History in China (1895–1906)*, pp. 97, 100–101.
73 Marques, *A Defeza*, p. 62.
74 Author's translation into English from the original in German.
75 Goethe (1749–1832) joined the Master of Lodge Amalia in Weimare on 23 June 1780.
76 Ann B. Shteir and Bernard V. Lightman, *Figuring it Out: Science, Gender, and Visual Culture*, Hanover, NH: Dartmouth College Press, 2006, pp. 61–62.
77 Manuel Teixeira, *A voz das pedras de Macau* (*Stone Voice of Macau*), Macao: Imprensa Nacional, 1980, p. 192.
78 Haffner, *The Craft in the East*, p. 401.
79 In 2004, the government of the MSAR hosted the fifth 'Encontro Macanese', a meeting point in Macao for the Macanese community in the diaspora, in particular those members of the 12 'Casas de Macau' ('Houses of Macao') worldwide.

4 The Holy House of Mercy and its impact on Macao's women

Leonor Diaz de Seabra

The Holy House of Mercy in Macao

The brotherhood dedicated to Our Lady of the Mercy was established by Queen Leonor (1458–1525) in 1498, in a chapel of the Cathedral of Lisbon. Initially, the brotherhood was known as the invocation of Our Lady of the Mother of God, Virgin Maria of the Mercy. However, soon it was known only as the Mercy or Holy House of Mercy.

The new brotherhood quickly extended throughout Portugal, as well as in its overseas establishments, thanks to the royal support. The fruits of this institution were soon felt. New hospitals were built and the existing ones were improved, asylums for old people were established and there were more and more orphanages appeared. The poor, in general, were taken care of and they were given material support. A system for caring for sick people in their own homes was created. Dowries for the maiden orphans to marry were instituted. The prisoners, the delinquents, those convicted and condemned to death were not forgotten. The Mercy extended its spiritual, judicial and material assistance to them.

Admission in the Mercies, in the category of brothers (member), was subject to different criteria, according to whether they were men or women. The participation of women as rightful sisters had been forbidden since the second half of the sixteenth century.[1] The women, initially admitted as 'members', or even as sisters were later considered only as children or widows of brothers, with the right to burial followed by the brotherhood. And, from the 1580s, their participation in the life of the brotherhood was forbidden, even in devotional terms.[2]

In colonial contexts, the criteria consisted of admitting people with identified male Portuguese origin, i.e. belonging to families who belonged to the colonial elite and who had the power of decision. These individuals were the ones who managed the finances of the Mercies, the collections and hospitals, distributed alms, granted marriage dowries to orphan girls and visited the poor in their homes. It was their task to effect distinctions, to submit the poor to complex selection processes similar to those that they had been submitted to in order to get to the position that they occupied in the Mercy.[3]

In the old regime, women made up the largest percentage of the poor in almost all categories of people in terms of economic and social vulnerability, although no definite criteria existed that granted these women priority regarding admission to the Mercy. However, it should be noted that women were dependent on men, whether they were married or unmarried. The only exception being widows, who enjoyed some autonomy if they were well off. When married, women did not have the same rights as their husbands.[4] Single women were dependent on their father or, in his absence, on their brothers. The vulnerable situation generally had its origin in the absence of masculine guardianship, or in its inefficacy (absent, invalid men, etc.). This inequality of woman also resulted in their lack of access to remunerated activities, especially those that were corporately regulated and excluded women. Female work was, therefore, more precarious and was usually domestic. Despite these limitations, work was indispensable for them to obtain any kind of social esteem.[5]

Therefore, the majority of the poor visited in their homes were women, who were the largest percentage of the 'ashamed poverty' and had been forced to assume the role of head of the family due to death, absence or invalidity of their husbands. Very often they were responsible for small children or handicapped people. The 'ashamed poor' also included the 'merceeiras' (those who received mercy), women over 50 years of age that received fixed and regular support from any institution besides the Mercy. Although the 'ashamed poor' were generally women, there was also a minority of men.[6] The attention to the 'ashamed poverty' had also captured the attention of the new brotherhoods and they devoted themselves, among their other obligations, to supporting these members of high social groups who had suffered disgrace or were ruined, favouring these 'new poor' in their religious and social activities.[7] This movement was immediately extended by the Franciscan movements that also deeply influenced the renovation of the brotherhoods, with the growth of the 'Mounts of Mercy' throughout the fifteenth century, turning their help of the poor into a wide mobilization of alms and charity.[8]

The foundation of the Portuguese Mercies is also connected to a wider movement of renovation of the European brotherhoods. They have some common religious and charitable purposes, such as, for example, providing assistance and support to prisoners.[9] In colonial societies, where the maintenance of the social statute was important, one of the great concerns of the charity was to support the people who, despite their higher social status, had fallen into situations of poverty, due to several kinds of adversity. It was, mostly, a secret kind of domiciliary help, the intention of which was to keep those (impoverished) people in an upper social status, in contrast to those whose poverty was openly recognized because they 'extended their hands in public'. For this reason, these people were called the 'ashamed poor'.[10] Helping them aided the maintenance of social hierarchies: on the one hand, the institution reaffirmed the hierarchies when helping the 'ashamed poor' maintain their existing distinctions, since it prevented the social order from being discredited; on the other hand, the receivers avoided the social exclusion of public aid. The aided poor, in this group, were generally widows, orphan girls without a dowry to get married, family units that lacked a father or a husband, etc. The 'ashamed poverty' constituted a level of descending social mobility that charity tried to prevent, even though the origins of these poor were the middle classes, but with some social credit. In this sense, the charity included, as one of its components, social reproduction.[11]

The Mercy's activities in Macao

In Macao, the Mercy was established by the Jesuit Bishop D. Melchior Carneiro who, upon his arrival in 1568, launched the construction of the brotherhood. For example, he himself went from door to door to beg for the funds he needed. After the Mercy was established in 1569, the Hospital of the Poor was soon created, as well as an isolated hospital to help the lepers, the Hospital of St. Lazarus, with a small church called Our Lady of the Hope (currently the Church of St. Lazarus) attached.[12]

From then on, other social projects were established, including institutions for the protection of abandoned children, orphans, widows, fallen women, etc. In 1571, for example, the Holy House already provided special support (without any racial discrimination, a great many of its protégées were Chinese) for the abandoned children, the orphans and captives, visiting the sick poor in their houses. All this assistance was maintained at the cost of alms from residents and the monthly fees from the brothers.[13]

Besides the Hospital of the Poor and the Lazarus, the Holy House had, almost since its beginnings, the House of the Displayed, or the 'Roda' as it was commonly called, in order to collect the funding, generally for the children of Chinese and slave women. The Holy House of Mercy took care of them through a governess and maids, whose choice was subject to very strict rules.[14] The rate of mortality among these abandoned children was very high and, more than saving their lives, the Mercy tried to save their souls through baptism.[15] Most of the children were female (normally non-desired), abandoned by their mothers after birth in the streets or delivered to the Hospital of the Rejected. Since there was not enough space to shelter them all, the foundlings were delivered to poor foster mothers, who received a small monthly subsidy to take care of the children until they were seven years old.[16]

After this period, the Mercy no longer provided assistance to the rejected, nor was it interested in their well-being anymore. As a result, the foster mothers forced the fostered children to beg for alms, in order to gain their sustenance. Most of them then became prostitutes.[17]

The Governor Jose Maria da Ponte e Horta forbade the 'Roda' in Macao with a governmental order in 1867, but without any practical results.[18] Only in 1876 was 'Roda' abolished, when the Holy House of Mercy trusted the Displayed ones to the Canossian Children of Charity who took care of them, at first in the building of the Displayed and later, in the Asylum of Holy Childhood, in Saint Anthony.[19]

Table 4.1 Registration of entries and releases of foundlings of the Holy House of Mercy (1850–1876)

Dates of entry			Names	Notes	Date		
Year	Month	Day			Year	Month	Day
1865	October	29	Isabel	Handicapped. Baptized.	Deceased 1867	November	15
1865	December	31	Ana Maria	Handicapped. Baptized.			
1866	February	9	Francisca Xavier	Handicapped. Baptized. Hospital: 5 June 1870. Release: 22 June 1870.			
1866	May	10	Micaela	Handicapped. Baptized.			
1866	May	22	Engrácia	Handicapped. Hospital, sick, at 18 September 1868, deceased.	Deceased 1868	September	30
1866	May	25	Maria de Jesus das Dores	Handicapped. Hospital on 27 May 1870. Release: 12 July 1870.			
1866	May	28	Esperança	Hospital: 7 January 1876. Release: 18 January 1876.	Deceased 1867	February	16
1866	June	12	João	Baptized.	Deceased 1867	August	23
1866	August	2	Josefa	Baptized.	Deceased 1867	July	7
1867	January	4	Maria Ana	Baptized. Hospital: 11 March 1869.	Deceased 1869	March	19
1867	April	10	Susana 15 April 1867	Delivered by Father Manuel Francisco do Rosário, with governmental order. Hospital: 15 January 1869. Release: 5 March 1869.			

Table 4.1 (cont.)

Dates of entry			Names		Notes		Date		
Year	Month	Day					Year	Month	Day
1867	April	15	Margarida	15 April 1867	Delivered by Father Manuel Francisco do Rosário, with governmental order. Hospital: 6 February 1869.	Deceased	1869	February	17
1867	April	15	Raquel	15 April 1867	Delivered by Father Manuel Francisco do Rosário, with governmental order. Hospital: March of 1869.	Deceased	1869	March	16
1867	April	15			Delivered by Father Manuel Francisco do Rosário, with governmental order.	Deceased	1867	May	30
1867	April	15	Lia		Delivered by Father Manuel Francisco do Rosário, with governmental order.	Deceased	1869	August	4
1867	April	15	Judite		Delivered by Father Manuel Francisco do Rosário, with governmental order.	Deceased	1869	August	22
1867	April	15			Delivered by Father Manuel Francisco do Rosário, with governmental order.	Deceased	1867	July	10
1867	April	15			Delivered by Father Manuel Francisco do Rosário, with governmental order.	Deceased	1867	May	5
1867	April	22	Francisco		Delivered by the Police, with governmental order.	Deceased	1868	November	15

1867	May	1	Maria	Delivered by Holy House of Mercy.	Deceased	1867	May	11
1867	July	29	Ana	Delivered by Holy House of Mercy.	Deceased	1867	July	29
1867	September	10	Ana	Delivered by Dr Leocádio.	Deceased	1867	September	10
1867	October	6	Maria do Rosário	Delivered by Dr Leocádio.	Deceased	1867	October	6
1867	October	21	Maria	Delivered by the police.	Deceased	1867	October	27
1867	November	21	Teodoro	Delivered by the Holy House of Mercy.	Deceased	1868	February	16
1868	September	11	Inocente	Delivered by the police, with governmental order. Baptized.	Deceased	1868	September	12
1868	September	25	António	Delivered by the police, with governmental order. Baptized.	Deceased	1868	September	26
1868	October	18	Maria	Delivered by the police, with governmental order. Baptized.	Deceased	1868	October	19
1868	October	22	Gentil António dos Remédios	Delivered by the police, with governmental order. Baptized. Later, he was delivered to his father, José do Rosário.		1869	August	31
1869	January	28	Maria	Delivered by Cláudio José da Silva, with governmental order. Baptized.	Deceased	1869	February	155
1869	February	4	Maria	Delivered by the police, with governmental order. Baptized.	Deceased	1869	May	7
1869	May	7	Maria	Delivered by the police, with governmental order. Baptized.	Deceased	1869	June	55

Table 4.1 (cont.)

Dates of entry			Names	Notes		Date		
Year	Month	Day				Year	Month	Day
1869	June	5	Esperança	Delivered by the Police, with governmental order. Baptized.	Deceased			
1869	July	17	Alina	Delivered by the police, with governmental order. Baptized.	Deceased	1869	July	17
1869	August	4	Maria	Delivered by Father António José Pereira with governmental order. Baptized		1869	August	4
1869	September	27	Ana Joaquina	Delivered by the police, with governmental order. Baptized.	Deceased	1869	September	28
1869	October	7	Maria	Delivered by the police, with governmental order. Baptized.	Deceased	1869	October	18
1869	November	6	Maria	Delivered by the police, with governmental order. Baptized.	Deceased	1869	November	7
1872	September	27	Maria do Rosário	Delivered by the police. Baptized. Hospital: 20 September 1872.				
1872	November	7	Teresa de Jesus	Delivered by the police, with governmental order. Baptized.				
1872	December	7	Teresa de Jesus	Order of the president of Holy House of Mercy. Hospitalized: 18 September 1876. Release.				
1875	April	18	Maria Rita	Hospital with order of president.				

Year	Month	Day	Name	Notes	Status	Year	Month	No.
1875	January	18	Helena	Hospital. Delivered to Ms Mariana Pereira Morais, 1 March 1873.				
1875	July	29	Marta	Delivered by the police, with governmental order. Baptized.	Deceased	1873	July	30
1875	April	17	Maria Rita	Hospital: 23 February 1876.				
1875	July	29	Anamita (girl)	With governmental order	Release	1875	August	17
1875	August	10	Anamita (girl)	With governmental order.	Release	1875	August	17
1875	August	11	Anamitas (6 girls and 1 boy)	With governmental order.	Release	1875	August	17
1875	August	11	Emília de Jesus	With order of the police.				
				Delivered 23 Foundlings to the Canossian Sisters.		1876	September	8

AH/SCM/286 – 'Book for registration entries and released of foundlings of the Holy House of Mercy (1850/11/20 until 1876/09/08)'

Table 4.2 List of foundlings, both adults and children, of the Holy House of Mercy delivered to the Sisters of Charity of the Order of the Congregation of Canossian, on 8 September 1876

No	Children		
1	Teresa de Jesus	4 years old	
2	Maria do Rosário	4 years and 6 months	
3	Emília de Jesus	7 years old	Delivered.
4	Maria Auta	1 year old	
5	Maria Filomena	10 years old	
6	Maria Severina	10 years old	
7	Maria Josefa	10 years old	
8	Susana do Rosário	10 years old	
9	Marta dos Remédios	10 years old	
10	Joana da Luz	10 years old	Died in the Hospital, 30 August 1877.
11	Maria Irenia	10 years old	
12	Francisca Rosa	10 years old	
13	Quintinal das Dores	10 years old	Released at 14 October to the house of Mr Maximiano A. dos Remédios.
14	Teresa de Jesus	14 years old	Delivered.
15	Maria da AssunçNewãNewo	10 years old	
16	Maria de Jesus	10 years old	Blind. Died 24 September 1877.
	Adults		
17	Teresa de Jesus	25 years old	
18	Ana Maria da AssunçNewãNewo	18 years old	Handicapped.
19	Sinforoza de Jesus	25 years old	Handicapped.
20	Maria de Jesus das Dores	17 years old	Blind.
21	Micaela de Santo	19 years old	Blind.
22	Francisca Xavier	19 years old	Blind.
23	Flora	32 years old	Blind.

Besides the Asylum of the Mercy there was the Asylum of Father Manuel Francisco Rosário de Almeida, for abandoned or sold children. It was maintained with the alms that this priest collected from door to door. The children received aid and education there and were later placed in 'honest houses'.[20]

The orphan girls were also object of the beneficence of the Mercy of Macao. In 1592 there were funds for dowries for the orphans, for their marriage. The dowries were requested by the orphans, or offered through proclamations, which invited the interested parties to present the request. They were often married in the Chapel of the Mercy, and the supplier and the board members attended the wedding.[21]

The Mercy was also in charge of the concession of dowries to single girls that needed them to achieve marriage. But to get a dowry they had to meet the criteria defined by the Mercies, such as an age limit, being fatherless, absolutely needing the dowry to marry. On the other hand, the brotherhood had to check on the poverty, honour and virtues of the candidates, whose 'sexual honour' was considered to be in danger as long as they remained single.[22]

In 1726, the need was recognized to take care of the orphans and widows in Macao, who were numerous at that time due to the frequent deaths of men in shipwrecks of the vessels that were doing commerce outside Macao. The statute was then approved and 30 widows and orphans were admitted. They received support, and the orphans were instructed to become mothers of families.[23] One of the orphans, the one who was considered the most deserving, was chosen annually to receive a dowry that consisted of a half per cent of the total commercial movement on the import duties. The Loyal Senate kept it for this purpose. This half per cent went up to 406 taels in 1726, but it was only 60 taels in 1737. From then on, the institution was suspended, until 1782 when the brotherhood made a proposal to establish a new asylum, in accordance with the Senate's rule, that was given 4,000 taels and the name of 'Female Hospice of Santa Rosa de Lima'.[24] This capital, which increased due to many donations and legacies, was loaned against cargo guarantees. The number of girls who could be admitted depended on the profits of these interest rates. Nobody was admitted without the permission of the bishop that nominated a chaplain (there was a chapel in the hospice), a superintendent, and a woman of good reputation for being 'community regent' (a sort of governess). A teacher taught the girls about religion, reading, writing, sewing and embroidery. The girls, whose parents would pay for the food, lodging, etc., could be admitted when there were vacancies and the bishop did not raise objections.[25] The orphans who had been educated there could, if the bishop allowed, be assigned as private teachers to any family, as well as accept a marriage proposal (if there was an appropriate suitor). In such a case the dowry was granted, but the amount of this dowry depended on the resources available to the institution and the bishop's good-will. The orphans' building – the Asylum for Invalids – was completed, in 1900, as was the Hospice of Indigents, designed for poor women and widows.[26] In 1925 the Holy House of Mercy had the Asylum for Invalids rebuilt.[27]

Another bishop, D. Marcelino José da Silva (1789–1803), founded the 'Female Hospice of Saint Maria Madalena' for suspected fallen women, that raised much criticism and eventually led to the bishop's resignation.[28] The 'Female Hospice', however, continued to exist and was soon full of women whose guilt had not been verified.[29] In the 'Female Hospice of Saint Maria Madalena' the girls learned spinning, weaving, sewing, etc. They lived on the income from their work as well as from donations, and were under the spiritual guidance of the vicar of St. Laurence's.[30] However, their belongings were badly managed – nobody made any inventories so that these belongings might be given back to others when the owner left.[31] As a result, many of those who had been regenerated 'for repentance, penitence or protection', had fallen again due to lack of means for living, and engaged in prostitution for survival.[32] By the decree of the Prince Regent of Portugal issued on 12 March 1800, this 'Female Hospice' was dissolved.[33]

The Mercy's impact on the fate and role of women in Macao

As we know, the first inhabitants of Macao did not join the Chinese population and the women they lived with were Japanese, Malays, as well as Indonesian and Indian slaves. Some Africans and numerous Timorese slaves were imported to Macao later, and they also contributed to the racial mixture.[34] The considerable mixture of Chinese blood that Macanese have absorbed throughout the centuries is mostly due to the cohabitation of the Portuguese and Eurasians with their 'muitsai' (female children not desired by the parents and sold by their parents as housemaids, for a given number of years, generally 40, or until the end of their lives).[35] This practice to sell the girls to the inhabitants of Macao started very early and continued for more than two centuries, in spite of the constant prohibitions of the Portuguese authorities as well as of the Chinese.[36] As female infanticide was not an unusual practice in China, many Chinese, because of their poverty, sold their children to the Portuguese, instead of killing them. Others stole or bought them from their countrymen and resold them in Macao. This commerce, of stolen or resold children, seems to have been more used to acquire 'muitsai', because the Chinese, in their majority, feared retaliation from their late ancestors, in case their descendants changed religion, and adopted those of the foreigners, when the children were sold to them directly. Many Chinese were not ashamed to practise this traffic with the Portuguese of Macao, and earned a great deal of money from it.[37] The Chinese female slaves were, generally, kidnapped by local dealers in their childhood, or were sold by their parents, and might be freed by someone who wanted to take them as concubines.[38] This practice was current in China where the Chinese appealed to the work from courtesans – the pei-pá-tcháis[39] – who were required to know music, painting and literature, thus becoming a pleasant company for the men in the evenings.[40]

Orphan girls and widows

Most of the charity given by last wills and testaments to the Macanese Holy House was directed to 'orphan girls', meaning that the Holy House worked to provide the dowries that were indispensable to guarantee the circulation of these female groups in the nuptial market of the territory. Some women would put forward significant monies in their will, directed specifically to aid this nuptial market circulation of orphan girls and widows. The origin of these funds for these last wills from women is especially important because it shows the appropriation of impressive mercantile fortunes by women resident in Macao, mostly of Chinese or Asian origin, who were usually widowed early and able to accumulate social power and prestige.[41]

There are also other cases in which the willed legacies state that not only their charity is to be given towards orphan girls and widows but also stipulate important moral conditions to be fulfilled. These conditions usually meant general categories of Christian ethic, such as 'good reputation', 'honesty', 'poverty' and 'homeless' but also, more interestingly, the hierarchization distinguishing the maiden – a virgin woman who is single – from the widow, who is relegated to a lower social status to be consoled, given a dowry and put (back) in the matrimonial market, functioning as a kind of demographic and nuptial reserve. Most of the orphans and widows that received general or particular legacies and support were of Chinese or Asian origin but suffered from completely opposite social conditions. It seems important to highlight this insistence in the chastity of these slaves, a doubly important condition, for their sale and circulation in the nuptial market of Macao. At the same time, there was a large interrelation of different female social types and their movement within the systems of customers and alliances that were established between the families of resident merchants established in Macao.[42]

These intersections of different types and circulations of Chinese and Asian women in a situation of slavery even made 'cativas' (captives) move into the houses of freed female slaves that had managed to use the dowries of their masters to marry and build their own family units. Starting, at least, from 1631, this type of legacy monies began to be strictly associated with 'cativas' and 'bichas'.[43] Identified so far as a term referencing infantile and juvenile female slavery of Chinese origin, the concept of 'bicha' is shown, in this documentation, to be broader, extending to other situations of Asian female slavery in the Macanese society of the sixteenth century.[44]

In other cases, there were testaments that treated their female slaves as if they were poor goddaughters. The concerns regarding freeing these female slaves of 'familial creation' and in assuring their circulation in the 'nuptial market' of Macao is found in some wills marked by a certain charitable tone, reminding us of the old biblical idea of 'reciprocal obligations' between masters and slaves.[45]

It should not be thought, however, that these kind of wills were regulated only by these examples of charity, leading to free setting and matrimonial dowry of this female domestic slavery. Sometimes, in testaments where the distribution of pious wishes is clearly marked, there are also signs of discrimination towards some of these captives. This kind of final settlement demonstrated the contradictions that were felt in large families when it was proposed that this other 'family' of employees, servants and slaves should be considered alongside the biological family.[46]

Throughout the eighteenth century, the merchants of Macao started to bring in great quantities of slaves from Timor, a large proportion of which were young females. These women then began to spread into private domestic units and even the public and religious institutions of Macao.[47] This enlargement of the slave population, however, would also end up increasing the collection of investments for their assistance that, together with the increase of situations of deep subjugation, caused the specialization and appearance of new social intuitions of sheltering and charity, such as the houses of exposed ('expostos') and foundlings ('enjeitados'), the gatherings ('recolhimentos') and colleges ('colégios').[48]

Whenever the documentation (from the Holy House of Mercy, in this case) seeks to discriminate the female Chinese slavery, mainly bought and exchanged at a tender age in the region of the Pearl River Delta, it uses local terms, derived from Cantonese, such as 'amui'. The circulation of these young women bought in Guangdong was very frequent in Macao but, as tentatively clarified by the council of the Leal Senado, complicated whenever the purchase and rescue caused problems between the local imperial authorities. For that reason, in July 1703, the Leal Senado forbade the sale of atais and amuis to avoid 'carias' (troubles) with the Chinese, deciding to not permit selling to any foreigner nor to sending them out of the territory due to the trouble that would follow.[49]

But the council knew perfectly well that, without these women brought in China, many with only months left to live, the Macanese society would have difficulty in reproducing: there would be a lack of 'offers' in the matrimonial market, a lack of domestic services and other more 'mundane' situations would be limited.

'*Meninas*' and '*moças*'

Despite this circulation of the more particular categorizations of captives and 'bichas' – or of the more generic terms of orphans and widows – underlining different social and judicial aspects of the socio-symbolic identification of female subjugation, the testament sources are still hard to perform a rigorous interpretation on. However, despite the instability of the social terminology of this documentation, it is noticed a preference for two general terms: 'menina' and 'moça' are the more abundant terms of qualification in this documentation and, as previously seen, they tend to accompany or precede some of those situations of subjugation of orphans, widows, 'bichas' and captives.

It is possible that, even at the end of the sixteenth century, the notions of 'menina' and 'moça' helped to distinguish, through formation of a judicial writing, types of social female subjugation of different ages and different social and symbolic groups, which this legacy documentation tried to manage from a fundamentally pious and charitable point of view. Despite finding both terms in the same document, a comparative study of available sources seems to suggest some differences in the utilization of these notions: 'menina' generally applies to a female slave or a female infantile or adolescent dependent, while 'moça' meant female slaves and female young adults of marrying age. Both terms have in common a predominant social subjugation, being mainly slaves or 'libertas' (free) of Asian origin or mixed race, circulating within domestic units of Macao under the shelter of a male protector/master who, either being a merchant or having strong connections to the business men, mobilized his earnings to give them a Christian education, shelter in his house (or that of a trustworthy person), food and clothing. This was done in exchange for favours that ranged from sexual services to domestic work.[50]

In other testament documents we found reverends, installed in Macao, funding the dowries for the marriage of some 'meninas' of their preference.[51] It should be noted in these types of testaments, just like in the previous ones, the generalized preference for the diminutive name of 'meninas' and it should be added a complementary option in supporting alternatively a future matrimony or entrance to the religious life that, in the case of women, always directed them to Clarisse's of Macao. This optional alternative also has the advantage of showing the ages of these women, still sufficiently far from access to the novitiate in the second order of minors that, in the more precocious cases, occurred between 10 and 14 years old, with generous and stable dowries.[52]

In age and even symbolic contrast, whenever we see again the notion of 'moça' or when in the same document this term is found together with the term of 'menina', it can be discerned with some approximate rigorous distinctions in the categorization and circulation of this female social subjugation destined to go into the matrimonial market of Macao.[53]

These concepts of 'menina' and 'moça' categorize age and socio-symbolic distinctions but do not properly explain the situations of female social inferiority: they do not overlap much with the notions of captives and 'bichas' and do not even touch much on the notion of the situation of orphans. For that reason, they tend to be categories with some leeway to their meaning with links to various ages and familial and social facets, frequently forcing these written sources to utilize other categories using moral values and alliances supporting the survival of these extensive families of Portuguese merchants installed in Macao. Sheltering many children, young women and other women in situations of subjugation and dependency, multiplying domestic units went on creating a true network of clients where some of the cross-links occurred thanks to the circulation and alliances, propelled by the power of supply to the matrimonial market of Macao with these many situations of female social subjugation. It is a kind of 'gift system', in which circulation through the social mobility of these women in situations of subjugation worked as a 'gift' fundamental for the movement of capitals that, under the guise of dowries, guaranteed alliances of families and interests from a matrimonial interchange.[54]

Goddaughters ('afilhadas') and damsels ('donzelas')

Whenever the legacies to the Holy House came from powerful persons, those of great authority and wealth, the types of protected female inferiority are widened but also specialized. For example, in 1664, the priest Manuel Pereira, owner of several slaves, left to the care of the Mercy his last will which enclosed an impressive amount of 'protected females' and 'goddaughters'.

It should be highlighted the great social importance of the circulation of these 'goddaughters', within the webs of influence and clientele, with whom it was used to organize the Portuguese merchant families installed in Macao. At the same time, the importance of control over these socially subjugated young women and their distribution can be seen as a true 'nuptial market', establishing dowries as well as access to marriage preferentially to 'Portuguese'. This circulation of women should end with marriage. Some singular testaments introduced, in these processes protection of female social subjugation, other categories creating other cultural and familial identifications, including the 'recognition' of natural daughters. The notion of 'damsel' should be associated to that recurrent presence of the concept of chastity that we keep finding in various testament documents, seeking to place, in the nuptial market of Macao, young women, not only protected by important dowries but also socially and morally elevated by their virginity, an indispensable condition for access to a Christian marriage.[55]

The finances of the Holy Mercy

How did the Mercies get funding for all their assistance and charitable actions? The Mercies had accumulated large patrimonies in real estate and furniture, mainly from the seventeenth century when these institutions had a greater number of donations, due to the vulgarization of the idea of Purgatory after the Council of Trent.[56] Thus, most of the funds of the Mercies were formed by 'estate of the dead', who donated their riches in benefit of their souls, stipulating a set of duties and obligations. A great part of the donated goods was dedicated to the celebration of a variable number of 'soul masses', depending on the value of the inherited goods. The rescue of the souls from Purgatory was also made through legacies for poor people, either wedding dowries for poor girls and orphans, donations for the poor sick people in the hospitals, money to help rescue captives (from religious wars) or even simple prisoners from the jails. The goods donated in these inheritances could be difficult to collect or insufficient for the obligations that had been set, but constituted the most significant part in the patrimony of the brotherhoods.[57] Thus the patrimonies of the Mercies were formed as the pious legacies were made, following the bonds that these instituted, because the merciful donations followed the popularity that some assistance duties of the Mercies received in detriment of others: the donations to displayed children were lesser, for example, while the legacies for dowries for marriage for orphans and widows

Table 4.3 Contracts of risks of the sea ('riscos do mar') – 1763

Contractor		Guarantor		Amount	Interest
Name	Profession	Name	Profession	Taels	
Simão Vicente Rosa	Merchant and shipbuilder			500	20%
Simão Vicente Rosa	Merchant and shipbuilder			1500	20%
Simão Vicente Rosa	Merchant and shipbuilder			1500	20%
Diogo de Mendonça Corte Real	Merchant	Bernardo Nogueira Carvalho da Fonseca		300	20%
Diogo de Mendonça Corte Real	Merchant	Bernardo Nogueira Carvalho da Fonseca		200	20%
Luís Coelho	Merchant and shipbuilder			2100	20%
Luís Coelho	Merchant and shipbuilder			2000	20%
João Francisco Belém	Merchant	Luís Coelho	Shipbuilder	500	20%
João Ribeiro Guimarães	Merchant and shipbuilder			1500	20%
João Ribeiro Guimarães	Merchant and shipbuilder			400	20%
Joaquim Lopes da Silva	Merchant	Joaquim Ribeiro Guimarães		500	20%
Joaquim Lopes da Silva	Merchant	Joaquim Ribeiro Guimarães		200	20% corruption suspicion
António José da Costa	Provedor			1600	20%
António José da Costa	Provedor			1400	20%
António José da Costa	Provedor			1100	20%

were more frequent and controlled the local nuptial market. There were other preferences of the donors, as is seen with the benefiting of hospitals or the legacies in favour of prisoners.[58] Not all the Mercies could administrate the same kind of institutions, which were in many cases totally different from those existing in the big cities where were many different hospices, dedicated orphans' houses and other institutions of public charity.[59]

The Mercy of Macao was devoted to financing maritime trade and loans with interests to private parties. The former was named 'riscos de mar' (risks at sea) and was granted directly by the brotherhood.[60] There were also smaller sums that with the Mercy, deposited at official or private institutions named 'ganhos de terra' (land earnings) rates at 6–7 per cent.[61]

Conclusion

In conclusion, we can say that some social constants are determined in Macao; necessarily those that are related with both the great malfunctions and social structures that are specific of the social organization of the territory. The great dysfunction of the structures of social cohesion of the territory throughout three centuries has its roots in the disequilibrium of the pyramid of ages in the territory in favour of women: not only was the female population more numerous but it also lived longer, settled and reproduced the basic kinships of the Macanese historical society. The Portuguese traders and adventurers who were installed in Macao since 1557 did not bring European women to the territory, because they were forbidden by the Chinese imperial authorities (as well the Portuguese Crown), to bring foreign women to Macao or to Canton.

The women who raised families, performed sexual services, did the housework and managed the 'houses' of Macao were systematically Asian slave women of various nationalities and backgrounds (Japanese, Malays, Indonesian, Indian, etc.), predominantly Chinese of low social condition, that had been bought, negotiated and abducted with the collaboration of local authorities. These 'muitsai', as they would later come to be known, represented the most fragile sector of the historical population of Macao. Mostly enslaved – and therefore deprived of any rights – they sometimes obtained emancipation through marriage or work, but were still liable to fall into strong dependency situations and marginality. The practice to sell these girls to the inhabitants of Macao started very early and went on for more than two centuries, in spite of the constant prohibitions from the Portuguese and Chinese authorities.

The bankruptcy of a merchant, a shipwreck, a crisis of supplies or an epidemic had a stronger echo among this population that had been thrown to the socially inferior borders of the city. However, in spite of their weakness, these female groups were absolutely crucial in the structure of a marriage market, which became vital in the formation of Euro-Asian kinships and in the reproduction of mercantile families, generating specialized forms of 'offers' and 'demand' for women, The Mercy of Macao supported these two movements: protecting and supporting the social feminine dependency in the territory, thus the brotherhood also knew how to lead these subaltern women to their marriages by means of dowries and alms.

Notes

1 Isabel dos Guimarães Sá, 'Estatuto Social e Descriminação: Formas de Selecção de Agentes e Receptores de Caridade Nas Misericórdias Portuguesas ao Longo do Antigo Regime' ('Social Status and Discrimination: Modes of Selection of Agents and Charity Receivers in the Portuguese Mercies Throughout the Old Regime'), in *Actas do Colóquio Internacional Saúde e Discriminação Social* (*Proceedings of the International Coloquium of Health and Social Discrimination*), Braga: Universidade do Minho (University of Minho), 2002, pp. 303–334.

2 Isabel dos Guimarães Sá, 'As Misericórdias nas Sociedades Portuguesas do Período Moderno' ('The Mercies in the Portuguese Societies of the Modern Period'), *Cadernos do Noroeste* (*Notebooks of the Northwest*), Série História (*History Series*), 15, 2001, pp. 337–358. Except the Holy House of Mercy in Nagasaki in the sixteenth century, following Rumiko Kataoka (Irmã Ignatia), 'Fundação e Organização da Confraria da Misericórdia de Nagasáqui' ('Founding and Organization of the Brotherhood of Mercy of Nagasaki'), *Oceanos: Misericórdias, Cinco Séculos* (*Oceans: Mercies, Five Centuries*), 35, July/September 1998, p. 116: 'The Nagasaki Holy House of Mercy had a peculiar characteristic that made it different from its Portuguese peers: the activity of the Nagasaki female members.'

3 Sá, 'Estatuto Social e Descriminação', p. 314.

4 Ibid., p. 315.

5 Ibid., p. 316.

6 Ibid.

7 Ivo Carneiro de Sousa, *Da Descoberta da Misericórdia à Fundação das Misericórdias (1498–1525)* (*From the Discovery of the Mercy to the Founding of the Mercies (1498–1525)*), Porto, Granito: Editores e Livreiros, 1999, p. 158.

8 Sousa, *Da Descoberta da Misericórdia à Fundação das Misericórdias*, pp. 166–167.

9 Ivo Carneiro de Sousa, *A Rainha D. Leonor (1458–1525): Poder, Misericórdia, Religiosidade e Espiritualidade no Portugal do Renascimento* (*Queen Leonor (1458–1525): Power, Mercy, Religiousness and Spirituality in Renaissance Portugal*), Lisbon: Fundação Calouste Gulbenkian/Fundação para a Ciência e Tecnologia, 2002, p. 399.

10 Sá, 'Estatuto Social e Descriminação', p. 311.

11 Ibid., p. 312.

12 Artur Levy Gomes, *Esboço da História de Macau (1511 a 1849)* (*Sketch of the History of Macao (1511 to 1849)*), Macao: Repartição Provincial dos Serviços de Economia e Estatística Geral, 1957, p. 62.

13 Gomes, *Esboço da História de Macau*, p. 63.

14 Leonor Diaz de Seabra (ed.), *O Compromisso da Misericórdia de Macau de 1627* (*The Duty of the Mercy of Macao of 1627*), Macao: University of Macau, 2003, pp. 87, 139.

15 José Caetano Soares, *Macau e a Assistência: Panorama Médico-Social* (*Macao and Assistence: Sociomedical Panorama*), Macao: Agência Geral das Colónias, 1950, p. 342.

16 Charles Ralph Boxer, *O Senado da Câmara de Macau* (*The Senate of the City Hall of Macao*), Macao: Leal Senado de Macau, 1997, p. 44.

17 Boxer, *O Senado da Câmara de Macau*, p. 45.

18 Manuel Teixeira, *As Canossianas na Diocese de Macau (1874–1974)* (*The Canossianas in the Diocese of Macao (1874–1874)*), Macao: Tipografia do Padroado, 1974, p. 26.
19 Manuel Teixeira, *Macau e a sua Diocese, vol. xii: Bispos, Missionários, Igrejas e Escolas* (*Macao and its Dioceses, vol. xii: Bishops, Missionaries, Churches and School*), Macao: Tipografia da Missão do Padroado, 1976, p. 286. In 1876 the 'Roda' was abolished definitively, when the Holy House of Mercy delivered the foundlings by the Canossian Sisters.
20 Soares, *Macau e a Assistência*, p. 145.
21 Seabra, *O Compromisso da Misericórdia de Macau de 1627*, pp. 89–92.
22 Sá, 'Estatuto Social e Descriminação', p. 317.
23 Anders Ljungstedt, *Um Esboço Histórico dos Estabelecimentos dos Portugueses e da Igreja Católica Romana e as Missões na China & Descrição da Cidade de Cantão* (*A Historical Sketch of the Settlements of the Portuguese and the Roman Catholic Church and the Missions in China and Description of the City of Canton*), Macao: Leal Senado de Macau, 1999, p. 62.
24 Luísa Arrais (trans.), George Bryan de Souza, *A sobrevivência do Império: os Portugueses na China (1630–1754)* (*Survival of the Empire: the Portuguese in China (1630–1754)*), Lisbon: Publicações Dom Quixote, 1991, p. 291.
25 Ljungstedt, *Um Esboço Histórico dos Estabelecimentos dos Portugueses e da Igreja Católica Romana*, p. 6.
26 J.S., 'A Misericórdia de Macau' ('The Mercy of Macao'), *Anuário de Macau* (*Yearbook of Macao*), 1927, pp. 137–148.
27 Manuel Teixeira, *Macau e a sua Diocese, vol. xii: Bispos, Missionários, Igrejas e Escolas* (*Macao and its Dioceses, vol. xii: Bishops, Missionaries, Churches and Schools*), Macao: Tipografia da Missão do Padroado, 1976, p. 284.
28 C.A. Montalto de Jesus, *Macau Histórico* (*Historic Macao*), Macao: Livros do Oriente, 1990. pp. 114–116.
29 Ljungstedt, *Um Esboço Histórico dos Estabelecimentos dos Portugueses e da Igreja Católica Romana*, p. 63.
30 Ibid., p. 64.
31 Ibid., p. 63.
32 Ibid., p. 64.
33 Ibid.
34 Boxer, *O Senado da Câmara de Macau*, p. 48.
35 Ibid.
36 Ibid., p. 49.
37 Maria de Jesus dos Mártires Lopes, 'Mendicidade e "maus costumes" em Macau e Goa na segunda metade do Século XVIII' ('Poverty and "Bad Habits" in Macao and Goa in the Second Half of the Sixteenth Century'), in *As Relações entre a Índia Portuguesa, a Ásia do Sudeste e o Extremo-Oriente. Actas do VI Seminário Internacional de História Indo-Portuguesa* (*Relations between Portuguese India, Southeast Asia and the Far East, Proceedings of the 6th International Seminar of Indo-Portuguese History*), Macao-Lisbon, 1993, pp. 65–82.
38 Luis G. Gomes (trans.), *Monografi a de Macau, por Tcheong-Ü-Lâm e Iân-Kuong-Iâm* (*Monography of Macao by Tcheong-Ü-Lâm e Iân-Kuong-Iâm*), Macao: Imprensa Nacional, 1950, pp. 120–124.
39 Isabel Nunes, 'Bailarinas e Cantadeiras: Aspectos da Prostituição em Macau' ('Dancers and Singers: Aspects of Prostitution in Macao'), *Revista de Cultura* (*Review of Culture*), 15, July/September 1991, pp. 95–117.
40 Luis G. Gomes, *Curiosidades de Macau Antiga* (*Curiosities of Old Macao*), Macao: Instituto Cultural de Macau, 1996, pp. 160–161.
41 About this subject see: Leonor Diaz de Seabra, *A Misericórdia de Macau (Séculos XVI a XIX): Irmandade, Poder e Caridade na Idade de Comércio* (*The Holy House*

of Mercy: Brotherhood, Power and Charity in the Age of Commerce), Macao: University of Macau, 2011.

42 Arquivo Histórico de Macau (AHM) (Historical Archive of Macao): Documents of Holy House of Mercy – Codex no.New 302, fl. 9v: 'The last wills and testaments made to the Holy House of Mercy (1592/08/16–1849/03/01)'

43 The (forbidden) condition of slaves caused the creation of a new category in the family structure of the Portuguese of Macao – that of 'criações' or 'crioulas', who were not slaves but also were not completely free. It was also still used the designations of 'nhins', 'nhons' and 'nhonhonha', 'amas' or 'aias', and 'bichas', as different designations of status of Macanese, Euro-asiatic and Chinese women – and even of other ethnicities – who made up part of the local families. 'Criações' were the children who were bought or the illegitimate daughters and sons (of the family head or of the 'nhons', their descendents), but had a status that was not quite that of the 'bicha', old slave or servant, but neither that of godchild. V. Ana Maria Amaro, *Filhos da Terra* (*Children of earth*), Macao: Instituto Cultural, 1988, pp. 24–25.

44 AHM/SCM/302, fls. 32–32v, and AHM/SCM/302, fls. 31–31v.

45 AHM/SCM/302, fl. 33v–34.

46 AHM/SCM/302, fl. 52v.

47 Ana Maria Amaro, 'A Mulher de Macau segundo os Relatos dos Viajantes' ('The Stories of Travellers About the Women'), *Review of Culture*, 15, 1991, p. 120.

48 AH/SCM/302 (1592/08/06–1849/03/01) and AH/SCM/303 (1667/00/00–1737/00/00).

49 'Termo feito em Junta de Homens bons sobre se não venderem Amuis ou atais para fora da Terra – 1703, Julho, 14' ('Decision on the meeting of the Senate about Amuis and Atais sold and sent out of their homeland – 14, July 1703'), in *Arquivos de Macau* (*Bulletin of Historical Archive of Macao*), 3rd series, 2(1), July 1964, pp. 44–45.

50 AHM/SCM/302, fl. 14 and AHM/SCM/302, fl. 4v.

51 AHM/SCM/302, fls. 9–9v and AHM/SCM/302, fl. 55v.

52 Manuel Teixeira, 'As Clarissas' ('The Clarisses'), in *Macau e a sua Diocese, vol. III* (*Macao and its Dioceses, vol. III*), Macao: Tipografia Soi Sang, 1956–1961, pp. 483–510.

53 BA, 49/V/5: *Principião as notas do ano de 1607. Testamento de Maria Gaya* (*Beginning the Notes About the Year 1607. The Last Will and Testament of Maria Gaya*), fls. 75–77.

54 AHM/SCM/302, fls. 40–40v.

55 AHM/SCM/303: The Last Wills and Testaments Made to the Holy House of Mercy (1667/00/00 a 1737/00/00)', fl.8; AHM/SCM/302: 'The Last Wills and Testaments Made to the Holy House of Mercy (1592/08/16 a 1849/03/01), fls. 74v–75.

56 Sá, 'As Misericórdias nas Sociedades Portuguesas do Período Moderno', pp. 337–358.

57 Ibid., 344–345.

58 Isabel dos Guimarãs Sá, *Quando o rico se faz pobre: Misericórdias, Caridade e Poder no Império Português, 1500–1800* (*From Riches to Rags: Mercies, Charity and Power in the Portuguese Empire, 1500–1800*), Lisbon: Comissão Nacional para as Comemorações dos Descobrimentos Portugueses, 1997, p. 82.

59 Ibid., p. 83

60 Soares, *Macau e a Assistência*, p. 311.

61 Sá, 'As Misericórdias nas Sociedades Portuguesas do Período Moderno', p. 350; See also Souza, *A sobrevivência do Império*, pp. 219–220: 'The administrative expenses of the Holy House of Mercy were paid with funds that came from the customs taxes of the Municipality Senate. Its capital was obtained through the administration of properties and legacies to widows or orphans. The Brotherhood invested within the limits of the property goods of the city and granted liability

loans at variable rates to independent traders, according to the destination of the vessel and to the risks of the respective voyage. Such loans were applicable for the preparation of sea-vessels and for the purchase of cargo. A financial guarantor was required. The Brotherhood also granted heavy loans to the municipality Senate for the payment of the expenses of the city and to residents, for land investment. That is why they are called "land profit" and the rates were fixed between seven and ten per cent.'

Part III

The impact of global forces

The presence and competition of
maritime powers in and around Macao

5   Dutch attacks against the Goa-Macao-Japan route, 1603–1618

André Murteira

The importance of the Goa-Macao-Japan shipping route to the history of Macao during the second half of the sixteenth century and the first half of the seventeenth century is well-known. With Macao serving as a regular port of call both in the Goa-Japan and in the Japan-Goa voyages, it is usually accepted that it was mainly this particular trade route that made the subsistence of the small entrepôt in China possible during the first 80 years of its existence, right until the closure of Japan to Portuguese ships in 1639.[1] The route was also the most important Portuguese shipping route in Asian waters and, as such, the ships that sailed it were obvious targets for the Dutch after they arrived in Asia at the end of the sixteenth century and entered into conflict with the Portuguese there.[2] In 1603 Jacob van Heemskerck took the carrack *Santa Catarina* in the Straits of Singapore, on its way from Macao to Malacca and Goa.[3] The capture was famously defended by Hugo Grotius in his renowned seminal work on international law, *De Jure Praedae*. It was also the first of a series of incidents that eventually led the Portuguese to stop using carracks and galleons on their voyages to Macao and Japan and to replace them with smaller ships such as galliots and pinnaces around 1618.

In this chapter, I attempt to analyse the Dutch attacks on Portuguese ships travelling between Goa, Macao and Japan before the change to small ships in 1618. Special attention is paid to how local contexts and the larger context of the Dutch-Portuguese conflict in Asia influenced the evolution of the Dutch threat to the route. The history of the Goa-Japan route was dealt with decades ago by Charles Boxer in a series of classic books, but his focus was mainly on the Macao-Japan part of the voyage, and the same can be said of later works by George Bryan Souza and Ana Leitão.[4] Their consideration of the Dutch privateering menace did not take into sufficient account of what happened west of the South China Sea, especially in the region commonly known as the Malacca and Singapore Straits. For the purposes of this chapter, it will be enough to recapitulate that between Goa and Nagasaki, in Japan. There were three important ports of call, both in the outward-bound and in the homeward-bound voyages: Cochin, in southwest India, Malacca, on the western coast of the Malay Peninsula, and, obviously, Macao. Ports of call, of course, were ideal places for pirates and privateers to lay in wait for prey. But

there were other potentially dangerous locations on the route, such as the narrow Singapore Straits, or the so-called 'point of Galle', in the southwestern
point of Sri Lanka, which most great ships entering and leaving the Western
Indian Ocean had to pass.

If we consider the regions where Dutch attacks were either carried out or
at least planned, we see, however, that the Indian Ocean was not especially
dangerous for Portuguese ships travelling to and from Macao and Japan during this period. The risk of meeting Dutch ships increased significantly while
entering the Straits of Malacca, and remained high until the arrival in Japan
and the subsequent return voyage to the Indian Ocean. In the following pages,
I shall analyse in a little more depth the background to Dutch privateering
actions in these areas.

The Straits of Malacca and Singapore

Starting with the Straits of Malacca and Singapore region, Dutch actions there
must be understood against the background of the regional rivalry between
Portuguese-held Malacca and the sultanate of Johor, on the southern tip of
the Malay Peninsula, which has been studied in detail by Peter Borschberg.[5]
In the first decade of the seventeenth century the newly arrived Dutch forged
an anti-Portuguese alliance with Johor, which presented the Portuguese in the
region with a very serious threat. Portuguese navigation to and from Macao
and Japan was especially vulnerable to Dutch-Johor cooperation, for the
sultanate was located near the strategic waterway of the Straits of Singapore,
which was, as outlined above, one of the most dangerous points on the Goa-
Japan route. Dutch-Johor relations actually started on the occasion of the
first known Dutch attack on a Portuguese ship on the Goa-Macao-Japan
route in 1603. The vessel in question was the previously mentioned carrack
Santa Catarina, which, on its way back to Goa from Macao was taken in
the Straits of Singapore by the Dutch captain Jacob van Heemskerck. The
capture was only made possible by vital information supplied by a ship sent
by the sultan of Johor, Ala'ud-din Ri'ayat Shah III, without which the Dutch
would have waited in vain for the Portuguese on a nearby island.[6]

The taking of the *Santa Catarina* became famous mainly because Hugo
Grotius defended it afterwards in *De Jure Praedae*. Peter Borschberg and
Martine van Ittersum have also analysed it in great detail in recent works.[7]
Apart from its importance as a legal precedent and the huge value of the
captured cargo – the richest ever recorded on the history of Dutch privateering against Portuguese navigation in Asia[8] – the capture was historically
significant because it marked the beginning of Dutch-Johor cooperation
against the Portuguese in the region of the Malacca and Singapore Straits.
Van Heemskerck took with him to Europe an ambassador from Johor to the
Dutch Republic, which shows how intent the sultan was on setting up a formal alliance. The ambassador died during the long voyage to the Netherlands,
but the alliance between the sultanate and the newly established Verenigde

Oostindische Compagnie (Dutch East India Company) – usually known as VOC – was formally sealed in 1606, in the form of two written treaties between the two powers.[9]

The first of these two treaties was signed on the eve of a joint military operation that marked the zenith of the Johor-VOC alliance: the siege of Portuguese-held Malacca in 1606. A joint taking of Malacca had probably been already discussed during van Heemskerk's visit to the sultanate in 1603 and was an aim of the VOC since practically its foundation.[10] The treaty stipulated that after the conquest of Malacca the VOC would keep the city for itself, while the sultanate would get the lands surrounding it.[11] The attempt, however, was a failure, due to the arrival of a huge relief fleet from Goa, which forced the Dutch to evacuate their land troops.[12] Another treaty was signed between the VOC and Johor immediately after the raising of the siege.[13] But it is clear that, from that time on, the two powers started to grow apart. The main reason for that was the inability on the part of the company to satisfactorily protect its ally from retaliatory measures from the Portuguese.

Since it allied itself with the Dutch, the sultanate was, in fact, subjected to regular naval blockades by Portuguese armadas from Malacca. Dutch ships proved themselves more than capable of breaking these blockades and of expelling the armadas from the Johor River estuary, as Jacob Pietersz van Enkhuizen did in 1603 with the armada of Teixeira de Matos, sent from Malacca to punish Johor for the help given to van Heemskerck in the capture of the *Santa Catarina*.[14] The problem was that the blockade was promptly resumed after the Dutch ships left. Without a permanent presence of VOC ships in the region, there was no way that the company could ensure the continuing protection of its ally. This inevitably led to the weakening of support for the alliance among power circles in Johor, where, as Peter Borschberg has shown, 'pro-Portuguese' and 'anti-Portuguese' factions competed for influence.[15]

It should be stressed that the anti-Portuguese alliance with Johor was a priority of the VOC's policy, as designed in the Netherlands, during most of the first decade of the seventeenth century. From 1602, the year of its foundation, until 1610, the VOC dispatched five large fleets to Asia. The commander of each of these fleets, who bore the title of admiral, was the supreme commander of all the company's forces in Asia during his stay there, since the VOC only nominated a resident governor for its possessions in the East in 1610.[16] From the dispatch of the second fleet onwards in 1603 all admirals were instructed to go to the Straits of Malacca and Singapore region to assist Johor in its war effort against the Portuguese in Malacca.

The history of this second fleet, however, already points to the fact that the company's resources at the time did not match its ambitions and that its regional priorities in the Indonesian archipelago could prevent it from paying the necessary attention to the Malacca and Singapore Straits region.[17] When the Dutch Admiral Steven van der Hagen arrived in Bantem, Northern Java in 1604, he was informed of the difficult situation of the Dutch outposts in the

Maluku and Ambon archipelagos, in Eastern Indonesia, where a Portuguese armada sent from Goa had carried out a series of punitive measures against local populations who had engaged in trade with the Dutch. He therefore diverted his fleet to the region, postponing his planned visit to Johor.[18] The Maluku and Ambon archipelagos were the only clove-producing region in the world at the time and, as such, had been a high priority for the VOC from the beginning, along with the neighbouring Banda archipelago, which produced nutmeg and mace.

The visit of the van der Hagen fleet to Maluku and Ambon proved a triumph: the two Portuguese fortresses in the region – at Ambon and Tidore – were taken by the Dutch, which effectively expelled the Portuguese from the area and established a permanent military presence there. Nevertheless, they would still face several challenges in the region during the following years, both from the local peoples – who resisted the VOC's monopolistic policies – and from the Spanish in the Philippines and the British East India Company – whose competition the VOC would also have to face in the Banda Islands. The recurring need to concentrate its still scarce resources on the defence of its positions on Maluku, Ambon, Banda and also Northern Java, was a permanent feature of the first two decades of the VOC's history and was probably the most important factor behind its failure to establish a permanent military presence in the Malacca and Singapore Straits region during the period, despite its often stated wish to do so.

Nevertheless, the region's most direct competitor when it came to the allocation of the VOC's resources was the Sunda Strait and its surroundings. This was the area first visited by the Dutch in Asia, during the 1595–1597 pioneering voyage of Cornelis de Houtman. In the next two decades, Bantam, in northwest Java, was their main port of arrival from Europe and they ended up setting the capital of their Eastern domains in the neighbouring port of Jakarta, or Batavia, occupied in 1619. The establishment of a proper capital in a harbour where the VOC could gather its shipping coming from and leaving for Europe (as the Portuguese did in Goa) was an early aspiration of the company. The two locations suggested since the beginning for this 'rendezvous' – as the VOC officers called it – were the Straits of Malacca and Singapore region, on the one hand, and the Sunda Strait and its vicinity on the other.[19] Both Malacca and Johor were considered but the final choice fell on Jakarta, near the Sunda Strait – an area easier to reach from Europe and where the Dutch, through their position in Bantam, had been present since their arrival in Asia.

The choice seemed to confirm the apparent loss of importance of the Straits of Malacca and Singapore region to the VOC during the second decade of the seventeenth century. It postponed the establishment of a permanent position of the company in the region to 1641, the year of the Dutch taking of Malacca. As such, its importance was considerable for the immediate future of the Portuguese presence in Asia. The failure of the VOC to either take Malacca or get instead a concession from Johor to build a fortress in its territory in the first decade of the seventeenth century seems relevant in this context. If it had succeeded in any of these two attempts, things in the following decade might have been different.

The most difficult moment for the Portuguese position in the region before 1641 was certainly the already mentioned 1606 siege of Malacca. The operation was led, on the Dutch side, by Cornelis Matelieff, admiral of the third VOC fleet, who, unlike his predecessor van der Hagen, actually obeyed the orders he had to visit the Malacca and Singapore Straits.[20] However, his successor, Paulus van Caerden, admiral of the fourth VOC fleet, was also unable to stop at the region.[21] After a detour through the western Indian Ocean in 1607, he attempted to sail to Johor from Bantam but was prevented from doing so by a monsoon and opted instead to proceed to Ambon.[22] Thus, when the admiral of the fifth fleet, Pieter Willemsz. Verhoeff, arrived at Johor in 1609 no Dutch ships had visited the sultanate for some time.[23] Verhoeff met thus with a fairly cold reception. His proposals to the sultan for a new joint attack against Malacca were rebuffed, as was his petition that the VOC should be allowed to build a fortress in Johor.[24] After Verhoeff's departure the sultanate was once more attacked by the Portuguese and – lacking any help from the absent Dutch – the sultan opted to make peace with the authorities at Malacca in 1609.

It is interesting to note that in 1614 the VOC finally obtained from the new sultan of Johor, Abdullah Ma'ayat Shah – previously known as Raja Bongsu, the former leader of the 'pro-Dutch' party at court and a brother of the old sultan – an invitation to build a fortress in his territory, but never took advantage of it.[25] Thus, the coming into power in Johor of a 'pro-Dutch' figure was not enough to significantly revive the Dutch-Johor alliance. This was important for the Portuguese navigation between Goa and Macao and Japan, for it meant that for a time the Dutch presence in the vital waterway of the Straits of Malacca and Singapore region was not as significant as it might otherwise have been. In 1615, a squadron of Dutch warships led by Steven van der Hagen destroyed a Portuguese armada off Malacca, and afterwards left the Straits of Singapore only two days before two carracks coming from Macao arrived there.[26] But otherwise the biggest threat to Portuguese navigation between Goa and Macao and Japan during this period was located in the area east of the Malacca and Singapore Straits, a region to which we must now turn our attention.

From Singapore to Japan

Pattani

Macao was the main port of call in the leg of the voyage between the Straits of Malacca and Singapore and Japan. However, until 1605 it sometimes happened that ships occasionally called at Pattani, on the eastern coast of the Malay Peninsula. A Dutch factory was founded there at the beginning of the seventeenth century, and in 1605 the Dutch gained permission from the local queen to attack the *Santo António*, a Portuguese carrack coming from Macao and bound for Malacca that had called at the port for repairs.[27] The permissions granted to the Dutch, first to set up their factory and then to seize the ship, were a consequence of worsening relations between Pattani and the Portuguese in Malacca. Thus, as in Johor, local cooperation based on pre-existing hostility to the Portuguese was essential for an important Dutch capture (the booty of the *Santo António* was second in value only to that of the *Santa Catarina*[28]). As a result of the incident, Portuguese ships stopped calling at Pattani. But in the second decade of the seventeenth century, the VOC presence at the harbour remained an important threat to Portuguese navigation between Malacca and Macao and Japan, in virtue of the route Pattani-Japan established by the company in 1609. To understand how that came about it is necessary, however, to first sum up the history of the Dutch's first contacts with China.

China

The first Dutch ships to ever call at the Chinese coast were two vessels commanded by Jacob van Neck, which arrived in 1601 at Macao.[29] There, the Portuguese captured 20 Dutchmen and executed 17 of them. Unable to do anything to help his captured countrymen, van Neck left for Pattani. This incident supplied Jacob van Heemskerck with the justification to carry out his previously mentioned attack on the *Santa Catarina*. Dutch historian and sinologist Leonard Blussé has argued that the executions were carried out in order to prevent Chinese authorities in Canton from contacting the Dutch captives, as they had explicitly demanded from the Portuguese. According to Blussé, the interest of the Chinese authorities for the captives reflected an interest on the part of some sections of the Chinese administration in opening up contacts with the Dutch, an interest that, Blussé speculates, must have died out after they were informed of subsequent Dutch attacks against Portuguese ships, which would have made them regard the 'red-haired Barbarians' as pirates and reject their overtures.[30]

One of these attacks resulted in the taking in Macao of a carrack bound to Japan in 1603,[31] which was one of the three biggest captures by the Dutch of Portuguese ships on the Goa-Macao-Japan route, along with the previously mentioned takings of the *Santa Catarina* in 1603 and the *Santo António* in 1605.[32]

It must be said that the original mission of the ships that took this carrack off Macao was to make contact with Chinese authorities in order to open up trade between the VOC and China. When the opportunity came for attacking the Portuguese in Macao instead, the mission was pushed aside. If Blussé is right, the Dutch should have started to lose favour among Chinese power circles then. When they attempted to open up trade relations afterwards, they were twice rebuffed: in Fujian in 1604 and in the Guangdong region in 1607.[33]

Nevertheless, a Chinese description of the Fujian expedition of 1604 used by Blussé points again to the existence of an internal debate among the Chinese administration regarding the position to take on the Dutch – a debate clearly won by the groups opposed to direct contacts with foreigners.[34]

Japan

The failure of the VOC to establish a position in China created a problem when the company did acquire a position in Japan, where it was authorized in 1609 by the Tokugawa shogunate to set up a factory at Hirado, in Kyushu, southern Japan.[35] However, without direct access to the Chinese market, the factory met with little commercial success in its early years. The VOC factory at Pattani was important in this context, because, to a limited extent, it supplied the Dutch with Chinese products that they could sell in Hirado. For that reason, the first VOC ships that went to Japan in 1609 stopped there, as did many of those that followed during the second decade of the seventeenth century.

The two ships that made the VOC's inaugural voyage to Japan in 1609 were also charged with a privateering mission. They were instructed to take any Portuguese carracks they met on their way to Japan, but they were not successful in the attempt.[36] From the moment the Dutch set a route to Japan that, in the area east of Singapore, coincided roughly with that of the Portuguese, it was predictable that they would try to combine trade and privateering against Portuguese ships travelling there. They did this in 1609 and after a few years of respite they started to attempt it again in 1615. Between 1615 and 1617, all VOC ships doing the annual Bantam-Pattani-Hirado voyage tried to take the famous 'carrack from Macao'.[37] They did not succeed but in 1615, the *Santo António*, a small Portuguese junk coming from Indochina, was captured near Japan.[38]

The Portuguese complained formally to the Japanese authorities, but the capture was nevertheless sanctioned by the shogunate. Adam Clulow has described in detail the process that led to the decision, pointing out how 'pro-Portuguese' and 'pro-Dutch' lobbies acted in support of the two groups of Europeans, with the *Daimyo* of Hirado supporting the Dutch and the *Bugyo* of Nagasaki the Portuguese.[39] This final decision gave the Dutch great satisfaction, encouraging them to proceed with their attempts to capture a carrack. There was, however, an important difference in that, unlike the *Santo António*, the carracks were given the so-called red-seal by the shogunate, which allowed them to formally conduct trade with Japan.[40] Nevertheless, in 1621 the shogunate felt the need to expressly forbid the Dutch and the English from attacking any ships in the waters close to the Japanese archipelago.[41] It should be remembered that, despite having illegalized Christianity in Japan and expelled all the Jesuit missionaries from the country in 1614, the Japanese authorities wished to maintain trade relations with the Portuguese and were therefore inclined to act as a neutral party in their conflict with the VOC. The

1621 prohibition was duly respected, and, from then on, Dutch ships ceased to be a threat to Portuguese shipping in the waters near the Japanese coast.

Epilogue

1617 was the last year in which a Portuguese 'kurofune', that is a great carrack, made the voyage to Nagasaki. The following year these sailing giants were replaced by squadrons of galliots, which were much smaller ships and, as such, could evade the VOC vessels more easily.[42] The great size of the carracks – which had ensured their protection against piratical attacks until the Dutch's arrival in Asia – became a liability after the power of the northern European ships' artillery proved enough to compel them to surrender, as was the case with the *Santa Catarina* and others. Unable to match their enemies' ships in firepower, the Portuguese eventually opted for a kind of vessel best suited to escape them.

The replacement of great ships by squadrons of small ones meant that no single capture could yield prizes comparable to those of the three big ships taken by the Dutch between 1603 and 1605 in the Goa-Macao-Japan route which I mentioned above: the *Santa Catarina* in the Straits of Singapore in 1603; an unnamed carrack in Macao, also in 1603; and the *Santo António* in Pattani in 1605. After these 'big three', there were no more captures of big ships on the route, although carracks and galleons still sailed it for more than a decade. The booties of these three prizes reached values that were never equalled in the history of Dutch privateering against Portuguese navigation in Asia.[43] Rich cargos such as these were typical of an age in which the Portuguese still dared to sail in Asia with their riches concentrated on big ships, something they ceased to do in the second decade of the seventeenth century.

The second decade of the century was also a period when the threat of Dutch attacks on the Goa-Macao-Japan route in the Straits of Malacca and Singapore seemed to recede for a while, due to the end of the alliance between the VOC and the sultanate of Johor. The relief was temporary, however. By the end of the decade the company started to send privateering fleets from Batavia to the region with regularity. The establishment of a VOC's post in the city of Jambi, in Sumatra, was instrumental in that respect, since it provided the fleets with a nearby basis similar to the one it planned for a time to set up in Johor. That, however, is a story for another article.

Notes

1 It is important to note, however, that Macao was not always a simple port of call, for there were several ships that made the voyage from Goa with Macao as their final destination, at least during the period studied in this article.

2 For the history of the Dutch in Asia in the seventeenth century see: F.S. Gaastra, *De Geschiedenis van de VOC* (*The History of the VOC*), 4th edition, Zutphen: Walburg Pers, 2002; L. Blussé and J. de Moor, *Nederlanders Overzee: de Eerste*

Vijftig Jaar, 1600–1650 (*Dutch Overseas. The First Fifty Years, 1600–1650*), Franeker: T. Wever, 1983, pp. 93–255; J. van Goor, *De Nederlandse Koloniën – Geschiedenis van de Nederlandse Expansie, 1600–1975* (*The Dutch Colonies – History of the Dutch Expansion, 1600–1975*), Den Haag: Sdu Uitgeverij Koninginnegracht, 1993, pp. 15–169. For the history of the Dutch-Portuguese conflict in the East see: S. Subrahmanyam, *The Portuguese Empire in Asia, 1500–1700: A Political and Economic History*, London: Longman, 1993, pp. 144–180; E. van Veen, *Decay or Defeat? An Inquiry into the Portuguese Decline in Asia, 1580–1645*, Leiden: CNWS, 2000, pp. 173–207.

3 P. Borschberg, 'The Seizure of the Sta. Catarina Revisited: The Portuguese Empire in Asia, VOC Politics and the Origins of the Dutch-Johor Alliance (1602–c.1616)', *Journal of Southeast Asian Studies,* 33(1), 2002, pp. 31–62; M.J. van Ittersum, *Profit and Principle – Hugo Grotius, Natural Rights Theories and the Rise of Dutch Power in the East Indies, 1595–1615*, Leiden-Boston: Brill, 2006, pp. 1–52.

4 C.R. Boxer, *The Great Ship from Amacon – Annals of Macao and the Old Japan Trade, 1555–1640*, Lisbon: Centro de Estudos Históricos Ultramarinos, 1963; *Fidalgos in the Far East, 1550–1770*, Hong Kong: Oxford University Press, 1968; *Portuguese Merchants and Missionaries in Feudal Japan, 1543–1640*, Aldershot: Variorum, 1986; *The Christian Century in Japan, 1549–1650*, Manchester: Carcanet Press, 1993; G.B. Souza, *Portuguese Trade and Society in China and the South China Sea, 1630–1754*, Cambridge: Cambridge University Press, 1986, pp. 1–63; A.P. Leitão, *Do Trato Português no Japão: Presenças que se Cruzam (1543–1639)* (*Portuguese Trade in Japan (1543–1639)*), unpublished MA dissertation, University of Lisbon, 1994; See also J.M. Flores, 'Macau: o Tempo da Euforia' ('Macao: The Age of Euphoria'), in A.H. de Oliveira Marques (ed.), *História dos Portugueses no Extremo Oriente* (*History of the Portuguese in the Far East*), Vol. I–II, Lisbon: Fundação Oriente, 2000, pp. 179–193.

5 P. Borschberg, 'Portuguese, Spanish and Dutch Plans to Construct a Fort in the Straits of Singapore, ca. 1584–1625', *Archipel (Archipelago)*, 65, 2003, pp. 55–88; 'Luso-Johor-Dutch Relations in the Straits of Malacca and Singapore, c. 1600–1623', *Itinerario,* 28(2), 2004, pp. 15–44. See also P.J. de Sousa Pinto, *Portugueses e Malaios: Malaca e os Sultanatos de Johor e Achem, 1575–1619* (*Portuguese and Malays: Malacca and the Sultanates of Johor and Aceh, 1575–1619*), Lisbon: Sociedade Histórica da Independência de Portugal, 1997; M. Lobato, *Política e Comércio dos Portugueses na Insulíndia: Malaca e as Molucas de 1575 a 1605* (*Portuguese Policy and Trade in the Malay-Indonesian Archipelago: Malacca and the Moluccas from 1575 to 1605*), Macao: Instituto Português do Oriente, 1999.

6 Van Ittersum, *Profit and Principle*, pp. 33–35.

7 P. Borschberg, 'Hugo Grotius, East India Trade and the King of Johor', *Journal of Southeast Asian Studies,* 30(2), 1999, pp. 225–248; 'The Seizure of the Sta. Catarina Revisited'; M.J. van Ittersum, 'Hugo Grotius in Context: Van Heemskerck's Capture of the Santa Catarina and its Justification in De Jure Praedae (1604–1606)', *Asian Journal of Social Science,* 31(3), 2003, pp. 511–548; Van Ittersum, *Profit and Principle*, pp. 1–52.

8 This amounted to 3,356,172 guilders, after the auction of the cargo in the Netherlands. See Borschberg, 'The Seizure of the Sta. Catarina Revisited', p. 57. Compare with the known values of cargoes of Portuguese ships taken in Asia by the Dutch in the period 1600–1661 in the table compiled by G.B. Souza in 'Commerce and Capital: Portuguese Maritime Losses in the South China Sea, 1600–1754', in A.T. de Matos and L.F. Thomaz (eds), *As Relações entre a Índia Portuguesa, a Ásia do Sueste e o Extremo Oriente – Actas do VI Seminário Internacional de História Indo-Portuguesa (Macau, 22 a 26 de Outubro de 1991)* (*Relations between Portuguese India, Southeast Asia and the Far East – Proceedings of the VI International Seminar of Indo-Portuguese History (Macao, 22–26 October*

1991)), Lisbon and Macao: Instituto de História de Além-Mar, 1993, pp. 340–347. It should be noted that the value ascribed by Souza to the *Santa Catarina* cargo – 1,694,886 guilders – is about half of that indicated by Borschberg. Even then, however, it is still the richest cargo captured by far, along with that of another ship coming from Macao, the *Santo António*, which I refer to below.

9   J.E. Heeres (ed.), *Corpus Diplomaticum Neerlando-Indicum. Verzameling van Politieke Contracten en Verdere Verdragen door de Nederlanders in het Oosten Gesloten* (*Corpus Diplomaticum Neerlando-Indicum. Collection of Political Contracts and Other Agreements Concluded by the Dutch in the East*), Vol. I, Martinus Nijhoff, 1907, pp. 41–45, 47–48.

10   Borschberg, 'Portuguese, Spanish and Dutch Plans to Construct a Fort in the Straits of Singapore, ca. 1584–1625', p. 68.

11   Heeres, *Corpus Diplomaticum Neerlando-Indicum*, Vol. I, p. 42.

12   'Historische Verhael van de Treffelijcke Reyse Gedaen... door den Manhasten Admirael Cornelis Matelief...' ('Historical Account of the Important Journey Done... by the Brave Admiral Cornelis Matelieff...'), in I. Commelin (ed.), *Begin ende Voortgangh van de Nederlantsche Geoctroyeerde Oost-Indische Compagnie. Vervattende de Voornaemste Reysen bij de Inwoonderen derselver Provinciën derwaerts Gedaan...* (*Beginning and Progress of the Dutch Chartered East India Company. Containing the Most Prominent Journeys Done There by the Inhabitants of the Same Provinces ...*), Vol. III, Amsterdam, 1646, account II, pp. 6–29; C.R. Boxer, 'The Affair of the "Madre de Deus" (A Chapter in the History of the Portuguese in Japan)', in *Portuguese Merchants and Missionaries*, article I, pp. 16–28; C.R. Boxer and Frazão de Vasconcelos, *André Furtado de Mendonça*, Macao: Fundação Oriente-Centro de Estudos Marítimos de Macau, 1989, pp. 61–72.

13   Heeres, *Corpus Diplomaticum Neerlando-Indicum*, Vol. I, pp. 47–48.

14   P. Borschberg, 'A Luso-Dutch Naval Confrontation in the Johor River Delta, 1603', *Zeitschrift der Deutschen Morgenlandischen Gesellschaft* (*Journal of the German Oriental Society*), 153(1), 2003, pp. 157–175.

15   Borschberg, 'Luso-Johor-Dutch Relations in the Straits of Malacca and Singapore, c. 1600–1623'.

16   For a detailed factual history of this period, see F.W. Stapel, 'De Nederlandsche Oostindische Compagnie in de Zeventiende Eeuw' ('The Dutch East India Company in the Seventeenth Century'), in F.W. Stapel (ed.), *Geschiedenis van Nederlandsch Indië* (*History of The Dutch Indies*), Vol. III, Amsterdam: N.V. Uitgevers Maatschappij.

17   For the history of this fleet, see 'Beschrijvinghe van de Tweede Voyagie... onder den Heer Admirael Steven vander Hagen...' ('Description of the Second Voyage... under the Lord Admiral Steven van der Hagen...'), in Commelin, *Begin ende Voortgangh van de Nederlantsche Geoctroyeerde Oost-Indische Compagnie*, Vol. III, account I; J.K.J. de Jonge (ed.), *De Opkomst van het Nederlandsch Gezag in Oost Indie* (*The Rise of Dutch Authority in East India*), Vol. III, Gravenhage: Martinus Nijhoff, 1865, pp. 26–46, 145–213.

18   Jonge, *De Opkomst van het Nederlandsch Gezag in Oost Indie*, Vol. III, pp. 29, 35.

19   Van Heemskerck was one of the first to discuss the question, in 1603, expressing his preference for Malacca or Johor over Bantam, in Northern Java, which meant opting for the Straits of Malacca and Singapore region instead of the Straits of Sunda. In 1608, Cornelis Matelieff, on the other hand, discarded Malacca as 'unconquerable' and advised instead to opt for Jakarta, in Java, although he also believed that the company should hold a position in Johor. Pieter Both, the first VOC governor-general, was ordered in 1610 to try to establish the desired rendez-vous in Jakarta. In 1612, Jacques l'Hermite advised the company's directors in the Netherlands that the governor-general should reside at Ambon or Banda. In 1614–1615, Jan Pieterszoon Coen, then director-general in Bantam expressed his

preference for the Straits of Sunda over the Johor region for establishing the rendezvous. In 1616, however, he seemed not to have totally discarded the option of establishing it alternatively in the Malacca and Singapore Straits, as Steven van der Hagen also considered doing the same year. Vom Ittersum, *Profit and Principle*, pp. 41–43; P.J.A.N. Rietbergen (ed.), *De Eerste Landvoogd Pieter Both (1585–1615), Gouverneur-generaal van Nederlands-Indië (1609–1614) (The First Governor Pieter Both (1585–1615), Governor-General of Dutch East Indies (1609–1614))*, Zutphen: Walburg Pers, 1987, Vol. II, pp. 197–198, 207–208, 219–220, Jonge, *De Opkomst*, Vol. III, pp. 381–384; H.T. Colenbrander (ed.), *Jan Pietersz. Coen – Bescheiden omtrent zijn Bedrijf in Indië (Jan Pietersz. Coen – Documents Concerning his Action in India)*, Vol. I, Gravenhage: Martinus Nijhoff, 1919, pp. 72, 89, 156–157, 205, 209, 214–217; P.A. Tiele (ed.), *Bouwstoffen voor de Geschiedenis der Nederlanders in den Maleischen Archipel (Materials for the History of the Dutch in the Malay Archipelago)*, Vol. I, Gravenhage: Martinus Nijhoff, 1886, pp. 128–130.

20 For the history of this fleet, see 'Historische Verhael van de Treffelijcke Reyse Gedaen… door den Manhasten Admirael Cornelis Matelief…'; Jonge, *De Opkomst van het Nederlandsch Gezag in Oost Indie*, Vol. III, pp. 46–63, 213–255. For an account of its long stay in the Straits of Malacca and Singapore, see 'Historische Verhael van de Treffelijcke Reyse Gedaen… door den Manhasten Admirael Cornelis Matelief…', pp. 6–51.

21 For the history of this fleet, see A. de Booy (ed.), *De Derde Reis van de VOC naar Oost-Indie onder het Beleid van Admiraal Paulus van Caerden, Uitgezeild in 1606 (The Third Journey of the VOC to East India under the Command of Admiral Paulus van Caerden, Departed in 1606)*, 2 vols, Gravenhage: Martinus Nijhoff, 1968–1970.

22 The prospect of taking a fleet of Portuguese carracks travelling from Macao to Malacca was a powerful incentive for van Caerden's insistence on trying to reach Johor from Bantam. Booy (ed.), *De Derde Reis van de VOC naar Oost-Indie*, Vol. I, pp. 48–51, 120, 192, Vol. II, pp. 135–136, 138; 'Historische Verhael van de Treffelijcke Reyse Gedaen… door den Manhasten Admirael Cornelis Matelief…', pp. 129–31; Jonge, *De Opkomst van het Nederlandsch Gezag in Oost Indie*, Vol. III, pp. 241–242, 247–248.

23 For the history of this fleet, see M.E. van Opstall (ed.), *De Reis van de Vloot van Pieter Willemsz Verhoeff naar Azië, 1607–1612 (The Journey of the Fleet of Pieter Willemsz Verhoeff to Asia, 1607–1612)*, 2 vols, Gravenhage: Martinus Nijhoff, 1972.

24 Borschberg, 'Portuguese, Spanish and Dutch Plans to Construct a Fort in the Straits of Singapore', pp. 71–78.

25 Ibid., pp. 80–86.

26 Tiele, *Bouwstoffen voor de Geschiedenis der Nederlanders in den Maleischen Archipel*, Vol. I, pp. 118–130.

27 For the history of Dutch presence at Pattani, see H. Terpstra, *De Factorij der Oostindische Compagniete Patani (The Factory of the East India Company at Pattani)*, Gravenhage: M. Nijhoff, 1938. For the capture of the *Santo António*, see P. Borschberg, 'The Seizure of the *Santo António* at Patani: VOC Freebooting, the Estado da Índia and Peninsular Politics, 1602–1609', *Journal of the Siam Society*, 90(1/2), 2002, pp. 59–72.

28 This amounted to 1,600,000 guilders after the auction of the cargo in the Netherlands, that is, about half of the 3,356,172 guilders generated by the auction of the *Santa Catarina*. See Borschberg, 'The Seizure of the *Santo António* at Patani', pp. 66–67. Compare with the known values of cargoes of Portuguese ships taken in Asia by the Dutch in the period 1600–1661 in the table compiled by G.B. Souza in 'Commerce and Capital', pp. 340–347. It should be noted that the value ascribed by Souza to the

Santo António cargo – 1,694,886 guilders – differs from that indicated by Borschberg (Souza also mistakenly dated the ship's capture from 1603). Nevertheless, it is still the most valuable cargo recorded in Souza's table, along with that from the *Santa Catarina* (which Souza also recorded as 1,694,886 guilders, well below the 3,356,172 guilders indicated by Borschberg).

29 For this episode, see L. Blussé , 'Brief Encounter at Macao', *Modern Asian Studies*, 22(3), 1988, pp. 647–664.

30 Blussé, 'Brief Encounter at Macao', pp. 654–658, 660–663.

31 'Historische Verhael van de Reyse Gedaen... onder het Beleijdt van... Wybrandt van Waerwijck...' ('Historical Account of the Journey Done... under the Command of... Wybrandt van Waerwijck'), in Commelin (ed.), *Begin ende Voortgangh van de Nederlantsche Geoctroyeerde Oost-Indische Compagnie*, Vol. II, account VIII, p. 72; W.P. Groeneveldt, *De Nederlanders in China – De Eerste Bemoeiingenom den Handel in China en de Vestiging in de Pescadores (1601–1624)* (*The Dutch in China – The First Attempts at Trade in China and the Settlement in the Pescadores Islands (1601–1624)*), Gravenhage: Martinus Nijhoff, 1898, pp. 14–15; Boxer, *The Great Ship from Amacon*, p. 67.

32 The value of the cargo was 1,400,000 guilders. See Groeneveldt, *De Nederlanders in China*, pp. 14–15; Souza, 'Commerce and Capital', p. 340.

33 Groeneveldt, *De Nederlanders in China*, pp. 16–35; Boxer, 'The Affair of the "Madre de Deus"', pp. 29–34. These two frustrated attempts were carried out by two of the VOC admirals in person, van Warwijck and Matelieff, which shows well the importance given by the company to the China trade.

34 Blussé and Moor, *Nederlanders overzee*, pp. 197–199.

35 L. Blussé, 'From Inclusion to Exclusiveness: The Early Years at Hirado, 1600–1640', in L. Blussé, W. Remmelink and I. Smits (eds), *Bridging the Divide: 400 Years of Dutch-Japanese Relations*, Leiden: Hotei Publishing, 2000, pp. 13–33.

36 Opstall, *De Reis van de Vloot van Pieter Willemsz Verhoeff naar Azië*, Vol. I, pp. 128–132, Vol. II, pp. 327–331, 337–341.

37 H.T. Colenbrander and W. Ph. Coolhaas (eds), *Jan Pietersz. Coen*, Vol. I, pp. 176–177, 203, 246, 254, 293–295, 345, 433–434, Vol. II, pp. 7, 12, 102, 107, 109–111, 113–114, 229, 236, 238–41, Vol. III, pp. 362–363, 393–396, Vol. VII-I, pp. 54–55, 192–193, 198, 215–216, 222, 288–289, 299–300, 307–8; E.M. Thompson (ed.), *Diary of Richard Cocks, Cape-Merchant in the English Factory in Japan, 1615–1622, with Correspondence*, London: Hakluyt Society, 1883, Vol. I, pp. 33, 105–106, 109, 118, 121–122, 135, 137, 174–175, 263–264, 266–267, 288–289, 336, Vol. II, pp. 4–5, 8–9, 17, 40, 43.

38 Colenbrander, *Jan Pietersz. Coen*, Vol. I, p. 203; Thompson, *Diary of Richard Cocks*, Vol. I, pp. 35–36; A. Clulow, 'Pirating in the Shogun's Waters: The Dutch East India Company and the *Santo Antonio* Incident', *Bulletin of Portuguese/Japanese Studies*, 13, 2006, pp. 65–80.

39 Clulow, 'Pirating in the Shogun's Waters', pp. 70–75.

40 Boxer, *The Great Ship from Amacon*, pp. 87–88; Clulow, 'Pirating in the Shogun's Waters', pp. 75–78.

41 From 1617 onwards, the use of Hirado as a basis for privateering against Portuguese and Spanish navigation in the South China Sea had increased. Blussé, 'From Inclusion to Exclusiveness', p. 28; A. Clulow, 'Pirating in the Shogun's Waters', pp. 78–79.

42 Boxer, *The Great Ship from Amacon*, pp. 95–97.

43 Compare with the known values of cargoes of Portuguese ships taken in Asia by the Dutch in the period 1600–1661 in the table compiled by G.B. Souza 'Commerce and Capital', pp. 340–347.

6 Early British presence in China

The first Anglo-Portuguese voyage to Macao

Rogério Miguel Puga

This chapter deals with the first voyage of an English ship to the Luso-Chinese enclave of Macao. Using Portuguese archival material and the East India Company Records (India Office Records, British Library, IOR), I retrace the adventures and analyse the aims of the British crew who travelled aboard the *London*, a ship chartered by the Portuguese viceroy of Goa to the East India Company, to travel to Macao in 1635, allowing the former to avoid the Dutch blockade. The Macao Portuguese defended their interests and tried to keep the newcomers as far away from the China trade as possible, while the East India Company factors tried to establish direct trade with the Chinese and compete with the Portuguese in Macao.

The English voyage East

References to Macao in the IOR are relatively scant, since, as is known, the China trade took place in Canton, the main destination for traders, who only lived in the Sino-Portuguese enclave because they were banned from living all year round in Canton. References to episodes in the lives of the British and to their experience of Macao that I found in the IOR cover mainly the periods between the trading seasons (March to September), when the supercargoes remained there. In turn, most English-language studies on the Western presence in southern China study the British presence in Canton, relegating Macao to a secondary place,[1] for, after 1700, the supercargoes of the East India Company (EIC) traded mainly in Canton and only resided in the enclave between trading seasons, with the latter acting as a 'means' to attain a commercial 'end'. My study, already published in Portuguese and English,[2] thus fills in what has hitherto been a historiographical 'vacuum'.

As we shall see, the voyages of the company's vessels to Macao – both the initially sporadic expeditions, decided by the English factories in the East, and the voyages organized in London – as well as the fruits of these expeditions, at first almost nil, testify to an initial (relative) lack of interest and the succession of forward and backward movement in English trade in southern China from the late 1630s, results that were also influenced by Portuguese interests and stratagems. The English maritime enterprise clashed early on with Iberian interests, and the first frictions of the fifteenth and sixteenth centuries foreshadowed later, more serious conflicts. During the dual monarchy of the Philips, the Anglo-Portuguese alliance remained 'dormant',[3] while a number of expeditions to distant Cathay departed from England, without success, however. In 1553, Sir Hugh Willoughby set sail for the East, but never reached it. In 1591, three English vessels, one of which was under the command of Sir James Lancaster, sailed beyond the Cape of Good Hope to avail themselves of Portuguese trade, as did the same sailor again in 1601, when he travelled to Banten (Java), where the Dutch had been since 1596, and which later became an English factory of strategic importance for the pepper trade. In 1596, the first official expedition to China left England, comprising three vessels (the *Bear*, the *Bear's Welp* and the *Benjamin*) under the command of Benjamin Wood. This fleet did not, however, reach its destination.[4] In 1602–1604, Sir Edward Michelborne obtained leave to travel to the East, notably to China and Japan, although this initiative bore no fruit.[5]

In Elizabethan England, Richard Hakluyt (c. 1552–1616) collected, translated and published, in *The Principal Navigations, Voyages and Discoveries of the English Nation* (1589–1600), dozens of European sources, including Portuguese,[6] in which Macao is a tenuous presence, functioning as a symbolic space of the riches and the experience which Portugal had imported from the Far East. Later, all this information was complemented by the collection published by Samuel Purchas (c. 1577–1626), *Hakluytus Posthumus or Purchas His Pilgrims* (1625),[7] in part comprising manuscripts inherited from Hakluyt, which encouraged English traders and investors to venture forth in the wake of Portuguese vessels. All these data on the Asian human and trading realities later became crucial in the clashes between the Portuguese and the English in the Eastern seas and were decisive in weakening the former and in the ensuing upset of the 'Carreira da Índia', the Portuguese kingdom being unable to defend its Eastern territories effectively. The annexation of Portugal by Spain in 1580 meant that the political reasons that had led England – within the context of the oldest political alliance in the Western world – to respect Portugal now waned. Attacks on Portuguese ships intensified in an attempt to weaken the Catholic Spanish enemy and demonstrate English naval superiority. The circumnavigations undertaken by Francis Drake (1577–1580) and by Thomas Cavendish (1586–1588), as well as the defeat of the Spanish Armada (1588), proved to England that it could compete on the sea with Philip II. Similarly, the lucrative Portuguese trade in the Far East drew the attention of the English, especially after the capture of the *Madre de Deus* (*Mother of God*) in 1592, by Sir John Burroughs, off the coast of the Azores. The cargo of the Portuguese vessel stimulated the covetousness of Elizabethan traders, who realized what riches would also be theirs should they upset the Portuguese trade monopoly in the East Indies. Approximately four years after the capture of the *Madre de Deus*, and 40 years before the first English vessel reached Macao, Laurence Keymis Gent concluded that England could become as powerful as the Iberian Peninsula, putting forward the following arguments in favour of the opening up of the *mare clausum*:[8]

1) Elizabeth I's nation had the same might, rights and capabilities as the Iberian Peninsula to create new trade networks.
2) Although the Papist Spanish enemy ruled Portugal, each Iberian country was a distinct political entity,[9] as shown by the Portuguese colonies' non-recognition of Philip II's might.
3) The West Indies, under Spanish rule, were divided and badly governed, which meant they could be easily taken by England, as could the Portuguese fleets that enriched Phillip's coffers.

It was in this context that naval battles were fought between the English fleets and Portuguese eastern territories, and in late December 1600, when the first Dutch vessels appeared on the coast of Macao, Elizabeth I authorized the founding of the Company of Merchants of London, trading into the East Indies, whose aim was to begin voyages to the East Indies, with a view to importing consumer goods and exporting English textiles; this event signals the beginning of English expeditions to Asia. Northern-European expansion, organized through private initiatives based on shareholder capital, differed from Iberian expansion, and the EIC's instructions for the second voyage advised Henry Middleton of the precautions he should take en route to the Moluccas, given the 'malice of the Portingalls toward our discovery of the trade to those parts'.[10] The arrival of English vessels in Surat – which, starting in 1613, would become the Anglo-Dutch base in the western Indian Ocean –[11] gave rise to clashes with the Portuguese, who took several vessels and led the EIC to address complaints to the authorities in London.[12]

Although England only turned towards the East in the seventeenth century, initial activity and clashes between the English and the Portuguese in the East Indies gave the former ever-greater knowledge of the trading space concerned, and this information gradually replaced what England had learnt indirectly from European, especially Iberian, sources during the sixteenth and early seventeenth centuries.

In 1602, two years before England and Spain signed their Peace Treaty, and in the wake of the Dutch,[13] the English, using their increasing naval military might and diplomatic activity, reached the Indian Ocean, gradually moving towards Macao. The recently-arrived 'enem[ies] from Europe',[14] faced with the defensive stance of the Portuguese, fought for the founding of the EIC factory in Surat in 1612, which, as reported by António Bocarro (c. 1594–1642) in 1635, caused the viceroy of Goa some concern.[15]

In early 1622 the English, in alliance with the shah of Persia, Abbas, took Ormuz, the most profitable customs house in the Portuguese Eastern empire, and thus acquired more and more territory, gained greater self-confidence and power in the East, where the Portuguese held the monopoly in trade, and where, since the Defence Treaty (1619) signed by the two Protestant enemies against the Catholics,[16] the combined English and Dutch fleets 'seek to master all shipping activity and trade' and attempt to infiltrate China.[17] In 1627, the director of the Batavia factory, in his conclusions on the factors to be considered when attempting to set up trade with China, stated that the Chinese did not allow foreigners to enter their country.[18] The Portuguese realized they could not keep the EIC away from Eastern markets, and English military support was essential for them in Asia, to resist Dutch attacks and the Dutch blockade, and in Europe, so that post-1640 Portugal could maintain its independence.

The Convention of Goa (1635) and the opening up of Eastern ports to the English

Following the 'firm peace and concord' signed in August 1604 by Philip II of Portugal and James I of England,[19] in 1630 Philip III and Charles I renewed the peace accords, which were to be observed in the overseas dominions of both nations.[20] In 1632 Count Linhares, the viceroy of India, wrote to Philip III, informing him of the proposal by the 'president of the English by which they would come to an understanding and practise in that State the peace which [the king of Portugal] had agreed with his Britannic Majesty'.[21] The king counselled peace with the English because 'that State [Portuguese Asian Empire] is in such a tight situation'.[22] According to the viceroy, this alliance would further result in benefit to the Crown's customs, through receipt of royal taxes,[23] while the Englishman William Methwold, who had arrived in Surat in November 1633, viewed this arrangement as an excellent strategy to revitalize English trade in Asia, which had fallen into decline.[24]

To face the Dutch forces, whose alliance with the English had ended in enmity after the massacre of Amboina (1623), the Convention of Goa was signed in January 1635.[25] This was a local peace and cooperation accord between Methwold and the viceroy of India,[26] which opened up the gate of the East to English vessels.[27] The Portuguese began to trade through EIC's ships, avoiding Dutch attacks, which continued despite the treaty signed between João IV and the United Provinces in November 1641, and which the Verenigde Oostindische Compagnie (VOC, Dutch East India Company), operating from Batavia, did not respect until 1645. Peace in the East came after a treaty was signed by the latter establishment and Goa in November of the preceding year. In 1635, the Convention of Goa put an end to almost half a century of maritime conflicts between the two oldest European allies but did not lead to the immediate weakening of their common enemy.[28] A new cycle of trade in the Estado da Índia began, as proved by the arrival of the *London*, an English vessel that, equipped with Portuguese weapons for defence against the Dutch,[29] set sail for Macao (Portuguese voyage). Its owners' condition was that English supercargoes could trade in Macao, which did not happen, as there were two Portuguese agents on board whose aim was to boycott English trade. The news of the signing of the Convention of Goa might not be favourably received by the local oligarchy, which proved in fact to be the case, since Macao's livelihood came from trade, and trade was its raison d'être from the very beginning, back in the sixteenth century. The English presence gradually took root in Asia, extending as far as Japan, where trade with Macao was banned in 1640 by the Japanese authorities, a measure that abruptly ended the city's first golden age.

The arrival of the English in Macao: the first vessel

'The Portugall, a watchfull eie and jealousie over us'.

'Henry Bornford at Surat to the Company, April 29, 1636', in Sir William Foster, *The English Factories in India 1634–1636*, Oxford, The Clarendon press, 1911, p. 227

The Convention of Goa signed between Goa and Surat aimed to face the growing Dutch power in the Far East, gradually opening the gateway to Macao for EIC vessels and those of private English traders. This alliance mirrored the problems with which the Estado da Índia had to concern itself in the face of its northern-European rivals and the strategies Portugal adopted to deal with the situation. The English first visited Macao when the Estado da Índia was beginning to contract, but the EIC only established itself in China in the early eighteenth century (1700). From early on, the arrival of these rivals displeased the municipality of Macao, which tried to defend its privileged status with the Middle Kingdom and keep its trade competitors away; four years later, these would facilitate the expulsion of the Portuguese from Japan, jeopardizing the survival of the 'City of the Holy Name of God' of Macao. On the other hand, imperial vigilance over Macao hampered the city's trade activity and its power, since the Chinese authorities viewed the enclave as part of China, under the authority of the emperor; and a perfect place where foreigners could be enclosed and controlled.

A group of Englishmen, accompanied by the Portuguese factor Gaspar Gomes, and as proposed by the viceroy of Goa, Count Linhares,[30] set sail from Goa on board the *London* in April 1635 and arrived in China on 23 July. The group was received in Macao with reluctance both by their fellow travellers, the Portuguese factors, and by the local oligarchy. The viceroy of Goa had secretly forbidden the crew to land, as a result of which the English supercargo trader Henry Bornford advised his directors that, should they want him to carry out a second journey to China, he would sail not to Macao but to one of the other ports or islands in the Pearl River Delta.[31]

In February of that year, and writing to Philip III about the benefits of the Convention of Goa, Count Linhares had informed the king that there was a cargo of copper and iron in Macao 'which could not be shipped because of the Dutch presence in the Straights of Singapore'. The viceroy had therefore chartered, from the president of the English factory in Surat, a vessel (the *London*) on which to carry these goods because as they [the English] are in no danger from the Dutch, they can bring them with great ease, and it does not cross my mind that the said English may divert this cargo, since, besides being men of their word, all their vessels will stand as security.[32]

It was agreed that the English would not contact or trade with the Chinese,[33] with Count Linhares defending his position thus:

my having agreed with this President that no English would land on Macao soil, and we would put in their vessel ... a captain with fifty sol-diers ... according to my thought that the Chinamen are treacherous, and that they might want to raid their vessel ... and, as for the cargo he much complimented me, and in fact it was agreed that I would name the price the vessel would pay to come here.[34]

In turn, and contrary to what the viceroy had written to Philip III, the instructions issued by the English factory in Surat advised the crew of the *London* that some of them would be allowed to settle on dry land.[35] Methwold's instructions to Captain Willes further advised him that both conflicts between the English and the Portuguese, to which the signing of the Convention had put an end, and the personal interests of the Portuguese community could bring to the boil adverse reactions on the part of the enclave's inhabitants towards the English during the 'first visit of an English vessel'. Thus, mistrust and the clash of trading interests marked the first contacts between Macao traders and the EIC. Methwold thus informed the *London*'s captain:

At his arrival at Macao, the Captain is enjoined to conform to direc-tions from the Portuguese governor, particularly in regard to persons sent ashore from the ship; and to avoid all occasions of giving offence: for it is to be apprehended, that as this is the first visit of an English ship there, under a friendly compact, so fears and jealousies; grounded as the former Enmity between the two nations, may be entertained by the Portuguese.[36]

In May 1635, the viceroy Miguel de Noronha wrote to the captain-general of Macao, Manuel da Câmara de Noronha, and announced the truce with the old allies (Convention of Goa), sending a copy of the document. The instructions from Goa were precise, listing the measures to be taken by the Portuguese when interacting with the English crew, and several times reiterating the need for the English to maintain a distance from the Chinese, for the former carried valuable goods with which to trade with Gaspar Gomes's assistance.[37] The *London*, the first English vessel to anchor in southern China,[38] despite having been secretly chartered by the Portuguese, triggered clashes between the Mandarin authorities and the administration of Macao, which was forced to pay a fine to the former because of the unwanted presence of the 'foreign' vessel,[39] after its departure on 20 October for Goa, where it arrived in early February 1636.[40]

On reaching Goa, the crew of the *London* refused to pay customs duties, just as they had done in Malacca, since they had bought their goods from Chinese residents of Macao and had not off-loaded them in India, as they intended to ship them on to England. After the *London*'s voyage, Manuel Ramos, the administrator of voyages to Japan, advised the viceroy of Goa to guard against monetary losses in Macao and to force the English to leave a deposit in Goa for the vessel's rendition.[41] Fully aware of the threat posed by the English vessels, the enclave at once joined forces with the Canton mandarinate in order to repel the unwanted foreign presence. Henry Bornford, 'the firste [Englishman] that negotiated ... business in those parts',[42] affirms in his travel log that while his apparent objective was to assist the viceroy of India to deal with the Dutch blockade, the underlying purpose of the EIC's mission was to launch direct trade with China. Bornford concluded:

> so far as the English could see, the averseness of the Chinese to inter-course with foreigners is exaggerated by the Portuguese, who also abuse other nations to the Chinese in order to keep the trade to themselves.[43]

The comments of the man in charge of the *London*'s voyage to Macao regarding Portuguese attitudes, including the comment I quote in the epigraph to this section, constitute the first English image about the city's dwellers, based on actual visual contact and interaction. From the beginning of the English presence in China, the Portuguese carried out a two-pronged strategy of interests that operated on two fronts and consisted of keeping other European nations away from China and denigrating their image among the higher echelons of Canton's provincial administration. However, Bornford listed the goods that could be most easily sold in Macao and reached the conclusion that, should peace between the Portuguese and the English come to pass, the latter would gain a part of this lucrative trade.[44] For his part, the Portuguese factor Gaspar Gomes, back in Goa, described the voyage to the new viceroy Pedro da Silva and stated that he had warned the English that, under the instructions they had received, they could not trade in Macao. Viceroy Pedro da Silva was highly suspicious of these expeditions and, in a report to Philip III of Portugal, he paraphrased the factor's account,[45] stating that the English

> did not wish to abide by this, but would rather have their own factory where they would sell and buy whatever was to be had, and became great friends with the local Chinamen, continuously giving them food and drink ..., taking them many goods and silver, and that they wanted no more than to be allowed to build two thatched houses outside the city and not sturdy houses like those of the Portuguese, and that they would offer them their goods cheaper by 30 per cent and 40 per cent than our prices,

and as the Chinamen did not allow them the goods which they requested, which will not be very difficult because those people always seek out their goods in larger quantities, and as those which we buy from them are in little quantity because of the lack of navigation and trade [due to the Dutch embargo in the Malacca Straights] they will easily make friends with the English, in this way harming this *Estado* [da Índia], especially when they [the English] come with such greed to return to China, as Gaspar Gomes tells me, and also here after they arrived I have heard that, even against our will, they will send out two of their brigs during the monsoon, and will do this every year.[46]

These accounts by Gomes and by the new viceroy reflected the interest felt by the supercargoes in Surat to approach the Chinese to request authorization to build a 'thatched' and not permanent factory, as were the Portuguese buildings, outside the walls of Macao where they would compete with the city's dwellers. Even before Gomes had arrived in Goa, Manuel Ramos had already warned the viceroy of the dangers of the return of the English and of trade with China and Japan passing into their hands, conveying similar facts to those which the factor would narrate *in loco*, as follows:

1) The English 'intent on continuing this trade', requested Chinese authorization to send two small vessels to Canton the following year and to build four 'very small totally unfortified' houses 'with no artillery', unlike those of the Portuguese in Macao, undertaking to sell to the Chinese merchandise at half the price practised by the Portuguese,
2) The English promised 'other things that would benefit them, much to our detriment', and tried to offer a Chinese man large annual payments to the Mandarins and to the emperor, making many other promises on this. Eventually, the Portuguese found out about the plan and convinced the man to take a Portuguese bribe to make him pretend to the English that he would go to Canton to intercede on their behalf,
3) If the English did not reach Macao from Goa, they would do so from Surat, thus jeopardizing Portuguese trade in the Far East.[47]

Pedro da Silva informed Philip III of the threat the English posed to the enclave's trade and of Surat's subversive intentions,[48] although voyages to China were not yet part of the trading policies of the EIC in London. However, many of the measures taken and much of the success of trading in the East derived from decisions made and strategies mapped out by the local factories without the prior approval of the directors in London.

Gaspar Gomes' account and Manuel Ramos' missive prove that the Estado da Índia had feared English competition from the moment the first EIC vessel had been sent to Macao, even though this had been the Portuguese wish. Pedro da Silva informed the king that he had admitted to his council, even before the vessel returned, 'how much he felt and regretted, already foreseeing the damage that would befall this Estado from sending this vessel to China',[49] describing how, after taking up his post, he had distanced himself from his predecessor's actions and forced the *London* to stay outside the port of Goa to check its cargo and exact the customs duties owed to the Portuguese Crown. The viceroy also wrote to the captain-general of Macao about the major drawbacks of the *London*'s voyage and enjoined him both to make every effort to ensure that no other European nation was received in any other Chinese port, as also letting him know that this voyage had incurred his displeasure; no other English vessel, he further wrote, should be sent to China, nor should any favours be extended to third parties.[50] Four years later, and fighting the Dutch blockade, the same viceroy, in the same type of move adopted by his predecessor with regard to the English, chartered a vessel from the Danish India Company, thus weakening the exclusive position of the English.[51]

After the *London*'s return, relations between Methwold and Pedro da Silva, who for three years did not pay the English for the chartering of the vessel, became tense to the extent that the truce enshrined in the Convention of Goa came close to being suspended.[52] For these same reasons, and having banned further English voyages to Macao,[53] the viceroy was considered by Surat as being 'irreconcilably adverse unto the English'.[54] In the same year, Madras, which would become known as Fort St. George, was acquired by the English, and, because of the Dutch blockade, the viceroy of Goa again proposed to the English that they send two or three vessels to Macao. This support was turned down by Surat, which informed London of the upset expressed by Goa with regard to what it felt was Portugal's abandoning of it, with the Portuguese even being prepared to become the subjects of a foreign king who would protect them from the Dutch. Surat also wrote of the need for English vessels to be sent to the East so as to profit from the advantageous wish expressed by the local Portuguese to cooperate in matters of trade: 'wee believe they would readily subscribe to furnish you with pepper, cinamon, and as much freedome & security in some of their forts (if not the fort itself)'.[55] In 1636 Surat informed London that they wished to set up direct trade with China, for which London would have to obtain authorization from Portugal, while the factory would pay the required taxes in Malacca. Three years later, when a Portuguese vessel anchored under the protection of the English fort at Armagon, because of a storm, the English approached the vessel to hoist their flag on it, but two Dutch vessels sent from Pulicat attacked the Portuguese vessel, whose crew decided to set fire to their ship after offloading part of its cargo.[56]

The voyage of the *London* and the other Portuguese proposals to use English vessels occurred as a result of the interests and in the name of the Portuguese in Goa. Therefore, this voyage cannot be considered the first English-driven mission to the Luso-Chinese enclave, especially as the EIC directors were unaware that Surat used its capital to send vessels to China, a practice that they later disapproved. London alerted Methwold to the danger of initiatives such as the chartering of the *London*, for the Dutch, should they find out those English vessels were carrying Portuguese munitions or goods, could easily take them in the Malacca Straights and confiscate the cargo,[57] as they did in 1643 when they captured the *Bona Speranza*. This English vessel was chartered by the viceroy of Goa, João da Silva Telo e Meneses, Count Aveiras, from Sir William Courteen's Commercial Association to transport Portuguese soldiers to Macao.[58] The vessel was escorted by two other English ships (the *Lesser* and the *Greater William*),[59] as a result of the difficulties posed by the Dutch blockade. As recorded by the viceroy in late 1643:

> the English vessel … which had set sail for China is also presumed to have been detained in the same fortress of Malacca, having fought with the Dutch, in which fight the English captain having died …, this leads us to believe that China must be suffering great hardship.[60]

Enmity and the initial fear of Anglo-Portuguese competition gradually gave way to cooperation as a strategy for the defence of both nations' interests in the face of the Dutch threat in the East,[61] and, thanks to the Convention of Goa, the Portuguese of Macao even started to travel to and from Lisbon via London onboard EIC vessels,[62] although peace between the two allies did not make them 'the masters of everything' as initially expected.[63] After the massacre of Amboina and the Dutch expulsion of the English from the spice trade, the EIC joined forces with the Portuguese to confront Dutch might, and it was in this context that, as we have seen, the Convention of Goa was signed and that the *London* arrived at Macao. Two years later a fleet owned by the William Courteen Association, and commanded by William Weddell, arrived in China, but the EIC would only establish direct trade with the Chinese in 1700. As we have seen, the Portuguese empire in Asia needed its English ally to help in the fight against the growing power of the Dutch enemy, but allies in Europe were rivals in Asia, and the Macao Portuguese defended their commercial interests and tried to keep the newcomers as far away from the China trade as possible. On the other hand, the East India Company factors tried to establish direct trade with the Chinese and compete with the Portuguese in Macao during their stay in the enclave.

Notes

1 P. Van Dyke's seminal *The Canton Trade*, is one of the only studies to devote more than a few paragraphs to the importance of Macao in the context of the China trade. P. Van Dyke, *The Canton Trade*, Hong Kong: Hong Kong University Press, 2005, pp. 35–48, 77, 119–167.

2 R.M. Puga, *A Presença Inglesa e as Relações Anglo-Portuguesas em Macau, 1635–1793* (*The English Presence and Anglo-Portuguese Relations in Macau, 1635–1793*), Lisbon: CHAM, 2009, pp. 19–51, republished in English as *The British Presence in Macau 1635–1793*, London: Royal Asiatic Society; Hong Kong: Hong Kong University Press, 2013

3 Cf. E. Prestage, 'The Anglo-Portuguese Alliance', *Transactions of the Historical Society*, 17, 1934, pp. 3, 12–23, and Charles R. Boxer, 'Vicissitudes das Relações Anglo-Portuguesas no Século XVII' ('Vicissitudes of Anglo-Portuguese Relations

in the 17th Century'), in Her Majesty's Government (ed.), *600 Anos de Aliança Anglo-Portuguesa* (*600 Years of Anglo-Portuguese Alliance*), London: Her Majesty's Government/British Broadcasting Corporation, n.d., p. 26.

4 G/12/1, fl. 1, and H. Cordier, *Histoire Générale de la Chine* (*General History of China*), Vol. II, Paris : Librairie Paul Genthner, 1920, pp. 191–192.

5 M.P. Smith, *Western Barbarians in Japan and Formosa in Tokugawa Days*, Kobe: J.L. Thompson, 1930, pp. 3–4.

6 The first account of China published in English is the *Treaty of China*, by the Portuguese Galeote Pereira, translated from Italian by Richard Eden and Richard Willes and published by the latter in *History of Travayle in the West and East Indies*, as well as by Hakluyt (see R.M. Puga, 'The Presence of the "Portugals" in Macao and Japan, in Richard Hakluyt, *Navigations*', *Bulletin of Portuguese/ Japanese Studies*, 5 December 2002, pp. 94–96).

7 R.M. Puga, 'Macau in Samuel Purchas's Hakuytus Posthumus, or Purchas His Pilgrimes (1625)', *Review of Culture,* 28 October 2008, pp. 16–41.

8 L.K. Gent, 'A Relation of the Second Voyage to Guiana, Performed and Written in the Yeere 1596', in R. Hakluyt, *Voyages*, Vol. VII, London: Dent, 1962, pp. 390–391.

9 On the Anglo-Spanish rivalry and the influence of the Portuguese voyages of exploration on Elizabethan literature, see R.M. Puga, 'The "Lusiads" at sea and the Spaniards at war in Elizabethan Drama: Shakespeare and the Portuguese Discoveries', in H. Klein and J.M. González (eds), *Shakespeare Yearbook: Shakespeare and Spain*, Vol. XIII, Lampeter: The Edwin Mellen Press, 2002, pp. 90–114.

10 Sir G. Birdwood and W. Foster, *The First Letter Book of the East India Company: 1600–1619*, London: Bernard Quaritich, 1893, p. 62.

11 On the Anglo-Dutch presence in Surat, see Maria Manuela Sobral Blanco, *O Estado Português da Índia: Da Rendição de Ormuz à Perda de Cochim (1622–1663)* (*The Portuguese 'Estado da India': From the Rendition of Hormuz to the Loss of Cochin (1622–1663)*), Vol. I, PhD Thesis, University of Lisbon, 1992, pp. 423–434.

12 Birdwood and Foster, *The First Letter Book of the East India Company*, pp. 219–220.

13 On the Dutch attacks on Portuguese possessions in the Indian Ocean, see K.M. Mathew, 'The Dutch Threat and the Security of the Carreira in India Waters', in Artur T. de Matos and Luís F. Thomaz (eds), *As Relações entre a Índia Portuguesa, a Ásia do Sueste e o Extremo Oriente* (*The Relations between Portuguese India, Southeast Asia and the Far East*), Macao: CNCDP, 1993, pp. 779–783 and Blanco, *O Estado Português da Índia* (*The Portuguese "Estado da India"*), Vol. I, pp. 393–451.

14 A. Bocarro, *Década 13 da História da Índia* (*Decade 13 of the History of India*), Lisbon: Tipografia da Academia Real das Ciências de Lisboa, 1876 [c. 1635], p. 429.

15 Bocarro, *Década 13*, p. 336.

16 K.D. Bassett, 'Early English Trade and Settlement in Asia, 1602–1690', in A. Disney (ed.), *An Expanding World, Vol. 4: Historiography of Europeans in Africa and Asia, 1450–1800*, Aldershot: Variorum-Ashgate, 1995, pp. 134–135.

17 Bocarro, *Década 13*, p. 303. In February 1628, the governor of India Frei Luís de Brito e Meneses mentions the great risk posed by the presence of English and Dutch corsairs in Asia (Arquivos Nacionais da Torre do Tombo (AN/TT, Lisbon), *Livros das Monções* (*Book of the Monsoons*), book 27, fls. 521–34v).

18 H.B. Morse, *The Chronicles of the East India Company Trading to China 1635–1834*, Vol. I, Oxford: Clarendon Press, 1926, p. 29.

19 In a letter to the viceroy of India, Phillip II refers to the articles, especially the ninth, of the first Anglo-Portuguese peace treaty of 1604, strengthened by that of 1630. See J.F. Biker (ed.), *Colecção de Tratados e Concertos de Pazes que o Estado*

da Índia Portugesa Fez (*Collection of Treaties and Agreements of Peace that the State of India Signed*), Madras: Asian Educational Services, 1995, Vol. I, p. 262, Vol. II, pp. 37–38.

20 India Office Records (IOR, British Library, London), G/12/10, fls. 67–80; Biker, *Colecção de Tratados* (*Collection of Treaties*), pp. 239–261. The 34 articles of the 1630 treaty seek to improve ties of friendship between the two nations, strengthen the free trade and protect their Asian domains against the Dutch (chs. 1–4, 7–8, 11–12).

21 'Exchange Made Between the Viceroy, the Count of Linhares and Guilherme Methewold', in Biker (ed.), *Colecção de Tratados*, Vol. II, pp. 50–51 (English version pp. 52–53).

22 Biker, *Colecção de Tratados*, Vol. II, pp. 263–264.

23 P.S.S. Pissurlencar, *Assentos do Conselho do Estado* (*Minutes of the Council of State*), Vol. II, Goa: Tipografia Rangel, 1954, pp. 3–5.

24 Sir W. Foster (ed.), *The English Factories in India 1634–1636*, Oxford: Clarendon Press, 1911, pp. 15–17, 79–80, 96.

25 IOR, G/12/10, fls. 69–74, J.F.B. de Castro (ed.), *Colecção dos Tratados, Convenções, Contratos e Actos Públicos Celebrados ente a Coroa de Portugal e as Mais Potências desde 1640 até ao Presente* (*Collection of Treaties, Conventions and Public Acts Celebrated between the Crown of Portugal and other Powers since 1640 to the Present*), Vol. I, Lisbon: Imprensa Nacional, 1856, pp. 102–103, M. Jesus, *Historic Macau*, Hong Kong: Kelly & Walsh, 1902, pp. 95–96; A. R. Disney, *Twilight of the Pepper Empire*, Cambridge, MA: Harvard University Press, 1978, pp. 148–154.

26 The 'Relação Breve, Geral das Principaes Couzas que Sucederão em a India o Anno de 1633' (The 'Brief General Relation of Things that Happened in India in 1633'), National Library of Portugal (Biblioteca Nacional de Portugal, Lisbon), *Fundo Geral* (*General fund*), cod. 7640, p. 60, lists the advantages of the peace agreement to be signed with England, especially the increase in trade and customs duties, as well as the weakening of the Dutch enemies.

27 Letter from the viceroy (1636) on the ceasefire with the English stating that it should be maintained due to the 'many enemies' and the difficult situation faced by the Portuguese empire (AN/TT, *Livros das Monções*, book 33, pp. 247–247v).

28 G.V. Scammell, 'England, Portugal and the *Estado da Índiac*.1500–1635', *Modern Asian Studies,* 16, 1982, pp. 177–192, summarizes Anglo-Portuguese conflicts through to the Convention of Goa.

29 On the context leading to the Anglo-Portuguese *entente cordiale* against the VOC in the seventeenth century, see G.R. Crone, *The Discovery of the East*, London: Hamish Hamilton, 1972, pp. 120–147, and Marcus P. M. Vink, 'The Entente Cordiale: The Dutch East India Company and the Portuguese Shipping through the Straits of Malacca, 1641–1663', *Revista de Cultura* (*Review of Culture*), 13(14), 1991, pp. 289–309. This latter author stated that the Dutch in Batavia were preparing for possible joint attacks from their Portuguese and English enemies. The study concludes that the Anglo-Portuguese *entente cordiale* is harmful in the long term to the Portuguese as, while the English did weaken the Dutch naval blockades and transport Portuguese goods, they were not able to protect all Portuguese possessions in Asia.

30 AN/TT, *Livros das Monções*, book 33, fl. 248, book 44, fls. 426–427, book 45, fls. 350–351, and Foster, *The English Factories in India 1634–1636*, pp. 103–104, 150, 177–178, 189–190, 226–230, which details under 'Consultation Held in Surat', pp. 102–103: 'an English ship "should be sent from Goa to Macau in China for freight goods…The voiadge in itselfe was generally approved…were it but *to experience the trade in those parts, which hath ever bene desired*"' (emphasis added, see IOR, G/12/1, fl. 24).

31 Foster, *The English Factories in India 1634–1636*, p. 228, and G/12/10, fl. 86–88.
32 Biker, *Colecção de Tratados*, Vol. I, p. 266.
33 *Arquivo Histórico de Goa* (AHG), *Filmoteca Ultramarina Portuguesa (Historical Archive of Goa (AHG), Overseas Portuguese Film Archive)* (FUP, Lisbon), *Livro dos Segredos* (*Book of Secrets*), no. 1, fls. 6–7.
34 Biker, *Colecção de Tratados*, Vol. I, p. 267.
35 Foster, *The English Factories in India 1634–1636*, pp. 105–106.
36 IOR, G/12/10, fl. 81.
37 This idea is repeated at the end of the letter (AN/TT, *Livros das Monções*, book 34, fl. 66) and in the instructions given to Manuel Ramos (fl. 73 and book 35, fl. 263).
38 For details of the vessel's route from Downs, via Surat, to Macao, see A. Farrington, *East India Company Ships, 1600–1833: Based on a Catalogue of the East India Company Ships' Journals and Logs 1600–1834*, London: The British Library, 1999, p. 386.
39 Letter from Manuel Ramos to the Viceroy of India (20 October 1635): AN/TT, *Livros das Monções*, book 35, fl. 253v.
40 Letter from the viceroy (18 February 1636): AN/TT, *Livros das Monções*, book 33, fl. 247v.
41 AN/TT, *Livros das Monções*, book 33, fl. 261.
42 'Henry Bornford at Surat to the Company, April 29, 1636', in Foster, *The English Factories in India 1634–1636*, p. 226, see also Cordier, *Histoire Générale de la Chine*, Vol. II, p. 211.
43 'Henry Bornford at Surat', p. 227.
44 Ibid., pp. 229–30.
45 AN/TT, *Livros das Monções*, book 33, fl. 248.
46 Ibid.
47 Ibid., book 35, fl. 267.
48 Ibid., book 33, fl. 248.
49 Ibid.
50 AHG, FUP (Lisbon), *Livro dos Segredos*, n. 1, fl. 11. Nevertheless, in 1639 Pedro da Silva told William Fromlin, Methwold's successor, that he would send someone to discuss with him the charters agreed both for Malacca and China (fl. 30).
51 In May 1639, Pedro da Silva warned the Danish traders that they could only negotiate with China with permission from the captain-general of Macao (AHG, FUP, *Livro dos Segredos*, fls. 31, 31v, 33).
52 AHG, FUP, *Livro dos Segredos*, fl. 583, n. 399.
53 'Copia do Conçelho sobre o Comerçio dos Ingleses' ('Copy of the Council about the Trade of the English'), in Pissurlencar (ed.), *Assentos* (*Minutes*), Vol.II, 1954, pp. 115–116.
54 IOR, G/12/1, fl. 58. Pedro da Silva informed Surat that Portuguese ports would not trade with English vessels and that these were only authorized to anchor for shelter or to take on supplies (Foster, *The English Factories in India 1634–1636*, pp. 152, 159). In another English document dated 1639 António Teles de Meneses, the governor of India who succeeded Pedro da Silva, is considered friendlier towards English interests (IOR, G/12/1, fl. 59).
55 IOR, G/12/1, fl. 60, and G/12/10, fls. 82–84.
56 IOR, G/12/1, fl. 60.
57 E.B. Sainsbury and W. Foster (eds), *A Calendar of the Court Minutes of the East India Company 1635–1639*, London: Clarendon Press, 1907, pp. 120–121.
58 In December 1635, Charles I granted a charter establishing the William Courteen Association, which was the first main competitor of the EIC in Asia. The interloping company was owned by the London merchant Sir William Courteen (1600–1649) and held the right to trade for five years at any Asian port in which there was no EIC factory already established. The company was poorly managed and

collapsed before 1646, but before that it sent several ships to Portuguese ports in Asia, including Macao.

59 IOR, G/12/10, fls. 107–110, Arquivo Histórico Ultramarino (AHU, Lisbon), *Macao*, box 1, doc. 42, AN/TT, *Livros das Monções*, book 48, fls. 287v, 294v, AHG, FUP, *Livro dos Segredos*, n. 1, fl. 67.

60 AN/TT, *Livros das Monções*, book 48, fl. 287v, book 50, fl. 124v. On the several Portuguese chartering of English ships, see Blanco, *O Estado Português da Índia* (*The Portuguese "Estado da Índia"*), pp. 552, 585 (footnotes 418–421), 586 (footnotes 422–424), which summarizes this Portuguese strategy to outflank the Dutch blockade. The author states that in 1644 the vessels *Hind*, from Swahili (Surat factory), and *William*, belonging respectively to the EIC and the Courteen Association, went to Macao in the service of the Portuguese Crown with munitions and gunpowder, which would be exchanged for cinnamon.

61 AN/TT, *Livros das Monções*, book 33, fl. 249.

62 IOR, G/12/68, fl. 6, G/12/89, fl. 65, IOR, R/10/6, fl. 192; Sainsbury and Foster, *A Calendar of the Court Minutes Etc. of the East India Company 1640–1643*, p. 151; Foster, *The English Factories in India 1642–1645*, p. 36.

63 Count Linhares, *Diário do 3.º Conde de Linhares, Vice-Rei da Índia* (*Diary of the Third Count of Linhares, Vice-Roy of India*), Lisbon: Biblioteca Nacional, 1937–1943 [1631–1634], p. 267.

7 The Cushing mission to Macao and US imperial expansion in nineteenth-century Asia*

He Sibing

Introduction: the China trade and the genesis of US-Asia relations

The late eighteenth century witnessed an entrepreneurial explosion of America's economic activities in the Asia-Pacific. The coming of Americans to Asia was marked by the historic voyage of the *Empress of China* to Macao in 1784.[1] This voyage not only initiated America's direct trade with Canton, but also marked the beginning of the age of American expansion into Asia.[2] Business entrepreneurs in the United States eagerly positioned themselves to explore the potential Asian markets. This development of American trade came at a time when England was rising in the East on the back of the opium trade while Europe's continental powers were declining.[3] The Napoleonic conquest of Holland created an opportunity for American traders to get involved in Dutch trade. They were commissioned to ship Dutch cargos to Nagasaki and Canton. This situation allowed the neutral Americans to replace continental European shipping, which averaged fewer than three arrivals at Canton per year by 1804 and dropped to non-arrival by 1809.[4] The French trading house in Canton was taken over by Americans. Thanks to the French Wars, US trade boomed in Asia. By 1800 more than 100 American trading ships had arrived in Canton via Macao, and in 1804 at least 74 American vessels visited Batavia.[5] American trading ships also began to call at Bangkok in 1821, and participate in the lucrative rice trade between Canton and the Spanish Philippines in the 1830s.[6]

American trade with Asia was the cardinal nexus out of which diplomacy, missionary activity and cultural exchange ultimately evolved. Following the free trade rationale, the United States utilized and refined the political technique of imperial expansion developed by the British and imposed the treaty of 'free trade and friendship' on weaker states in Asia.[7] Following the model of the Anglo-Siamese Treaty of 1826, American envoy Edward Roberts successfully concluded the Treaty of Amity and Commerce between Siam and the United States at the royal city of Bangkok in 1833. A decade later, in the wake of Britain's victory over China in the First Opium War, upon the petitions of the China traders led by partners of Russell and Company,[8] President John

Tyler appointed Caleb Cushing, a Massachusetts congressman closely associated with the China traders, as the first American minister to China. On 3
July 1844, the United States concluded the first treaty with China at Wangxia,
a village on the outskirts of the Portuguese coastal settlement of Macao.

American merchants in the Canton trade formed a mercantile community
in Macao that became the first Sino-American meeting place. The presence
of an American community in Macao was responsible for the relationship
between the opium smuggling business and the Treaty of Wangxia. The origins of American policy toward China lay among the American residents in
the Canton-Macao area. The first Sino-American treaty included all those
provisions the China traders desired, which laid the foundation for an imperial American sovereignty in Asia and the Pacific in the nineteenth century. As
a traditional entrepôt and the sole European settlement on the China coast,
Macao functioned as a nexus between the old celestial empire and the emerging
imperial state in the new continent, playing a pivotal role in the evolution of
the early Sino-American relations.[9] Written as a research survey,[10] this chapter
reviews the literature on the Treaty of Wangxia and reassesses Caleb Cushing's
diplomatic endeavours in Macao from the perspective of American imperial
expansion in Asia. It also provides a sketch of Cushing as a critical observer
during his six-month sojourn in Macao, discussing his keen observations of
social customs, cultural differences, and daily life of the common people in the
Portuguese outpost on the periphery of a 'pagan state' in the Orient.

Historiographical survey

Cushing's mission to China has been a much-studied subject in the literature
on the early American-East Asian relations. Researchers often view this
mission in the context of their own historical period, defining issues partially
in terms of present concerns. Interpretations about the origins of US China
policy therefore have been subjected to constant challenge and modification.
One long-standing thesis holds that the primary objective of the United States
in East Asia in the mid-nineteenth century was to boost American economic
and sentimental interests in China. Therefore, the initial policy of maintenance
of an 'open door' and the integrity of China was adopted. Tyler Dennett's
standard account of US Asia policy, *Americans in Eastern Asia*,[11] emphasizes
America's intent to cooperate with European powers in China to allow Asian
nations to maintain independence and strengthen themselves.[12] Subsequent
studies continued to view the Cushing mission as the origin of a consistent US
East Asia policy, culminating in the 'open door' notes of 1899–1900.

The first doctoral dissertation on the Treaty of Wangxia was completed
in 1918 by Harry G. Dildine. In this comprehensive study of the first Sino-
American treaty, the author believes that in Cushing's treaty the United States
established a special relationship with China. Compared with their European
colleagues, according to Dildine, the Americans were more pacific and hon-
ourable. Due to lack of access to either Cushing's manuscripts or Chinese

diplomatic documents, this study could not effectively assess the negotiating process and the impact of the American diplomacy on the Chinese empire.[13] Claude Fuess was perhaps one of the first scholars to have access to Cushing's personal manuscripts. His classic account published in 1923 was the only biography of Cushing that researchers heavily relied on until John Belohlavek's new biographical study of Cushing came out in 2005.[14] In his essay published in 1933, Ping Chia Kuo provides revealing insights into the Cushing mission by utilizing the then recently published Chinese diplomatic documents relevant to the treaty negotiations, *Chouban Yiwu Shimo* (*The Beginning and End of the Management of Barbarian Affairs*).[15] The negotiating process, Kuo points out, was facilitated by a difference between imperial commissioner Qiying and Cushing's respective purposes. To prevent Cushing from attempting to proceed to Beijing was Qiying's primary concern. The concession of commercial privileges to the Americans was merely a moderate importance on the imperial commissioner's agenda. Due to his ignorance of international law, Qiying paid little heed to the question of extraterritoriality. However, Kuo's study could not fully analyse the combination of the Cushing papers, the US official correspondence and the newly-released Chinese documents. The objective of a balanced study is achieved in Ming-shun Chiao's 1954 doctoral dissertation, which combines the American diplomatic correspondence, the Cushing papers and the Chinese documents in an analysis of the Cushing mission and the Treaty of Wangxia.[16] It illuminates the proceedings in a way Fuess' biography of Cushing failed to achieve, specifically by relating Cushing's early political experience in Congress to the mission and by highlighting Cushing's relationship in Macao to his missionary advisers Peter Parker and Elijah Bridgman. The political-economic background is the focus of this dissertation and its conclusion is consistent with the previous studies on the subject. The historical appraisal had remained much the same since the 1920s, as Richard W. Welch, Jr. concludes in his survey published in 1957.[17]

In a heavily used survey of the early Chinese-American diplomatic relations, which was first published in Taibei in 1961, revised in 1979, and then reprinted in Beijing in 1997, Li Dingyi devotes a chapter to the Sino-American treaty negotiations in Macao.[18] This study is primarily based on the documents in *Chouban Yiwu Shimo* and a limited use of secondary works by American scholars. Although it contains an in-depth analysis of the Chinese documents, this study is hindered by the lack of use of primary sources from the United States. Much more bi-archival research still remains to be done. In a doctoral dissertation completed in 1976, Jeffrey Robert Biggs attempts to weigh the Cushing papers, American official correspondence and the English translation of Chinese diplomatic documents against each other in order to gain a more balanced interpretation. He argues that the 'treaty provisions lay quite outside the official instructions and can be interpreted only as an expression of Cushing's "gentleman-scholar" approach to diplomacy'.[19] This assertion indicates that the author fails to perceive Cushing's imperial aspirations. Motivated by his sense of mission, Cushing actually acted as an aggressive empire-builder rather than a 'gentleman-scholar' in Macao. The extraterritorial privileges Cushing added in his treaty, in practice, justified the use of military power to protect American commercial interests in its informal empire. Biggs also misinterprets Cushing's personal manuscripts and Secretary of State Daniel Webster's instructions and claims that reaching Beijing was a clearly designated objective of Cushing's mission. The next significant study of the subject appeared in 1977. In 'The Treaty of Wanghia', a chapter in his book on the early Sino-American relations, Earl Swisher extensively examines the Chinese diplomatic documents in *Chouban Yiwu Shimo*, revealing how imperial commissioner Qiying's false perception of the foreigners affected his negotiating strategy.[20]

During the last two decades of the twentieth century, a disproportionally large number of studies on American diplomatic history focused on the contemporary period. The preoccupation with the newly available records of the Cold War era has resulted in an increasingly serious problem: the post-World War II period is overemphasized while the earlier periods, especially the nineteenth century, are generally neglected. This, as Professor Michael H. Hunt noted, has led to 'an ironic diminution of historical perspective on the part of historians'.[21] The only significant study relevant to the Treaty of Wangxia published in this period is perhaps Jacques M. Downs' meticulous study of the American commercial community in Canton.[22] Three chapters of this book deal with the treaty negotiation.

The new century saw a reviving scholarly interest in the Cushing mission and the Wangxia treaty. In 2005, *American Quarterly,* the journal of the American Studies Association, published international law scholar Teemu Ruskola's essay on Cushing's invention of American imperial sovereignty in the Treaty of Wangxia.[23] Historian Belohlavek's new biography of Cushing was also published in the same year, a chapter of which is devoted to the China mission, providing new insights on Cushing's activities in Macao.[24] In 2007, the journal of the Society for Historians of American Foreign Relations, *Diplomatic History*, published independent historian Macabe Keliher's article on the origins of US China policy, which reinterprets the Cushing mission.[25] This recent scholarship will be discussed further in the following analyses of the Cushing mission.

Launching the mission to Macao

The 1842 Sino-British Treaty of Nanjing legitimated what the opium trade had already established, and required China to end its traditional tribute system and to accept the European conception of international relations. However, the extent to which the United States would share in the privileges obtained by the British was uncertain. This situation rendered necessary the sending of an American commissioner to China. The major task of the China mission would be to determine whether American ships could obtain equal access to the trading ports opened by the Sino-British Treaty. The justification for dispatching a commissioner to China, as President John Tyler stated in his message to Congress on 30 December 1842, was that 'the commercial interests of the United States connected with China' required 'at the present moment a degree of attention and vigilance'.[26]

Because of the unstable politics in Washington, the US Senate did not take final action on the China mission until 3 March 1843. Congress approved the bill to establish 'the future commercial relations of the United States with China on terms of equal reciprocity', and the Senate Foreign Relations Committee endorsed the president's recommendation and approved an appropriation of $40,000 for a China mission. Tyler nominated Caleb Cushing, a lawyer from Newburyport, Massachusetts, and a powerful member of the House Committee on Foreign Affairs, to head the mission. Raised in a family of seafaring tradition, Cushing had wide connections with the China traders. Cushing's close association with the families of the China trade raised concerns among political insiders as well as merchants.[27] Despite his political opponent's criticism, as a trusted confidant of the president, Cushing confidently forged his new career as diplomat.

Before this appointment, Cushing had been exerting his influence to pressure the Tyler administration to dispatch a mission to China. In December 1842 Cushing told Tyler that while Britain did not seek privileges 'for her own benefit only', other countries that desired 'like advantages' would have to engage China to acquire them on their own account. He strongly endorsed the petitions of American traders in Canton and Macao, and those of Boston and Salem, all of which urged the sending of a 'respectable national force' to China. Cushing proposed that the president should send 'an Agent' not only to China, but, after the successful conclusion of treaty negotiations, also to Japan 'for the same purpose'.[28] In his message to Congress at the end of 1842, which was written by Daniel Webster, President Tyler fully agreed with Cushing that the new situation after the Opium War required an American diplomatic presence in China.

China traders and the formulation of China policy

To base his China policy on sufficient available intelligence, on 20 March 1843, Webster issued a circular on behalf of the Department of State asking 'intelligent persons' who were acquainted with China and who had been 'concerned extensively in the trade between it and the United States' to provide the department with 'opinions and suggestions' on how to cultivate 'friendly relations' with that nation and on how to open and enlarge 'commercial intercourse between the two countries'. 'The general objects of the mission', the circular states, would 'sufficiently indicate the points to which these suggestions may refer'.[29] The merchants associated with the China trade quickly responded to Webster's circular. The carefully considered responses were not only helpful to Webster in preparing the instructions for Cushing but also provided important sources of historical information about the China trade under the Canton system and the attitudes of the American merchants toward the Chinese empire.

The most important response Webster received was from John M. Forbes, a former partner of Russell and Company who was designated by the Boston merchants engaged in the China trade to be their spokesman.[30] Forbes expressed the primary concern of those who responded to the circular: American trade should be admitted to the China market 'upon the same footing with the most favored nation'.[31] The China traders proposed to send diplomats with warships to intimidate China. On the other hand, they understood that their government was not ready to use military forces in China. Having carefully considered the British role in the Sino-Western relations, they believed that the best US policy would be to follow and to ride the coattails of England, sharing the privileges gained by them.

The opinions and suggestions of those who responded to the circular had a perceivable impact on the instructions of 8 May 1843, which Webster prepared with unusual care. Based on the information provided by the China traders, Webster specified three goals for the Cushing mission: the 'leading object of the Mission' was 'to secure the entry of American ships and cargoes into these ports, on terms as favourable as those which are enjoyed by English merchants' and to try to see the emperor in person, although this was a secondary objective and used primarily as a threat with which to coerce Beijing to grant American commercial rights. Cushing was given the option to abandon the trip to the Chinese capital if it endangered securing 'most favoured nation' status in China. Cushing's directive was to negotiate a treaty equalling or surpassing the concessions granted to Britain.[32] These instructions to Cushing established the basis of American foreign policy toward China and led to the establishment of formal relations between the two nations in 1844.

Cushing's diplomatic endeavours in Macao

Following Webster's directives, Cushing left for China on 31 July 1843. A squadron was assigned to escort the mission, which included four warships mounting more than 200 guns. In Canton, the American merchant consul, Paul S. Forbes of Russell and Company, informed the Chinese authorities in October 1843 of Cushing's impending arrival and his intention to proceed to Beijing.[33] Imperial Commissioner Qiying notified Forbes that the American mission to Beijing was unnecessary since he had been authorized 'to settle all commercial intercourse with foreign nations'. Strongly opposing Cushing's journey to the capital, the commissioner urged Forbes to detain Cushing in Guangdong.[34] Besides, the Chinese authorities did not think it was necessary to negotiate a treaty with the United States for all privileges obtained by the British had been extended to the Americans. Forbes agreed to try to stop the mission but refused to make any promise. In his report to the State Department, however, he suggested that 'the point would be yielded if insisted upon'.[35]

On 24 February 1844, the vessel *Brandywine*, carrying the Cushing legation, dropped anchor in Macao Roads. Cushing declined an offer from Forbes to quarter him in Russell and Company's factory, but remained on the warship for four additional days and did not land in Macao until 27 February, after renting a house on the 'Praia Grande' belonging to a former Portuguese governor as the legation's residence.[36] Cushing appointed Peter Parker and Elijah Bridgman, both American missionaries in China, as 'Chinese Secretaries' who would serve as translators. Bridgman was the editor of *The Chinese Repository*, a forceful organ of militant Protestantism in China, which advocated war against China.[37] Parker had met Cushing before when he visited the United States in 1841 to request the American government to send a minister to Beijing to secure trading privileges.[38] As a missionary doctor in Canton, Parker had become well-acquainted with the Hong merchants as well as Qiying and other Chinese officials. These connections enabled Parker to play a crucial role in the treaty negotiations.[39]

The arrival of the Cushing legation caused a sensation among the American community in Macao. American merchants now demonstrated mixed feelings toward Cushing's mission, because the situation had greatly changed since 1839, when American merchants petitioned Congress on the eve of the Opium War for a commissioner to acquire a commercial treaty. As Cushing settled in Macao, he received news from US Minister Edward Everett in London. A supplementary Anglo-Chinese treaty negotiated in 1843 had granted 'most favoured nation' status to all foreign merchants. Cushing immediately dispatched a member of the legation to Hong Kong to visit Governor Henry Pottinger to ask advice regarding how to negotiate with the Chinese. The British official cordially received the American diplomat and provided him with the supplementary Anglo-Chinese treaty signed in Humen (the Bogue). Meanwhile, Qing officials reaffirmed that American traders would receive the privileges granted to the British. Cushing's mission now seemed to become unnecessary. In the view of some traders, this mission would be harmful if Cushing conducted prolonged and perhaps offensive negotiations since these might destroy their favourable trade environment and so jeopardize rather than improve their commercial relations with the Chinese.[40]

Notwithstanding the debatable need to continue his mission, Cushing still firmly believed that the United States should secure respect and privileges by negotiating its own bilateral agreement with China rather than relying on a treaty obtained by the British. To Cushing, it was a matter of national honour. He therefore decided to press on. Under these circumstances, however, Cushing was in no strong position to insist on going to Beijing. Dissuaded by the Chinese officials from proceeding northward and lacking sufficient naval forces to intimidate the Chinese, Cushing stayed in Macao to communicate with the acting governor-general of Guangdong while awaiting the arrival of the imperial commissioner from Beijing. In practice, a personal interview with the emperor was not a genuine objective of the mission, but used essentially as a means to pressure Beijing to yield to American demands. This means of coercion proved to be very effective. On the other hand, by remaining in Macao, the legation could conveniently solicit whatever assistance it needed from the US merchant-consul and the commercial-missionary establishments in the Macao-Canton area. Meanwhile, the American diplomats could also enjoy Anglo-American social life in the exotic European enclave.

To detain Cushing on the periphery of the Chinese empire in order to maintain the emperor's sense of distance was apparently Qiying's major concern. He was determined at all costs to prevent Cushing's trip from going to Beijing. Macao was the ideal place to contain the barbarians and to minimize their contact with the Chinese people. By basing himself in Wangxia, just outside the walled city of Macao, the imperial commissioner could stay comfortably on his own turf, which was securely controlled by the Chinese authorities, yet conveniently close enough to allow him to interact with the American legation within the city. Canton might have been an alternative venue, but although the 1842 Treaty of Nanjing had made that city one of the treaty ports opened to foreigners, at that time the Cantonese, led by the local gentry, were still consistently denying foreigners access to their city. The presence of American officials within Canton would have undoubtedly stirred up unrest among the masses, with potentially serious consequences. Indeed, even in Macao robbers made five assaults on the residence of the American legation, and on one such occasion succeeded in gaining entry, so that the American officials habitually carried arms for their own protection. Qiying could not guarantee the safety of the American representatives in Canton. It was probably due to these considerations that he opted to deal with Cushing in Wangxia and Macao. To show the Chinese that Americans were not sided with the British, Cushing would not propose to negotiate with the imperial commissioner in Hong Kong. Therefore, he accepted Qiying's arrangements.

While the two sides spent several months engaged in prolonged exchanges of correspondence, the impatient Cushing ordered warship *Brandywine* to sail up the Pearl River on 13 April to pay a 'courtesy call' on Governor Cheng at Huangpu. Cushing also informed Cheng that, in addition to the long-delayed *St. Louis* and the *Perry*, two of the four warships assigned to escort the legation to Macao, the East India Squadron would arrive on the Chinese coast soon. With the arrival of additional naval ships in early June, Cushing became even more aggressive. He reported the change of his strategy to the State Department, stating that if negotiation with Qiying in Macao did not go well, he was now ready to proceed north with the squadron available to compel the Chinese to yield to his demands.[41]

After making these demonstrations of military force and threatening that if the Chinese declined to meet with him, this would be 'considered an act of national insult, and a just cause for war', on 21 June Cushing finally met Imperial Commissioner Qiying, at the American legation's residence in Macao. The first meeting of the two commissioners focused on the impossibility of Cushing visiting Beijing. The Chinese court was not prepared to receive foreign legations, explained Qiying. If Americans were allowed to go to the imperial capital, then other nations would make the same demands, and the Chinese would not be able to manage them. Cushing returned the visit the following day at the headquarters of the Chinese legation in Wangxia. At this meeting, Cushing stressed that the United States desired for peace and friendly relations and did not demand territorial concession from China. Qiying asked for a draft of the treaty the American desired. The specific terms of the treaty, both sides agreed, would be worked out by the two commissioners' top subordinates. Their negotiations lasted less than three weeks, taking place alternatively in Wangxia and in Macao. Fearing that, if Cushing's demands were not satisfied, he would proceed north to Beijing with his naval squadron, on 3 July 1844 Qiying hastily signed a Treaty of Peace, Amity and Commerce with the United States at the Temple of the Goddess of Mercy (Guanyin Tang) in Wangxia. Backed by a small squadron as well as the presence of the US naval forces in the Pacific, Cushing thus easily won the favourable treaty he sought. Under its terms, China was obligated to allow Americans to trade freely in Canton as well as in four other previously closed ports. Moreover, Americans obtained the right of extraterritorial jurisdiction in China. By accepting the principle of 'most favoured nation' treatment, China established a precedent for future arrangements with Western powers.

Cushing as a critical observer

Scholarship by diplomatic historians has generally neglected the social and cultural environment in which the Cushing mission took place. Only the new biography by Belohlavek offers some insights into Cushing's perception of the local society and people in Macao. During his six-month sojourn in Macao, Cushing remained a shrewd observer of the environment, which would have seemed totally exotic to a New Englander. He recorded street life, culture, language, geography and climate in detail. He even developed a taste for Chinese art and called a prominent Chinese painter he met a 'genius'. Cushing began to learn Chinese on his long journey to China. In Macao, while continuing his language studies, he frequented bookstores in the Chinese quarter despite the fact that he was often surrounded by scores of curious spectators on such occasions. A library of more than 200 Chinese books that he accumulated in Macao later became the nucleus of the Library of Congress' Orientalia Collection.[42]

Cushing made extensive observation on daily life of the boat people, beggars, lepers, thieves and prostitutes in Macao, but he did not show any sympathy for these unfortunate people, which was consistent with his attitude toward social problems in America and Europe. Cushing was 'a critical observer, not a social reformer', as his biographer Belohlavek observes. The practice of foot-binding was also the subject of Cushing's scrutiny. Comparing it with the popular American fashion of corseting and crushing the chests of women, he claimed that foot-binding 'would be no more absurd, but uncomfortable to the individual and less dangerous'. He often compared his own observations with those written by the British. In contrast to an observation by an English authority who described the Chinese as a dirty, 'noisy, nasty, and nefarious people', Cushing believed that the Chinese appeared to be cleaner than the

English or Americans of the same social class. The creativity, manners and work ethic of the Chinese people were highly regarded by Cushing. The hard-working and muscular Chinese labourers, he noted, could be easily trained to be good soldiers who 'under Tartar or European leaders might conquer the world'. Cushing not only developed a good working relation with his Chinese counterpart Qiying, but actually held a deep respect for him. Before Cushing's departure for the United States on 27 August 1844, Qiying sent him a life-size portrait. This appeasement technique had been used by the imperial commissioner repeatedly to cultivate intimate friendships with Western diplomats and it seemed effective. Soon after his return to Old Essex, Massachusetts, Cushing honoured the Chinese commissioner by christening a new family ship the *Keying* (*Qiying*).[43]

According to Belohlavek, Cushing arguably 'had greater respect for the Chinese than the resident European community'.[44] Interestingly, Cushing regarded the multilingual Portuguese as an intelligent and gentlemanly people who were 'superior to other foreigners in knowledge and character'. In contrast, he disliked the English and American merchants, believing that most of them were 'money grubbing traders and not particularly intellectual in their taste'. Cushing didn't have much respect for the Protestant missionaries either, saying that they were 'mere school wardens to children' and that their missionary works were 'a misappropriation of funds'. It is ironic that the minister felt contempt for the commercial-missionary community that fervently supported his mission. The resident American community in Macao in fact had great respect for their diplomatic representative. For example, soon after the welcome party for Cushing in Macao, Mrs Nathaniel Kinsman, the wife of a partner in Wetmore and Company, reported enthusiastically to her husband in Canton that 'the Minister looked splendidly'.[45] At the end of the mission, the American community in Canton sent Cushing a letter signed by 25 merchants to express their gratitude. Nevertheless, their good feeling toward him didn't affect his keen observation and intuition.

The Cushing mission and the founding of America's informal empire in Asia

The first US mission to China was, as Daniel Webster called it, the most important American diplomatic mission of his times. Webster's instructions to Cushing of 8 May 1843 constituted the first coherent US policy toward China, establishing the basis of American foreign policy for the next half a century. In this sense, the instructions could be viewed as the foundation of the Open Door doctrine of 1899–1900. Although Webster did not concern himself with China's sovereignty, he did insist that all countries maintain equal access to China's markets and not fall under the influence of a single Western power.[46]

In addition to the commercial concessions of the Treaty of Nanjing and a clause granting 'most favoured nation' status, Cushing's treaty included four significant provisions: first, it validated and extended the doctrine of extraterritoriality; second, it laid out procedures for establishing formal diplomatic exchanges and relations; third, it gave Americans rights to build hospitals, churches and cemeteries in the treaty ports; and fourth, it stipulated that at the end of 12 years either nation could renegotiate the treaty. This provision for treaty revision later provided aggressive Westerners with an opportunity to seek further concession from China and resulted in the Second Opium War. Throughout modern Chinese history, the condition of extraterritoriality remained a contentious issue. Under American military coercion and lacking basic knowledge of international law, Qiying made no objection to the provisions for extraterritoriality because he thought the concept of extraterritoriality was consistent with the traditional Chinese mode of handling barbarians by letting them regulate themselves. The result was that, from 1844 until 1943, American citizens in China were subject only to the laws of the United States.

To obtain the right of extraterritoriality was not part of Webster's instructions to Cushing. In his memorandum to the State Department, Cushing justified the addition of the extraterritoriality clause to the treaty, explaining why this clause was 'essential' to the 'honour' of the United States. The origins of extraterritoriality, according to Cushing, could be traced back to the religious exemption of Christians from the jurisdiction of the Ottoman Empire. He argued that the general principles of international law 'only apply to the intercourse of no states but those of Christendom'. The United States had previously signed extraterritoriality treaties with 'the Barbary states', the Porte and the Imam of Muscat, he stated. According to his religious justification of the doctrine of extraterritoriality and historical precedents, the right of Western extraterritoriality certainly could apply in the 'pagan' states of Asia, including China. But as comparative law professor Teemu Ruskola points out, the historical precedents of extraterritoriality given by Cushing omitted the important fact that most of the treaties between the United States and the Barbary States included a reciprocal right of extraterritorial jurisdiction.[47] The Treaty of Wangxia, however, stipulated no such reciprocity. The 1833 Treaty of Amity and Commerce with Siam, of which Cushing made no mention whatever, stipulated American submission to Siamese jurisdiction. Reviewing other relevant precedents, Ruskola finds that none of the US treaties with the Sandwich Islands (1826), Tahiti (1826), Samoa (1839) and Sulu (1842), provided for American extraterritoriality. In practice, the 1844 Treaty of Wangxia became the model for subsequent American extraterritoriality treaties with other nations in Asia and the Pacific, including the treaties with Borneo (1850), Japan (1857), Samoa (1878), Korea (1882) and Tonga (1886). In 1856 the United States also acquired extraterritoriality in Siam through treaty revision. The Wangxia Treaty can therefore be regarded as representing the beginning of a new era in the American political relations with Asia.

The United States did not merely exercise its power abroad through economic and military might. International law has also been utilized as an important instrument in American overseas expansion. In the early republic, American leaders held the 'liberal notion of sovereign equality' to serve the country's own national interests in order to survive in a hostile international environment. By the mid-nineteenth century, this notion had been replaced by 'an imperial American sovereignty in the Pacific'. In his China mission, Cushing revised the early diplomatic history of the United States by inventing a tradition of US extraterritoriality in 'Oriental' states. 'This extraterritoriality,' as Ruskola notes, 'in turn protected American commercial interests in Asia, while real or alleged violations of extraterritorial privileges justified the occasional use of military power to protect America's "rights" under the law of nations'.[48]

Until the outbreak of the Opium War in 1839, it appeared that the United States in practice respected the sovereign equality of China and other Asian nations despite Britain and other European powers had already utilized extraterritoriality to deal with peoples in non-Western world. Thomas Jefferson, for example, made an exception to the Embargo Act for a Chinese in 1808 because he believed that China as a sovereign nation deserved the respect. In the 1833 treaty with Siam, the United States admitted that American citizens in Siam would be subject to Siamese law. The Treaty of Wangxia signified that the United States no longer recognized the sovereign equality of the Asian nations. With the extraterritorial privileges, the treaty established imperial American sovereignty in the Pacific in the second half of the nineteenth century. It also became the model for European powers to acquire their own extraterritoriality treaties in the age of imperialism.[49]

Driven by his sense of mission, Cushing not only intended to open China for America's 'free trade', but also aggressively planned to forge America's informal empire in Asia through imposing treaty of 'free trade' on other Asian states. In January 1844 when he was still on his way to Macao, Cushing sent a private letter to Tyler requesting permission to proceed to Japan after completing the treaty negotiation in China. But Tyler lacked confidence in such a mission and expressed that 'little probability exists of effecting any commercial arrangement with that country'. He was reluctant to give sanction to the Japan mission in an election year because he feared that a diplomatic failure would affect his prospects for re-election. Not until August 1844 did Tyler and Secretary of State John C. Calhoun grant Cushing the approval requested. When Cushing received Calhoun's instructions for the Japan mission, however, he had departed from Macao for several months.[50] The diplomatic mission to Japan did not materialize until the Perry expedition of 1853 when Webster served as Secretary of State under President Millard Fillmore. When Webster instituted the Japan mission, the China market was still his primary concern.[51] Anticipating the eventual establishment of a line of steamships between California and Shanghai, he wanted Japan to supply fuel for the China trade because he believed that the creator had deposited coal 'in the depths of the Japanese islands'. This view was expressed explicitly in his instructions to John Aulick, the commander of the East India Squadron.[52]

Webster shared the same imperial inspiration with Cushing for establishing an American trading empire in Asia and the Pacific. He successfully instituted the Japan mission Cushing attempted to undertake years earlier, acquiring an open door to the markets and ports of the Pacific region without territorial expansion. The foundation of this informal empire was commercial expansion supported by a willingness to maintain 'the freedom of trade' by using military force to guarantee unhindered access to the markets on a 'most favoured nation' basis.

Historians have presented various interpretations on why US politicians and officials became interested in direct intervention in China in the mid-nineteenth century, and thus constructed the foundational China policy. In his article in *Diplomatic History*, Macabe Keliher argues: 'It was bitter rivalry with Britain for markets and influence in the Pacific that forced US politicians and bureaucrats to assume a positive role in East Asia in the early 1840s.'[53] He notes that before the Opium War, American traders in China had repeatedly appealed to Washington for governmental support of their commercial endeavours, but the US government remained inactive until Britain gained new trading concession and territory in the conclusion of the First Opium War in 1842. This situation compelled Washington to dispatch a mission to China to negotiate a treaty for securing rights that matched those that the British had gained. Otherwise, the United States would lose a huge market to Britain. Keliher concludes: 'The mission to China and the treaty resulted from it was the reflection of a strong and autonomous China policy, a policy that found another voice in the Open Door notes half a century later.'[54] Dismissing the conventional interpretations that the United States and Britain were predominantly cooperative in regard to China and that, prior to the Open Door policy, the United States did not have its own independent policy in China but merely followed Britain's lead, Keliher emphasizes the rivalry and antagonism between the United States and Britain in China. He continues:

> It was the threat of British monopoly of the Pacific markets that forced the U.S. government to move from a passive to an active role in Americans' interaction with China, and which led to the direct articulation of a China policy in the form of the Wangxia Treaty of 1844.[55]

While undoubtedly shifting the emphasis from the cooperation to the antagonism between the United States and England, Keliher's revisionist arguments neglect the extensive evidence found in the China trade archives about the lives of those conducting trade missions and shaping diplomatic policy. Since the Americans arrived in China in the late eighteenth century, the EIC had been allowing US vessels to trade with British India, and the company had to compete with American firms on equal terms in Calcutta. American traders were also permitted to do business in the British East Indies by black-letter law. The Jay Treaty of 1794, which was designed to hinder dispute between America and Britain from turning into open hostilities, granted the United States 'most favoured nation' status in EIC possessions. US merchantmen therefore could go to any ports open to the British.[56] Correspondence between Russell and Company and Jardine Matheson and Company reveal partners of the Russell firm had good working relations with their British counterparts in the Canton-Macao area.[57] In Canton, American traders worked closely with the British beginning with the arrival of the *Empress of China*; and in Macao residents of both nationalities socialized intimately with each other, sharing both a pride in their Anglo-Saxon heritage and similar racial prejudices. During the pre-treaty days, an extensive Anglo-American social life developed within the European enclave. Protestant missionaries from both countries often preached together and cofounded and worked for the same benevolent organizations, cooperating to advance their spiritual enterprises in China.[58] There was little evidence to indicate that American diplomats regarded the British officers as their rivals. Upon his arrival in Macao, Cushing – whom Keliher describes as Anglophobic[59] – immediately contacted the governor of Hong Kong for advice regarding how to deal with the Chinese in treaty negotiation. The British governor cordially sent him copies of the treaty negotiated with China. The bitter rivalry and antagonism between the United States and Britain in other parts of the world did not carry over into China where corporations from different nations collaborated in setting the conditions of 'free trade'. The Treaty of Nanjing did not deny American access to the China market and all the privileges that the British had gained through war were automatically granted to other nations, including the United States. It is nevertheless true that American statesmen such as Daniel Webster and John Tyler firmly believed that the United States should secure respect and privileges by negotiating its own bilateral agreement with China rather than relying on a treaty obtained by the British. To Cushing, it was a matter of national honour. But this was not a bitter rivalry with England.

Before the Opium War when the US government maintained a lax attitude toward China, American traders were compelled to improvise their strategies as they negotiated with Cohong merchants and pursued their commercial interests. The key elements in their improvised policies were maintaining the equal conditions of trade and insisting on a formal stance of neutrality in the conflicts between Great Britain and China. They did not always follow the lead set by the British. During the opium crisis of 1839, for example, American traders in Canton did not follow the British retreat to Macao. They instead remained in Canton to carry on their lucrative business, taking advantage of the absence of their business competitors. Even this competitive advantage was not a sign of bitter rivalry and the American trading presence in Canton during this period proved beneficial for both British and American traders.[60] These 'bizarrely competitive and cooperative connections' between the Americans and British in the East, as a recent study of Anglo-American East Indies trade observes, endured in the nineteenth century.[61]

Before the Sino-British war, when the partners in Russell and Company repeatedly requested Washington to send diplomats with warships to protect their economic interests in Canton, they were well-aware that their government was not ready to use military forces in China. They therefore suggested that the best US policy was to follow other Western powers led by Britain in order to share the privileges gained by them. After the Treaty of Nanjing was signed in 1842, when the Chinese authorities had been severely weakened, the China traders seized this opportunity to call upon Washington to negotiate a treaty with China, demanding privileges similar to those granted to the British. The Treaty of Wangxia reflected the China policy formulated by the Canton traders and exemplified that the Americans had utilized and refined the free trade rationale and the political technique advanced by the British to forge its own informal empire in East Asia in the nineteenth century.

Epilogue: 'The Great Chinese Museum' and the justification of the Cushing mission

Shortly after Cushing's return to the United States from his triumphal mission on 31 December 1844, an exhibit called 'The Great Chinese Museum' was opened in Boston on 8 September 1845. This exhibit, which was funded by American missionaries and Chinese merchants, included items assembled by at least two of the China mission's members: Cushing and John R. Peters, Jr., one of the four volunteer attaches of the legation. After Cushing's departure, Peters stayed in China to collect Chinese artefacts for his father, John Peters, Sr., who was to set up a massive expo on China to exhibit the 'Largest Collection of the Kind in the Nation'.

The handbook to the exhibit was supposedly written by Peters, Jr. The exhibition opened with a life-size tableau of the Chinese emperor (instead of the imperial commissioner) holding a brush as reference to the signing of the Treaty of Wangxia. This distorted representation of the treaty-signing ceremony was obviously intended to aggrandize the Cushing mission and clearly underscored the political implications of this exhibit. A life-size portrait of Qiying provided by Cushing was also among the objects displayed in the museum, but it was overshadowed by the fabricated image of the emperor. By showcasing Chinese products and artefacts within the context of enlightened relativism, the museum intended to convey the images that China was more 'a complex civilization amenable to diplomatic trade relations than as a culturally destitute land ripe for Euro-American conquest'. This exhibit, therefore, served to justify Cushing's diplomatic efforts leading to the conclusion of the first Sino-American treaty.[62]

Notes

* An earlier version of this chapter appears in *Review of Culture*, International Edition, 35, July 2010, pp. 135–152.

1 On this voyage, see Philip Chadwick Foster Smith, *The Empress of China*, Philadelphia, PA: Philadelphia Maritime Museum, 1984; and Samuel Shaw, *The Journals of Major Samuel Shaw, the First American Consul at Canton*, Boston: Wm. Crosby and H.P. Nichols, 1847.

2 Arthur Power Dudden, *The American Pacific: From the Old China Trade to the Present*, New York: Oxford University Press, 1992; Arrel M. Gibson, *Yankees in Paradise: The Pacific Basin Frontier*, Albuquerque: University of New Mexico Press, 1993; Donald D. Johnson with Gary Dean Best, *The United States in the Pacific: Private Interests and Public Policies, 1784–1899*, Westport, CT: Praeger, 1995.

3 Leonard Blussé, *Visible Cities: Canton, Nagasaki, and Batavia and the Coming of the Americans*, Cambridge, MA: Harvard University Press, 2008.

4 Yen-p'ing Hao, 'Chinese Teas to America – A Synopsis', in Ernest R. May and John K. Fairbank (eds), *America's China Trade in Historical Perspective*, Cambridge, MA: Harvard University Press, 1986, p. 15.

5 Foster Rhea Dulles, *The Old China Trade*, Boston: Houghton Mifflin, 1930, p. 210; Blussé, *Visible Cities*, p. 64.

6 For America's early contact with Siam, see Edmund Roberts and W.S.W. Ruschenberger, *Two Yankee Diplomats in 1830s Siam*, Bangkok: Orchid Press, 2002. For the development of the US Canton trade, see Jacques M. Downs, *The Golden Ghetto: The American Commercial Community at Canton and the Shaping of American China Policy, 1784–1844*, Bethlehem, PA: Lehigh University Press, 1997; and Paul Van Dyke, *The Canton Trade: Life and Enterprise on the China Coast, 1700–1845*, Hong Kong: Hong Kong University Press, 2005. For the rice trade, see Benito J. Legarda, *After the Galleons: Foreign Trade, Economic Change and Entrepreneurship in the Nineteenth Century Philippines*, Quezon City: Ateneo de Manila University Press, 1999, pp. 157–178.

7 For the British free trade rationale and political technique of imperial expansion, see John Gallagher and Ronald Robinson, 'The Imperialism of Free Trade', *Economic History Review*, second series, 6(1), 1953, pp. 1–15; Bernard Semmel, *The Rise of Free Trade Imperialism*, Cambridge: Cambridge University Press, 1970; and Martin Lynn, 'British Policy, Trade, and Informal Empire in the Mid-Nineteenth Century', in Andrew Porter (ed.), *The Oxford History of the British Empire, Vol. 3: The Nineteenth Century*, Oxford: Oxford University Press, 1999, pp. 101–121.

8 For Russell and Company, see He Sibing, 'Qichang Yanghang yu Meiguo dui Guangzhou zaoqi maoyi, 1818–1844 nian' ('Russell and Company and Early American Trade with Canton, 1818–1844'), in Ye Xianen, Xie Pengfei and Lin Youneng (eds), *Fan Zhusanjiao yu Nanhai maoyi* (*The Pan-Pearl River Delta Region and the South China Sea Trade*), Hong Kong: Xianggang chubanshe, 2009, pp. 237–268; and He Sibing, 'Russell and Company and the Imperialism of Anglo–American Free Trade', in Kendall Johnson (ed.), *Narratives of Free Trade: The Commercial Cultures of Early US–China Relations*, Hong Kong: Hong Kong University Press, 2012, pp. 83–98. This chapter adopts material previously published by the author in the studies listed above.

9 He Sibing, 'Macao in the Making of Sino–US Relations: From the *Empress of China* to the Treaty of Wangxia, 1784–1844', in Priscilla Roberts (ed.), *Bridging the Sino–American Divide: American Studies with Chinese Characteristics*, Newcastle: Cambridge Scholars, 2007, pp. 332–361.

10 The diplomatic historian Michael H. Hunt defines 'research survey' as a hybrid of conventional research monograph and derivative survey in his critically acclaimed book, *The Making of a Special Relationship: The United States and China to 1914*, New York: Columbia University Press, 1983, p. xi. This study attempts to adopt this research strategy.

11 Tyler Dennett, *Americans in Eastern Asia: A Critical Study of the Policy of the United States with Reference to China, Japan, and Korea in the 19th Century*, New York: Barnes and Noble, 1922.

12 Dorothy Borg (ed.), *Historians and American Far Eastern Policy*, New York: East Asian Institute, Columbia University, 1966, pp. 34–35.

13 Harry G. Dildine, 'The Treaty of Wangxia', PhD dissertation, Northwestern University, 1918.

14 Claude M. Fuess, *The Life of Caleb Cushing*, 2 vols, New York: Harcourt, Brace, 1923; John M. Belohlavek, *Broken Glass: Caleb Cushing and the Shattering of the Union*, Kent, OH: Kent State University Press, 2005.

15 Pin-chia Kuo, 'Caleb Cushing and the Treaty of Wanghia, 1844', *Journal of Modern History,* 5(1), 1933, pp. 34–54.

16 Ming-shun Chiao (Qiao Mingshun), 'The Beginning of American–Chinese Diplomatic Relations: The Cushing Mission and the Treaty of Wangxia of 1844', PhD dissertation, University of Notre Dame, 1954. This thesis is rewritten in Chinese and published as a book in 1991 titled *ZhongMei guanxi de diyiye: 1844 nian Wangxia tiaoyue qianding de qianqian houhou* (*The First Page of China–US Relations: The Signing of the Wangxia Treaty of 1844*), China: Social Sciences Academic Press. This work stands out among scores of historical studies on the subject by scholars in China.

17 Richard E. Welch, Jr., 'Caleb Cushing's Chinese Mission and the Treaty of Wanghia: A Review', *Oregon Historical Quarterly,* 53, March–December 1957, pp. 328–355.

18 Li Dingyi, *ZhongMei waijiao shi* (*History of China–US Diplomatic Relations*), Taibei: Lixing Shuju, 1961; revised edition published as *ZhongMei zaoqi waijiao shi* (*History of the Early Sino-American Diplomatic Relations*), Taibei: Lixing Shuju, 1979, and reprinted by Beijing University Press in 1997.

19 Jeffrey Robert Biggs, 'The Origins of American Diplomacy with China: The Cushing Mission of 1844 and the Treaty of Wang-Hsia', PhD dissertation, George Washington University, 1976, pp. x–xi.

20 Earl Swisher, 'The Treaty of Wanghia', in Kenneth W. Rea (ed.), *Early Sino–American Relations, 1841–1912: The Collected Articles of Earl Swisher*, Boulder, CO: Westview Press, 1977, pp. 56–107.

21 Michael H. Hunt, 'The Long Crisis in US Diplomatic History: Coming to Closure', *Diplomatic History,* 16, Winter 1992, p. 120.

22 Downs, *The Golden Ghetto*.

23 Teemu Ruskola, 'Canton is Not Boston: The Invention of American Imperial Sovereignty', *American Quarterly,* 57(3), 2005, pp. 859–884.

24 John M. Belohlavek, The Road to China, 1843–1844', in *Broken Glass*, pp. 150–180.

25 Macabe Keliher, 'Anglo–American Rivalry and the Origins of US China Policy', *Diplomatic History,* 31(2), 2007, pp. 227–257.

26 President John Tyler's Message to Congress, 30 December 1842, in Kenneth E. Shewmaker (ed.), *The Papers of Daniel Webster: Message and Papers*, Hanover, NH: Dartmouth College and University Press of New England, 1983–1988, Vol. IV, pp. 211–214.

27 Charles Hall to John C. Calhoun, 30 November 1844, in Robert L. Meriwether and W. Edwin Hemphill (eds), *The Papers of John C. Calhoun*, 21 vols, Columbia: University of South Carolina Press, 1963–1993, Vol. XX, pp. 405–411.

28 Jules Davids (ed.), *American Diplomatic and Public Papers: The United States and China, Series 1: The Treaty System and the Taiping Rebellion, 1842–1860*, 21 vols, Wilmington, DE: Scholarly Resources, 1973, Vol. I, p. xlii.

29 Circular, 20 March 1843, in Shewmaker, *The Papers of Daniel Webster: Diplomatic Papers*, Vol. I, pp. 901–902.

30 Sarah Forbes Hughes (ed.), *Letters and Recollections of John Murray Forbes*, 2 vols, Boston: Houghton, Mifflin & Co., 1899; Reprinted, New York: Arno Press, 1981, Vol. I, p. 115.
31 John Murray Forbes et al to Daniel Webster, 29 April 1843, in Shewmaker, *The Papers of Daniel Webster: Diplomatic Papers*, Vol. I, pp. 917–921.
32 Daniel Webster to Caleb Cushing, 8 May 1843, in Shewmaker, *The Papers of Daniel Webster: Diplomatic Papers*, Vol. I, pp. 922–926.
33 P.S. Forbes to Imperial Commissioner Kiying (Qiying) and the Governor of Canton, 3 October 1843, in Davids, *American Diplomatic and Public Papers, Series 1*, Vol. I, pp. 157–158.
34 Imperial Commissioner Kiying and Governor-General Ke to Consul P. S. Forbes, 12 October 1843, in Davids, *American Diplomatic and Public Papers, Series 1*, Vol. I, pp. 164–169.
35 P.S. Forbes to the Secretary of State, 7 October 1843, in Davids, *American Diplomatic and Public Papers, Series 1*, Vol. I, pp. 159–163.
36 Downs, *The Golden Ghetto*, p. 290.
37 Murray A. Rubinstein, 'The Wars They Wanted: American Missionaries' Use of *The Chinese Repository* Before the Opium War', *American Neptune,* 48(4), 1988, pp. 281–282.
38 Peter Parker to Daniel Webster, 30 January 1841, in Shewmaker, *The Papers of Daniel Webster: Diplomatic Papers*, Vol. I, p. 885.
39 On Parker's role, see Edward V. Gulick, *Peter Parker and the Opening of China*, Cambridge, MA: Harvard University Press, 1973, pp. 113–124.
40 *Niles' National Register*, 21 September 1844, quoted in Belohlavek, *Broken Glass*, p. 162.
41 Belohlavek, *Broken Glass*, pp. 166–167.
42 Fuess, *The Life of Caleb Cushing*, p. 450; Belohlavek, *Broken Glass*, p. 174; Margaret C.S. Christman, *Adventurous Pursuits: Americans and the China Trade, 1784–1844*, Washington, DC: Smithsonian Institution Press, 1984, p. 160.
43 Wang Ermin, 'Qiying de waijiao' ('Qiying's Diplomacy'), in *Ruoguo de waijiao* (*Diplomacy of a Puny Nation*), Guilin: Guangxi shifan daxue chubanshe (Guangxi Normal University Press), 2008, pp. 55–76; Belohlavek, *Broken Glass*, pp. 177–178.
44 Belohlavek, *Broken Glass*, pp. 175–177.
45 Christman, *Adventurous Pursuits*, p. 150.
46 Kenneth E. Shewmaker, 'Forging the "Great Chain": Daniel Webster and the Origins of American Foreign Policy Toward East Asia and the Pacific, 1841–1852', *Proceedings of the American Philosophical Society,* 129(3), 1985, pp. 225–259.
47 Ruskola, 'Canton Is Not Boston'.
48 Ibid.
49 Ibid.
50 Melohlavek, *Broken Glass*, p. 173.
51 Shewmaker, 'Forging the "Great Chain"'. For the Perry mission see also Peter Booth Wiley, *Yankees in the Land of the Gods*, New York: Viking, 1990; and George Feifer, *Breaking Open Japan: Commodore Perry, Lord Abe, and American Imperialism in 1853*, New York: Smithsonian Books/Collins, 2006.
52 Daniel Webster to John Aulick, 10 June 1851, in Shewmaker, *The Papers of Daniel Webster: Diplomatic Papers*, Vol. II, pp. 289–290. Aulick was named commander of the East India Squadron in 1851 but was replaced by Mathew C. Perry for the mission to Japan.
53 Keliher, 'Anglo–American Rivalry and the Origins of US China Policy'.
54 Ibid.
55 Ibid., pp. 228–229.

56 James Fichter, *So Great a Proffit: How the East Indies Trade Transformed Anglo–American Capitalism*, Cambridge, MA: Harvard University Press, 2010, pp. 173–204.
57 See Letter 183, 198, and 201, in Alain Le Pichon (ed.), *China Trade and Empire: Jardine, Matheson & Co. and the Origins of British Rule in Hong Kong, 1827–1843*, Oxford: Published for the British Academy by Oxford University Press, 2006; and W.E. Cheong, *Mandarins and Merchants: Jardine Matheson & Co., A China Agency of the Early Nineteenth Century*, London: Curzon Press, 1979.
58 Rosmarie W. N. Lamas, *Everything in Style: Harriett Low's Macau*, Hong Kong: Hong Kong University Press, 2006; Murray A. Rubinstein, *The Origins of the Anglo–American Missionary Enterprise in China, 1807–1848*, Metuchen, NJ: Scarecrow Press, 1996.
59 Keliher, 'Anglo–American Rivalry and the Origins of US China Policy'.
60 Robert B. Forbes, *Personal Reminiscences*, 2nd edn, Boston: Little, Brown and Company, 1882, pp. 155, 152–153.
61 Fichter, *So Great a Proffit*.
62 Ronald J. Zboray and Mary Saracino Zboray, 'Between "Crockery-dom" and Barnum: Boston's Chinese Museum, 1845–47', *American Quarterly*, 56(2), 2004, pp. 271–307.

Part IV
Cosmopolitanism
The transnational and transitional politics, society and identity of Macao

8   Macao

An early modern cosmopolis

Iona Man-Cheong

Macao as cosmopolis[1]

Macao as a port city and a mercantile entrepôt – the place where goods and commodities are transferred – is, according to most leading scholars on the subject, exemplary in establishing the earliest and most long-lasting maritime frontier contact zone for China. Its liminality established the place as non-threatening in the eyes of metropolitan authorities in both Europe and China; its geopolitical location also meant it was a place where the differences in peoples and cultures allowed ideas and social practices to mix and, as is evident today, to produce a vibrant, unique assemblage now self-named as 'Macanese' culture.

How did this early cross-cultural mix come about and how was it able to cohere as an entity? How did this local brand of cosmopolitanism continue to exist yet seem to have so little effect on later Sino-European relations? The Portuguese governed Macao for some four centuries – it was the last colonial outpost in China, Portugal withdrawing and Macao reverting to Chinese rule in 1999 – yet it was not an imperial colony seized by force of arms.[2] In fact, not until the mid-nineteenth century did it become a colony in the strict imperial definition of the term. My argument here is that while Macao's liminality gave it a unique position in terms of power and space (even the establishment of Hong Kong in the 1840s under very different conditions of political inequality and coercion did not alter that position), Macao's vitality and vibrancy was due to its position as a place of hybridity and drift (terms I define later in this chapter), able to create a cosmopolis of itself on terms negotiated daily by its denizens. I conclude with the suggestion that the administrative system that constituted its ruling framework was comprised of men who, without a common spoken language, had in their elitist governing ideologies nonetheless an assumed commonality that allowed their jurisdictions to interact and thrive well into the nineteenth century. These elitist assumptions of administrative rationality bore some resemblance to the Enlightenment ideas of cosmopolitanism as set forth in the eighteenth century, while Macao itself exemplified the durability of the hybrid, creating a heterotopia that is even today (consider the present culture of gambling casinos, theme parks, multinational corporations and the ongoing Macanese way of life) filled with significance.[3]

This project began as a way of looking at how the great eighteenth-century ideal of cosmopolitanism was actually practiced on the ground. The French *philosophe* Denis Diderot devised the term 'cosmopolis' to refer to the urban centres where intercultural encounters and exchanges occurred. While most often it was the violence of empire-building that underlay these meetings, it was the everyday practices of ordinary people that illustrated how difference could be *lived* and *thought*. In that sense, Macao has always worked to provincialize the centrality of Europe. Nor were these encounters solely an invention of modernity, for they emerged from an older system of mercantile exchange that had fostered transcultural cosmopolitanism before the term was understood in its modern, Enlightenment sense.[4] It is these trans- and intercultural linkages of ordinary people – sailors, slaves, merchants, administrators and womenfolk – that established the wider global relations through which modern national and cosmopolitan imaginaries could exist.

Macao's cosmopolitanism is due in large part to its position as a city of liminality, of transience and of drift. These terms capture the various marginalities that gave this cosmopolis its strengths.[5] Eighteenth-century Macao was doubtless liminal to China's ruling Manchus, who were not interested in expansion into an overseas empire, as it was to the declining Portuguese imperialists, who, with the closure of Japan to overseas trade, lost their advantageous access to Japanese silver and no longer felt the need to exclude other countries from using the port.[6] However, as a point of entry, Macao regarded both empires as a threshold and thus an important node of communication.

As a place of hybridity, Macao captures Foucault's meaning of a 'heterotopia' – a place that is 'capable of juxtaposing in a single real place several spaces, several sites that are in themselves incompatible'.[7] So while the rulers of empires might describe the Macanese cosmopolis as geopolitically marginal, its very existence challenged and, at the same time, gave meaning to the nation-state narrative of territorial borders, purity of blood, and singularity of language and culture. Macao was utopian in very few respects: it was not a romanticized, ideal entity, but one that existed in its messy day-to-day practices; nor was it a rational space despite the attempts by all parties to make it so; and only in our retrospective view can it be described as progressive or forward thinking. It is as a space of transience and drift, where intercultural and interracial exchanges were negotiated and equivocated upon, that Macao achieves its greatness before being overtaken by more paranoid nation-state regimes. As a heterotopia, a space of creative hybridity, a place where difference generated distinctive identities and cultures, Macao comes into its own, challenging its so-called masters in its pre-eminence as an East Asian cosmopolitan port city.

Liminality, more than mere marginality, also signifies a place of transformational betweenness. Because Macao was neither fully Portuguese nor fully Chinese, it created the conditions for a space of transformation. The reason for this betweenness was twofold. Macao had been an important way station in Portugal's lucrative sixteenth- and seventeenth-century trade with Japan, the source of its famous Black Ships' cargoes of gold and silver. Japan's closing of this trade in the 1630s ended Macao's importance to Portugal as well as introducing Japanese refuges into China – Christian converts escaping persecution.[8] These Japanese, especially the women, became one of the earliest groups to intermarry with the Portuguese in Macao. From the Chinese side, Macao had also the possibility to become the port of trade for China-Europe exports instead of Canton. Kangxi, emperor of the newly established Qing empire, was fascinated with the knowledge and skills that the Jesuits had brought to the capital, and so offered the monopoly of the export trade twice to the Portuguese in Macao; but the authorities refused, fearing a difficult-to-control influx of foreigners from all parts of Europe.[9] This was undoubtedly a loss to Portugal since, instead of being the central trading port, Macao became the dormer town for the Canton trade upriver. But this also contributed to Macao's particular character as a bustling, cosmopolitan port filled with people waiting to do trade in Canton (where no foreign residence was allowed) before the trading season began or as a place of residence once the season was over, both dependent on the all-important trade winds. Those who settled in Macao thrived on the trade with the transient population of traders and merchants, slaves and sailors. By the later eighteenth century, Macao was so central that the British East India Company built its own offices there for off-season residence.[10]

Located at the mouth of south China's Pearl River Delta, Macao was in many respects a place of transience, filled with a mostly floating population of sailors and the smaller, more settled part of the population who serviced them, such as tavern keepers, store owners and prostitutes; merchants and their slaves from Africa, Southeast Asia and the Middle East; and European missionaries who established orphanages, schools, churches, convents, monasteries and hospices, in competition with local Chinese institutions; and a handful of administrators, both Chinese and Portuguese, who struggled to ensure order, stability and security without having any explicit common language. At this point, the geo-ecological idea of 'drift' becomes salient: it describes the way sediment moves along the shore, pushed by the effect of wind on water, creating patterns and dividing the shoreline into cells that can be independent of one another while keeping to the broader connection of the overall shoreline.[11] The movement of drift, in Macao, operated via the transient, mixed populations that throughout its existence created small cells of settlers, who in the semi-permanence of their lives created a singular culture of mixed-race families linking them more closely with transoceanic networks of other port cities than it did to the hinterland of China. It is the sedimentation, layer upon layer, of this drift that created a vibrant, hybrid community. Each of these characteristics – the liminality of place, the transience of peoples, and the drift of their residence and settlement patterns – points to how, when practised on the ground, cosmopolitanism allows for agency in the creation of identity for those who live by their own labour and depend on their wits.

A 1797 case involving five European sailors especially illustrates how Macao's cosmopolitanism allowed the multiple nationalities resident in

Macao to slip between the jurisdictions of authorities and to use language differences to their advantage in employment opportunities.[12] Chinese government troops rescued the five European sailors from a small boat in difficulties during a storm. The men alleged to the Chinese authorities, who took them into custody, that they had left their English ship to take employment on a Dutch ship. However, finding that their new jobs were even harder than their last, the sailors allegedly ran away from the Dutch ship back to their English one from which they had probably deserted. The Chinese authorities were most concerned, however, to discover whether in fact the whole story was a fabrication and if these five were in fact pirates trying to avoid capture. These are the basic dynamics of the encounter: Europeans, as was common practice, taking advantage of better employment opportunities in this international port; Chinese authorities as the local security forces fighting piracy; and the lack of a common language beyond simple pidgin. If the sailors were English they probably did not speak Dutch, adding another layer to the mix. First, the Chinese launched an investigation to find out to which ship the sailors actually belonged. The sailors' names were carefully transliterated phonetically into Chinese; the authorities then requested the Portuguese provide them with a list of names of any men claimed missing from the English ship. Their plan was to compare the lists and to return those correlating to the English ship. We can only guess at the complications faced by an interpreter comparing lists of names written in Chinese and English. The record does not provide the final outcome of the case, but clearly the men had used their international circumstances to find better employment or, to escape capture as pirates, and the Chinese and Portuguese authorities cooperated to resolve the matter – an unromantic but rough-and-ready example of cosmopolitanism as practiced on the ground.[13]

Macao, although always a port, had only a small 'native' population of Chinese.[14] Described as 'a tiny, barren peninsula, about three miles long and less than half a mile wide', Macao was separated from the main part of the island by an isthmus. The Chinese, in an attempt to maintain control, had early on in 1574 constructed a wall to barricade the foreigners in, to keep them isolated and to restrict European access to China's hinterland. By the eighteenth century, a gate garrisoned with a permanent Chinese guard was built into the wall, allowing Chinese to enter Macao to service the port city with supplies, builders, artisans and peddlers – and allowing Chinese authorities to exert pressure on the foreign settlement by stopping daily supplies. Macao was also unique among European outposts. Rather than being seized and held by military force, Macao was rented by the Portuguese until well into the nineteenth century; the Portuguese paid a small annual ground rent (from 500 to 2,000 ounces of Chinese silver).[15] Fragrant Island (Xiangshan), of which Macao was a portion, was set among an archipelago of islands located on the western side of the Pearl River Delta: attractive for access to both licit and illicit water traffic. Macao's wide, protected harbour was also conveniently located just 40 miles downriver from Canton – the central point

of the export trade – which had become the benefactor of the Qing monopoly export trade, given Macao's earlier refusal to take this responsibility.[16]
Although the Portuguese did retain their own military force in Macao, the
force was more for local security than for repelling Chinese advances.

Cosmopolitan populations and cross-cultural encounters

The population of Macao fluctuated hugely between the seventeenth
and nineteenth centuries, growing as high as 19,000 during the heyday of
Portuguese trade with Japan, but falling to just a few thousand by the early
eighteenth century. But Macao grew again as trade with Europeans picked
up with the re-establishment of connections with the Qing authorities at the
end of coastal evacuation in 1684.[17] Only when Hong Kong was established
as a second trade entrepôt on the eastern side of the Pearl River Delta did the
population fall again and Macao lost its pre-eminence.[18] The population also
fluctuated with the trading season. With the monsoon blowing in, trading
in Canton began and sailors inundated the town. Under the Canton trading
system European sailors could expect to be in port for as many as six months
before the season ended.[19] The sailors constituted a mixed group of mainly
European, Lascar and Chinese sailors (hired to replace Europeans for the
homeward voyage). At these moments, the population was wildly diverse
and as such the possibility of both conflict and tension and cooperation was
always present.[20] The merchant population of Macao was the transient group
most responsible for the exchange of goods and labour. Their numbers were
small, but they brought their employees, slaves and ships' crews with them.
Merchants added to the wealthier part of the cosmopolitan mix and derived
from many cultural backgrounds. Besides the British, Danish and Swedish
from the various European monopoly East India Companies, merchants also
included Armenians, Parsees (a sub-ethnic group from South Asia who had
their own religion and were famous as men of business) and Goans (many
of whom were mixed race merchants from Portugal's earliest colony on the
Indian subcontinent).[21] Many in this last group were better known for their
involvement with the private or country trade contracted to the various
European East India Companies to supplement their own ships bringing
cotton and later opium from the subcontinent. The merchants sometimes
brought their families, especially through the eighteenth century, when lavish
mansions were built as off-season residencies for the periods they were not
permitted to stay in Canton; foreign women were never allowed to reside in
Canton. Some became long-term residents, adding to the settled population
of Macanese. With the growth of population, a perennial area of contention
was the building of houses, and the necessity of housing construction and
repairs. While construction often relied on slave labour supplied by merchants,
house repairs depended upon Chinese artisans and builders. Local court
records are replete with complaints from both Chinese contractors and their
European customers about overly high prices, cheating, unfulfilled contracts

and cost overruns.[22] The Chinese authorities eventually introduced a system of officially licensed contracts to forestall further complaint and maintain good community relations.

With the merchants came the populations that made up the bulk of the transient populations: the slaves and the sailors. Slaves – African, Malays from Southeast Asia, and South Asians – had come with the merchants. Besides the usual manual work of carrying goods, they were also involved in building construction and, when not working for their masters, were paid wages. Chinese records include a significant number of cases identified as involving slaves; their presence in Macao from the sixteenth century ensured some Chinese were early aware of African and Arab slaves.[23] The Chinese sources recording the most serious conflicts between black slaves and the local Chinese population provide evidence also of their prevalence in Macanese society. For example, in 1795, a Chinese man carrying a large bundle of firewood allegedly accidentally bumped into a black slave who was himself carrying a small boat on his back.[24] The black slave, infuriated, dragged the Chinese man into a doorway and proceeded to beat him ferociously; another Chinese man trying to intervene was also attacked. The slave was finally overcome and taken into custody. The Portuguese and Chinese local authorities were asked to carry out a joint investigation into the circumstances, to find out the name of the slave assailant and whether he had been deliberately provoked. In this case, a cooperating, multicultural supervising body was empowered to resolve a cross-cultural conflict. Naturally, examples of cooperation between the same two groups do not get recorded in these sources.

Slaves in their free time mixed with ordinary society in the town's bars and taverns, including the most transient of Macao's mixed population: the seafaring people. The eighteenth-century transoceanic, East Asian arc of trade linked these seafarers from the Atlantic world with those of the Indian Ocean and South China Sea who all came into Macao after a long and often difficult voyage ready for shore leave. A small but relatively prosperous group of innkeepers and tavern owners (one document mentions a total of nine premises) provided convivial places to congregate, often promoting local sex workers' services as well. Speaking multiple languages, usually with pidgin Portuguese as a common link, slave and sailor rubbed shoulders.[25]

Such a volatile mix of slaves, sailors and their support services could sometimes erupt into violence, disturbing social order and worrying the authorities as we see in 1799. Tavern keepers, not wanting to lose any opportunity to profit from their clientele, had apparently taken to selling alcohol on credit.[26] Fighting and brawling spilled out into the streets when sailors were prevented from rejoining their ships without paying their tab. The Chinese magistrate was deeply critical of this unscrupulous mode of profiteering and even more concerned about the public disturbance. He ordered the Portuguese authorities to have all incoming sea captains inform their crew that the purchase of liquor on credit was strictly forbidden. But apart from issuing prohibitions and public orders, little else could be done; at least they could ensure all incoming ships' crews received advance warning. Fictional depictions of the mayhem of sailors in international ports of call certainly reflect part of the reality of Macao, but crews could be in port for several months at a time, which meant there was also less exuberance and some moments of quiet living.

The Chinese authorities, in a spirit of cooperation reflecting a cosmopolitan outlook, endeavoured to mediate disputes among ordinary transients and to apportion blame correctly, especially when cases involved both Chinese and non-Chinese, including cases involving slaves or, as in one 1777 case, a Chinese man who attacked and injured a foreign sailor.[27] During the fight that broke out between Rong Yagou, a Chinese, and Antonio Jose, a Portuguese sailor, Rong hit Jose harder on the head than he probably intended, resulting in serious injury; Rong Yagou was arrested for grievous bodily harm. By the time the case came before the Chinese magistrate, the condition of the victim was unclear. Reflecting the care the authorities took over such incidents, the magistrate requested his Portuguese counterpart visit the injured man and report. When it was discovered that Antonio Jose had completely recovered, the Chinese assailant was charged with the lesser crime of causing injury during an affray.

Women played a vital social role in developing a hybrid community, as wives, vendors, mistresses and sex workers not to mention those who became associated with the Christian Church.[28] At one point, Macao was actually known as the 'city of women': out of a total population of 19,500 near the end of the seventeenth century, 16,000 were women, including some slaves.[29] Although the total population had dropped by 1830, nonetheless 2,600 of the total 4,400 were women; the rest included 900 Portuguese and 800 enslaved men. Interestingly, while the ethnicity of the 100 free blacks employed as soldiers was noted, that of the slaves was not.

While Portuguese colonial policy relied on an influx of women to establish the settled community, this policy hardly accounts for such high numbers.[30] Portuguese policy, unlike Britain's more ambivalent stance, encouraged colonists to intermarry with the local population.[31] As intermarriage with Chinese was less of an option in China, those residing in Macao brought women from other transoceanic places including Japan, India, Malacca, the Philippines and other Southeast Asian Malay settlements.[32] Though there is little in-depth research on the history of women in Macao, we can be sure that news of the enclave's need for women spread and contributed to their numbers.[33] A significant number also derived from the efforts of both Catholic missionaries and slave traders. Macao was the main point of entry for pre-nineteenth century Christian missionary activities in China and the place where the missionaries established their first religious institutions such as churches and schools. The Misericordia were institutions of refuge, most often run by nuns; they offered refuge for single women and also housed children they believed had been abandoned, the vast majority of which were unwanted girls, both babies and children. Besides offering refuge, such institutions were employers of women. Simultaneously, and no doubt contributing to a negative image of their activities, especially in the seventeenth and earlier eighteenth century, there was a thriving trade in Chinese and Japanese slaves. Although forbidden by Portuguese law, the fashion for Chinese and Japanese slaves in Portugal meant that children were in great demand, and this continued to foster the trade. The trade in the kidnapping and sale of children, especially girls that some Chinese families would sell for cash, was brisk. Of course, many of the girls stayed in service in Macao and did not leave for Portugal. Whether abandoned, kidnapped or runaways, these girls became a focus of Catholic conversion. When adult, many eventually married either the transient sailors or foreign settlers, creating the mestizo and creole populations of Macao.[34] Others, without the protection of the Church, entered the thriving sex trade either as prostitutes or, in many cases, providing sex as part of their domestic duties. Marriage to Chinese women was not an option until 1793, when Chinese migrants were permitted to settle in Macao for the first time.[35] The ethnic variety of women in Macao was probably not limited to the South Asians, Goans, Malays, Japanese and Chinese women for whom we have evidence – only further research can provide answers – but together they contributed to Macao's cosmopolitan mix at all levels of society.[36] Portuguese and European seafarers and merchants who intermarried with Malay and Chinese women joined with descendants of previous generations of mixed-race people, for example, the children of Japanese Christian martyrs who had escaped to Macao in the seventeenth century. These mixed-race Eurasian children had strong ties to the settled community and were among the creative elements of Macanese hybrid culture. As multilinguists they were invaluable and were in demand as translators and interpreters both in Macao and in other parts of the empire, communication and cross-cultural translation being a crucial link in Chinese and European endeavours. Mixed-race unions, already common in Macao, were also carried back to their places of origin, with those in the upper ranks of Portuguese society occasionally holding high position. Antonio de Albuquerque Coelho, the Governor of Macao (1718–1720), was the Portuguese son of a mulatto mother (Angela de Bairros 'who had both Indian and Negro blood in her veins'), and as an illegitimate son, he looked overseas for a career. As his father once declared, 'even we pure Christians are all descended from heathens in a remoter or nearer degree', and entrepôts such as Macao were accepting environments.[37]

One final small but important section of women, widows, often with wealth and/or property, found themselves in an important niche. In addition to the already high mortality rates of the times, husbands settled in Macao could become the casualties of conflicts in the Portuguese empire; seafaring husbands could desert their wives or die while away at sea, leaving their wives in port. A widow could be a woman of property and considered an important catch for any man of either reputation or substance trying to make a life on shore.[38]

Of course it would be a mistake to assume Macao – with its ethno-racial mix and social divisions between white Europeans, peoples of different classes and Chinese – was completely free from racial prejudice and discrimination. While all who were born in Macao were considered free citizens, there were always limitations to the extent that a 'free Portuguese subject' (that is, an individual of mixed race born in Macao or any other Portuguese territory) could achieve social advancement, or rise through official ranks in either the civil or military services.[39] C.R. Boxer suggests that the differences between white and mixed-race Europeans was certainly not as great as that faced by native Chinese – but even in that case, many found ways of making their way through society.[40]

Assumed cosmopolitanism: the framework for cosmopolitan practice

While Macao's society exhibited a rich hybrid mix, the institutional and administrative arrangements established the frameworks within which the vitality of its creative hybridity flourished.[41] One impression gained from a reading of the Chinese cases collected from the local magistrate's court is that, given the lack of common language between the Portuguese and the Chinese authorities, there still existed a common elitist spirit of administration that, without any previous agreement, but relying on similar class assumptions, allowed a cross-cultural administrative operation to run smoothly. The officers from both sides were selected from the educated social elites of their societies; their class-specific backgrounds, dispositions and assumptions coloured their views and generated another commonality that might be described as a kind of cosmopolitanism. Just as the educated European elite of the eighteenth century thought of themselves as the social and cultural arbiters of society, so too did the educated Chinese literati, the backbone of the Chinese empire's bureaucracy. Educated eighteenth-century Europeans, like the educated Chinese, understood the social distinctions of rank and gender; more importantly, both equated the 'moral' with the 'social', regarding correct social relations as fundamental. For much of the eighteenth century this assumption seemed to undergird the relatively smooth relations between the two sets of local authorities, producing a local cosmopolitanism. The Portuguese judicial authorities were elected, while the Chinese assistant magistrate, housed in a building adjoining the barrier gate, was an appointed official,[42] but these kinds of differences seemed to have less impact. Only when the power dynamics engendered by free trade capitalist ideology and backed by guns helped produce the increasingly prevalent nineteenth-century brand of imperialism, both nationalistically and culturally, did this relationship change. But for much of the period up through the eighteenth century, it seemed that both the Portuguese and Chinese authorities were in agreement that the lower orders had to be restrained and controlled, that this duty fell to them as members of the elite, and that their adjudications and cooperation were necessary to keep order and provide stability.[43]

As the nineteenth century progressed, the trust engendered by these mutual assumptions began to fray on both sides, especially in cases involving the increasingly dominant British in South China. As the commercial aspirations of the British grew, their characterization of the Chinese legal system as barbaric and unjust provided a rationale for their own hostile reactions, as the 1807 case involving the British ship *Neptune* illustrates.[44] Sailors on leave from the ship had gotten into a major fight with the local Chinese. Apparently local vendors had cheated and robbed them; infuriated, the British-employed sailors were out for revenge. They attacked the local Chinese with cudgels, the locals retaliated with stones and bricks, and a Chinese man was killed during the ensuing melee. The Chinese, as had been customary, expected the perpetrator to be surrendered and tried according to Chinese law. But with growing European xenophobia and the demonization of Chinese culture, the resident British authorities decided, on principle, to protect their men, down to the lowliest sailor. They would do everything to prevent them from falling into what they characterized as the malevolent clutches of Chinese law. The case dragged on for several months with British obfuscations and the slow wheels of Chinese bureaucracy grinding forward. After several show trials, no British would confess to the murder, but a likely suspect was agreed upon and fined the equivalent of £4 sterling. Such responses were to be increasingly common as the nineteenth century advanced, culminating in the Opium War, with the Europeans trying to shield their own from Chinese justice and the Chinese increasingly mistrustful of foreign intentions.[45]

So what are we to make of the earlier cross-cultural mix and cultural commonality? For its time, Macao was a unique part of China. Arguably, the shift of mercantile capitalism into the newer free-trade mode offers one explanation for this exceptional period of history. If the earlier period was characterized by mutual understanding between local Chinese and local European of the terms of monopoly trade, the latter period's mode of aggressive national competitiveness was less conducive to cultural exchange.

As the contact zone between cultures, Macao accrued its own significance as an early modern cosmopolis – a place of hybridity, vitality, and cultural encounter – with its vibrant mixture of transient sailors and slaves, merchants and settlers. Administrators – themselves not necessarily self-conscious cosmopolites – acted within a kind of cosmopolitan framework determined more by common class ideology than negotiation, holding the whole loosely together. Thus the sustained and daily practices and experience of cross-cultural encounter implanted roots of cosmopolitanism deep in the interstices of empire.

Notes

1 For a critical introduction to cosmopolitanism, see Carol A. Breckenridge, Sheldon Pollock, Homi K. Bhabha and Dipesh Chakrabarty, *Cosmopolitanism*, Durham: Duke University Press, 2002.

2 The date for the settlement of Macao is 1555–1557, see C.R. Boxer, *Portuguese Society in the Tropics: The Municipal Councils of Goa, Macao, Bahia and Luanda*, Madison: University of Wisconsin Press, 1965, p. 65.

3 For the concept of heterotopia, see Michel Foucault, 'Of Other Spaces', in Nicholas Mirzoeff (ed.) *The Visual Culture Reader*, New York, London: Routledge, 2002, pp. 229–236.

4 For the question of Enlightenment ideals, see Michael Scrivener, *The Cosmopolitan Ideal in the Age of Revolution and Reaction, 1776–1832*, London: Pickering and Chatto, 2007, pp. 6–32. For discussions on decentering a Eurocentric focus, see Dipesh Chakrabarty, *Provincializing Europe: Postcolonial Thought and Historical Difference*, Princeton: Princeton University Press, 2000.

5 For a discussion of Macao as a place of liminality, transience and hybridity, see Christina Miu Bing Cheng, *Macau: A Cultural Janus*, Hong Kong: Hong Kong University Press, 1999, pp. 1–5, 197–217; for liminality, see Bjorn Thomassen, 'The Uses and Meanings of Liminality', *International Political Anthropology*, 2(1), 2009, pp. 5–27.

6 C.R. Boxer, *Four Centuries of Portuguese Expansion, 1415–1825: A Succinct Survey*, Berkeley: University of California Press, 1969, pp. 41, 90; George Bryan Souza, *The Survival of Empire: Portuguese Trade and Society in China and the South China Sea, 1630–1754*, Cambridge: Cambridge University Press, 1986. For Ming and Qing dynasty relations with China, see John Wills, 'Maritime Europe and the Ming', in John E. Wills, Jr. (ed.), *China and Maritime Europe, 1500–1800*, Cambridge: Cambridge University Press, 2011, pp. 24–77; Jane Kate Leonard, *Wei Yuan and China's Rediscovery of the Maritime World*, Council on East Asian Studies, Cambridge, MA: Harvard University Press, 1984.

7 Michel Foucault, 'Of Other Spaces', p. 233. For hybridity meaning a creative interaction of two or more cultures producing many varied and mixed cultural practices, see Homi Bhabha, 'Signs Taken for Wonders', *Critical Inquiry*, 12(1), 1985, pp. 144–165; Lisa Lowe, *Immigrant Acts: On Asian American Cultural Politics*, Durham: Duke University Press, 1996.

8 This description of the cosmopolitan nature of Macao society is indebted to C.R. Boxer, *The Portuguese Seaborne Empire, 1415–1825*, New York: Knopf Books, 1969; Cesar Guillen-Nunez, *Macau*, Oxford: Oxford University Press, 1984. For a very good, if now outdated bibliography, see Richard L. Edmonds (ed.), *Macau*, Oxford: Clio Press, 1989.

9 Anders Ljungstedt, *An Historical Sketch of the Portuguese Settlements in China and of the Roman Catholic Church and Mission in China & Description of the City of Canton*, Hong Kong: Viking Hong Kong Publications, 1992 reprint of 1826 edition, pp. 68–69; Guillen-Nuñez, *Macau*, p. 32. As Souza (*The Survival of Empire*, pp. 194–212) makes no mention of such an event, it is perhaps fictitious.

10 H.B. Morse, *The Chronicles of the East India Company Trading to China, 1635–1834* Oxford: Oxford University Press, 1926, reprint Ch'eng-wen Publishing Company, 1966, Vol. IV, p. 152.

11 Washington State Department of Ecology, Net Shore-Drift, Washington, 2002, www.ecy.wa.gov/services/gis/data/shore/driftcells.htm (accessed 13 January, 2009).

12 The court cases in this chapter all derive from the published reports in Liu Fang (ed.) *Qingdai Aomen zhongwen dang'an huibian* (*Qing Dynasty Macao Chinese Document Collection*, hereafter *Aomen huibian*). These reports are copies of case records sent up to the provincial authorities from the local magistrate's office, there are no corresponding copies of instructions sent back instructing the local authorities how to proceed, nor what the final outcomes were. The collection of Qing dynasty routine memorials held by the First Historical Archives was not available to researchers at the time I was completing this research. Despite this limitation, the examples here still provide a great deal of information useful for understanding the dynamics of Macanese society in the period.

13 *Aomen huibian*, document nos. 1465, 15 January 1797 (Chinese date: Jiaqing 1/12/18).

14 Jonathan Porter, *Macau: Imaginary City*, Boulder, Colorado: Westview Press, 2000, pp. 33–59, 62–69 discussing Macao's geographic setting, its unique position as a rental property, and its walls and defense fortifications. See also, Ljungstedt, *An Historical Sketch*, pp. 12–13.

15 Porter, *Macau*, pp. 36–43, 48–49, 63.

16 Ljungstedt, *An Historical Sketch*, pp. 68–69, Porter, *Macau*, p. 52.

17 David Faure, *Emperor and Ancestor*, Stanford: Stanford University Press, pp.172–175; for impact of the end of the Qing coastal evacuation, see Philip A. Kuhn, *Chinese Among Others*, Lanham, Maryland: Rowman and Littlefield, 2009, p. 35.

18 See Porter, *Macau*, pp. 88–95; Patrizia Carioti, 'The Portuguese Settlement at Macao' in *Revisita de Cultura* (*Review of Culture*), 8, 2003, pp. 25–39.

19 A.J.R. Russell-Wood, *A World on the Move: The Portuguese in Africa, Asia, and America, 1415–1808*, New York: St. Martins Press, 1992, pp. 37–41. For a comprehensive exposition of the Canton system, see Paul A. Van Dyke, *The Canton Trade*, Hong Kong: Hong Kong University Press, 2005.

20 Roderich Ptak, 'The Demography of Old Macao, 1555–1640', *Ming Studies*, 15, 1982, pp. 27–35; Souza, *The Survival of Empire*, pp. 31–39.

21 For a series of fascinating articles concerning this group of merchants, see Carl T. Smith, 'Muslims in the Pearl River Delta, 1700–1930', *Revisita de Cultura* (*Review of Culture*), 10, 2004, pp. 16–25; Carl T. Smith and Paul Van Dyke, 'Armenian Footprints in Macao', 20–39; Guo Deyan, 'The Study of Parsee Merchants in Canton, Hong Kong and Macao', *Revisita de Cultura*, 8, 2003, pp. 51–69.

22 For building of residences, see Porter, *Macau*, p. 89; also the many records concerning clerks and runners in *Aomen huibian*.

23 C.R. Boxer, Souza and other authors of Macao history have emphasized the prevalence of slaves in Macanese society from early Portuguese settlement until nineteenth century. The research of Lúcio de Sousa (University of Tokyo) of slaves in Macao will open up this relatively unworked field of research.

24 *Aomen huibian*, document no. 587, 10 January 1795 (Chinese date: Qianlong 59/12/20).

25 Ibid., document no.835, 5 November 1799 (Chinese date: Jiaqing 4/10/8).

26 Ibid.

27 Ibid., document no. 584, 14 December 1777 (Chinese date: Qianlong 42/11/15).

28 The most detailed historical work on women in the Portuguese empire to date is C.R. Boxer, *Women in Iberian Expansion Overseas*, New York: Oxford University Press, 1975.

29 Ljungstedt, *An Historical Sketch*, pp. 28–29, for foreign residency; Boxer, *Portuguese Society*, p. 63, for 'city of women'; Porter, *Macau*, pp. 129–135, for population figures and their ethnic breakdown (also Souza, *The Survival of Empire*, pp. 31–39).

30 Porter, *Macau*, pp. 131–135; Boxer, *Portuguese Society*, pp. 63–67.

31 Boxer, *Four Centuries of Portuguese Expansion*, p. 61.

32 Philippe Pons, *Macao*, London: Reaktion Books, 2002, pp. 101–103.

33 See C.R. Boxer, *Fidalgos in the Far East, 1550–1770: Fact and Fantasy in the History of Macao*, The Hague: Martinus Hijhoff, 1948, pp. 255–268 for the conditions for *mui-tsai* (girls who were somewhere between slave and domestic servant, and sometimes mistress).

34 Boxer, *Portuguese Society*, p. 51.

35 Boxer, *Fidalgos in the Far East*, pp. 222–241.

36 See also Porter, *Macau*, pp. 76–77.

37 C.R. Boxer, 'A Fidalgo in the Far East, 1708–1726: Antonio de Albuquerque Coelho in Macao', *The Far Eastern Quarterly*, 5(4), 1946, p. 388.

38 Boxer, *Portuguese Society*, p. 145.

39 C.R. Boxer, *Race Relations in the Colonial Portuguese Empire, 1415–1825*, Oxford: Clarendon Press, 1963, pp. 70–71; also in Boxer, *Portuguese Society*. While creole

is now often used in a much broader sense, the distinction between mestizo and creole was much simpler. *Mestizo* meant a person of mixed race. Creole refers to either a language created out of local languages or, people born in the colony either mixed or not; primary identity would be with the place of birth. See Boxer, *Race Relations* for an in-depth discussion.

40 Boxer, *Race Relations*.
41 Boxer, *Portuguese Society*, pp. 42–71.
42 Ibid., pp. 5–7, 50–53 for election of Portuguese officers; for Chinese appointment system, see I. Man-Cheong, *The Class of 1761: Examinations, State and Elites in Eighteenth-Century China*, Stanford: Stanford University Press, 2004, pp. 144–196.
43 For examples of the basic approach of Chinese and Portuguese officials, see the abstracts to Chinese magistrate court cases in both Chinese and Portuguese versions (the latter are not direct translations of the Chinese abstracts, but Portuguese abstracts from the original Chinese documents) in Fang Li (ed.), *Putaoya guoli Dongpota dang'an guan guicang Aomen ji dongfang dang'an wenxian: Hanwen wenshu* (*Macau and Eastern Documents Held in the Torre do Tomro National Archives of Portugal: Chinese Documents*), Macau: Institute of Culture, 1997, and the Portuguese index of same title.
44 See *Aomen huibian*, document no. 1397, 10 June 1807 (Chinese date: Jiaqing 12/5/5) and Morse, *The Chronicles of the East India Company*, Vol. III, pp. 26–49.
45 Many scholars have discussed the trajectory leading to open hostilities, see for example, Lydia H. Liu, *The Clash of Empires: The Invention of China in Modern World Making*, Cambridge, MA: Harvard University Press, 2004; see Frederic Wakeman, Jr., 'The Canton Trade and the Opium War,' in John K. Fairbank (ed.) *Cambridge History of China*, Vol. X, part 1, Cambridge: Cambridge University Press, pp. 163–212.

9 Macao's urban identity question, 1557–1999/2009

Spatializing territory

Paula Morais

This chapter looks at Macao's urban identity from the period of 1557–1999/2009, yet it particularly concentrates on the post-handover decade and the territory's identity question in relation to recently accelerated urban change. The analysis examines the processes of urban transformation at the peninsula and observes how current rapid urbanization is severely questionable in sustaining local qualities, sense of place and identity as Macao urban space is becoming largely unidentifiable. Furthermore the Pearl River Delta region is witnessing an exceptionally fast development, particularly in the last decades, which scale of growth has superseded long-established administrative boundaries of individual governments.[1]

> The Greater PRC City-region has all along been China's leading region pioneering reform and open door policies, and is also the major area of cooperation among Hong Kong, Macao and the Mainland. The successful cooperation among Guangdong, Hong Kong and Macao in the past 30 years has created a city-region which is one of the most unique in the world.[2]

The Pearl River Delta Mega City-Region Strategic Spatial Planning Report,[3] published in October 2009, defines a *9+2* city region: i.e., greater PRC townships (9) and Hong Kong and Macao (2), in pursue of 'Building Coordinated and Sustainable World-Class City-Region'.[4] One of the main strategies previews the 'Optimization of the Spatial Structure' reorganizing space into three new metropolitan areas: i.e. Guangzhou/Foshan, Hong Kong/Shenzen and Macao/Zhuhai.[5] Hence present urban identity question in Macao is not only a result of spatial change enforced by rapid urbanization but also a scale question. Yet, the superimposition of this new urban-regional scale means that this will not be a simple geographical boundary of socio-cultural relations but it will constitute an 'active, socially produced and politically contested moment of those relations'.[6] Macao's urban form role as a producer of identity and difference and as a frame for everyday socio-cultural relations is fading in the name of the homogenizing forces of local, regional and world-scale capital accumulation and state rescaling.[7]

Table 9.1 Periodization table of Macao political system and spatial orders projects' classification from 1557 to 1999 and 2009 (2049)

Macao political system	Time	Spatial order project	Spatial strategies and defining context
Macao as 'Chinese Imperial Territorial Concession'	1557–1849	the *territorialization* project	Portuguese flexible urbanism and the significance of Sino-Portuguese foreign relations in urban form
Macao as a 'Restricted Autonomy'	1849–1887		
Macao as 'Portuguese Territory in Chinese Land'	1887–1987		
	1987–1999	the *deterritorialization* project	Accelerated urbanization, spatial erasure and homogenization; public narratives of loss
Macao as 'Special Administrative Region of the People's Republic of China', SAR	1999–2009		
	2009–2049	the *reterritorialization* project	PRC Mega City-Region Strategic Spatial Planning – new Macao/Zhuhai metropolitan area rescaling

Hence this study argues that Macao's urban space and identity have a multidimensional responsibility in spatializing territories, in contextualizing and providing for identification among societies and their places, serving different projects and intents at different times. As such, Macao's urban identity history can be defined by three main spatial order projects: the one of a 'territorialization' exerted by the Portuguese administration particularly evident in the period framed by the 1887 bilateral treaty,[8] and until the Sino-Portuguese Joint Declaration in 1987,[9] which aimed primarily at securing their presence in the territory as it was constantly questioned by China (i.e. the 'Macao question'[10]), and the one of a 'deterritorialization' led by post-1987(1999)[11] capitalist economy project and globalization. Globalization forces in Macao are enforcing a process of 'deterritorialization' in the service of a pro-growth political position and a future city-regional scale 'reterritorialization': i.e. the reconfiguration and rescaling of forms of territorial organization. Thus the Pearl River Delta (PRC) new urban-region will become a hinge for China's global economic competitiveness. A brief conclusion proposes that urban space, through the means of a sustainable urbanism that capitalizes cultural and spatial differences (i.e. identity), can play a role in equilibrating the path of social and economic development in the changing territorial production and organization of twenty-first-century global capitalism landscape.

Methodology: the study analysed primary and secondary sources, narratives, documents and maps from both Portuguese and Chinese sources. It concentrated on the two key dimensions in the history of urban transformation: political and spatial forms integrating some notes on the socio-cultural and economic, as well as planning and governance dimensions. The study is defined by an interdisciplinary and mix-methodology approach in which spatial analysis and ethnographic methods have been applied: i.e. morphological analysis of maps, on-site observations and in-depth interviews. The author has personally conducted 60 in-depth interviews with decision-makers, academics and the public, from Chinese, Portuguese and Macanese resident communities during 2008 and 2009. Yet this study has chosen a Portuguese perspective due to the complexity of the subject examined and plurality of interpretations regarding the 'Macao question'.

Theoretical framework

Periodization note: 1557, 1887–1987, 1999/2009

It is essential to refer that the periods addressed in this chapter are part of a wider project (a work in-progress) that includes a full detailed analysis and periodization of Macao's urban transformation from its founding in 1557 until the handover in December 1999,[12] and in the last decade, therefore marking all primary spatial changes in the territory in relation to its political status – i.e. Macao as a 'Chinese Imperial territorial concession' in the first period (1557–1849) formally acknowledged by China in the 1887 Luso-Chinese Friendship and Commercial Treaty; as a 'restricted autonomy' and Portuguese sovereignty affirmation attempt during the 'colonial' period, which according to the juridical concepts of the West was exercised from 1849 until the 1887 treaty;[13] as a 'Portuguese territory in Chinese land' from 1887 until 1999, and later post-1999 as a People's Republic of China Special Administrative Region (SAR) under the framework of 'one country, two systems' (Table 9.2).

The 'Macao question'

The divergence between Portuguese and Chinese authorities regarding the Portuguese presence in Macao were based on the difference of interpretations that both powers had about the question of sovereignty and true status of the territory: i.e. the 'Macao question'. Until the Luso-Chinese Friendship and Commercial Treaty in 1887, the 'Macao question' was essentially based on the problems of China in defining and recognizing the Portuguese presence in Macao.[14]

The ambiguity of the political system and indeterminacy of place was then reflected in the territory's historiography as it differed mainly according to Chinese and Portuguese perspectives. This diversity of analysis relates primarily to Macao as an extremely complex entity to classify by one single perspective or discipline. Macao was an intricate case, and its unusualness has long been an intriguing object of study for Chinese, Portuguese and scholars globally. Vasconcelos de Saldanha spoke about Macao as an 'autonomous

Table 9.2 Periodization table of Macao looking at urban transformation (seven periods), demography (census of resident population), and Macao, Portugal and China's primary political instances and Sino-Portuguese treaties from 1557 to 1999–2009[a]

Macao: urban transformation periodization from 1557 to 1999 and 2009

Time	Peninsula morphological periods	Peninsula km2 [b]	Total resident population[c]	
1557–1640	1st period of founding and early settlement	3.4	400	12.500
1640–1849	2nd period of consolidation of the citadel	3.4	12.500	30.000
1849–1927	3rd period of affirmation and expansion	3.4	30.000	157.175
1927–1949	4th period of compression	5.2	157.175	374.737
1949–1987	5th period of decay and recovery	5.8	188.896	241.729
1987–1999	6th period of densification	6.5 to 7.8	355.693	437.455
1999–2009	7th period of erasure	9.3	427.400	544.100

Portugal and China: primary political periods and instances, and World Wars

	Portugal political periods and instances	World Wars	China political periods and instances	
1385–1580	House of Aviz – the Far East exploration and empire		Ming dynasty	1368–1644
1580–1640	House of Habsburg – the Restoration War in 1960		Qing dynasty	1644–1911
1640–1834	House of Braganza – Liberal Wars 1828–1834		Opium Wars	1839–1842 1856–1860
1834–1910	House of Braganza-Coburg		First Sino-Japanese War	1894–1895
1910–1926	First Republic founding	1914–1918 WW I	Republic of China founding China Civil Wars 1912–28	1911–1949
1926–1974	Second Republic – Portuguese Colonial Empire 1930–1951	1937–1945 WW II	Second Sino-Japanese War Chiang Kai-shek period PRC Founding 1949	1937–1945 1928–1948
1974	Third Republic – Carnation Revolution in 1974		Mao's death	1976
1986	Portugal joins the EU		Economic Reform 'One country, two systems'	1987

Table 9.2 (cont.)

Macao: primary political instances and Sino-Portuguese treaties

1557	Founding of Macao – according to Chinese scholars in the 14th and the 36th Year of Ka Tcheng (Jiajing) of Ming dynasty (1535–1557)
1849	Portuguese Governor Ferreira do Amaral attempt for independence – Macao stops paying land rent to China and expels Chinese officials
1887	Sino-Portuguese Friendship and Commerce Treaty (ratified 28 April 1888)
1928	Renewal of Sino-Portuguese Friendship and Commerce Treaty
1937–1945	Second Sino-Japanese War (1937–1945) and World War II (1939–1945) – Macao claimed neutrality
1966–1967	'123' Incident and PRC agreement in 1967
1987	PRC–Portugal's Joint Declaration of the Government of the People's Republic of China (PRC) and the Government of the Republic of Portugal on the Question of Macao.
1999	Handover of Macao to China in December 1999 – Macao becomes a Special Administrative Region (SAR) of PRC

[a] Paula Morais, 'Macau's Urban Transformation 1927–1949: The Significance of Sino-Portuguese Foreign Relations in the Urban Form', in Izumi Kuruoshi (ed.) *Entwined Perspectives on the Construction of the Colonized Land: East Asia and WWII*, Aldershot: Ashgate Publishing, forthcoming.
[b] DSCC, Cartography and Cadastre Bureau of Macau.
[c] C. Cónim and M. Teixeira, *Macau e a sua População 1500–2000, Aspectos Demográficos, Sociais e Económicos*, Macao: Imprensa Oficial de Macau, 1998, information originally obtained from a compilation of Macao censuses that refers to the total resident population including the islands of Taipa and Coloane.

community in the heart of China' and about 'conventions' (and 'convention practices') between China and Portugal and carefully pointed that the examination of Macao's four and a half centuries phenomena was too vast to be analysed and defined based on contemporary concepts of state, international community or international law.[15] Therefore a diversity of concepts, in its nature and objectives of power, state conceptions, tributary systems, empires that integrate territorial parcels with different levels of subordination to the centre, all these were facts that constituted the reality of the complex international system that Portugal found in Asia from the sixteenth century until the nineteenth century.[16] Therefore, and from a Portuguese perspective, the historiography of the Sino-Portuguese spatial-political relations from 1557 until 1999 will be centred on the conditions of Macao's existence as stated in the periodization note (see Table 9.1) the spatial structure of which evolved amid Chinese and Portuguese forces.[17]

Globalization and urban identity

Human identity requires the identity of a place.[18] Places are centres of significance for individuals, and these can span from the home to the neighbourhood, to the city and the region, and to the level of the sovereign state.[19] This study looks at the theoretical enquiry of territorial place-making in anthropology and urban studies – i.e. ideas of 'territorialization', 'deterritorialization' and 'reterritorialization' – looking at the question of 'space' and 'cultures' in relation to identity construction and to the forms of its territorialization – in particular in the service of state and capitalist economy projects. Macao provides evidence that the production of urban space is indeed part of the production of society as a whole, and its multiple driving forces, not limited to architectural and planning participation: i.e., a spatial political economy, presently must be analysed in the context of globalization.[20] It adds to the debate about the significance of urban space in defining identity, which in turn sustains processes of spatialization of territory. As Lisa Malkki argued, 'having roots involves an intimate relation between people and places' and '"deterritorialisation" and identity are intimately linked'.[21]

At present modernity and globalization have been accompanied by a new fluidity of capital, culture and people. Today's cities observe a constant inter-play between a relatively stable physical dimension and an unfixed public sphere. Due to this interplay, urban identity is increasingly complex to define since it flows among languages of global, national and local belonging. It is clear, particularly in an era of perceived flux and instability, that individuals need a strong sense of belonging to anchor themselves in civil society and to identify with and accept the legitimacy of their political institutions.[22] And this sense of group or territorial belonging depends on what significant char-acteristics are shared in a given place and time. So urban space, in its physical dimension, can have a role in endorsing a sense of belonging or else we find space and society in an equal state of unrest.

Urban identity in Macao

> Where do I belong? [...] As a constant lament it refers to dislocation felt by displaced subjects towards disrupted histories and to shifting and transient national identities. Equally it refers to university departments and orders of knowledge, to exhibiting institutions and marker places and, not least, to the ability to live our complex and reflexive identities which acknowledge language, knowledge, gender and race as modes of self-positioning.[23]

This study is about territorial space, identity and change in Macao. It addresses the production of urban space, which defines the historical emergence of the spatial political economy formation of territorial space presenting a synopsis of Macao's urban identity from its foundation in 1557 until present times.[24] The central argument of this investigation is that the history of Macao's urban identity question can be defined by three main spatial order projects: the one of a 'territorialization' (1557–1987), the one of a 'deterritorialization' led by

Figure 9.1 Leal Senado square in 1915 (photograph by M. Russel, in IICT/Arquivo Histórico Ultramarino, Lisbon). An example of how Portuguese identitary references were already well-expressed in the main civic square at the time, both in the buildings and in the traditional cobblestone pavement, i.e., *calçada Portuguesa* (Paula Morais, 'Macau's Urban Transformation 1927–1949: The Significance of Sino-Portuguese Foreign Relations in the Urban Form', in Izumi Kuruoshi (ed.) *Entwined Perspectives on the Construction of the Colonized Land: East Asia and WWII*, Aldershot: Ashgate Publishing, forthcoming).

post-1987 capitalist economy project and globalization forces as Macao is experiencing an incremental 'deterritorialization' process in the service of a pro-growth politics, and then the one calling for a future urban-regional 'reterritorialization' in the PRC.

'Deterritorialization' has been considered one of the key ideas in a large and leading body of literature on globalization studies. Stephan Feuchtwang argued that 'deterritorialising projects do have the expected characteristics of abstraction, destroying or emptying what was centred and meaningful, making space out of place'.[25] Feuchtwang also pointed out that 'deterritorialization' is usually in the service of 'reterritorialization' – either that of a capitalist economy or as a state project, usually both.[26] For Deleuze and Guattari,[27] capitalism needs no territory as it is the axiom of the commodity – it turns everything into a plane of abstract values and of functions.[28] Their theory of territories define these as 'sets of environmentally embedded triggers of self-organizing processes, and the concomitant processes of "deterritorialization" (breaking of habits) and "reterritorialization" (formation of habits)'.[29] Hence 'reterritorialization', after 'deterritorialization', turns the abstraction of codes, of the single plane into new relations with other planes and codes – it returns space into place, yet a new place.[30]

From 1557 to 1987 (1999) Macao produced a distinctive territorial place: i.e., the production of a particular context and identity, which is now being interrupted by modern forces of disruption – i.e. globalization and a blind capitalist economy – that will turn the plurality of Macao codes into 'the abstraction of a single space of function and matter'.[31] Macao's territory was thus spatialized and fixed in space hence identifiable,[32] and with a strong sense of uniqueness, where the notions of 'difference' are still present in the territorial and residents' discourse (Table 9.3). The urban identity of Macao means something distinctive and with the meaning of individuality as 'a workable image requires first the identification of an object'.[33] Therefore, there is no 'original identity of a place' since identity is inherently dynamic.[34] Yet, if place is an organized world of meaning then it requires a necessary static concept, which means that if places or territories would be in constant change then it would be impossible to develop any sense of place.[35] So there seems to be an interdependence of concepts: of those of change and of continuity. This dynamic is best described as 'rhizomatic',[36] i.e. as allowing immediate connections between any of its points, which is additionally stated by Hebdige in his study of Caribbean music and cultural identity:[37]

> Rather than tracing back the roots ... to their source, I've tried to show how the roots themselves are in a state of constant flux and change. The roots don't stay in one place. They change shape. They change colour. And they grow. There is no such thing as a pure point of origin ... but that doesn't mean there isn't history.[38]

The 'territorialization' project, (1557) 1887–1987 (1999)

> Time would pass, old empires would fall and new ones take their place, the relations of countries and the relations of classes had to change, before I discovered that it is not quality of goods and utility that matter, but movement: not where you are or what you have, but where you come from, where you are going and the rate at which you are getting there.[39]

From 1557 until 1987, Macao's political state of affairs was unclear as the Portuguese presence was continuously questioned by China, thus Portugal had to constantly explore ways of affirming its existence. Urban space had a significant role in this affirmation intent through promoting spatial strategies and protecting a state identity.[40] The Chinese demographic majority endorsed the sense of a 'Chinese city',[41] hence Portuguese identitary references had to be further expressed by the spatial structure in order to assist for authority assertion, so urban form was firstly political vision.[42] Furthermore Macao's uncertainty led to a constant planning flexibility and negotiation for development as there was never an 'absolute ruler' in the territory hence the inexistence of an unconditional decision-maker. Macao's spatial political

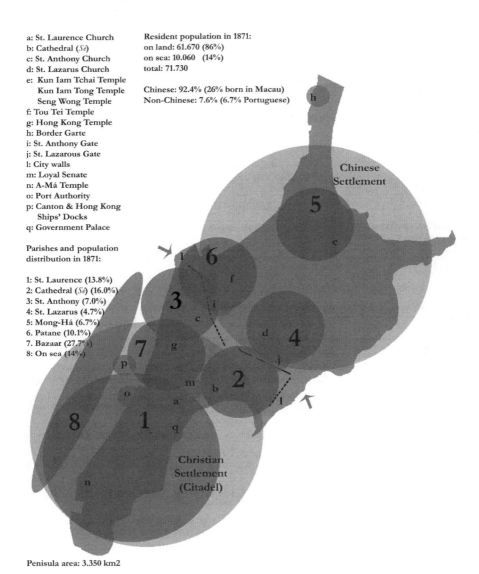

a: St. Laurence Church
b: Cathedral (*Sé*)
c: St. Anthony Church
d: St. Lazarus Church
e: Kun Iam Tchai Temple
   Kun Iam Tong Temple
   Seng Wong Temple
f: Tou Tei Temple
g: Hong Kong Temple
h: Border Garte
i: St. Anthony Gate
j: St. Lazarous Gate
l: City walls
m: Loyal Senate
n: A-Má Temple
o: Port Authority
p: Canton & Hong Kong
   Ships' Docks
q: Government Palace

Parishes and population
distribution in 1871:

1: St. Laurence (13.8%)
2: Cathedral (*Sé*) (16.0%)
3: St. Anthony (7.0%)
4: St. Lazarus (4.7%)
5: Mong-Há (6.7%)
6. Patane (10.1%)
7. Bazaar (27.7%)
8: On sea (14%)

Resident population in 1871:
on land: 61.670 (86%)
on sea: 10.060 (14%)
total: 71.730

Chinese: 92.4% (26% born in Macau)
Non-Chinese: 7.6% (6.7% Portuguese)

Chinese Settlement

Christian Settlement (Citadel)

Penisula area: 3.350 km2

Figure 9.2 (from left to right) 1889 map (diagrammatical outline) and 1889 map (illustration based on a Map of 'Macau Peninsula' by António Heitor (15th March 1889), Sociedade de Geografia de Lisboa, Litografia da Imprensa Nacional (Lisbon Association of Geography, National Lithography Press), Colecção CJ/BC. in Infante *et al* 1997, p. 26). This map illustrates Macao right after the 1887 Bi-lateral treaty. It shows two main circles that correspond to the Portuguese citadel and Chinese village of Mong-Há that were previously divided by the citadel walls which are by now fairly destroyed (dashed and continuous lines (l) represent fully destroyed walls and existing parts of it respectively). The smaller circles represent the seven parishes (1–7, in which 8 defines the maritime population area) and the little circles locate symbolic buildings, i.e. churches and temples, which act as reference points for the identity of these places (a–q), which still exist in today's urban fabric. (Paula Morais, 'Macau's Urban Transformation 1927–1949: The Significance of Sino-Portuguese Foreign Relations in the Urban Form', in Izumi Kuruoshi (ed.) Entwined Perspectives on the Construction of the Colonized Land: East Asia and WWII, Aldershot: Ashgate Publishing, forthcoming.)

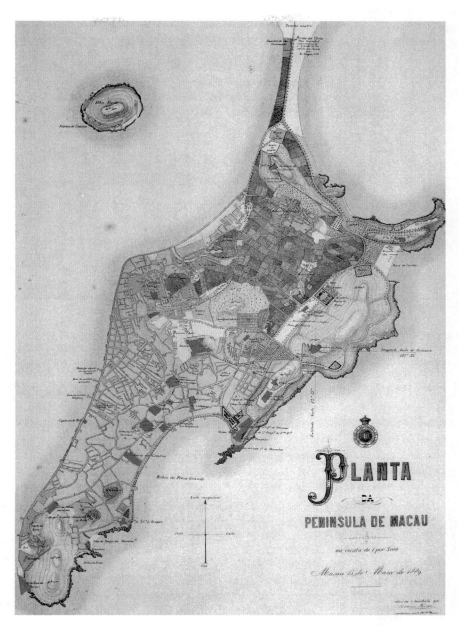

Figure 9.2 (cont.)

Figure 9.3 Leal Senado Square in the 1960s: an example of how Leal Senado Square constituted a host for both cultures: celebrating China's national day and holding the statue of Coronel Vicente Nicolau de Mesquita (right) which was strategically placed in the square in 1940 to reinforce the status quo of Macao as Portuguese and to further secure neutrality as this was during World War II and Portugal was neutral (photo owned by the author).

economy and urbanism culture during the nineteenth and twentieth centuries were of an unusual flexible nature and Portugal's spatial strategies were particularly evident.[43] In short, Macao's 'indetermination' called for a constant reinvention, flexibility and strategies' exploration to pursue the development of the territory and that aimed to secure the Portuguese presence through the means of a spatial identity until the Sino-Portuguese Joint Declaration in 1987.[44] These conditions produced a unique urban setting in Macao, which, with identity difference, provided the basis for Deng Xiaoping's politics of 'one country, two systems' in establishing the territory as a Special Administrative Region (SAR) of the People's Republic of China (Figure 9.1).

Portuguese urbanism culture entailed a strong adaptation to local contexts so the spatial patterns created across the globe in the sixteenth century were diverse.[45] The impermanence of Macao's condition, surrounding political instability and its ever-changing market led to the necessary flexibility in the territory's planning allowing the Portuguese exploring new development strategies hence its 'flexible urbanism' culture.[46] Macao had to opt between a spontaneous and successive form (assembled) and the ideal urbanism that is planned (shaped).[47] Besides, intent precedes design so urban form was firstly political vision or strategy hence the adopted politics of a flexible nature in the city design combined both previous approaches.[48] So the lack of a statutory planning system was then pragmatically accepted by the Portuguese administration and the Chinese commercial elite, who held the private investment capacity. However, during the 1970s, the 1980s and the 1990s there were several attempts by the Portuguese administration to create some form of legal planning system for Macao in which some urban studies and master planning were commissioned but never fully implemented, continuing being only referential. Planning continued to be flexible, as overall plans were administered by the Public Works Bureau and regulated by the General Regulation of Urban Construction (RGCU, Regulamento Geral de Construção Urbana) and land law.[49] In fact post-1949 planning was indeed business-oriented management as planning guidance was primarily based on land-use and its market-oriented flexibility, as often it was the use conditioned by the geographical placement in the peninsula. An additional guidance was the superior quality of the cartography that provided an accurate foundation for any plans and designs, and finally the protection that the Portuguese administration conceded to the architectural profession requiring that all projects were to be designed and surveyed by architects.[50] To conclude, over time the original 3.4km^2 peninsula of Macao was radically transformed and rose to 7.8km^2 in 1999 (Table 9.2), which led to significant alterations in its coastline and overall urban form. Visionary plans and extensive land reclamation projects occurred essentially from 1910 to 1927 and roughly continued until the early 1930s, however, urban development persisted in a relatively slow pace until 1987. It was primarily due to the 1985 changes in land law,[51] i.e. the new horizontal property regime, that the legal basis for a higher densification and urban block rescaling is set hence fostering the beginning of rapid urbanization. Lastly, it is important to refer that urban development in Macao, particularly between 1887 and 1987, was primarily linked to politico-diplomatic and contextual strategies supporting the Portuguese presence in the territory and Chinese business interests but it was also guided by the intent of enhancing the quality of urban life.

From (1557) 1887 to 1987, 'Macao' was thus spatialized and fixed in space hence 'recognizable' and with a strong sense of uniqueness,[52] where the notions of 'difference' are still present in the territorial and residents' discourse (see Table 9.3). To conclude, the significance of Macao's urban identity legacy is visible not only in its cosmopolitan society, free-market economy or culture but most deeply in its physical space. Urban form was strategic in building a state identity during the Portuguese administration particularly throughout the twentieth century. However in this constant negotiation over urban form, designs inevitably intertwined so urban space reflected both Portuguese and Chinese design traditions. Macao is indeed different, and this difference is reflected in the polysemics of its urban space – a value globally recognized by the World Heritage award given by UNESCO in 2005 to its urban centre. It demonstrates living evidence of how a territory can provide for multicultural inclusion and develop a society and space that can navigate in ever-changing contexts as 'such communities provide further examples on the human dimension in a world on the move'.[53]

The 'deterritorialization' project, (1987) 1999 /2009

The sound of jackhammers chipping away at the rocks on the street below is a reminder that change is constant – Macao has always been rebuilding. If there were no jackhammers in the eighteenth century, even then they were tearing down the buildings of the previous decades and putting up new ones in their places. In cities like Macao, time, especially architectural time, never stands still. Cities are, in many ways, very fragile constructions, ephemeral creations that endure only through a process of perpetual change. ... Modern machines make changes more rapidly – and more ruthlessly – now, and in one sense, that is all that is different about the process of change for Macao. ... the past itself was endangered. ... Will the past become a nostalgic illusion conjured only in the memory by occasional, isolated and lifeless fragments and glimpses of what once was?

[...] For several days afterwards, I felt an oppressive sense of loss – the loss of the old Macao that seemed to be disappearing everywhere before my eyes.[54]

Figure 9.4 (from left to right) Macao 2009 photographs taken by the author reveal the severe changes in the urban centre in the last decade: first is a view from the main axe of St. Paul's Ruins which has been considered the reference of Macao's identity; second a photograph of fake money paper that is usually burned to help the deceased members of the family in the underworld or appease evil spirits (this is a traditional Chinese ritual still present in Macao's everyday life), and finally an overall image of how changes in the traditional urban centre have become largely unidentifiable. The map of Macau in 2006 represents the peninsula contour at the time (in white), the original landscape in 1887 (in grey) and the areas under the present protection of UNESCO and Macao's Cultural Institute (in dark grey).

At present a new spatial order is being imposed to Macao.[55] As a result old places are disappearing and new ones are being formed. In the last decade the territory has been experiencing a 'spatial erasure' generated by the blend of three main factors:[56] first, the economic growth created by the end of gambling industry monopoly in 2002 has fostered accelerated urbanization; second, by the inexistence of a statutory planning system and effective development control; and finally, the withdrawal of the Portuguese administrative presence in Macao since 1999 means that there is now one single decision-maker –prior public administration and private investment were divided among Portuguese and Chinese elites respectively. Macao's identity 'difference' is being radically altered through uninterrupted and unplanned urban transformation hence leading to a strong spatial erosion, densification and homogenization: i.e. no difference. Furthermore, Macao's socio-cultural structures and relations are being progressively decontextualized from place hence generating a rupture and a 'sense of loss' in local residents, transversal to all cultural groups (see Table 9.3). The worst examples of spatial disruption are being experienced outside the historical centre but even its most significant heritage sites are experiencing a disturbing impact from the increasing decline of Macao's urban environment (see Figures 9.4 and 9.6).[57]

To conclude, governance's pro-growth politics and the limitation of the heritage policies are strongly endangering the territory's urban identity and soon this erasure will provide the path for 'deterritorialization' and the building of 'new identitary referents'.[58] Yet, it can be argued that Macao process of 'deterritorialization' initiated after the 1987 Sino-Portuguese Joint Declaration, which was supported by 1985 land law changes,[59] which provided the legal basis for higher densification and urban block rescaling, hence promoting rapid urbanization.

Accelerated urbanization, public narratives of loss and spatial homogenization

Macao's accelerated urbanization has been an uneven process that inevitably produces social tensions, conflicts and public and institutional protest,[60] as is widely evident in local and international media.[61] Two key examples are the Guia Lighthouse case and UNESCO's increasing concerns. UNESCO has issued consecutive alerts stating the increasing concern with Macao's urban environment and conservation areas.[62] The Guia Lighthouse controversy in October 2006 was a defining moment of public awareness and action of how seriously unprotected heritage landscape is. Several civil society groups concerned with the territory's historical environment were formed, from which two examples are the 'League of Guia Lighthouse Protectors' and the 'Guia Lighthouse Protection Concern Group'. These civil society actions led Macao government to reply to UNESCO concerns and guarantee that the territory would 'put forth the biggest effort' to 'ensure that current and future construction projects will not deteriorate the urban environment outside the buffer zones'.[63]

Several institutions, academics and decision-makers have stressed the importance of maintaining and developing Macao's cultural identity as a social, political and economic asset.[64] The president of the Association for Macao Historical and Cultural Heritage, Cheang Kok Keong,[73] stated that, particularly since the post-2002 gambling liberalization, 'Macao's "unique identity" has been in constant danger of sinking under the weight of skyscrapers, casinos and the quest for wealth'. Liu Tik Sang,[66] a cultural anthropologist, has argued that the fundamental requirement for heritage conservation is that local people have 'the heart' in doing so: if the people are proud of it (the heritage) then they will be willing to spend time preserving it, yet Sang also stressed that the government and academic institutes must play a part in supporting this goal – as 'the heart' of the government must be as willing as 'the heart' of the public. This argument about the significance of 'the heart' is found in the analysis of a recent survey of 600 residents in Macao, conducted by the Polytechnic Institute of Macao (IPM), which revealed that 49 per cent of them are proud of belonging to Macao. Present government politics of 'loving the motherland and loving Macao' has raised the importance of local and national identity awareness and affection, and this 'dual love' is a reason for the territory success of the 'one country, two systems' policy according to the study findings.[67] In 2004 President Hu Jintao made a strong call for the development of an inclusive and harmonious society in Macao stating that: 'All citizens, regardless of their stratum, circle and religion, can and should unite for the grand goals of loving the motherland, loving Macao and maintaining Macao's long-term prosperity and stability.'[68]

In short the IPM study showed that 77 per cent of the residents declared that their quality of life had generally improved, 16 per cent confirmed it remains the same and only 5 per cent claimed the decline of the quality of life. These findings were significant in understanding current population's perception of local and territorial changes. However all research results are delimited by the criteria in which questions are designed: i.e., the definition of 'quality of life'. If economic growth and financial stability are the main indicators then life in Macao has definitely improved. However the author's in-depth interviews enquired about the urban environment, social relations and culture and found that there were fundamental concerns and senses of loss (see Table 9.3).[69] A note must be made that this sample does not aim to generalize the feelings of the population of Macao but to present an example of public narratives in Macao today. Nevertheless this study provides evidence that there are several issues of concern that should be addressed and assessed further through a wider survey. Further quantitative and qualitative studies should be conducted in order to accurately assess public opinion regarding the urban environment and residents' lifestyles quality and changes. In short, the main objective of presenting this qualitative study is to provide evidence of how Macao identity is perceived as 'different', or 'special' or 'unique', as Macao is perceived by residents as a place with a 'sense of history' and 'difference', not only for its gambling industry character.

Table 9.3 Macao's urban identity definition by residents and perceptions of current changes

Resident	Place of birth	What is the identity of Macao? Can you give a description of what Macao is for you?	What do you think of Macao today? (positive, negative, other)
P1	Hong Kong	A city with a sense of history.	I feel positive – Hong Kong does not have history; it is all modern and history is important.
P7	China	A Chinese city with Portuguese style. Macao is very special.	I feel positive – Macao is capable of attracting many tourists.
P10	China	It feels like old Shanghai.	I feel positive – I come here because is cleaner but there are too many people. Before 1999 it was not so crowded.
P12	Macao	A place that still has some Portuguese culture and still have many special features. I would try not to mention the casinos.	I feel negative – too crowded with Chinese tourists! They do not know how to value their own culture. They are low educated and should be more concerned about our culture and do not use and abuse our space so much.
P13	Macao	Beautiful place, Different cultures, East and West.	I feel negative – so many things are unfair. The government goes against the resident's will.
P15	Hong Kong	Quite special place that you should go to try the experience.	I feel negative –many citizens cannot catch up with the standards of life. I do not know the past. It has been changing so fast so I cannot describe very well.
P17	Macao	Casinos and old heritage houses.	I feel negative – too many casinos and the air is bad.
P24	China	Freedom. You can be free in Macao! No one is going to constrain you.	I feel positive – I was born in China, but would not move to China now – my roots are here in Macao. The economy has developed, the government has money, so the economy is good.
P25	China	Good for living and eating –when I die I will stay here.	I feel positive – I came here to escape the Japanese war. I have my own shelter and three meals. So I am OK and the 5000 MOP per year is good!
P28	China	Gambling – I do not recognize Macao anymore. Leal Senado does not represent Macao – gambling does!	I feel negative – bad environment! Gambling industry. The government should use the tax to educate people – give them skills! I used to love Macao – I swore that I would never leave this place. But now Macao is a total failure – Macao doesn't care about the next generation!

Table 9.3 (cont.)

Resident	Place of birth	What is the identity of Macao? Can you give a description of what Macao is for you?	What do you think of Macao today? (positive, negative, other)
P30	China	Macao is like gambling – there are lots of opportunities if you venture. If you win you can win a lot; if you lose, you are lost.	I feel negative – I live here because I have no choice. I have money but I am not happy. People in Macao have no true relationships. After 30 years I am still not used to Macao. People are too indifferent and the neighbours do not know each other
P32	Macao	Macao is like Macanese food: Chinese ingredients with Portuguese seasoning.	I feel negative – before it was simple and pure. The special features of Macao have changed – it is a modern city – the Portuguese tried to maintain the heritage, today the government does not maintain the heritage well.
E1	Macau	Macao is an eccentric place, we are not China but we are not Portugal either.	I feel negative and positive – rationally I feel positive due to the economic growth and opportunities. Emotionally I feel negative as I do not identify with the newly produced spaces and architecture – I am horrified to think that Macao in 2049 will have no traces of history!
E3	Portugal	Macao is found in the Leal Senado square. It is found in the history of places.	I feel confused – identity must be represented locally and the priority is the Portuguese local context as a differentiator of Macao from the rest of China. The casinos are imposing Anglo-Saxon values now so these will start dominating the territory.
E7	US	Multicultural: you can identify with the city itself, which includes lots of things, and you use your own specific cultural background to relate to that larger sphere!	I feel negative and positive – I feel happier than in the US but the urban planning here is a mess! Macao is overcrowded … you get tense and stressed. People sort of fight each other over public space.
E13	Portugal	Macao is a shelter. I feel proud of Macao.	I feel negative – after 1999 the external interests are stronger than the local, so there is an annihilation of the culture to accommodate international interests. There is an incremental destruction.
E18	China	Macao is so small but has contributed a lot to the world in the sense of East–West and as a gateway to China, interactions in culture, in trade, in many ways … in history.	I feel negative – the Portuguese government in Portugal did not care anymore about Macao. You signed a joint declaration that we both have the responsibility to see what it isn't going well. You just let it go as it was not your business anymore – it is your business. What happened to the joint declaration, is it only a paper? You need to care! Portugal needs to care.

E19	China	*Confused!*	*I feel negative – people think only about money and do not know what to do about it.*
E20	Portugal	*A plural and vibrant city.*	*I do not know – because with the new casinos the Macao landscape changed so much. … Macao now is confusing, because there are good things, but also bad things. Before 1999 the image was not so good, but it was better than it is now.*
E23	Macao	*Macao today is not a place to live anymore. The old Macao had 91 cars, the Av. Almeida Ribeiro would become full after the 11am Sunday mass; the Tap Seac street had 9 to 13 house s… Everyone that arrived in Macao left with a 'memory'.*	*I feel negative – before 1966 I liked Macao. Today life is different and to go back is impossible. I do not like the tall buildings, the density and the scale – the buildings that existed before were maximum three storeys high.*
E28	China	*Macao is a mixed culture so we should capitalize on that – for tourism – but then the government must also consider residents' needs – tourists are important but what about us?*	*I feel negative – Macao is developing casinos but no social development – we will have to pay for creating an imbalanced society. It is very sad but we are losing all the people with knowledge – a generation of elite people is gone.*
E31	Portugal	*The idea is 'protection', this is my image from Macao. Do you know the story of the lotus flower? Macao is built in a lotus flower that is open but when the danger comes the lotus closes and protects the people.*	*I feel positive – I do feel affected by the latest urbanization and development – I care more about people than buildings. But in Macao there is a claustrophobic phenomenon that impels me to leave every three months! Also we are like phantoms [like glass] nobody talks to you. The problem is not in space but in the culture. But I am not here to maintain the Portuguese legacy or the Portuguese culture.*
E33	Macao	*Macao is like a Portuguese house with Chinese furniture (the people are Chinese but the houses are European).*	*I feel negative – this is not my home! after 1999 Macao has become a 'house of tatterdemalions', the bad people are born now out of 'too much money and too little education', and ambition.*
E37	Portugal	*Fortune! It is the word that symbolizes Macao is a promise that the city promotes for the Chinese, Portuguese, Filipino … it is a 'lollipop city'.*	*I feel positive – to be honest I like the new image. It is much more dynamic, and I am not nostalgic, plus I like mistakes. Macao space reflects what it is in reality and its values, and when there are no values the city makes more neons!*

Table 9.3 presents a sample of individual descriptions of what Macao identity is and how residents feel about the latest urban changes. This is a sample illustration of the 60 in-depth interviews conducted with residents by the author in different locations and urban public spaces of Macao, hence providing for a diversity of public narratives. The main places for public interviewing were the squares of Leal Senado, Lilau, Hong Kung Temple, Carlos da Maia, Triangular, Tap Seac and Lotus. Furthermore the sample includes the public (P), academics and decision-makers in Macao (E) from Chinese, Portuguese and Macao cultural groups.

In the end, the Portuguese group did not bring 'European history' to people without it. They brought individual histories that were far less predictable than we may have been inclined to think. Macao is one of those places that provides evidence that global forces played in local contexts and forms in unexpected ways, changing known structures into unusual spatial and cultural settings:[70] i.e., 'different'. A critical evidence of the outstanding universal value of Macao's urban identity (and spatial structure difference) is the World Heritage Committee's recognition of Macao historic centre in 2005 as a living embodiment of the city urban culture.[71] Macao was indeed a unique urban interface for East and West civilizations; individuals came to Macao due to a diversity of reasons, but primarily due to political and economic interests. It was a place of 'indetermination',[72] which gradually created a very polysemic and complex urban space. But above all Macao was 'different'. The elimination of this difference will constitute a loss not only for Macao's identity and its citizens but it will also remove a critical asset of its political economy.[73] So, Macao has acquired a new value for China due to its bridging role for economic cooperation between the Portuguese speaking-countries and the mainland. For Portugal, the new value of Macao may be in recapturing its economic, financial and commercial significance,[74] so new strategies must be designed based on common interests that will maintain and strengthen the relations between Macao, Portugal and China:

> While Macau's current special status almost guarantees that the territory's unique character will fade rather than disappear overnight, the process can only be slowed further by heavy investment from Portugal or the emergence of a new special character for the territory.[75]

These strategies must be cultural, essentially commercial and economic,[76] yet they must also be spatial. Macao government has an unclear vision and uncoordinated decision-making processes as it lacks a long-term vision for development, strategy and the necessary planning tools for development control. Planning in Macao has been management (not planning) and MSAR development vision appears contradictive in practice – as if Macao is to be a 'World Centre of Tourism and Leisure' then it must carefully consider the quality of its urban environment (see Figures 9.4 and 9.6). MSAR has finally commissioned to Guangdong Provincial Urban and Rural Planning Research Institute a project to develop a planning law for the territory – 'Projecto da Lei do Planeamento Urbanístico e das Ideias Conceptuais dos Diplomas Legais Complementares'[77] – which was recently under public consultation (25 April until 5 June 2012) as the inclusion of the civil society in the planning process is also essential. This project was based on an initial study carried out in 2008 as the last decade's growth and public demand urgently required development control action, and also due to the central government's approval in 2009 of a new reclamation plan for 350 hectares that will require robust planning guidance.

Finally the urbanism culture requires an in-depth analysis and diagnosis of urban structures and patterns in order to produce evidence-based plans. It needs a careful assessment of what constitutes spatial inheritance that can represent a pattern of continuity by different stakeholders and cultural groups (i.e. Chinese, Macanese and Portuguese institutions and overall civil society) thus 'what to erase and what to keep' will define its future spatial narrative. Macao's significance and future ambitions should be more than to aspire for the profits of historical tradition to be reorganized as 'a museum culture ... of local history'.[78] Places are also the homes of people that need fundamental association with their environment – as places of history and the ones of memories are not necessarily the same. If places are going to continue being erased and ignored in the name of placelessness then the future can only hold an environment where places do not matter.[79] Architects and urbanists have been fighting for a new thought of city renovation, of buildings, that must be a reflexive process and not only a place for inventions and originalities

> that means we must go back, pick up the narrative of the city and continue it. If we could do that would be great. I only did it in fact with a serious urbanism, I think of the past in order to propose for the future.[80]

A serious urbanism entails concepts of sustainability, which in turn contains the need for diversity and identity continuity that will promote a 'sense of history' as 'of place'.[81] Suggestions for ensuring sustainable urban development lay at the level of urban governance, statutory planning and urban design.

In the end the factual value of Macao is how a territory can provide for multicultural inclusion and develop a society and space that can navigate in ever-changing contexts with no fundamental conflict. The territory politico-economic structure was divided amid Portuguese and Chinese forces hence creating a polysemic space that is ambiguous and with multiple meanings. And as Kevin Lynch pointed out,[82] space should be open-ended and adaptable to change allowing individuals to continue and organize reality. Macao had an exemplary recipe of how to build a harmonious society, the ingredients of which are a division of powers, a plural society and a polysemic space.

The 'reterritorialization' project 2009 and onwards

Modernity in the West has been understood as a process of historical transformation that encompasses concepts of freedom, human rights and

Figure 9.5 Leal Senado Square in 2010: an example of spatial continuity on the main civic square as the main buildings remain and the traditional cobblestone pavement has been reapplied with a similar wave pattern design as the one in 1915 (i.e., *calçada Portuguesa*).

individuality.[83] Marc Augé uses the concept of 'supermodernity' to describe the logic of late capitalist phenomena,[84] which is defined by a logic of excess: of information, of homogenization of space and of consumption. Additionally latest literature on globalization reveals that nationally organized politico-cultural identities are being 'deterritorialized',[85] as there is an apparent disembedding of social relations from their local-territorial preconditions.[86] Neil Brenner's central thesis states that processes of 'reterritorialization' – i.e. the reconfiguration and rescaling of forms of territorial organization such as cities and states – must be viewed as an intrinsic moment of the current round of globalization.[87] Furthermore the relationship between cities and territorial states is being significantly eroded, generating new geographies of global urbanization and capital accumulation whose control goes beyond state territorial powers.[88] In short, Brenner points out that in spite of the diversity of analysis of globalization theses are relatively confluent in stating that there is an:

> accelerated circulation of people, commodities, capital, money, identities and images through global space. These accelerated, globally circulating

flows are said to embody processes of deterritorialisation through which social relations are being increasingly detached and disembedded from places and territories on sub-global geographical scales. ... Globalisation is conceived here as a reterritorialisation of both socioeconomic and political-institutional spaces that unfolds simultaneously upon multiple, superimposed geographical scales.[89]

There is, once again, a new spatial order project for Macao now. Last decades path of 'deterritorialization' has served a pro-growth economic project that has generated a severe decline in the urban environment and identity essentially due to the inefficiency of development control. However, globalization forces in Macao are also enforcing the need of a future city-regional scale 'reterritorialization': i.e. the reconfiguration and rescaling of forms of territorial organization in the Pearl River Delta in the name of global economic competitiveness.

The Pearl River Delta Mega City-Region Strategic Spatial Planning Report was designed as a cross-boundary study based on the spatial plan framework of 'one country, two systems' and it defines a 9+2 city region: i.e. greater PRC townships (9) and Hong Kong and Macao (2), in pursuit of 'Building Coordinated and Sustainable World-Class City-Region'.[90] It previews the reorganization of space into three new metropolitan areas: i.e. Guangzhou/Foshan, Hong-Kong/Shenzen and Macao/Zhuhai. The spatial aspect is indeed one of the main characteristics of the study in which three major development strategies for the Greater PRC city-region are recommended, namely the optimization of spatial structure, high accessibility and quality environment. It promotes a positive shift from regional competition to cooperation in order to capitalize on individual advantages, and hopefully will further enforce sustainable development control at regional and local levels. However, to benefit from individual advantages territories must retain their individuality, including the spatial differences in which Macao tourism economy is strongly based: 'a World of Difference, the Difference is Macao – so if Macao is not different, then it is not Macao'.[91]

> If two things have absolutely nothing which distinguishes them from each other, they are identical, then they are the same thing.[92]

Urban identity difference is necessary for a sustainable development framework for Macao and the PRC city region – in particular spatial difference preservation and production. Primary reasons for this are: first, urban identity difference is imperative for the success of Macao's economy and its diversification,[93] in particular its tourism industry. The PRC strategy addresses this matter through stating that the main purpose of it is to facilitate the establishment of the three economic zones but allowing the specialized development of individual places. However the subject of individuality is still timidly addressed, hence Macao will have to ensure

Figure 9.6 (from top to down) photos taken by the author in 2009: Guangzhou, Hong Kong and Macao. These are examples of how previous distinctive cities are becoming spatially similar.

the question and meaning of individuality. Therefore, the second step is to secure economic individuality through socio-spatial and cultural diversity, which in turn will be ensured by a statutory planning system and sustainable urbanism culture. China planning system and urbanization have long been criticized for ignoring local differences and enforcing a large homogenization of space,[94] 'Stop making Chinese cities look the same!'[95] This was the main statement of a planning forum in Suzhou in 2010 in which academics and urban planners gathered to urge China to stop building lookalike cities with 'identical faces', encouraging planners and designers to preserve local identities and to 'provide nutrition or inspiration to new Chinese building styles'.[96] A similar phenomenon is visible in Macao and the PRC city region (see Figure 9.6). Hence Macao spatial identity preservation and a new creative architectural production should be secured through the means of promoting a rich architectural and urbanism culture. Also, urban-regional scale integration is a complex matter of governance and planning, and it will be particularly difficult to implement socially and culturally. Environment is a transversal aspiration as it is by nature an integrative ingredient. But the plurality of socio-cultural forms will be difficult to manage in this new urban-regional territorial order, hence the preservation of local identities will be critical. Local identities can promote positive city-regional scale 'reterritorialization' as SARs' socio-cultural identities continuity will lessen any 'deterritorialization' process through neither creating sudden ruptures nor disembedding social relations from their places, thus assisting a stable socio-cultural environment. A note must be made that 'deterritorialization' processes are occurring in other places in China and the world,[97] as capitalism needs no territory since it is the axiom of the commodity that turns places into spaces.[98] In time and through a 'reterritorialization' that favours plurality and a natural process of socio-spatial embedding it is possible that Macao will acquire a new 'sense of place' and belonging continuing to honour the prosperous formula of 'loving the motherland and loving Macao'.

So Macao needs to guarantee urban identity and difference by planning (not managing) strategies, coordinated at the local level and between the urban-region scales – i.e., cooperation on a win-win basis,[99] securing the continuation of local socio-cultural and environmental capital.

Conclusion

Space matters! And a different space matters even more. Macao has proved that urban space has served different state projects and intentions over time. The materialization of urban form is not an irrational process as it constitutes a significant interface between political economy and urban design.[100] Macao is a symbol of the significance of space and the power that spatial structures can exert for state's controlling its actions and empowering nationality, for developing local-global economy competitiveness and territorial rescaling.

Hence the history of Macao urban identity quest can be defined by three main spatial order projects:

1. From (1557) and particularly from 1887 to 1987, Macao had an ambiguous political status (i.e. the 'Macao question') hence the Portuguese aimed primarily at securing their presence in the territory as it was constantly questioned by China. Urban space was critical in affirming at state identity, which in turn sustained political and economic strategies: i.e. the 'territorialization' project.
2. Yet, since 1987 urban space in Macao has been experiencing large changes, most intensely since post-1999 due to MSAR strong pro-growth politics and inadequacy of development control. Spatial structure erosion and urban environment decline are enforcing a disembedding of social forms from place, hence generating a vast sense of loss in the public. Furthermore spatial erasure and newly produced forms are creating a largely homogeneous and unidentifiable landscape. Macao increasing identity loss is providing the way for 'deterritorialization'.
3. Finally globalization and the reconfiguration and rescaling of territorial organization forms in the PRC are initiating a process of an urban-regional 'reterritorialization'.

In short, Macao unique urban identity and difference are disappearing in the name of the productive forces of local, regional and world-scale capital accumulation and state rescaling.[101] This spatial erasure will soon provide for an identity shift, which will have severe impacts on local socio-cultural forms and relations, environmental distinctiveness and finally in the local economy as identity is a serious value for the territory's development. Hence Macao needs a vision, coordinated strategies within the different planning scales: i.e., national and regional, territorial and neighbourhood – as for too long the territory has lacked fundamental tools for development control through the means of a statutory planning system. Present heritage policies are insufficient to ensure sustainable development and to fully honour China's long-term goal of creating an 'inclusive and harmonious society'.

> As long as Macao's overall and long-term interests and China's national interests are truly cherished, Macao can achieve a broad-based unity in its society and make concerted efforts to usher in an even brighter future for the Macao people.[102]

To conclude, China's harmonious society project needs the necessary tools to be implemented and become successful. Thus this study argues, based on a Macao case study, that urban identity has a multidimensional responsibility in spatializing territories, in contextualizing and providing for identification among societies and their places, serving at different times, different projects and intents. It is precisely the paramount value of space and cultural plurality spatialization that Macao has so clearly demonstrated through history that must be recognized. Individuality in the new PRC urban-region is possible for Macao through the means of a sustainable urbanism that capitalizes on socio-cultural and spatial differences. Therefore, sustainable development must place a strong note on the cultural features of societies in relation to social, economic and environmental.[103] 'Loving the motherland and loving Macao', creating harmonious and sustainable places means to ensure that social and economic development are 'mutually reinforcing' in the rapid transforming landscape of the twenty-first century.[104]

Notes

1 Guangdong Provincial Government, Macao SAR and Hong Kong SAR Governments, *Building Coordinated and Sustainable World-Class City-Region Consolidated Final Report 2009*, p. 2.
2 Ibid., p. 3.
3 The 'Planning Study on the Coordinated Development of the Greater Pearl River Delta (PRC) Townships' (the 'Greater PRC Study') is the first strategic planning study undertaken with the agreement among the Hong Kong and Macao Affairs Office of the State Council and the governments of Guangdong Province, Hong Kong Special Administrative Region (SAR) and Macao SAR – its commission originated from 2004 at the Hong Kong/Guangdong Cooperation Joint Conference.
4 Ibid., p. 1: Planning study report title – *Building Coordinated and Sustainable World-Class City-Region Consolidated Final Report*.
5 *Building Coordinated and Sustainable World-Class City-Region Consolidated Final Report 2009*, p. 8.
6 Brenner, 'Globalisation as Reterritorialisation: The Re-scaling of Urban Governance in the European Union', *Urban Studies*, 36(3), 1999, p. 446
7 Henri Lefebvre, *The Production of Space*, London: Wiley-Blackwell, 1974, 1978; Brenner, 'Globalisation as Reterritorialisation'.
8 Luso-Chinese Friendship and Commercial Treaty.
9 In 1846 all Chinese officials were expelled from Macao by Governor Ferreira do Amaral (later assassinated) hence originating the need of the 1887 Treaty. In 1987 Portugal and China the signed the Joint Declaration that specified the handover of Macao to China on 20 December 1999.
10 The divergence between Portuguese and Chinese authorities regarding the Portuguese presence in Macao were based on the difference of interpretations that both powers had about the question of sovereignty and true status of the territory: i.e. the 'Macao question', which is explained further in this chapter.
11 It can be argued that in fact spatial erasure and urban change initiated after the PRC-Portugal's Joint Declaration in 1987 – this period until 1999 already experienced heavy spatial densification. Yet, it is after 1999 that fundamental changes occurred.
12 A.H. de Oliveira Marques, *História dos Portugueses no Extremo Oriente: Macau e Timor no Período Repúblicano* (*History of the Portuguese in the Far East: Macau and Timor in the Republican Period*), Vol. IV, Lisbon: Fundação Oriente, 2003; according to Chinese historians the funding is thought to be around the 14th and the 36th Year of Ka Tcheng [Jiajing] of Ming dynasty (1535–1557), in Tan Shibao, 'Estudos sobre a Lenda das Aldeias na Península de Macau antes da sua Fundação' ('Studies about the Legend of the Villages of the Macau Peninsula before its Foundation'), *Revista de Cultura*, 1, 2002, p. 20–33 and Fok Kai Cheong,

Estudos sobre a instalação dos Portugueses em Macau (*Studies about the Portuguese settlement in Macau*), Lisbon: Gradiva, 1996.

13 Antonio Vasconcelos de Saldanha, *Estudos sobre as relacoes Luso-Chinesas* (*Studies about the Luso-Chinese relations*), Lisbon: Instituto Superior de Ciências Sociais e Políticas & Instituto Cultural de Macau, 1996.

14 Saldanha, *Estudos sobre as relacoes Luso-Chinesas* (*Studies about the Luso-Chinese relations*); M. Calado et al, 'Macau: Memorial City on the Estuary of the Pearl River', *Review of Culture*, second series, 36–7, 1998, p. 615; Moisés Silva Fernandes, *Macau na Política Externa Chinesa 1949–1979* (*Macau in the Chinese Foreign Policy 1949–1979*), Lisbon: Imprensa de Ciências Sociais, 2006.

15 Saldanha, *Estudos sobre as relacoes Luso-Chinesas* (*Studies about the Luso-Chinese relations*).

16 Ibid., p. 16.

17 Ibid., p. 615.

18 Norberg-Schulz, *Genius Loci: Towards a Phenomenology of Architecture*, New York: Rizzoli International Publications, 1980, p. 22.

19 Yi-Fu Tuan, *Space and Place: The Perspective of Experience*, Minneapolis: University of Minnesota Press, 1977, 2007, p. 179.

20 Cuthbert, 'A Debate from Down-Under', pp. 223–224; Scott Lash John Urry, *Economies of Signs & Space*, London: Sage, 1994; J. Brian McLoughlin, *Urban and Regional Planning: A Systems Approach*, London: Faber and Faber, 1994; Peter Saunders, *Social Theory and the Urban Question*, London: Routledge, 1989; A.D. King 'The Social Production of Building Form: Theory and Research', *Environment and Planning D. Society and Space*, 2(4), 1984, pp. 429–446; Manuel Castells, *The City and the Grassroots, A Cross-Cultural Theory of Urban Social Movements*, Berkeley: University of California Press, 1983. Henri Lefebvre, *The Production of Space*.

21 Liisa H. Malkki, 'National Geographic: The Rooting of Peoples and the Territorialization of National Identity among Scholars and Refugees', *Cultural Anthropology*, 7(1), 1992, p. 24.

22 UNESCO, *Towards a Constructive Pluralism Report*. Extract from opening address by Chief Emeka Anyaoku, Commonwealth Secretary-General on Pluralism for the 2000 International Year for the Culture and Peace, 1999, p. 7.

23 Irit Rogoff, *Terra Infirma: Geography's Visual Culture*, New York and London: Routledge, 2000, p. 14.

24 A.R. Cuthbert, 'A Debate from Down-Under: Spatial Political Economy and Urban Design', *Urban Design International,* 10, 2005, pp. 223–234.

25 Stephan Feuchtwang, *Making Place: State Projects, Globalisation and Local Responses in China*, New York and London: Routledge-Cavendish, 2004.

26 Ibid.

27 Ibid.

28 Gilles Deleuze and Felix Guattari, *A Thousand Plateaus: Capitalism and Schizophrenia*, London: Continuum International Publishing Group Ltd., 1988, 2004; Feuchtwang, *Making Place*.

29 Daniel Smith and John Protevi, 'Gilles Deleuze', in Edward N. Zalta (ed.), *The Stanford Encyclopedia of Philosophy*, Stanford: Stanford University Press, 2008.

30 Ibid.

31 Deleuze and Guattari, *A Thousand Plateaus*.

32 Anthony D. Smith, *The Ethnic Origins of Nations*, New York: Blackwell, 1986, p. 1.

33 Kevin A. Lynch, *The Image of the City*, Cambridge, MA: MIT Press, 1960.

34 UNESCO, *Towards a Constructive Pluralism Report*; Deleuze and Guattari, *A Thousand Plateaus*; Milton and Rose D. Friedman, *Free to Choose*, London: Secker and Warburg, 1980, Lynch, *The Image of the City*.

35 Tuan, *Space and Place*, p. 179.
36 Deleuze and Guattari, *A Thousand Plateaus*, p. 3.
37 Malkki, 'National Geographic', p. 37.
38 Dick Hebdige, *Cut 'n' Mix: Culture, Identity, and Caribbean Music*, New York and London: Routledge, 1987, p. 10.
39 C.L.R. James, *Beyond a Boundary*, Durham: Duke University Press Books, 1993, p. 116–117.
40 Morais, 'Macau's Urban Transformation 1927–1949'.
41 Chinese population was in general about 95 per cent of the total population in particular between 1887 and 1999. Portuguese population was indeed a minority and varied from being 6.7 per cent (1889), 2.4 per cent (1927), 0.6 per cent (1980) and 0.9 per cent (1996) – population data in Cónim CNPS & Teixeira MFB, *Macau e a sua População, 1500-2000*.
42 Nuno Portas, *Os tempos das Formas, Volume 1: A Cidade Feita e Refeita* (*The times of Forms, Volume I: The City Made and Remade*), Braga: Universidade do Minho, 2005.
43 Cuthbert, 'A Debate from Down-Under'; Scott Lash John Urry, *Economies of Signs & Space*; J. Brian McLoughlin, *Urban and Regional Planning: A Systems Approach*; Peter Saunders, *Social Theory and the Urban Question*; A.D. King 'The Social Production of Building Form: Theory and Research'; Manuel Castells, *The City and the Grassroots, A Cross-Cultural Theory of Urban Social Movements*; Lefebvre, *The Production of Space*.
44 Morais, 'Macau's Urban Transformation 1927–1949'.
45 Ibid.
46 Ibid.
47 Kostof, *The City Assembled: The Elements of Urban Form Through History*, London: Thames & Hudson, 1992.
48 Portas, *Os tempos das Formas, Volume 1*.
49 RGCU was a set of planning rules that guided construction and urban design (e.g. height, typology, occupation rates, etc).
50 Morais, 'Macau's Urban Transformation 1927–1949'.
51 Macao government sets up a new *Regime Jurídico da Propriedade Horizontal, Decreto-Lei 31/85/M* (*Horizontal Property Regime*).
52 Smith, *The Ethnic Origins of Nations*, p. l.
53 Russel-Wood, *The Portuguese Empire, 1415–1808: A World on the Move*, Baltimore: The Johns Hopkins University Press, 1992, 1998, p. xvi.
54 Porter, 1996: 191–193.
55 Morais, 'Macau's Urban Transformation 1927–1949'; Paula Morais, 'Macao Culture of Space and Time', *Review of Culture* (International Edition), 31, 2009, pp. 8–27.
56 Ibid.
57 Ibid.
58 Ibid.
59 Macao government sets up a new *Regime Jur í dico da Propriedade Horizontal* (*Horizontal Property Regime*), *Decreto- Lei 31/85/M*.
60 Two examples are presented: UNESCO latest expert formal alerts and the Guia Lighthouse case.
61 UNESCO, Convention Concerning the Protection of the World Cultural and Natural Heritage, 35th session, Paris: UNESCO Headquarters, 2011; and examples of press news in 'History in Ruins', *Macao Closer*, 2009; 'Heritage Protection Hindered by Lack of Laws', *Macao Daily Times*, 2011; 'Reclamações sobre Lei do Património Cultural enviadas à UNESCO' ('Complaints sent to UNESCO regarding Heritage Law'), *Hoje Macao* (*Macao Today*), 2012.
62 'Reclamações sobre Lei do Património Cultural enviadas à UNESCO'.

63 'Central Govt Urges Explanation of Guia Lighthouse Conservation', *Macao Daily Times*, 14 August 2008.
64 Morais, 'Macao Culture of Space and Time'; Thomas Chung, 'Valuing Heritage in Macau: On Contexts and Processes of Urban Conservation', *Journal of Current Chinese Affairs*, 38(1), 2009, pp. 129–160; J.L. Sales Marques et al, *ACE Macau: Architecture Culture Environment*, Macao: Politecnico di Milano, 2007; Richard Engelhardt, 'The Management of World Heritage Cities: Evolving Concepts, New Strategies', in David Lung (ed.), *The Conservation of Urban Heritage: Macao Vision*, Macao: Instituto Cultural do Governo da R.A.E. de Macau, 2004, pp. 33–48; Fok Kai Chong, 'The Existence of Macau: A Chinese Perspective', in *Macau on the Threshold of the Third Millennium*, Macao: Macau Ricci Institute, 2003, pp. 13–38; Carlos Marreiros, 'Macau Mixed Architecture and Urbanisation', in *Macau on the Threshold of the Third Millennium*, Macao: Macau Ricci Institute, 2003, pp. 205–241; Roderich Ptak, 'Macau: China's Window to the Latin World', in Arthur H. Chen (ed.), *Culture of Metropolis in Macau: An International Symposium on Cultural Heritage Strategies for the Twenty-first Century*, Macao: Instituto Cultural do Governo da RAE de Macau, 2001, pp. 327–336; Gary M.C. Ngai, 'Macau's Identity: The Need for its Preservation and Development into the Next Century', *Portuguese Studies Review*, 7(2), 1999, pp. 112–128.
65 'History in Ruins,' Macu Closer, March 2009
66 'Heritage Protection Hindered by Lack of Laws', *Macao Daily Times*, 16 July 2011.
67 'IPM revela dados sobre estudo aos cidadãos sobre a política 'um país, dois sistemas' ('IPM reveals data about the study done to the citizens regarding the policy of "one country, two systems"'), *Hoje Macao*, 11 July 2011.
68 President Hu Jintao made this call during a celebration gathering marking the fifth anniversary of Macao's return to the motherland and the inauguration of the second-term government of the Macao SAR, in *China Daily*, 20 December 2004.
69 Morais, 'Macao Culture of Space and Time'.
70 John L. Comaroff, *Ethnography and the Historical Imagination*, New York: Westview Press, 1992.
71 The World Heritage Committee's decision is based on the cultural criteria (ii), (iii), (iv), and (vi) as set out in the 'Decisions adopted at the 29th Session of the World Heritage Committee, Durban 2005' in WHC-05/29.COM/22, 130–1 (WHC 2005), Chung, 'Valuing Heritage in Macau'.
72 Joao de Pina-Cabral, *Between China and Europe: Person, Cultures and Emotion in Macao*, New York and London: London School of Economics Monographs on Social Anthropology, Continuum London-New York, 2002, p. xi.
73 Morais, 'Macao Culture of Space and Time'.
74 Moisés Silva Fernandes, *Macau na Política Externa Chinesa 1949–1979*, p. 16; Richard Lewis Edmonds, 'Macau in the Pearl River Delta and Beyond', *China Perspectives*, 44, 2002, pp. 18–29.
75 Francisco Murteira, 'Algumas Reflexões sobre o Triângulo China-Macau-Portugal' ('Some Reflections about the China-Macau-Portugal Triangle'), *Povos e Culturas* (*Cultures of Peoples*), 5, 1996, pp. 385–386; Moisés Silva Fernandes, 'Após Macau: Perspectivas sobre as Relações Luso-Chinesas depois de 1999' ('After Macau: Perspectives on the Luso-Chinese Relations after 1999'), in *Ação do IV Congresso Português de Sociologia – Sociedade Portugesa: Passados Recentes, Futuros Próximos* (*Action of the Fourth Portuguese Conference of Sociology-Portuguese Society: Recent Past, Near Future*), Coimbra: Universidade Federal do Rio de Janeiro, Instituto de Filosofia e Ciências Sociais, 2000, p. 15.
76 Fernandes, *Macau na Política Externa Chinesa 1949–1979* (*Macau in the Chinese Foreign Policy 1949–1979*), p. 15.
77 DSSOPT (2012) – Ideias conceptuais do projecto de proposta de Lei do Planeamento Urbanístico e dos diplomas complementares (Texto de consulta)

(Conceptual ideas for the Urban Planning Law and complementary diplomas' proposal – consultation text).

78 David Harvey, *The Urban Experience*, Baltimore: Johns Hopkins University Press, 1989, p. 303.

79 Edward Relph, *Place and Placelessness*, London: Pion Ltd, 1976.

80 Nuno Portas, 'Entrevista a Nuno Portas conduzida por Carlos Vaz Marques' ('Interview to Nuno Portas by Carlos Vaz Marques'), *Revista LER* (*LER Journal*), July/August 2012.

81 John Locke, *'Of Identity and Diversity'*, in *An Essay Concerning Human Understanding*, ed. Raymond Wilburn, London: J.M. Dent & Sons, 1947, pp. 162–174; Ljubinko M. Pušic, 'Sustainable Development and Urban Identity: A Social Context', *Spatium*, 11, 2004, pp. 1–6.

82 Lynch, *The Image of the City*.

83 William S.W. Lim, *Asian Ethical Urbanism: A Radical Postmodern Perspective*, Singapore: World Scientific Publishing Co., illustrated edition, 2005.

84 Marc Augé, *Non-Places: Introduction to an Anthropology of Supermodernity*, New York and London: Verso, 1995.

85 Aejun Appadurai, *Modernity at Large: Cultural Dimensions of Globalization*, Minneapolis: University of Minnesota Press, 1996.

86 Brenner, 'Globalisation as Reterritorialisation'.

87 Ibid.

88 P. Taylor, 'World Cities and Territorial States: The Rise and Fall of their Mutuality', in P. Knox and P. Taylor (eds), *World Cities in a World-System*, New York: Cambridge University Press, 1995, pp. 48–62.

89 Brenner, 'Globalisation as Reterritorialisation'.

90 *Building Coordinated and Sustainable World-Class City-Region Consolidated Final Report 2009*, p. 5.

91 MSAR, Macao Government Tourism Office.

92 Gottfried Wilhelm Leibniz (1646–1716) – the *Identity of Indiscernibles* is a principle of analytic ontology first explicitly formulated by Wilhelm Gottfried Leibniz in his *Discourse on Metaphysics*, Loemker, 1969, p. 308.

93 Chung, 'Valuing Heritage in Macau'; Fok, 'The Existence of Macau: A Chinese Perspective'.

94 'City Planners Urged to Stop Building Look-Alike Cities with Identical Faces', *People's Daily* Online 2010; and Lu Yongyi, Li Yu and Wang in personal interviews to the author in 2008.

95 'City Planners Urged to Stop Building Look-Alike Cities with Identical Faces'.

96 Ibid.

97 China creation of mega-city regions – e.g. PRC and Yangtze River Deltas, and Beijing- Tianjin-Bohai Area.

98 Deleuze and Guattari, *A Thousand Plateaus*; Feuchtwang, *Making Place*.

99 *Building Coordinated and Sustainable World-Class City-Region Consolidated Final Report*, 2009.

100 Cuthbert, 'A Debate from Down-Under'.

101 Henri Lefebvre, *The Production of Space*; Brenner, 'Globalisation as Reterritorialisation'.

102 'Hu Envisions Better Future for Macao SAR', *China Daily*, 20 December 2004.

103 Keith Nurse, *Culture as the Fourth Pillar of Sustainable Development*, London: Commonwealth Secretariat, 2006; Ljubinko M. Pušic, 'Sustainable Development and Urban Identity'; UNESCO, *Records of the General Conference 31st Session Paris*, 15 October to 3 November 2001, Vols I and II, 2002; OECD, *Sustainable Development: Critical Issues*, Paris: Organization for Economic Co-operation and Development, 2001.

104 WCED, *Our Common Future*, Oxford: Oxford University Press, 1987, p. 54

10 State, market forces and building national identity in China's Hong Kong and Macao

Bill K.P. Chou

Introduction

This chapter compares the building of national identity in postcolonial Macao and Hong Kong. Their former colonial rulers never seriously built national identities of any sorts in the two city-states. After the retrocession of the sovereignty to China, the governments of the two Special Administrative Regions (hereafter SARs) are pursuing the reintegration of the people to the national identity of China as the people in both Macao and Hong Kong have not yet identified themselves fully with the mainland. They are conscious of the distinction between their mainland Chinese counterparts and themselves, and between the mainland and their home city. The success of building a state-defined national identity in these two city-states is contingent on the strength of local identities as much as political elites' intentional efforts. Macao identity is weaker than Hong Kong identity; Hong Kong identities contrast considerably with the Chinese national identity on the views towards civil liberty, legal concepts and linguistic culture. Behind the contrasts are the effectiveness of the colonial governance and the vibrancy of the mass media (together with the pop culture created).

Meanwhile, the market forces in the two postcolonial city-states shape the trajectory of national identity-building in different ways. It is argued that the identity of the new sovereignty has become more receptive among the Hong Kong Chinese communities due to the business and personal opportunities available in the mainland. Nevertheless, the Hong Kong identity became stronger with the emergence of the ill impact of certain Chinese policies, namely intensifying intervention in Hong Kong politics and increasing economic integration with Hong Kong. In Macao, a local identity revolving the cultural and historical heritage has quietly emerged out of the government's economic rationality in promoting the city's cultural tourism.

Formation of Hong Kong and Macao identities

National identity is a sense of common history and culture shared by the communities within the boundary of a nation. In the period shortly after

World War II when many former colonies went independent, building national identity was an urgent task for these newly-formed countries as a common national identity is necessary to the cohesion of the societies.[1] It is able to strengthen territorial integration and maintain social stability – fundamental conditions for any modern state to augment the capacity of their governance, promote national economic development and improve the welfare of the public. This function is especially essential for the countries composed of two or more significant ethnic groups without other common values, languages, religions and/or understanding of their own histories. As a result, building national identity is always high on the political agenda of modern nation-states upon their establishment.

National identity is shaped by the education system and mass media along with other elements such as market forces. Through their impact on education and mass media, the authorities may influence what people know, believe and treasure. During the colonial era, the education system and mass media of Hong Kong and Macao played negative roles in inculcating a sense of belonging to China.[2] The education system in Hong Kong during colonial era was characterized by depoliticization. In the 1950s, the Chinese nationalistic sentiments that pro-Beijing schools perpetuated were deemed threatening to the colonial government. Out of the Cold War mentality and fear of communism, the colonial government closed down some of these schools. It aligned students' thinking with the market-driven ideology in two ways. First, the utilitarian aspect of education was emphasized by adapting the British education system to the local system. English teaching was promoted. Students studying in the schools with English as instruction medium were favoured in further studies in both local and overseas higher institutes, as well as in future career advancement. With higher English proficiency, Hong Kong people are able to connect with the global economy and migrate to English-speaking countries in the developed world. In the wake of emigration waves since the early 1980s until the mid-1990s for 'political insurance' against possible political instability in future, many Hong Kong people developed familial ties with Canada, Australia and New Zealand. Their political and cultural outlooks are more diverse than their ethnic background suggests. In the meantime, the British and Western liberal approach in historical education, which places stress on the analytical and critical thinking is at odds with the mainland's patriotic education, which requires students to embrace a shared national identity uncritically.[3] In other words, an international dimension of Hong Kong identity that is uncomfortably accommodated with Chinese identity has been created.

The second way to foster a market-oriented mentality is to depoliticize the curricula. The modified British education system was intended to develop a productive labour force rather than to promote the understanding and appreciation of British or English culture. Few students took the subjects contextualizing the UK, such as English literature and British history. Since the colonial government did not attempt to inculcate a British identity and remove students' Chineseness, Hong Kong's English education did not trigger a backlash from local Chinese nationalists. Besides that, model syllabi were introduced. Textbooks could not be published without official approval. The coverage of Chinese history subject excluded much of the modern time of China. The effective end-date was extended to 1911 in 1965. Then it was further to 1945, 1949 and 1976 in 1972, 1979 and 1995 respectively; the curriculum related to contemporary Chinese politics and the context of Hong Kong were minimized. Therefore the curriculum did not create among students a consciousness of a shared past. Without the approval of the director of education, no schools were allowed to hold discussion on politics or display flags and symbols with political nature until the countdown to the handover.[4]

The riots of 1966 and 1967 uncovered the widespread of grievances towards the colonial rule. In response, the Hong Kong government resorted to civic education to instil in students a sense of belonging to the colony. The civic education curriculum underscored the city's economic success. However, discussion on political issues was still prohibited so as not to draw public attention to their restricted political rights and freedom. Through education, the colonial government hoped to cultivate law-abiding citizens to improve its quality of governance and, above all, legitimacy. The issue of national identity was irrelevant to this colonial strategy and therefore almost nonexistent.[5] The civic-related subjects of Hong Kong's education in colonial era, in the words of Tse, was

> alien, conformist and depoliticized in nature, alienating students from their indigenous nationality and local politics and fostering students as 'residents' or 'subjects' in a colonial state rather than 'citizens' in a nation-state.[6]

Political education was not felt necessary until the early 1980s. The British government had to prepare for the handover of Hong Kong's sovereignty to China and phase in a more democratic political system. It was necessary to equip students with political skills and cultivate them civic values to deal with the forthcoming political changes with increasing political participation and mobilization. In 1985, the government reformed the curriculum by issuing its first civic education guidelines – *The Guidelines on Civic Education in Schools*. But the guidelines were depoliticized and vague; the definition of civic education was broad, including any topics that may help students become 'good citizens'. School teachers were free to avoid the 'sensitive' topics (that is, political and ideological debates). As a result, the government dropped its ban on discussion of political issues in 1990 and issued the narrower but more clearly-defined *Guidelines on Civic Education in Schools* in 1996. The guidelines explicitly defined that the teaching of civic education should cover the understanding of students' community, country and the global village. Beyond factual knowledge, the guidelines required teachers to teach students life skills and cultivate students with affective cognition to their community, country and the global village. Clearer definition could not preclude schools from freely choosing what to teach and even whether to teach. Many school administrators and teachers were educated in the old curricula that avoided political issues and were therefore reluctant to teach politically controversial issues.[7]

Education in Macao is also apolitical but for different reasons. Unlike Hong Kong's school curricula under tight control of the colonial government, a laissez-faire approach was characteristic of Macao's education policies. Different schools were allowed to design their own history curriculum and discuss political and ideological issues, depending on the schools' tradition, school teachers' personal choice and the orientation of the universities enrolling their graduates. As the most popular destinations for the students to pursue higher education are China, Taiwan, Portugal and the territories adopting the British education system, the education systems and curriculum of these territories coexist in Macao.[8] The political ideologies behind the diverse curriculum, if any, cancelled out each other and had limited impact in orientating the identity outlook of the student body as a whole.

Unlike the education curriculum in Hong Kong, however, the Macao curriculum neither instilled in the students a sense of belonging to the city nor played any significant role in identity-building. The casino-based economy does not require Macao to connect with the global economy; most casino-goers are mainland Chinese and Hong Kong people with linguistic traditions similar to those of Macao people. Many Macao people have no urgent needs to learn foreign languages or pursue higher education, and therefore an international dimension of identity can hardly be created. Macao schools may either use their own teaching materials or adopt the textbooks from Hong Kong or the mainland given that the book market of Macao is too small for any textbook publishers to flourish there. The context that the textbooks portrayed is usually irrelevant to Macao. A collective image or pride about Macao can hardly be conveyed through the school system. These factors are unfavourable for forming a local identity.[9] Without a strong sense of local identity, Macao people are more likely to be proud of China than Macao (see Table 10.1).

The mass media shaped the identity of Hong Kong, not Macao. Hong Kong is at the centre of distinct film traditions; Hong Kong people's identities are strongly connected with a cinematic impression of Hong Kong people being efficient, smart and able to make a fortune. The negative discourse on the mainland Chinese people in films and other forms of mass media enhanced their sense of superiority over their mainland compatriots.[10] The impact of Hong Kong mass media extends beyond Hong Kong to other Chinese communities, including Macao. A physical fitness instructor told the author that owing to the influence of Hong Kong media, she thought mainland Chinese were wicked and untrustworthy in general.[11] Although the negative narrative of the mainland Chinese has faded due to the business consideration of opening the markets of China, removing the negative image will take some time.

Table 10.1 Identification with China and Macao

Year	Proud to be Chinese	Proud to be Macanese
1991	66.9%	53.6%
1999	74.1%	38.8%
2006	79.5%	65.8%

Source: Yu Chun, Lü Guomin, 'Dazhong zhengzhi wenhua'
('Popular Political Culture'), in Huang Shaolun, Yang Yuwan,
Yun Baoshan and Zheng Hongtai (eds), *Aomen shehui shilu:
Cong zhibiao yanjiu kan shenghuo suzhi* (*Macao Society: A
Quantity Analysis of Quality of Life*), Hong Kong: Institute of
Asia-Pacific Studies, the Chinese University of Hong Kong,
2007, p.306.

There was a difference in the impact of the mass media on the two cities. While the mass media contributed to the rise of Hong Kong identity, Macao did not undergo the same transformation. Macao films are almost absent and are narrowly restrictive within the small art scene. Macao people viewed Hong Kong TV as often, if not more often than local TV programmes. The collective image presented by the media is primarily the image of Hong Kong and Hong Kong's way of interpreting the world. Because of their limited influence, local media could neither create an imagined community of Macao nor articulate values commonly shared by Macao people. Most respondents interviewed by the author could hardly identify what Macao constituted; they were more confident of claiming that they were Chinese rather than Macao people when travelling overseas. When the author asked the interviewees about their perceptions towards Macao, almost all of them shared the same appreciation of Macao's tranquil and simple lifestyle, as well as intimate interpersonal relations.[12] A customs officer characterized Macao people as confrontation averse, pointing out that most participants in the protests against various government policies since 2006 were born in mainland China, not Macao. The collective image about Macao was based more on the personal daily encounters than the information and image conveyed by mass media or perpetuated through schooling. O'Regan stated that films are useful for framing the histories, stories and national or regional distinction of a community and shaping the community's identity.[13] The absence of popular local films and TV programmes in Macao makes it difficult to create a solid identity. Owing to a lack of an obvious Macao identity commonly embraced by Macao people and taken pride in by them, pursuing a Macao identity was a very popular theme in the local art scene.[14]

It is true that Macao has a longer history than Hong Kong does, and has a richer cultural heritage symbolized by Portuguese and Chinese-style architecture. Macao once was the centre for the spread of Christianity and Western civilization to East Asia. It has a longer tradition of rule of law and shows more respect to civil liberty and individual rights than China does. These

Table 10.2 Some key socio-economic indicators

Year	Real GDP growth	Nominal GDP per capita (US$)*	Unemployment rate	Monthly median income (US$)	Inflation rate
2003	14.2%	17,774	6.0%	598	–1.6%
2004	28.3%	22,604	4.8%	643	1.0%
2005	6.7%	24,297	4.1%	718	4.4%
2006	16.6%	28,317	3.8%	832	5.2%
2007	27.6%	36,144	3.1%	975	7.35%

* In May 2009, US$ 1 approximately = 8 Macao patacas (MOP) Source: *Major Statistical Indicators*, www.gov.mo/egi/Portal/s/dsec/dsec_stat_tc.html (accessed 8 February 2009); *Monthly Income, by Industries*, www.dsal.gov.mo/pdf/work/chinese/8_SalCAM_a.pdf (accessed 8 February 2009).

were cultural prides of being Macanese, said Jorge Rangel – the last secretary for public administration, education and youth before the handover of sovereignty.[15] However, none of the Macao Chinese interviewed by the author appreciated this part of history.

The emergence of Hong Kong identity was partially attributed to the rapid economic growth between the end of the 1960s and the turn of the twenty-first century and the competence of the people to stand out in the global economy. The success of the casino-based economy in Macao, however, fails to bring a sense of pride and cultivate a local identity to any of the interviewees. Since the casino liberalization in 2002 and the mainland's relaxation of outbound tourism in 2003, Macao has recorded high rates of economic growth (see Table 10.2). The GDP per capita is almost doubled in four years and exceeds the four 'little tigers' of Asia.

Nevertheless, most interviewees dismissed the economic growth as a pride of Macao. Two 20-year-old university students lamented that Macao had nothing to be proud of. A mechanic in his fifties said that the economic boom did little good and just created widespread materialism among young people. He believed that this 'money first' mentality undermined Macao's familial values and the 'tradition' of seeking a balanced lifestyle and displaying one's talent fully. A customs officer aged 30-plus said that the economic development was 'unbalanced'. Casinos and high-rise buildings were constructed at the expense of natural environment. The green zone was not enough. Roads became more crowded.[16] Macao people are not generally proud of the economic success partly because the lopsided economic growth has benefited only a small number of people and bred corruption in the public sector, especially in the sectors related to infrastructure and real estate development. On the contrary, the majority had to bear the cost of economic growth, such as rocketing property prices, competition from migrant and illegal workers for jobs, more crowded roads and worsening pollution.[17] Market-driven value might be useful for explaining the emergence of Hong Kong identity and the reluctance of some Hong Kong people to be integrated into Chinese national identity after the handover of sovereignty.[18] But apparently this approach is of little use to understand Macao people's mentality towards their identity. Without a strong sense of local identity, Macao people are more ready to accept the state-defined Chinese national identity than their Hong Kong counterparts.

The report of China news is relevant to the explanation for the Macao people's relative ease to integrate with the national identity of China. For the purpose of saving money, the only television channel in the territories, the government-run TDM, has no reporters stationed in Beijing to cover Chinese news. Instead, it solely relies on China Central Television's footage.[19] In case of newspapers, the news reports of New China News Agency are extensively used in order to cut costs. Besides that, professional reporting does not seem to be a high priority in the minds of both media managers and journal editors.[20]

The political orientations of civic associations and demographic factors are relevant in the discussion of identity issues. The Macao government adopted a corporatist model to organize the civic associations in a hierarchy led by the dual authorities of the Macanese and Chinese governments. The most significant civic associations were pro-Beijing in their political inclination. These pro-Beijing civic associations played an active role in providing social services at the time when Macao's colonial government was either uninterested or unable to supply them. As a result, major civic associations enjoyed wide community support. Their leaders were coopted by both the colonial government for better governance and higher legitimacy, and by the Chinese government to be its agents in dealing with the colonial government.[21] In the meantime, the mainland-born residents (237,000, or 47.1 per cent of the population) in Macao outnumbered the local-born residents (213,000, or 42.4 per cent) in 2006.[22] In Macao, mainland-born residents make up a larger percentage of the population than they do in Hong Kong (2,100,000, or less than one third of the population), where more than 4 million residents (almost 60 per cent of the population) were born in Hong Kong.[23] Given that mainland-born residents have usually received some education in the mainland and have been more used and receptive to mainland Chinese culture and values, these people are more likely to identify themselves with the mainland than their adopted land.

Macao-born Chinese tend to manifest stronger emotional detachment from China in comparison to their mainland-born counterparts. When asked why they were patriotic, the self-proclaimed patriots who stated that being patriotic was natural tended to be mainland-born. A mainland-born interviewee said that she would prefer a Macao SAR passport to a Portuguese passport if she had free choice on either one of them.[24] The ethnic-based national identity, however, is not common among Macao-born Chinese. They are inclined to link their patriotic feeling with China's economic success. Like the Hong Kong students reported by Mathews, Ma and Lui,[25] the expression of love was offered in conditional, situational terms.

The utilitarian and rational consideration reflects that these Macao people do not have natural passion towards China. Rather, they are akin to many Hong Kong people's utilitarianism, which emphasizes the contribution of 'patriotic feeling' (meaning good relations with Chinese authorities and good understanding of China) to expanding their business opportunities and life chances in China.[26] Two university students claiming to attach strong sentiment to China and the People's Liberation Army said that they preferred Portuguese passports to Macao SAR passports.[27] In addition to the privilege of entering more countries visa-free, one of them thought that her Portuguese passport entitled her the right to work in European Union countries and study in their universities at local tuition fees. The examples show the flexible and utilitarian conception towards citizenship. Like their Hong Kong counterparts, many Macao people are ready to pick up foreign citizenships as long as foreign citizenships are useful to them.

Existing literature stated that Macao people are patriotic. The interviews conducted by the author suggest another story.[28] No interviewees showed strong emotional attachment to China. Rather some may find it uneasy to identify themselves as patriots. They may tactically evade the question related to their patriotic feelings. A university student embarrassingly queried: 'Is the question whether I am patriotic meaningful at all?' Another undergraduate burst into laughter when asked whether she was patriotic. These respondents' hesitation to tell whether or not they are patriotic is no different from their Hong Kong counterparts but contrasts with the mainland Chinese students who are always ready to claim a love for China, as documented by Mathews, Ma, and Lui.[29]

The misconception that Macao people were very patriotic can be traced to local media. According to a Macao media observer, widespread patriotic rhetoric in mass media emerged only after the handover. Criticism against the Macao government, let alone the Chinese government, was regarded by some media managers and senior journalists destructive to the 'one country, two systems' policy, and was therefore restrained. The management of *Aomen ribao* (*Macao Daily*), the Chinese-language newspaper with the largest circulation in Macao, even considers itself a member of the 'governing coalition'.[30] In addition, some media managers and senior journalists were coopted by the Chinese and Macao governments into various symbolic positions of consultative committees.[31] Professional journalism and neutrality of news reports are placed on a lower priority than throwing support behind the Chinese and Macao governments.

Macao people are reluctant to fully embrace the Chinese national identity for several reasons. The first is the sense of distinction with mainland compatriots. All the interviewees said that Macao people are not smarter than mainland Chinese in making money, but are more hygienic, honest and willing to comply with law and order. Mainland Chinese are considered rude and selfish. As discussed above, Hong Kong mass media played a role behind this perception.

The second reason is the authoritarian regime of China and its bloody history in revolutionary era. A mechanic asked the author: 'What do you mean by patriotism? Does patriotism include loving the Chinese government or Communist Party of China? If the answer is affirmative, I am afraid I am unpatriotic.' Hong Kong's mass media may be an explanation for this mentality, but their power should not be overexaggerated. From time to time, Hong Kong's mass media replayed the image of the 1989 Tiananmen Square incident, especially around its anniversary. The processions and vigils in Hong Kong memorizing those killed at Tiananmen Square are widely reported by Hong Kong media. These events, together with the frequent reports on the corruption and blunders of the Chinese government, are believed to have caused huge psychological impacts that have deterred Hong Kong people from identifying themselves with China. In response to the authors' enquiry on their feelings towards the Tiananmen Square incident, none of the Macao respondents expressed strong emotion regarding the tragedy or against the Chinese government. As discussed above, the positive image of China and the Chinese government portrayed by local media plays a role here.

The third explanatory factor is education. The Macao government never unifies the curriculum or seriously controls what is to be taught. The schools run by the government and by the Catholic and Protestant Churches do not enthusiastically inculcate a sense of belonging to China. Even the history teachers of pro-Beijing schools were reluctant to adopt all official Chinese points of views and interpretation of modern history to make their teaching more objective but less ideological.[32] Most respondents, including those having spent years in pro-Beijing schools, said that their schools did not spare much time teaching them to understand or belong to China. They were not aware of some China's current issues regarded as common sense in China.[33] Most interviewees said they did not regard China's national flag with any feelings of attachment. Certainly education has the power of subliminally shaping the respondents' mentality by the wide adoption of Chinese (Cantonese) as instruction medium, the use of history and geography textbooks published in the mainland, the China tours in their final year of secondary schooling, the singing of Chinese songs compiled by mainland Chinese composers during music lessons, and the occasional national flag-raising ceremonies. However, this does not suffice to deny that Macao people in general do not display a strong sense of patriotism.

The fourth reason is that some Macao people associate patriotism with negative connotations. It was not until the handover of sovereignty that Chinese-language newspapers were filled with patriotic rhetoric. 'Loving the motherland and loving Macao' has become a cliché for pro-Beijing politicians, business leaders and social elites. Macao does not have a true democracy. It is easier for politicians to obtain political offices and power through toeing the Beijing line than appealing to the public to get elected. The transparency and consistency of the administration are far from satisfactory, exemplified by the former Secretary for Transportation and Public Works Ao Man Long's intervention in the tendering process to assure that his friends and those who gave bribes could obtain the contracts of public construction projects.[34] Many people submit to the authorities by openly claiming their allegiance to China in hopes of obtaining favour from the authorities in return. Nevertheless, such behaviour is not universally acceptable on moral grounds. A respondent was cynical of the 'patriotic' civic associations. She said that many leaders of these civic associations were not really patriotic but selfish and greedy. The banner of patriotism was only used by these associations to get close to the Macao and Beijing governments for particularistic treatments in their pursuits of business opportunities, political aspirations and career advancement.

Building national identities in postcolonial Hong Kong

Having reviewed the history of state-formation in Europe, Rokkan argued that the strength of territorial centres built up on economic/technological resources and cultural/religious heritages is negatively related to the ease of state-formation and national integration.[35] Strong territorial centres tend to resist state power. Hong Kong is a strong territorial centre. Economically, it has long eclipsed its neighbouring regions as a regional hub of trade and communication, as well as becoming a magnet for foreign direct investment and talents. The distinctive political, social and legal cultures fostered by the status of strong territorial status, in turn, strained the China–Hong Kong relations.[36]

Before and after the handover, Beijing was worried about keeping Hong Kong in the orbit of its control due to such issues as the assistance to the Chinese student leaders in the student movement in 1989, the triumph of democracy camp and defeat of pro-Beijing forces in the elections of the legislative council, municipal councils and district councils (or district boards before the handover), and the wave of emigration to escape the communist rule. The building of national identity in postcolonial Hong Kong is far more difficult and controversial. Building a national identity defined by the Chinese authorities was deemed urgent. Soon after the handover of the sovereignty, the then Chief Executive Tung Chee-hwa repeatedly called for more emphasis on national education to cultivate a sense of belonging and pride to Chinese history and culture, saying that schools should deepen students' understanding of contemporary China, and China's achievements in particular. With Tung's support, the social force emphasizing patriotic education gained the upper hand over the advocates of democratic values and human rights education in the debate on the content of civic and national education.[37] Schools were required to teach students the national anthem and raise the national flag to cultivate allegiance to China on the part of students. Government subsidies were offered to schools and non-governmental organizations to organize exchange tours for students to visit mainland China. Independent civic education subject was introduced to step up the teaching of Chinese history and culture. The curricula of history-related subjects were also revised to increase the components on contemporary China and the China–Hong Kong relationship. China issues were related to students' lives to strengthen their conception that Hong Kong is subordinate to China. As pointed out by Vickers and Kan, the new syllabus of local history at the level of junior high school highlighted the themes of China's contribution to Hong Kong's development and Hong Kong's transition to become a part of China. Hong Kong's successes were attributed to the benevolence of China, such as cheap supplies of food and drinking water, and the capital and entrepreneurship from China after 1949. In contrast, Hong Kong's contribution to China's modernization was not mentioned. The historical narratives that were contradictory to the Beijing and Han ethnic-centred perspectives – such as the 'cleansing' of the aboriginal tribes by Han troops in the twelfth century and Hong Kong's role in 1989 Beijing student movement – were ignored.[38]

In 2012, the government published 'Moral and National Education Curriculum Guide (Primary 1 to Secondary 6)' to replace the civic education guidelines adopted in 1985 and later revised. The curriculum aims at 'cultivating students' positive values and attitudes through a continuous and systematic learning experience. It enables students to acquire desirable moral and national qualities'. National qualities include building 'identities in different domains; to care for family, society, the country and the world; to become informed and responsible family members, citizens, nationals and global citizens'.[39] A professor from Beijing Normal University was invited to draft teaching materials. The curriculum placed high emphasis on the achievement of the Chinese government whereas the controversial and sensitive political issues were downplayed. Many liberal-minded politicians, educationalists and students were outraged by the government's attempt to brainwash the students, to inculcate in them a narrow set of value judgements and indoctrinate them with an uncritical sense of patriotism.[40] With little emphasis on developing students' political efficacy and improving their competence in political participation, the national education in post-handover Hong Kong is little different to that in colonial Hong Kong: the education in both periods seeks to turn the people into obedient subjects.

It is evident that after the handover, Hong Kong people's identification with China is growing while identification with Hong Kong was going down until 2009 (see Figure 10.1). With China intensifying its intervention in Hong Kong politics and increasing its economic integration with Hong Kong, the alienation of Hong Kong people from China resurfaced. On 1 July 2003, half a million people took to the streets in Hong Kong to protest against the legislation of the human rights violating State Security Bill. The mass protest powerfully demonstrated the public resentment of Hong Kong's economic stagnation since the 1997 Asian Financial Crisis and the first Chief Executive Tung Chee-hwa's mishandling of several controversial issues.[41]

Since the protest, the Chinese government became more proactive in exercising political control over Hong Kong. Economically, China tried to integrate Hong Kong's economy so that Hong Kong's economy and, consequently, the

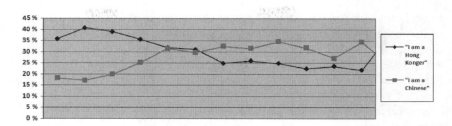

Figure 10.1 Hong Kong people's self-declared identity, December 1997–December 2011

legitimacy of the Hong Kong government would be boosted. Meanwhile, closer integration offered the Chinese government more leverage over Hong Kong's economy and built up its support among Hong Kong businesspeople and professionals whose business and career development depended on the China market. The strategies of tighter political control and closer economic integration mirrored China's integrative project on the borderlands, namely Xinjiang and Tibet.[42]

To step up its political control, Chinese government was active in Hong Kong's electoral campaigns. It negotiated various pro-Beijing political factions to avoid direct competition in the elections of legislative council and district councils to increase the chance of getting elected. It called upon pro-Beijing businesses and China's state-owned businesses to contribute donations to pro-Beijing political parties so as to strengthen their abilities in mass mobilization for electoral campaigns, advocacy of policies that favoured the Chinese government, and opposition of policies that the Chinese government disliked. In the 2012 chief executive election, it threw its support behind the candidate, Henry Tang, who represented the interests of big businesses but had limited public support and work competence. With more support from the public and, more significantly, the pro-Beijing factions representing the long-time supporter of Beijing, former convener of the executive council Leung Chun-ying joined the elections. In the electoral campaigns, the two candidates were mocked with various scandals, such as extra-marital affairs, manipulation of bidding of public construction projects and illegal construction in residence. Many Hong Kong people were enraged by the Chinese government's meddling into Hong Kong's domestic politics, which they supposed Hong Kong had the autonomy to handle.[43]

In regards to closer economic integration, the Chinese government relaxed its outbound tourism 'Individual Visitor Scheme' in 2003. Since then, mainland Chinese tourists to Hong Kong have increased drastically and contributed substantially to Hong Kong's economy. The Closer Economic Partnership Agreement (CEPA, a free trade pact) was signed with Hong Kong to lower the entry barrier for Hong Kong's exports to China's market, and for Hong

Kong's professionals to China's service industries.[44] Nevertheless, the influx of capital also propped up Hong Kong's property market and increased the cost of living for most Hong Kong people, whose salary rise cannot catch up with the property and rental prices. Many Chinese pregnant women went to Hong Kong to give birth to their babies to circumvent China's control on population growth and help their babies apply for permanent residence in Hong Kong. This practice put enormous strain on Hong Kong's medical services. The difference of mainland Chinese visitors, migrants, students and professionals in their attitude towards hygiene, manner and other personal habits triggered territory-wide discontent, especially in cyberspace, where abrasive words were common in netizens' criticism. Their resentment was culminated by a Peking University professor's accusation of Hong Kong people of being the 'running dogs of colonial rule'. To fight back, Hong Kong netizens portrayed the mainland Chinese as locusts predating Hong Kong.[45]

Building national identities in postcolonial Macao

In the case of Macao, the government has held or subsidized societal association to hold celebration for National Day and Macao SAR Establishment Day, or activities condemning 'secessionist movement' in Tibet and Taiwan. In a written reply to a legislator, Secretary for Administration and Justice Florinda da Rosa Silva Chan said that patriotic education was an integral component of Macao's fundamental education. To produce teaching and reading materials, the Education and Youth Bureau commissioned People Education Press, a Beijing-based publisher, to compile textbooks for the subject of 'moral and citizen education'.[46] Through a semi-official publisher of China, the content of the textbooks would be convergent with the Beijing's ideology and official interpretation of patriotism

The Education and Youth Bureau also launched a website and education resources centre to advise school teachers on matters related to patriotic education, such as the procedure of raising the national flag and the expected responses when the national flag is raised and the national anthem is played. Since 2004, the bureau subsidized Macao schools to organize China study tours for students. Through these tours, students may pay a visit to China's 'patriotic bases' – historic sites and venues that evidence imperialist invasion into China since the mid- nineteenth century, display the exhibits boasting China's cultural legacy and scientific advancement, and/or are related to the achievement of the Communist Party of China. By January 2009, more than 18,000 students had participated in this type of study tour. Since 2008, the bureau has fully subsidized school students to participate in the training camps in Whampoa Military Academy – a legendary military academy that graduated many military commanders for the Communist Party of China and the Nationalist Party of China in the Republican era.[47] By presenting to young people a positive image of the People's Liberation Army (PLA) – a symbol of Chinese authority – it is hoped to inculcate among young people a sense of belonging to China.

Following Hong Kong government's production of a short TV film with a soundtrack of China's national anthem before the evening news, Macao's government-run television broadcast channel TDM produced films promoting patriotism. Meanwhile, TDM showed documentaries produced by China's television broadcast channel to disseminate a positive image of China. The influence of the Macao government on the mass media has implications on the national identity of the Macao people. Since 2004, the Macao government sponsored the managers of mass media and senior journalists to attend training courses in Beijing every year. According to official explanation, the courses were aimed at helping Macao journalists better understand the politico-economic development of China and China's foreign policies. In the training course of 2009, for example, the areas covered included Tibetan issues, financial tsunami, cross-strait relations and China–US relations. The guest speakers of the course included senior officials from the National Development and Reform Commission, Ministry of Commerce, National Bureau of Statistics, State Administration of Religious Affairs, General Administration of Press and Publication and Associations of Cross-Strait Relations, as well as Peking University's economists and strategists.[48] Through its influence on the journalists' thought, it is believed that the central government is able to influence the public opinions in favour of Beijing.

At the same time, the Portuguese culture and influence that do not fit in the government's framework of economic development are ignored. To diversify its casino-based economy, the government has promoted cultural tourism in recent years. One of the promotion strategies is to highlight Macao's European and Portuguese elements, such as architecture, decoration and food, in order to attract the tourists uninterested in gambling. Therefore the government applied and successfully convinced UNESCO of designating some traditional Portuguese and Chinese architecture as World Heritage Sites in 2005. Since then, these UNESCO designated sites have come under the limelight of government's promotion campaign.

On the contrary, the heritages enshrining the Portuguese influence and contribution to China and Macao's modernization are seldom mentioned. Between 1993 and 1999, for instance, the colonial government erected nine pieces of public art symbolizing the Sino-Portuguese friendship and Portuguese presence on the soil of China for more than 400 years. The official website of the government Tourist Office only mentioned two of them: the Gate of Understanding and Kun Iam Ecumenical Centre.[49] The Education and Youth Bureau maintained a webpage 'Loving China, Loving Macao' to assist school teachers in preparing for the course materials of civic-related subjects. These course materials mention not much about Portuguese accomplishments, such as making Macao a window for China to understand astronomy and Christianity, technology for making cannons, providing a haven for

Chinese refugees during World War II and other political upheavals in China, and bringing Macao a membership of the developed world. Instead, the website highlighted the point that students should love their motherland of China unconditionally.[50]

In addition, guidelines for moral and citizenship education are made. Macao is used as a context to introduce students to the knowledge, skills and attitude of a wide array of issues, such as the political system, civic liberty and citizen's rights and duties. However, the schools are so well-established and well-connected with political elites that the government is reluctant to compel the schools to follow the guidelines.[51]

Market forces in action

Market forces play a different role in the building of national identity of Hong Kong and Macao in the post-handover era. Similar to the colonial era, competition for foreign-direct investment and export markets requires the preservation of the international dimension of local identity: English is still much emphasized in education and commerce. Places in local international schools and schools in English-speaking countries are sought after as better English learning environments. The government provides working adults with subsidies for learning English in the workplace. Since the international dimension of local identity is practical, building-up national identity at the expense of local identity is resisted by the local population, as is testified by the large number of local students giving up places in government-subsidized schools that some parents frown upon for placing too much emphasis on promoting Chinese (Cantonese and Mandarin) as the instruction medium after the handover.[52] Thanks to their parents with passports obtained from English-speaking countries in the 1980s and 1990s through emigration, many students are able to enrol in the public education system of some English-speaking countries at subsidized levels.

In the meantime, market forces contributed to fostering an identity of China in Hong Kong. Some local mass media were taken over by tycoons with substantial investment in mainland China and coopted by the authorities. For example, *South China Morning Post* – the highest circulated and oldest English newspaper – was acquired by Chinese Malaysian Robert Kuok from Murdoch's News Corporation in 1993. His business in China includes bottle companies for Coca-Cola, 50 per cent ownership of the Beijing World Trade Centre, and oil refining and commercial properties. Before the handover, he was invited to be Beijing's adviser on Hong Kong affairs.[53] In 2003, Charles Ho – a Standing Committee member of the National Congress of Chinese People's Political Consultative Conference and CEO of British American Tobacco Hong Kong – acquired a Chinese newspaper *Sing Dao Daily* and an English newspaper *Hong Kong Standard Daily*. The news reports that Chinese government disapproves are deemed to be undesirable to the tycoon's businesses in China and are censored.[54] Since their taking over of these media, the editors and senior journalists of the media were told to tune down their criticism against the Chinese government. Journalists from the mainland were appointed to senior positions while those critical of Beijing were sacked or forced to resign; self-censorship in Hong Kong media was pervasive. The negative news reports of the Chinese government's corruption and brutality – most notably the reports of 1989 Tiananmen Square incident – have deterred many Hong Kong people from identifying with China.

In Macao, market forces shape the identity of the people in another way. The postcolonial economic development has cultivated a local identity revolving around the cultural relics. It is believed that Macao's overdependence on gambling will increase the volatility of the economy. After the handover, the government proposed several measures of economic diversification, such as setting up cross-border industrial zones, offshore business centres, trading centres for the global Chinese business community, dialogue platforms between China and Portuguese-speaking countries, and business centres for enterprises based in Western Guangdong province. However, these have met with only limited success. Thanks to the liberalization of China's outbound tourism and Macao's casino industry, Macao's GDP was propelled from MOP 82 billion in 2004 to MOP 170 billion in 2009. The rise of casino revenue from MOP 44 billion (54 per cent of GDP) to MOP 122 billion (72 per cent of GDP) in the same period indicated the increasing dependence of Macao's economy on the casino industry, not economic diversification.[55]

Meanwhile, the government wants to use the city's heritage to attract tourists other than gambling tourists. Cultural tourism centred on heritage can be traced back to the Portuguese national legislation that listed the most significant colonial sites in 1953. In 1976, Macao passed its first heritage protection law. After the handover, the government stepped-up promotional campaigns and successfully listed the representative Portuguese and Chinese architectures on UNESCO's World Heritage Sites. In 2009, the government enacted a new heritage protection law to align with the international best practice of heritage protection.[56]

All the people interviewed by the author said that they loved the built heritage. It is expected that some people are vigilant in preserving the heritage when there are any development projects that might affect the appearance or the spatial relations of this architecture with the surrounding regions. The strong identification of Macao people is evidenced by the preservation of the Guia Lighthouse. Guia Lighthouse was one of the earliest lighthouses along China's coasts. It was built with a fortress for maritime defence and was an integral part of a grouping of architecture with a fortress, a chapel and air-raid shelters. Now it is open for the public to visit. Below the lighthouse is a park that is regarded as one of the greenest places in the concrete forest of the Macao peninsula, the region inhabited by 85 per cent of the population. In August 2006, the government announced it had approved of construction projects beside the hill topped by the lighthouse. The projects included several high-rise buildings measuring over 100 metres, including the new headquarters of the Central Liaisons Office (the representative of the Beijing government in Macao).[57]

Upon completion, the view of the lighthouse would be entirely blocked. The public would no longer be able to view it from a distance. The construction plans provoked public outcry; mass campaigns such as demonstrations, signature campaigns and seminars were organized against the construction project. Complaint letters were sent to UNESCO. Later on, UNESCO's representatives went to Macao to investigate and alerted the Beijing government of the threat to the lighthouse. Soon afterwards, the Macao government announced to lower the height of the projects to below 90 metres. The Central Liaison Office followed suit and lowered their new headquarters to 88 metres, with three floors less than its original plan.[58]

The mass campaign over Guia Lighthouse is unusual in Macao. Macao people seldom take to the streets or openly confront the authorities due to the small size of the city and the consequential vast control of the authorities over political resources, business opportunities and even personal pursuits. The open protests in the past usually revolved around the issues of livelihood, for instance, the competition for jobs from migrant workers and the right of abode of the children born on the mainland to Macao residents. The campaign for conserving Guia Lighthouse is different from past protests in the sense that the campaign is related to preserving a collective memory over a historical heritage – something intangible but cherished by many Macao people.

Another case of collective action against the threat to historical heritage occurred in 2006. The Social Welfare Bureau was reportedly planning to redevelop its headquarters 'Little Blue House' – a Portuguese-style mansion – into a 14-storey new headquarters. 'Little Blue House' has a history of less than 80 years; it is not included in the World Heritage List and is far less important than Guia Lighthouse historically. However, it is an integral part of St. Lazarus Parish – a region with heavy concentration of Portuguese-style architecture. Its authentic value impresses many local people, so the news of demolishing the 'Little Blue House' provoked another outcry. To settle the disputes, an expert commission was formed to collect public opinion. It was found that around 47 per cent of the 10,000 respondents wanted to preserve the whole 'Little Blue House' and 38 per cent said that they wanted to preserve the exterior walls of the 'Little Blue House'. Only 15 per cent agreed with redevelopment.[59] In the end, the government dropped the plan of redeveloping the 'Little Blue House' and looked for another site to construct the new headquarters.

These two examples illustrates that it is their historical heritage that many Macao people value. They have strong urge to protect it when it is endangered. The survey undertaken in the controversy over the planned redevelopment of the 'Little Blue House' demonstrates that the better-educated people tend to be more supportive of conserving the architecture with historical value. With the expansion of the tertiary education and the increasing proportion of the population with higher education attainment, more and more local people will be identified with the richness of historical and cultural heritage. Historical heritage can therefore be considered to be a part of Macao identity emerging among the government's attempt to diversify the casino-based economy.

Conclusion

Building national identity has been on the agenda of the two city governments for further integrating into the mainland. With the forces of state and market in action, it is unimaginable that the people of the two cities will vehemently resist the integration process. The younger generation who are immersed in an environment witnessing the rise of China in the global politics and economy and taught to love China will be more receptive to China than their parents and grandparents, who personally experienced the hardships under the communist regime. What is interesting in this research is that the alienation of Hong Kong people from China has spilled over to Macao through mass media, but strong resentment against the polity of China is always absent there. The feeling of alienation in Hong Kong, once lessened, was worsened due to the intensification of China's political influence and the downsides of economic integration with China.

Identity-shaping evolves in more than one direction. While the two cities are found to be developing a Chinese identity defined by the state, Macao's local identity centred on its cultural heritage has quietly emerged. The emotional attachment to the cultural heritage can be traced back to the government's effort to diversify an economy overdependent on gambling industries. The market force of developing the tourist industry through better use of cultural heritage also plays a role. This contrasts with the economic logic in Hong Kong that helps to connect the local identity with the national one.

Notes

1 Liisa Malkki, 'National Geographic: The Rooting of Peoples and the Territorialization of National Identity Among Scholars and Refugees', *Cultural Anthropology*, 7(1), 1992, pp. 24–44; Benedict Anderson, *Imagined Communities: Reflections on the Origin and Spread of Nationalism*, London: Verso, 1991.
2 For the literature about national identity in Hong Kong, see Edward Vickers and Flora Kan, 'The Re-Education of Hong Kong: Identity, Politics, and History Education in Colonial and Postcolonial Hong Kong', in Edward Vickers and Alisa Jones (eds), *History Education and National Identity in East Asia*, New York: Routledge, 2005, pp. 171–202; Gordon Mathews, Eric Kit-wai Ma and Tai-lok Lui, *Hong Kong, China: Learning to Belong to a Nation*, London; New York: Routledge, 2008, and Elaine Chan, 'Defining Fellow Compatriots as "Others" – National Identity in Hong Kong', *Government and Opposition*, 35(4), 2000, pp. 499–519. For the literature about national identity in Macao, see Gary M.C. Ngai, 'Macau's Cultural Identity: Its Preservation and Development Before and After 1999', in Ruifino Ramos et al (eds), *Macau and Its Neighbours in Transition: Proceedings of the International Conference Held at the University of Macau*, Macao: Faculty of Social Sciences and Humanities, University of Macau, 1997, pp. 125–136.

3 Edward Vickers, *In Search of an Identity: The Politics of History as a School Subject in Hong Kong, 1960s–2002*, New York and London: Routledge, 2003, pp. 199–226.

4 Vickers and Kan, 'The Re-Education of Hong Kong', pp. 171–202; Wing On Lee, 'Citizenship Education in Hong Kong: Development and Challenges', in Wing On Lee, David L. Grossman, Kerry J. Kennedy and Gregory P. Fairbrother (eds), *Citizenship Education in Asia and the Pacific: Concepts and Issues*, Hong Kong: Comparative Education Research Centre, University of Hong Kong; Kluwer Academic, 2004, pp. 59–80.

5 Sai Wing Leung and Wing On Lee, 'National Identity at a Crossroads: The Struggle between Culture, Language and Politics in Hong Kong', in Geof Alred, Mike Byram and Mike Fleming (eds), *Education for Intercultural Citizenship: Concepts and Comparisons*, New York: Multilingual Matters, 2006, p. 23; Agnes S. Ku and Ngai Pun, 'Introduction: Remaking Citizenship in Hong Kong', in Agnes S. Ku and Ngai Pun (eds), *Remaking Citizenship in Hong Kong: Community, Nation and the Global City*, London and New York: Routledge Curzon, 2004, p. 4.

6 Thomas Kwan-Choi Tse, 'Civic Education and the Making of Deformed Citizenry: From British Colony to Chinese SAR', in Ku and Pun (eds), *Remaking Citizenship in Hong Kong: Community, Nation and the Global City*, p. 55.

7 The paragraph is based on the personal observation of the author who was a high school teacher between 1992 and 1997 and a civic education master between 1996 and 1997. The author once invited a democrat as a guest speaker in a high school in 1997. The Chinese authorities were never on good terms with Hong Kong's democrats. The author was therefore criticized as politically insensitive by a school administrator who worried that the invitation may imply the school's support of the democrats and was harmful to the school's long-term interests.

8 Kang John Tan, 'Secondary School History Curricula', in Mark Bray and Ramsey Koo (eds), *Education and Society in Hong Kong and Macau: Comparative Perspectives on Continuity and Change*, Hong Kong: Comparative Education Research Centre, University of Hong Kong, 1999, pp. 171–194; Kwok-Chun Tang and Mark Bray, 'Colonial Models and the Evolution of Education Systems: Centralization and Decentralization in Hong Kong and Macau', *Journal of Education Administration*, 38(5), 2000, pp. 468–485.

9 Tan, 'Secondary School History Curricula'; Tang and Bray, 'Colonial Models and the Evolution of Education Systems'.

10 Eric Kit-Wai Ma, 'Re-Nationalization and Me: Hong Kong Story After 1997', *Inter-Asia Cultural Studies*, 1(1), 2000, p. 174.

11 The data about Macao in this section, unless specified, is derived from the interviews of 31 Macao citizens with permanent identity cards. The interviews were conducted between December 2008 and May 2009.

12 The author interviewed 21 Macao permanent citizens between August 2008 and March 2009. In addition, the author has reviewed the interviews by Jill McGivering in *Macao Remembers*, Hong Kong: Oxford University Press, 1999.

13 Tom O'Regan, 'A National Cinema', in Graeme Turner (ed.), *The Film Cultures Reader*, London: Routledge, 2002, pp. 139, 155–156.

14 Interview with a Macao visual artist in August 2008.

15 McGivering, *Macao Remembers*, p. 19. There are two definitions of Macanese. A broad definition refers to Macao people. A narrower definition adopted by the author refers to the Macao people who are Eurasians with Portuguese blood.

16 Interestingly, most of the younger interviewees said they loved China because of China's economic success. Apparently, the official discourse of China's economic development conveyed in the mass media is influential on identity building.

17 Bill K. P. Chou, 'The Paradox of Macao's Development', in Maria Antonia Espadinha (ed.), *Law and Social Sciences: Proceeding of the First Seminar*, Macao: University of Macau Publication Centre, 2009, pp. 229–242.
18 Mathews, Ma and Lui, *Hong Kong, China*.
19 Interview with a former TDM reporter in November 2008.
20 Take the example of the reaction of Macao's media towards 2008 Sichuan Earthquake. The magnitude 8.0 earthquake occurred in May 2008 and killed 69,000 people. The TV footages from Hong Kong and Mainland about the disaster-stricken zones and the grief of the deceased's beloved were sensational and caused strong urges among Macao Chinese to lend a helping hand. Local media remained inactive but continued to rely on the sources from Hong Kong and the mainland. Two weeks after the earthquake, a medical team from Macao leased a chartered flight and invited the media to follow them. Although the air transportation was free of charge, several newspapers still did not send their reporters to the site. A reporter told the author that the disaster had already been widely reported by other media. It was unnecessary for Macao reporters to go (interview in May 2008). The journalists seemed to regard themselves as 'human recorders': Their job is simply to record and report certain facts; they have little incentive to critically analyse existing reports, examine official statements and documents, interview informants, and provide a new angle for understanding the causes, processes, and impacts of the disaster. With heavy reliance on the mainland's official sources for China news, Macao media cannot but convey a positive image of the mainland.
21 Bill K.P. Chou, 'Interest Groups in Macao', in Conor McGrath (ed.), *Interest Groups & Lobbying: Volume Three – Latin America, Africa, the Middle East, and Asia*, Lewiston, NY: The Edwin Mellen Press, pp. 317–340; Huasheng Lou, *Zhuanxing shiqi Aomen shetuan yanjiu: duoyuan shehui zhong fatuan zhuyi tizhi jiexi* (*A Research of Macao Interest Group at Transitional Period*), Guangzhou: Guangdong People's Press, 2004, pp. 309–315.
22 Statistics and Census Bureau, Macao SAR Government, *Global Results of By-Census 2006*, www.dsec.gov.mo/Statistic/Demographic/GlobalResultsOfBy-Census2006.aspx (accessed 11 April 2009).
23 Census and Statistics Department, Hong Kong SAR Government, *2006 Population By-Census*, www.bycensus2006.gov.hk/data/data3/statistical_tables/index_tc.htm#G1 (accessed 11 April 2009).
24 Chinese people who were born in Macao before 1981 or born to Portuguese passport-holders are qualified for both Portuguese and Macao SAR passports.
25 Mathews, Ma and Lui, *Hong Kong, China*, p. 117.
26 Ibid., pp. 95–114.
27 Interview with two students in March 2009.
28 Herbert S. Yee, *Macao in Transition*, Hampshire: Palgrave, 2001; Shiu Hing Lo, *Political Development in Macao*, Hong Kong: Chinese University of Hong Kong Press, 1995, pp. 23–46.
29 Mathews, Ma, and Lui, *Hong Kong, China*, pp. 115–130.
30 Interviews in March and April 2009.
31 Bill K.P. Chou, 'Interest Group Politics in Macao after Handover', *Journal of Contemporary China*, 14(43), 2005, pp. 191–206.
32 Kang John Tan, 'Secondary School History Curricula', in Mark Bray and Ramsey Koo (eds), *Education and Society in Hong Kong and Macau: Comparative Perspectives on Continuity and Change*, Hong Kong: Comparative Education Research Centre, University of Hong Kong, 1999, pp. 171–194.
33 The argument is based on the experience of the author who was the instructor of an undergraduate course 'Politics of China' several years ago, and is currently the

instructor of another undergraduate course 'Public Administration: China' at the University of Macau.

34 Tiago Azevedo, 'The Executive Strikes Back', *Macau Business*, March 2009, p. 54; Alexandra Lages, 'Web of Deceit', *Macau Business*, March 2009, p. 55.

35 Stein Rokkan, *State Formation, Nation-Building, and Mass Politics in Europe: The Theory of Stein Rokkan: Based on His Collected Works*, ed. Peter Flora with Stein Kuhnle and Derek Urwin, Oxford: Oxford University Press, 1999, pp. 145–147.

36 Pitman B. Potter, 'Theoretical and Conceptual Perspectives on the Periphery in Contemporary China', in Diana Lary (ed.), *The Chinese State at the Borders*, Vancouver and Toronto: UBC Press, 2007, pp. 240–264.

37 Yan-wing Leung and Shun–wing Ng, 'Back to Square One: The "Re-Depoliticizing" of Civic Education in Hong Kong', *Asia Pacific Journal of Education*, 24(1), 2004, pp. 43–60

38 Vickers and Kan, 'The Re-Education of Hong Kong', pp. 189–191.

39 The Curriculum Development Council, Education Bureau, HKSAR, *Moral and National Education Curriculum Guide (Primary 1 to Secondary Six)*, p. 12, www. edb.gov.hk/FileManager/EN/Content_2428/mne%20guide%20%28eng%29%20 final.pdf (accessed on 14 June 2012).

40 'Neidi jiaoyu bu cheng wu canyu zhiding bengang guomin jiaoyu kecheng' ('Mainland Chinese Education Ministry Has Not Participated in Drafting Hong Kong's National Education Curriculum'), *Shangye diantai (Commercial Radio)*, 13 June 2012, www.881903.com/Page/ZH-TW/newsdetail.aspx? ItemId=521517&csid=261_341 (accessed on 14 June 2012); 'Renquan jiancha jiu 'deyu ji guomin jiaoyu kecheng zhiyin' zixun gao lichangshu (2011.8)' ('The Opinions of Hong Kong Human Rights Monitor on the Consultative Paper of Moral and National Education Curriculum Guide, 2011.8'), *Duli meti (Independent Media)*, 27 August 2011, www.inmediahk.net (accessed on 14 June 2012).

41 Ngok Ma, 'Civil Society in Self-Defense: The Struggle against National Security Legislation in Hong Kong', *Journal of Contemporary China*, 14(44), 2005, pp. 465–482

42 Potter, 'Theoretical and Conceptual Perspectives on the Periphery in Contemporary China'.

43 'The Rigging Unravels: China Faces Unpalatable Choices for Hong Kong's Next Chief Executive', *The Economist*, 3 March 2012, www.economist.com/ node/21549001 (accessed 6 March 2012).

44 Bill K.P. Chou, 'Economic Integration of China's Hong Kong and Macao: Regional and International Dimensions', in Albert Tavidze (ed.), *Progress in Economics Research Vol. 18*, New York: Nova Science, 2011, pp. 71–89.

45 'Dog and Locusts: Old Divisions Find a New Expression', *The Economist*, 4 February 2012, www.economist.com/node/21546051 (accessed 3 March 2012).

46 'Chen Limi: Duoyuan huodong tui aiguo jiaoyu' ('Chen Limin: Promoting Patriotic Education through Diverse Activities'), *Aomen ribao (Macao Daily)*, 30 January 2009, B6.

47 Ibid.

48 'Xinwen jie guoqing yanxiuban jin kaike' ('Training Course of Understanding China for Journalists Begin Today'), *Aomen ribao*, 23 March 2009, B4.

49 Macau Government Tourist Office, *Discovering Macau*, www.macautourism.gov. mo/en/discovering/sightseeing_detail.php?catid=43 (accessed 20 April 2009).

50 Education and Youth Bureau, *Aiguo aiao (Loving China, Loving Macao)*, www. dsej.gov.mo/cre/lovechimo/macau_history/index.html (accessed 20 April 2009). Interestingly, the Portuguese and English version of the webpage do not list the 'Loving China, Loving Macao' series, implying that the patriotic education is restricted to Chinese-speaking students.

51 Interview with a former high school teacher, November 2008.
52 Vickers and Kan, 'The Re-Education of Hong Kong', pp. 183–184.
53 'Secretive Billionaire Forsakes Retirement', *The Standard*, 14 September 1993, p. 4.
54 Carol P. Lai, *Media in Hong Kong: Press Freedom and Political Change, 1967–2005*, London: Routledge, 2007.
55 Calculated from the statistics of Macao government issued in various years.
56 Hilary du Cros, 'Emerging Issues for Cultural Tourism in Macau', *China Aktuell: Journal of Current Chinese Affairs*, 1, 2009, pp. 76–77.
57 'Baohu denta jingguan shangwei chenggong, Aomen shimin rengxu nuli' ('Lighthouse Has Not Been Protected Successfully. Macao Citizens Must Still Be Vigilant'), *Songshan Denta* (*Guia Lighthouse*), http://guialighthouse.blogspot.com (accessed 3 March 2009).
58 Ibid.
59 'Shegongju lanwuzai ni chaijian re guanzhu' ('The Plan to Demolish Social Welfare Institute's Blue House Arouses Attention'), *Aomen ribao*, 1 June 2006, B3; 'Lanwuzai mindiao, zhuanjia he duoshu shoufangzhe ren you baoliu' ('Experts and the Majority of the Respondents in a Survey Believed that Blue House Should Be Preserved)', *Huaqiao bao* (*Jornal Va Kio*), 20 January 2007, www.jornalvakio.com/index.php?tn=viewer&ncid=1&dt=&nid=16249 (accessed 30 January 2007).

11 The implications of the Special Administrative Regions for the international system
Macao as a successful case study

Carmen Amado Mendes

Introduction

This chapter focuses on the international impact of the ten years of existence of the Macao Special Administrative Region (SAR), after the transfer of the Portuguese administration to the People's Republic of China (PRC) in 1999. Theoretically, it is argued that the handover of Macao (as the one of Hong Kong) can hardly be considered as a process of pure decolonization or pure retrocession, being rather a hybrid between the two. The SARs are special instances of decolonization or rather cases of retrocession for three main reasons. First, China never considered Hong Kong and Macao as colonies, framing them in the retrocession of concession territories in the 1920s and 1930s, such as Weihaiwei, Shanghai and Taiwan in 1945. Second, especially during the last period of its administration, Britain and Portugal did not consider Hong Kong and Macao as full formal colonies, partly due to their perception of the legitimacy of Chinese claims. Third, Hong Kong and Macao did not become independent: what was at stake was not their independence but their return to mainland China. The negotiation processes for the British and Portuguese withdrawals did not take place between the metropolis and the colonies but between the metropolis and a third country, which was expected to assimilate the colonies.

The chapter does not aim at constructing a new model but rather to provide a case study (the Macao SAR) for testing a conceptual scheme (the 'one country, two systems' formula). Following this line, an original issue to be raised by this study concerns the impact that the success of this concept may have on its replication in other anomalous cases of the international system. It may therefore provide a useful theoretical basis for the understanding of similar international situations, such as Gibraltar or the Falklands. The chapter begins by examining the existing literature on withdrawal from empire, focusing on special instances of decolonization and cases of retrocession, particularly Hong Kong and Macao.

Decolonization vs. retrocession

Colony is

> a domination imposed by an external political power ... with a ten-
> dency to subordinate the resources and institutions of the dependent
> region to the interests of the political power and the ethnical or cultural
> dominant group.[1]

This chapter considers two main kinds of colonies: colonies of white
settlement thoroughly colonized with colonists that overwhelm the indigenous
people, and dependencies where colonization was minimal, consisting of the
exploitation of the territory by metropolitan authorities. These territorial
possessions are often taken as part of empire largely for resource extraction.
Within this latest category, there is a group of dependencies that never
achieved full independence. Hong Kong and Macao fall in this group.[2]

An enclave is by definition a 'detached portion of a state territory completely
surrounded by the territory of another state',[3] 'except for those parts where
it is limited by sea'.[4] The colonial enclave is usually claimed by the adjoining
state without regard to the principle of self-determination.[5] The dominant
international norm regarding colonial enclaves is that they are 'integral parts
of the political unit to which they belonged at the time of the colonial conquest or of the successor of this unit'.[6] The third state sovereign retains the
right to retrocession of the territory, as it happens with the 'leased territories'.[7] The administrative authority, limited by treaty or otherwise to dispose
of territory only in a certain way, is left with the only option of decoloniz-
ing the enclave by transferring it to the enclaving state.[8] The wishes of the
enclave's population are not considered since the inhabitants are regarded as
too few to constitute a separate people.[9]

This chapter therefore considers two main processes of withdrawal: decolonization and retrocession. By decolonization it means the 'measures intended
eventually to terminate formal political control over colonial territories and
to replace it by some new relationship'.[10] Retrocession covers the cases that
do not follow the norm of decolonization towards independence. They refer
to special instances of decolonization, where the withdrawal of the colonial
powers does not imply the right to self-determination but the full sovereignty
of another country over them. History provides us with some examples, when
a particular country (usually one that has lost a war) was forced to cede a
small part of its territory to another country. Hong Kong and Macao are two
such rare international situations of 'decolonization without independence',[11]
or rather retrocession. Instead of bringing them independence, decolonization integrated the two enclaves in a larger territory.[12]

To an extent, modern decolonization took place before the Second World
War: the British colonies of white settlement – Canada, Australia, New

Zealand, South Africa and Northern Ireland – have obtained through the 'Dominion Status' near-total independence while retaining some links with Britain, and later constituted the Commonwealth.[13] But the most significant movement of withdrawal from the empire was after 1945, and by the late 1960s the majority of the European colonies had achieved independence.[14] The Portuguese dictatorship maintained colonialism in Africa until the mid-1970s, but this was rather an exception. Historians and international relations theorists have largely covered the subject of decolonization. Among the most known historian explanations are those of John Darwin, Muriel Chamberlain, John Gallagher, Robert Holland and Nicholas White. Among international relations theories, the literature on late decolonization can be grouped into two types of account: the realist and the normative account.

The most common power politics explanations of decolonization are the emergence of mass nationalism in colonial societies at a time of decline in the economic and military strength of the European powers due to the Second World War, and the emergence of the two superpowers: the United States and the Soviet Union.[15] The fact that the Allies were losing the war on the Japanese front until 1943 proved that white men and their states could be defeated by Japan, and the United States and the Soviet Union assumed anti-colonial positions.[16] Most realist authors assume that there is a positivist connection between the Second World War and the decolonization process, especially in Africa. They say this is particularly true for Britain and France, the biggest colonial powers in Africa. Portugal managed to keep its African colonies longer because it was not involved in the war and because of the small scale of this metropolis and its possessions.[17] Besides, realism argues that the changes in the international system created new economic opportunities in intra-European relations. Colonies were not seen as vital for their metropolis anymore, and in some cases they even became a burden.

From a normative perspective, the change of norms in the international society and the shared belief in the universal right to self-determination, in the context of a new non-imperialist world order, pushed the colonial powers to withdrawal from their empires. European powers often presented normative justifications for holding their empires and decolonization took place when those justifications were no longer accepted. The British government, which always tended to use 'indirect rule' in its colonies, was among the first to put in practice the new approach towards colonialism. By contrast, in Portugal, the dictatorship delayed the infiltration of new norms as much as possible. Only after overthrowing the regime could the revolutionaries fight for changing the colonial policy.

Thus, after the Second War World, the trend in international politics was devolution and secession:[18] several new countries were born as larger units broke down to give rise to independent states. This section will focus on the colonial enclaves, where the tendency is exactly the opposite: here, small units are expected to join bigger ones. These, then, are special instances of decolonization, or retrocession, where dependencies do not achieve independence but are absorbed in a larger country. The specificity of the colonial enclaves is mainly responsible for the existence of outstanding colonial disputes that are far from being resolved, as the principle of the 'territorial integrity of a country' may clash with the 'right to self-determination' of another territory.[19]

Although both principles are affirmed in the same declaration, the United Nations regards self-determination as the cardinal rule. Therefore, 'territorial integrity' takes over the 'right of self-determination' only 'in the case of small non-viable territories claimed by a contiguous state'.[20] The reversion of territorial enclaves applies only 'in the most limited circumstances': small territories adjacent to the claimant state and territories ethically and economically derivative of that state.[21] If the territories are not by definition enclaves, as is the case, for example, of small islands, they are immediately granted the full right to self-determination.[22] Thus, while Gibraltar is a colonial enclave, which gives Spain the right of reversion, the Falklands are not, which gives the Falklanders the right to self-determination disregarding the claims from Argentina.

Colonial disputes

It is worth analysing briefly those two cases. Gibraltar, once part of the Spanish territory, was ceded by Spain to Britain 'in perpetuity' by the Treaty of Utrecht on 13 July 1713. But, as it often happens with the colonial enclaves, the treaty does not clearly state a cession of sovereignty and provides a right of pre-emption in favour of Spain, which is entitled to first preference if Britain alienates Gibraltar.[23] Spain, basing its claims in the principle of the territorial integrity, argues that even if Gibraltar is allowed to choose independence she could exercise its right of pre-emption, while Britain defends that the Treaty of Utrecht does not oppose the right to self-determination of the Gibraltarians.[24] It is however arguable that the only valid argument why the Spanish territorial integrity legally takes over the right of the Gibraltarians to self-determination does not lay in the Treaty of Utrecht, but in the fact that Gibraltar is a colonial enclave and that Spain is territorially contiguous and was the former sovereign.[25] Finally, there are reasons to believe that Spain will absorb Gibraltar if Britain leaves, and in the referendum of 1967 the Gibraltarians voted strongly against being assimilated into Spain, thus making it difficult to solve the impasse.

Both the Gibraltarians and Falklanders are British citizens, which makes them different from all the other remaining British imperial possessions.[26] As with the Gibraltarians, the Falklanders also wish to remain British citizens for fear of being swallowed up by Argentina. To defend them from an Argentinean invasion, Britain even went to war in 1982, but that did not make Argentina give up the idea of reunifying the islands under her. Argentina's claims are not considered in the United Nations due to the fact that the Falkland Islands do not fit into the category of the colonial enclaves: they are islands – which by definition do not constitute an enclave – and they are too big and too far from Argentina. From the British point-of-view the Falklands (and Gibraltar) should be entitled to self-determination but this was never accepted by the General Assembly,[27] which thinks that Britain and Argentina should solve the dispute between themselves.[28]

Puerto Rico is another case where neither self-determination nor devolution has yet taken place. It was ceded by Spain to the United States as a result of the Spanish–American War of 1898. Although Spain has not claimed the territory back, Puerto Rico seems far from achieving independence, remaining in semi-colonial status. It continues to suffer American cultural assimilation and receives financial and diplomatic advantages in exchange. Cases where the process of retrocession effectively took place are rare. One main reason for this, as was discussed previously, is the theoretical impasse about whether the territory should achieve self-determination or reverse to the claiming state. Besides, the use of force by the third sovereign state is condemned by the United Nations. The prevailing norm is that:

> states suffering from territorial amputations as a result of colonial conquest do not have the right to reconquer colonial territory in respect of which they may have a valid claim to sovereignty.[29]

Goa, for example, was returned to India in 1961 after a military invasion by the Indian state quickly overwhelmed the Portuguese garrison. India considered Goa 'ethically, geographically, historically, and legally one with the rest of India and the Indian people', therefore she was entitled to respond in self-defence against Portugal's aggression of 450 years.[30] There was little support in the United Nations for this argument even if India received some sympathy due to Portugal's intransigence in maintaining her overseas possessions at a time of decolonization.[31] The fact that India's annexation of Goa was not condemned was rather an exception to the legal principle prohibiting the acquisition of territory by force:[32] it took place within the colonial context in which the new norm of decolonization conflicted with the old norm of the prohibition on the use of force.[33] In any event in the case of Goa (a colonial enclave), self-determination meant unity with India.

China and retrocession

China remains an exception in experiencing several cases of retrocession. The primary example of retrocession is that of Taiwan, a Japanese colony from 1895, returned to mainland China in 1945 after Japan's defeat in the Second World War. Yet, throughout the 1920s and 1930s, China had been exposed to what is now termed 'retrocession', when her foreign concessions, (except Hong Kong and Macao) were returned to her. 'Retrocession' in the 1920s and 1930s came after a long period of foreign control over territory that had been conceded by China. The European imperial powers had long aspired to set foot in Chinese territory – especially after the Portuguese established themselves in Macao in 1557 – and China's defeat in the First Opium War provided the ground to force China to concede to them extraterritorial rights (exempting them from Chinese justice) and treaty ports (where they controlled the administration). The lease of several Chinese territories through these 'unequal treaties', as China has called them, provided Britain, France, Germany, Russia, Japan and the United States with privileged military and commercial positions within China.[34] Britain clearly led the scene until the First World War: it had the Crown colony of Hong Kong and had concessions at Xiamen, Jinjiang, Jiujiang, Hankou and Tianjin. Besides, Britain dominated the International Settlement of Shanghai and had the entire Yangzi valley as a sphere of influence.[35]

Soon after the First Word War, in which she slightly participated, and at the Versailles conference in 1919, China claimed in vain the abolition of the privileges that the treaty system had given to the foreign powers.[36] Although China self-conscientiously entered 'international society' (Bull and Watson conception) in 1918–1920, accepting the international rules and norms,[37] she soon found that the success in treaty revision laid in bilateral negotiation.[38] The Chinese claims for the retrocession of the foreign concessions were strengthened by the anti-imperialist Chinese Nationalist revolution in 1923–1928 against 'the domestic and foreign enemies of the Chinese people'.[39] Due to Britain's powerful position, British imperialism became a prime target. Anti-British agitation affected the Shanghai and the Yangzi regions in particular, but a strike was also organized in the foreign concession of Xiamen, and Hong Kong was boycotted from July 1925 to October 1926. The movement aimed to put an end to the foreign political and economic domination in China.[40] The turning point was the pacific retrocession of Hankou to China. 'By the early 1930s, negotiations had restored Chinese control over maritime customs, tariffs, postal communications, salt monopoly revenues and almost two-thirds of the foreign concessions in China.'[41]

The currents of Chinese nationalism also arrived in the British colony of Weihaiwei in the 1920s. Weihaiwei had been leased by China to Britain in 1898, along with the New Territories of Hong Kong, but it ended up being of minor importance to the British.[42] The only purpose of the lease had been to constitute a naval base to maintain the supremacy of the British vis-à-vis other foreign powers in China at a time when Russia had occupied Port Arthur (now Lüshun) and Dalian and the Germans' Jiaozhou (Kiaochow Wan). The lease was to expire when Russia left Port Arthur, but Britain managed to hang on to Weihaiwei after Russia was forced to give up Port Arthur to the Japanese following her defeat in the 1904–1905 war.[43] After a protracted negotiation process, the rendition of Weihaiwei took place in 1930, at a time when the British were glad to leave to avoid the development of an anti-British movement in a colony that had ceased to be of any importance.[44]

Although the two leaseholds were practically identical, Britain was much more committed to the New Territories than it was to Weihaiwei. While the inhabitants of the New Territories were naturalized as British subjects, those of

Weihaiwei remained Chinese citizens. Being part of the Crown colony of Hong Kong, Britain did not recognize China's continuing sovereignty over the New Territories as she tacitly did over Weihaiwei.[45] China, however, never recognized any difference of principle over its foreign concessions. They were all the result of 'unequal treaties', and as such should all return to China's sovereignty as soon as possible. Hong Kong and Macao did not escape this logic of retrocession, although they remained for a longer time under colonial authority.

The 'one country, two systems' formula

There are three main reasons why studies on the British and the Portuguese withdrawals from Hong Kong and Macao are better framed in the theory of retrocession rather than of decolonization. The first is China's refusal to recognize them as colonies, and claiming their retrocession to its sovereignty. The second reason pertains to British and the Portuguese attitudes to Hong Kong and Macao: they always treated these territories as special cases. Finally, Hong Kong and Macao did not achieve independence but they were integrated into a third sovereign country.

As stated above, China's position was that the British and the Portuguese occupation of these territories was the outcome of the 'unequal treaties'. Beijing considered the treaties unequal for three reasons: the rights and privileges accorded to foreigners were not accorded to the Chinese; the treaties were imposed on China by force of arms; and under the 'most favoured nation' clause, China had to extend to all other powers the concessions made to one. The principle of extraterritoriality was at the root of the inequality because it granted foreign powers special rights and privileges that helped to develop the imperialism of free trade and foreign investment in China. Besides, China argued that the treaties should be considered void because the context in which they were signed had changed.[46]

After winning the Opium War, Britain forced China to sign the Treaty of Nanking on 29 August 1842, surrendering Hong Kong and five treaty ports. When the treaty was ratified, by 26 June 1843, Hong Kong was declared a Crown colony. The Kowloon Peninsula was added to the colony by the convention of Peking in October 1860 and the New Territories were leased for 99 years in a convention signed in Peking on 9 June 1898.[47] Although the People's Republic of China considered them as void, the existence of the three treaties gave the British government grounds to negotiate with China: there was a part of the Chinese territory that under international law as understood on the West, was part of the British Crown.

Regarding Macao, China never ratified the only treaty that formally recognized Portugal's sovereignty over the territory. The Portuguese government had therefore to accept that it was not, strictly speaking, a colony. In Portugal the opinions diverge. According to some, it should be classified as leasehold (Cessão por Arrendamento) because the Portuguese paid ground-rent to the Chinese for a certain period of time.[48] Others say that the Portuguese permanence in Macao was the result of a special understanding and correlations of interests between them and the Chinese: the Portuguese were aware of depending on the Chinese good will and China never ceased to demonstrate its sovereignty over the territory.[49] There was also the argument that Macao is a case of 'shared sovereignty' because China always tried to limit the Portuguese juridical powers in the territory.[50]

Thus, Hong Kong and Macao had different historical backgrounds and different legal status. Hong Kong was occupied by the British since the nineteenth century, being the Hong Kong island and Kowloon a Crown colony and the New Territories a leasehold. Macao was a Portuguese establishment since the middle of the sixteenth century (although not a stable one, as the border on the peninsula moved north and there were serious conflicts) but it was never formally ceded by China. However, for the PRC the situations of Hong Kong and Macao were very similar: both were the product of an era of European imperialism that forced China to accept 'unequal treaties'. The British and the Portuguese presence was illegitimate, therefore Hong Kong and Macao could not be considered colonies.

China constantly treated Hong Kong and Macao as internal affairs. In August 1949, China's nationalist government stated to the UN Special Committee on Information from Non-Self Governing Territories that it should stop transmitting information on Kowloon and the New Territories.[51] This was based on the argument that the United States had previously developed for the Panama Canal Zone: 'The fact that sovereignty over a territory rested with a state other than the administering power was a reason for ceasing to transmit information to the Special Committee.'[52] In 1963, the Taiwan government stated in the General Assembly that

> any question about the status of Hong Kong and Macao should be discussed between the states concerned and that these territories do not seem to belong to the same category as other non-self-governing territories to be examined by the Committee.[53]

As soon as the PRC replaced Taiwan in the United Nations (UN) as the legitimate China, the Chinese government objected to the UN categorization of Hong Kong and Macao as colonies:

> The settlement of the questions of Hong Kong and Macau is entirely within China's sovereignty right and does not at all fall under the ordinary category of 'colonial Territories'. Consequently, they should not be included in the list of colonial Territories covered by the declaration on the Granting of Independence to Colonial Countries and Peoples.[54]

The PRC's ambassador to the UN stated that they should be removed from the UN list of colonial territories. This was granted to China at the meeting of the Special Committee on Decolonization on 17 May 1972.

Some say that this decision did not alter the legal status of Hong Kong as a non-self-governing colonial territory and that its inhabitants were still entitled to the right of self-determination. This is based on the argument that the right of self-determination has been crystallized into a norm of international law that cannot be set aside even by treaty. It is a right primarily enjoyed by the inhabitants of the colonies and Hong Kong was a colony under both domestic and international law. Its inhabitants were therefore free to determine its political status.[55] The right of self-determination in the case of Hong Kong is questioned by others who say Hong Kong was never a 'state' and that Britain had the obligation to return the New Territories to China in 1997.[56]

In any case, the pronouncement of the Committee of 24 would prove in the long term to have deprived the people of Hong Kong of fighting for its right to self-determination.[57] The fact that the British government did little to avoid this stands in contrast with its attitude regarding the Falklands and Gibraltar, cases in which Britain always defended the right of its inhabitants to self-determination. The British government considered Hong Kong as a case *suis generis* and agreed with China the transfer of sovereignty without holding a referendum.[58] The colony of Hong Kong was primarily an economic identity; its political identity was always secondary. The prime concern of the British administration was to ensure the social harmony and the political stability necessaries for trade.[59] Furthermore, the principles of self-government and self-determination that Britain traditionally applied to its colonies before withdrawing were probably very difficult to apply in Hong Kong. Instead, when Beijing demanded Hong Kong back in 1982, London negotiated the maintenance of the colonial system in the territory for 50 years, with a high degree of autonomy.[60] This model would soon be adopted by Lisbon for Macao.

In fact, the British and Portuguese perception of the legitimacy of the Chinese claims also shaped their withdrawal from Hong Kong and Macao as a process of retrocession. At an age in which both Britain and Portugal had neither the strength nor the (normative) will to hold on to these anachronistic colonial survivals, Chinese claims were perceived as having some legitimacy. The same causes (weakening power of the metropolis, normative shifts, etc.) that had led Britain and Portugal to decolonize pushed them to withdraw from Hong Kong and Macao, but the consequence in these two cases was retrocession to the PRC. After the First World War, the treaty system and the policy of coercion towards China was morally unjustifiable and unpopular within Britain.[61] British public opinion had become anti-interventionist and anti-imperialist and would not accept any military intervention in China.[62]

Thus, Hong Kong and Macao did not follow the usual path of decolonization towards independence. Instead, when they ceased to be 'colonies' they were integrated into a sovereign state; under the concept of 'one country, two systems',[63] Hong Kong and Macao became Special Administrative Regions of the PRC in 1997 and 1999. All negotiations on the two transitions were held between Britain and the PRC, and between Portugal and the PRC. The people of Hong Kong and Macao were not even awarded third party status in the negotiation process. China argued that negotiations should be held between sovereign states and opposed the inclusion of representatives of the Hong Kong and Macao governments and peoples.[64]

This formula, promoted by Deng Xiaoping, established a very unique framework for the handover of the British and Portuguese administrations to the People's Republic of China: the social and economic systems of the two territories and its main laws would remain unchanged and the administrations of the new SARs would be carried on by their own inhabitants with high degree of autonomy. In part due to their anomalous history, Hong Kong and Macao exceed the classical autonomy model observed within federated states: they have, for example, their own currency, issue autonomous passports and hold formal frontiers and maintain separate customs controls from inland China.[65]

From the central government point of view, the financial markets of Hong Kong continue to play a key role while Macao assumes an important function within China's foreign policy. The permanent secretariat of the Forum for Economic and Trade Cooperation between China and Portuguese-Speaking Countries (known as the Macao Forum) created in 2003,[66] was located in this SAR, using the historical specificities of the enclave as a traditional bridge between East and West. The history of more than five centuries of 'lusophone' presence distinguishes Macao from the other Chinese regions and provides it with affinities with the Portuguese-speaking countries, namely the language and cultural, legal and administrative legacies. Several events are organized in Macao, such as the lusophone games, lusophone food fairs, the lusophone festival and the 'cultural week of China and the Portuguese-speaking countries' which officially aims

> to display the popular cultures of different Portuguese-speaking countries and to stimulate the conviviality between the communities which share a common language, and to assume the importance of the lusophone culture as an intrinsic part of Macau's identity.[67]

By promoting its 'own cultural model', this SAR creates a 'familiar' atmosphere where leaders of that group of countries feel more comfortable to negotiate. The political, economic and business elite of those countries participate in different training courses organized by the Macao Forum, not only receiving technical information on their areas of interest but also shaping their perceptions of China and its development model. The Macao SAR is thus helping China develop its strategy of soft power in the Portuguese-speaking world.

Conclusion

There are many contemporary outstanding colonial disputes that are far from being solved; cases where neither independence nor retrocession took place.

Macao plays a unique role, being an example for other anomalous cases of the international system, such as Gibraltar or the Falklands, and the model of autonomy of the SARs may yet inspire other cases of retrocession.

The two Chinese SARs have been a successful implementation of the 'one country, two systems' formula. From the central government point of view, they give a very positive contribution to the policy of national reunification, being used as political showcases: Beijing expects them to be an example of the applicability of that formula to Taiwan. For Hong Kong and Macao, this guarantees their autonomy from the mainland, at least until the conflict on the Taiwan Strait is solved. The Macao SAR has also assumed an official role in China's external relations, as a platform of cooperation with the Portuguese-speaking countries, reinforcing its own identity by being acknowledged as a Chinese region with 'lusophone characteristics'.

Notes

1 António de Sousa Lara, Modern Colonisation and Decolonisation, Lisbon: ISCSP, 2000, p. 14.
2 Some argue that Macao only fitted in this pattern by the nineteenth century, when the Chinese outnumbered the Portuguese.
3 James R. Fox, *Dictionary of International and Comparative Law*, New York: Oceana, 1992.
4 A. Rigo Sureda, *The Evolution of The Right of Self-Determination*, Leiden: Sijthoff, 1973, p. 176.
5 James Crawford, *The Creation of States in International Law*, Oxford: Clarendon Press, 1979, p. 377. Self-determination here means *external* self-determination: the population of the colonial enclaves is limited to *internal* self-determination within the limits of the claimant state. Sureda, *The Evolution of The Right of Self-Determination*, p. 282.
6 Sureda, *The Evolution of The Right of Self-Determination*, pp. 176–177, 219.
7 Crawford, *The Creation of States in International Law*, p. 380.
8 Ibid., p. 227.
9 Peter Malanczuk, *Akehurst's Modern Introduction to International Law*, 7th edn, London: Routledge, 1997, p. 331.
10 John Hargreaves, *Decolonization in Africa*, 2nd edn, London: Longman, 1996, p. xvii.
11 The term 'decolonization without independence' was developed in previous academic analysis on Hong Kong such as: James Tang, 'From Empire Defence to Imperial Retreat: Britain's Postwar China Policy and the Decolonisation of Hong Kong', *Modern Asian Studies*, 28(2), 1994, p. 317; Siu-kai Lau, *Decolonization without Independence: The Unfinished Political Reforms of the Hong Kong Government*, Hong Kong: Hong Kong Institute of Asia-Pacific Studies, Chinese University of Hong Kong, 1987.
12 Boaventura de S. Santos and Conceição Gomes, *Macao – The Tiny Dragon*, Porto: Edições Afrontamento, 1998, pp. 5, 8.
13 Muriel E. Chamberlain, *European Decolonisation in the Twentieth Century*, London: Longman Companions to History, 1998, pp. 43–44.
14 John Darwin, *Britain and Decolonisation*, London: Macmillan Education Ltd., 1988, p. 334.
15 Ibid., p. 17.

16 Eric Hobsbawm, *Age of Extremes*, London: Abacus, 1995, pp. 216–217.
17 Only a minority of realist authors say that the war actually intensified colonialism. Being aware of the weaknesses in its empire already in the interwar years the British government exploited wartime emergencies to strengthen its position in the colonies. Henry Wilson argues that these two views on the effects of the Second World War are not necessarily contradictory. He says that more important than asking if the war affected the process of decolonization is to ask how it influenced the outcome in the different cases. David Clive Wilson, 'Britain and the Kuomintang, 1924–28: A Study of the Interaction of Official Policies and Perceptions in Britain and China', unpublished PhD thesis, SOAS, University of London, 1973, pp. 53–54, 63.
18 Devolution implies the consent of the former sovereign while the absent of this consent leads to secession, revolutionary creations of new states. Crawford, *The Creation of States in International Law*, pp. 215, 247.
19 'Declaration on the Granting of Independence to Colonial Countries and Peoples', General Assembly Resolution 1514 (xv) of 14 December 1960, Article 6 and Article 2.
20 Crawford, *The Creation of States in International Law*, p. 378.
21 Ibid., pp. 383–384.
22 Sureda, *The Evolution of The Right of Self-Determination*, pp. 176–177.
23 Ibid., p. 282; Crawford, *The Creation of States in International Law*, pp. 381 n. 126.
24 Britain refers to *internal* self-determination only, not willing to treat Gibraltar as a third sovereign part, but Spain opposes all kinds of self-determination arguing that even internal self-determination could allow Gibraltar to become independent, being only formally depending on Britain within the Commonwealth. Sureda, *The Evolution of The Right of Self-Determination*, pp. 282–284.
25 Sureda, *The Evolution of The Right of Self-Determination*, p. 288.
26 The remaining British possessions are: Anguilla, Bermuda, British Antarctic Territory, British Indian Ocean Territory, British Virgin Islands, Cayman Islands, Falkland Islands, Gibraltar, Montserrat, Pitcairn Islands, St. Helena and dependencies, South Georgia and the South Sandwich Islands, and the Turks and Caicos Islands. Klaus Dodds, 'Towards Rapprochement? Anglo-Argentine Relations and the Falklands/Malvinas in the late 1990s', *International Affairs*, 74(3), 1998, p. 617.
27 Crawford, *The Creation of States in International Law*, pp. 383–384, 381 n. 126.
28 Malanczuk, *Akehurst's Modern Introduction to International Law*, p. 332.
29 Sharnon Korman, *The Right of Conquest*, Oxford: Clarendon Press, 1996, p. 276.
30 Ibid., pp. 267–268.
31 John Dugard, *Recognition and the United Nations*, Cambridge: Grotius Publications Limited, 1987, p. 116.
32 Korman, *The Right of Conquest*, pp. 274–275.
33 Dugard, *Recognition and the United Nations*, p. 116.
34 Clarence B. Davis and Robert J. Gowen, 'The British at Weihaiwei: A Case Study in the Irrationality of Empire', *Historian*, 63(1), 2000, p. 87.
35 Edmund S.K. Fung, *The Diplomacy of Imperial Retreat: Britain's South China Policy, 1924–31*, Hong Kong: Oxford University Press, 1991, p. 2.
36 Ibid., p. 14.
37 Yongjin Zhang, *China in the International System, 1918–20*, London: Macmillan, 1991; William C. Kirby, 'The Internationalization of China: Foreign Relations At Home and Abroad in the Republican Era', *The China Quarterly*, June 1997, p. 443.
38 Kirby, 'The Internationalization of China', p. 443.

39 Fung, *The Diplomacy of Imperial Retreat*, p. 30.
40 Ibid., pp. 35–44.
41 Kirby, 'The Internationalization of China', pp. 440–441.
42 Six years after the British leasehold of Weihaiwei, the Colonial Office and the Foreign Office already debated its retrocession to China. The British found Weihaiwei to be militarily worthless and too poor to prosper economically. Thanks to its exceptional climate, it ended up being used mainly as a summer retreat for the British navy and expatriates. See for example N.J. Miners's foreword to Pamela Atwell, *British Mandarins and Chinese Reformers: The British Administration of Weihaiwei (1898–1930) and the Territory's Return to the Chinese Rule*, Hong Kong: Oxford University Press, 1985, p. ix; Davis and Gowen, 'The British at Weihaiwei', pp. 90–91; Julia C. Strauss, *Strong Institutions in Weak Polities: State Building in Republican China 1927–1940*, New York: Oxford University Press, 1998, p. 158.
43 Miners in Atwell, *British Mandarins and Chinese Reformers*, pp. vii–x.
44 Strauss, *Strong Institutions in Weak Polities*, p. 160.
45 Miners in Atwell, *British Mandarins and Chinese Reformers*, p. ix.
46 Fung, *The Diplomacy of Imperial Retreat*, pp. 25–26 for the last paragraph.
47 Gerald Segal, *The Fate of Hong Kong*, London: Simon & Schuster, 1993, pp. 11–16.
48 Adriano Moreira, *Overseas Policy*, Lisbon: Ministério do Ultramar, 1956, pp. 31–32; Benjamim Videira Pires, 'The Rent of Macao's Floor', *Jiameishi Xueyuan Jianbao (Bulletin of the Luís de Camões Institute)*, 1(4–5), 1976; and Almerindo Lessa, *The History and the men of the First Democratic Republic of the East*, Macao: Imprensa Nacional, 1974.
49 See António V. Saldanha, *Luso-Chinese Relations Studies*, Lisbon: ISCSP and ICM, 1996; Jorge Morbey, *The Challenge of the Transition*, Lisbon: Gráfica Monumental, 1990.
50 Francisco G. Pereira, *Portugal, China and the 'Macao Issue'*, Macao: Instituto Português do Oriente, 1995, p. 11.
51 The United Nations Special Committee on Information from Non-Self-Governing Territories was replaced in 1961 by the Special Committee on Decolonization, known as the Committee of 24. Its role was to monitor the progress of the colonial territories towards self-government.
52 'Fletcher-Cooke to CO', confidential, tel. no. 170, 26 August 1949, Creech Jones to Grantham, secret, no. 53, 19 November 1949, and other correspondence and minutes in CO537/4800, in Peter Wesley-Smith, *Unequal Treaty 1898–1997*, revised edition, Hong Kong: Oxford University Press, 1998, p. 244.
53 'Higham to MacLehose', secret, 12 March 1964: FO371/175888, in Wesley-Smith, *Unequal Treaty 1898–1997*, p. 251.
54 A/AC. 109/3968 of 8 March 1972, UNGA A/AC.109/L.795 of 15 May 1972 and FO371/175931.
55 Nihal Jayawickrama, 'The Right of Self-Determination', proceedings from a seminar on the Basic Law, held at the University of Hong Kong, 5 May 1990, pp. 93–94, 86–89, for the whole paragraph.
56 Georg Ress, 'The Hong Kong Agreement and Its Impact on International Law', in Jürgen Domes and Yu-ming Shaw (eds), *Hong Kong, A Chinese and International Concern*, Boulder: Westview Press, 1988, p. 132.
57 Wesley-Smith, *Unequal Treaty 1898–1997*, p. 251.
58 Ress, 'The Hong Kong Agreement and Its Impact on International Law', p. 132.
59 Rup Narayan Das, 'Politics of the Democratic Process in Hong Kong', *International Studies*, 34(4), 1997, p. 410.
60 Jermain T.M. Lam, 'Sino-British Relations over Hong Kong during the Final Phase of Political Transition', *International Studies*, 34(4), 1997, p. 442.

61 Fung, *The Diplomacy of Imperial Retreat*, p. 240.
62 Kirby, 'The Internationalization of China', p. 442.
63 Li Pang-Kwong, 'Executive and Legislature: Institutional Design, Electoral Dynamics and the Management of Conflicts in the Hong Kong Transition', in Li Pang-Kwong (ed), *Political Order and Power Transition in Hong Kong*, Hong Kong: Chinese University Press, 1997, p. 54.
64 Ibid., p. 57.
65 Paulo Cardinal, 'Macau: The Internationalization of an Historical Autonomy', *Boletín Mexicano de Derecho Comparado*, XLI(122), 2008, pp. 639, 674.
66 The forum includes the PRC and seven Portuguese-speaking countries: Portugal, Brazil, East Timor, Mozambique, Angola, Cape Verde, Guinea-Bisau; and São Tomé and Principe, as an observer (for maintaining diplomatic ties with Taiwan). Its official aims are promoting closer cooperation and economic links among its members. www.forumchinaplp.org.mo.
67 Macao Government 2007.

Glossary

A
Á Van Kai　下環街
Aomen Jiefang Lianhe Zonghui　澳門街坊聯合總會
Aomen Qingzhou Fangzhong Huzhuhui　澳門青洲坊眾互助會
Aomen Qingzhoushan Tudi Miaohui　澳門青洲山土地廟會
Aomen Xue　澳門學
Appeaser of Villains　解小人

B
Banying Fang (Pan Ieng Fong)　板營坊
Beidi　北帝

C
Caibo Xingjun (God of wealth)　財帛星君
Caichuanwei Jie (Chai Sun Mei Kai)　柴船尾街
Cai Shen Ye, (God of wealth)　財神
Caodui Hengjie (Chou Toi Wang Hong)　草堆橫巷
Caodui Street (ChouToi Street)　草堆街
Capitalism　資本主義
Censer　香爐
Cessãopor Arrendamento – (Leasehold)　租赁权
Chen Shuk Bo (Qin Shubao), Gate God　秦叔宝，門神
Cheng-Kuoc-Sim-Lam　正覺禪林
Cheong-Chao　漳州
Cheung Chau Island　长洲岛
ch'i (fixed cosmic order of the world)　氣
Chinese opera shack　大戲棚
Confucianist　儒家
Cultural Heritage　文化遺產

D
Dan Jia　蜑家
Dashenggong　大聖公

Donation name list   捐贈者名單
Dra. Ana Maria Amaro   安娜 玛里亚阿马罗

F
Fanfang (foreign quarter)   番坊
Fu Lu Shou   福祿壽
Fude Ci   福德祠
Fudetang Paohui   福德堂炮會
Fuheshe (FokWo Se)   福和社
Furnace for burning paper offerings   燒冥鏹爐

G
Gantang Szekwan   庵堂寺觀
Ge Yi   格義
Globalization   全球化
Glocalization   全球本土化
Gongsuo   公所
Guangdong Tushuo   《廣東圖說》
Guangsubing   光蘇餅
Guanyin Gumiao (Kun Iam Tchai)   觀音古廟
Guolanjie (Kuo Lan Kai)   果欄街

H
Haiyang Wenhua (maritime culture)   海洋文化
Heishawan (HakSa Wan)   黑沙灣
Historical education   歷史教育
Hongbao   紅包
Hongrendian   弘仁殿
Hongsheng Dawang   洪聖大王
Hua Tao, (God of doctor)   華佗, 醫神
Huangpu   黃埔
Humen   虎門

I
Identity   同一性
Individual Visitor Scheme   自由行政策

J
Jao Chong/Zhou Cang   周倉
Ji   稷
Ji Gong, (Living Buddha)   濟公, 活佛
Jiandui   煎堆
Jianlongshe (Kin Long Se)   建隆社
Jiefanghui   街坊會
Jing   境

Jingtian (respect heaven)　敬天
Julongjie (Rua de Choi Long/Choi Long Kai)　聚龍街

K
Kai Jing　鷄頸
Kai Mountain　鷄山
Kai Paddle　鷄拍
Kai Pohao　鷄婆好
Kangxi (emperor)　康熙
Kuaiziji (Fai Chi Kei)　筷子基
Kuaiziji Fangzhong Huzhuhui　筷子基坊眾互助會
Kwan Ping (Guan Ping), Adopted son　關平，養子
Kwan Tai (Kwan Ti/Guan Di)/Kwan Kung/Beidi/Mou Tai, God of War　關帝/
　　關公/北帝/武帝，戰神
Kwan Tai (Kwan Ti/Guan Di/Mou Tai)-Tin Hua Temple　關帝天后廟
Kwan Ti (Kwan Tai/Guan Di)/Kwan Kung/Mou Tai, God of War　關帝/關
　　公/武帝，戰神

L
Li　里
li　(natural law)　理
Lianfeng Miao　蓮峰廟
Lianluoshe　聯絡社
Local identity　本地身份認同
Longtian (*Long Tin*)　龍田
Luís Gonzaga Gomes　高美士

M
Mage　媽閣
Mage Miao　媽閣廟
Manuel Teixeira　文德泉
Market force　市場力量
Mass media　大众傳媒
Mazu　媽祖

N
Nanjing　南京
National education　國民教育
National identity　國民身份認同
National integration　國家整合
Nezha　哪吒

O
Offerings table　祭祀枱

P

Padroado (Patronate)　保教權
Pai Fang, gateway　屏風
Pak Tai Temple　北帝廟
Pao　炮
Paojin　炮金
Piaose　飄色
Place-making　場所營造
Pro-Beijing associations　親北京社團
Pu　鋪
Puji Chanyuan (Pou Chai Sim Iun)/Guanyintang (Kun Iam Tong/Templo de
　　Kun Iam Tong)　普濟禪院/觀音堂

Q

Qiangpao　搶炮
Qingzhou(Cheng Chao)　青洲
Qiying　耆英
Queziyuan (AvenidaConselheiro Ferreira de Almeida e Rua da Mitra/Cheok
　　Chai Un)　雀仔園

R

Rhizomatic (rhizome)　根莖
Rui Brito Peixoto　路易
Ruyi, cloud-shaped gong　如意

S

Sam Po Temple　三婆廟
Sanjie Huiguan (Templo de Sam Kai Vui Kun/Sam Kai Wui Kun)　三街會
　　館
Sense of place　地方意識
Shalitou (Sa Lei Tau)　沙梨頭
She　社
Shuangchong Xiaozhong (double loyalty)　雙重效忠
Solve Villain　解小人
Spatial political economy　空間政治經濟
Staff area　員工辦事處

T

Table of incenses and candles　香燭枱
Tai Shan (Toi San)　臺山
Tang　堂
Tanka　蜑民
Tao ch'I (Great Ultimate)　太極
Teng Mei　丁未

Tin Hau, empress of heaven　天后
Tiyuhui　體育會
To ask the gods for an oracle　解簽
To Dei Kung/Tu Di Kung (earth god)　土地公
Tsinmeaou　寢廟
Tudihui　土地會

W

Wan Kuok-koi (Broken Tooth Koi)　尹國駒　（齙牙駒）
Wang Xia Guanyintang　望夏觀音堂
Wangxia (Mong Ha)　望夏
Wangxia Fangzhong Huzhuhui　望夏坊眾互助會
Wangxia Jiefanghui　望夏街坊會
Wat Chi King Tak, Gate God　尉遲敬德，門神
Weapons, (Kwan Kung, Kwan Ping, Jao Chong)　武器
Wei　圍
Wish fulfilling god　心想事成公仔
Wong Tai Sin　黃大仙

X

Xiahuan (Ha Wan)　下環
Xiangshan Xianzhi　香山縣誌
Xinglongshe　興隆社

Y

Yisi　乙巳
Yongfu Society (Weng Fok Se)　永福社
Yonghetang Huapaohui　永和堂花炮會
Yongxingshe (Weng Heng Se)　永興社

Z

Zhang-Quan-Chao　漳泉潮
Zhaoqing　肇慶
Zheng De　[明]正德
Zheng He　]鄭和
Zhongheshe (Chung Wo Se)　中和社
Zhou Zanhou (Zhou Feixiong)　周飛熊
Zhuojiacun (Cheok ka Chuen)　卓家村

Index